The Summons of Death
on the
Medieval and Renaissance
English Stage

The Summons of Death on the Medieval and Renaissance English Stage

Phoebe S. Spinrad

Ohio State University Press
Columbus

A shorter version of chapter 4 appeared, along with part of chapter 2, as "The Last Temptation of Everyman, in *Philological Quarterly* 64 (1985): 185–94. Chapter 8 originally appeared as "*Measure for Measure* and the Art of Not Dying," in *Texas Studies in Literature and Language* 26 (1984): 74–93. Parts of Chapter 9 are adapted from my "Coping with Uncertainty in *The Duchess of Malfi*," in *Explorations in Renaissance Culture* 6 (1980): 47–63. A shorter version of chapter 10 appeared as "Memento Mockery: Some Skulls on the Renaissance Stage," in *Explorations in Renaissance Culture* 10 (1984): 1–11.

Library of Congress Cataloging-in-Publication Data

Spinrad, Phoebe S.
    The summons of death on the medieval and Renaissance English stage.

    Bibliography: p.
    Includes index.
    1. English drama—Early modern and Elizabethan, 1500–1700—History and criticism. 2. English drama— To 1500—History and criticism. 3. Death in literature. 4. Death— History. I. Title.
PR658.D4S64   1987   822'.009'354   87-5487
ISBN 0-8142-0443-0

To
Karl Snyder and Marjorie Lewis
without whom none of this
would have been

Contents

Preface   ix

I Death Takes a Grisly Shape
Medieval and Renaissance Iconography   1

II Answering the Summons
The Art of Dying   27

III Death Takes to the Stage
The Mystery Cycles and Early Moralities   50

IV Death as Educator
Everyman   68

V Death Takes an Alias
The Late Moralities and the Secular Mode   86

VI Medieval Summons,
Renaissance Response
Tamburlaine, Parts I and II   123

VII The Summons to Hell
Doctor Faustus   143

VIII The Kindly Summons
Measure for Measure   162

IX The Summons of Nothingness
The Duchess of Malfi   184

X Memento Mockery
The Old Iconography Begins to Slip   214

XI A Choice of Deaths
The Last Decades of Renaissance Theater   250

Epilogue
Some Last Words and a Last Play   277

Notes   287

Bibliography   317

Index   331

Preface

THE HUMAN MIND IS AFRAID OF NOTHING. . . .
Depending on how we read such a statement, it may seem
either a truism or an absurd (if gallant) falsehood. To clarify the
statement, we may try a simple mental exercise.
Picture infinity. Populate it with infinite worlds, infinite possibilities, parallel universes, time and space running in all directions, always expanding, always (if necessary) returning and
beginning again. It is confusing, but not impossible. We tend to
pick out highlights as exempla of what exists beyond what we
are able to imagine, to say "et cetera" and go on to something
else, and finally to yawn and stretch and go away, promising ourselves that we will think of more later.
Now picture finity. This is much easier; we can place a frame
around our "et ceteras" and feel a comfortable sense of closure—
until we are asked to imagine what lies outside the frame. Now
the message is clearer: The human mind is afraid of Nothing.

It is at the moment of death that Everything and Nothing
meet, and throughout the history of humankind, art has struggled
to make them both less frightening by transmuting them into
Something, a something that can be borne. The greatest art,
indeed, has been not about love, as we often like to think, or

about duty or the class struggle or sex or God or military victories, but about endings: the deaths of heroes, the passing of innocence, the discarding of illusions, the saving of one precious object from the wreck of many others. The endings themselves may be seen as fortunate, as in the slaying of the dragon or the resolution of a love triangle; but, as Samuel Johnson has pointed out, in each ending we see and struggle with our own end:

> We always make a secret comparison between a part and the whole; the termination of any period of life reminds us that life itself has likewise its termination; when we have done any thing for the last time, we involuntarily reflect that a part of the days allotted us is past, and that as more is past there is less remaining. . . . [B]y vicissitude of fortune, or alteration of employment, by change of place, or loss of friendship, we are forced to say of something, this is the last. (Idler, No. 103, in Rasselas, Poems, and Selected Prose, ed. Bertrand H. Bronson [New York: Holt, 1971], 214–15.)

In the great age of the English drama, death walked the stage in many guises, constantly reminding Renaissance man and woman that all endings were one end. But such a vivid reminder was not new to the Renaissance audience, and in fact was not only a mutation but a muting of the Death that had frightened and comforted audiences for two centuries before. Without the medieval Legends and Dances of Death, without the Dreary Deaths that brandished spears from medieval painting and stage, there would have been no Doctor Faustus, no Bosola, no Yorick.

It is the purpose of this study, then, to examine the way in which four centuries of art managed to grapple together Everything and Nothing into the greatest drama of the English language—only to lose sight, at the end, of what they were grappling with, and to wrestle helplessly with the scenery as the curtain came down.

Since drama does not exist in a cultural vacuum, I have thought it advisable to provide a background against which the moving figure of Death may best be seen. My first two chapters block in this background: a description of the changing iconography and theology of death during the fourteenth through seventeenth centuries, exclusive of the drama itself. In this I depart from the method of Theodore Spencer, whose seminal work, *Death and Elizabethan Tragedy*, provided the impetus for my study. Spencer describes each generation separately in terms of the art, philosophy, poetry, and drama of the given age. But it is my intention to observe how the ideas of one age mingled with another, how some artists hung back from change while others leaped ahead, how some followed one diverging path while others followed a second one or retraced their steps. And in order to see patterns within such apparently random motion, we ought first to have an idea of the overall pattern in all its permutations. Therefore, I have postponed actual discussion of the plays until the background is established.

In beginning with medieval ideas and medieval drama, I do not mean to suggest that the Middle Ages are either the beginning or the standard from which all death literature is to be measured; however, we must begin somewhere, and I have chosen to begin with the earliest staged English drama, with all its ideas and influences in place, and to trace changes from there to the closing of the theaters in 1642. Obviously, just as the Renaissance was influenced and reacted against conventions of the previous period, so the Middle Ages also had its influences and contrasts. For readers who would like to explore earlier conventions, I highly recommend both Spencer's work and Frederick Parkes Weber's *Aspects of Death and Correlated Aspects of Life in Art, Epigram, and Poetry*, as well as the other works listed in my bibliography.

In selecting texts for this study, I have tried to combine the flavor of the original with the fluidity of the modern. Although in some cases I may have preferred an old-spelling edition of a Renaissance play—for example, F. L. Lucas's edition of Webster—I have used instead the best modernized text available, to avoid making some plays seem "quainter" than others of the same period. For the medieval plays, and the prose and poetry of all four centuries, I have generally used the old spelling, but with certain modifications: the substitution of *th* and *y* for thorn and yok, respectively, and minor adjustments as indicated in the text where oddities of spelling would have interfered with intelligibility.

I am deeply indebted to Karl Snyder, Marjorie Lewis, and Bob Frye of Texas Christian University, who helped more than I can say with the original research on this manuscript; to Gloria K. Fiero of the University of Southwestern Louisiana, who steered me toward many of the medieval representations of Death that appear in my discussion; and to my colleagues at Ohio State University, without whose suggestions and encouragement I might have despaired of ever completing the final version.

This work does not pretend to be a comprehensive study of all that was written, painted, and sung about death in the fourteenth through seventeenth centuries; my difficulty lay not in finding examples to include but in deciding what I could bear to leave out. Like all human endeavor, the result is only a finite representation of infinite possibilities, an attempt to blend Everything and Nothing into Something.

I

Death Takes A Grisly Shape

Medieval and Renaissance Iconography

IT HAS BECOME A HISTORICAL COMMONPLACE to speak of four-
teenth- and fifteenth-century Europe as a society obsessed with
death. Many reasons have been advanced for this "obsession":
the violence of the age; the preaching of the mendicant friars,
whose appeals to the emotions and whose continual cries of
"memento mori" were designed to bring the worldly or heretical
home to Mother Church; and the onslaught of the Black Plague,
which left corpses piled in the streets or in huge communal graves.
But valid as all these reasons may be for an obsession with death,
to posit them *as* reasons is to beg the question—to assume that
the obsession existed.

There is an old story about the traveler who stopped in a
rural village where modern civilization had not yet spread its blessings. Appalled at the primitive conditions in the village, he asked
a local resident, "My good man, what is your death rate here?"
The villager thought for a moment and replied: "Hundred percent. Everybody dies."

The death rate of the human race has always been one hundred percent, and few societies have failed to notice the fact. Indeed, the very historians who speak of the late medieval "obsession" with death cannot help mentioning the extensive death
literature of other ages; Johan Huizinga speaks of the long history

of the *ubi sunt* lyric, dating back to ancient Greece; Leonard P. Kurtz describes the "skeleton at the feast" used as memento mori in ancient Rome; Theodore Spencer deals at great length with the death literature of Graeco-Roman antiquity, as well as with the *contemptus mundi* literature of the early church fathers; and Willard Farnham traces death literature from Greek tragedy through Seneca and the early church fathers, and finally to the great twelfth-century *De Contemptu Mundi* of Pope Innocent III.[1] the "old, old fashion, Death," as Dickens calls it,[2] has never been far from the human mind. The question, then, is not why the fourteenth and fifteenth centuries were more concerned with death than was any other age, but how they chose to cope with a perennial problem: the hundred percent death rate of humankind.

The most prominent figures of death in this period, are, of course, the decomposed corpse and the skeleton. Indeed, we have grown so accustomed to this type of personification that we hardly recognize any other symbol; but other forms were occasionally attempted. At Pisa, in the Campo Santo fresco of the Last Judgment (ca. 1350), death is represented by a bat-winged woman shrouded in long veils, who flies over the world reaping groups of young people with her scythe.[3] And in the late-fourteenth-century poem *Death and Liffe*, Death is a hideous old crone armed with a mace and darts:

> Her eyes farden as the fyer that in the furnace burnes;
> They were hollow in her head, with full heavye browes;
> Her leres were leane, with lipps full side;
> With a marvelous mouth, full of main tushes;
> & the nebb of her nose to her navell hanged.
> & her lere like the lead that latelye was beaten.[4]

"Dame Death," in this poem, has a basilisk gaze from her hollow eye-sockets, and whatever she touches dies. "The greene grasse in her gate she grindeth all to powder" (193); the very birds of the air lose their power to fly, and the fish forget how to swim, "Ffor dread of Dame Death that dolefully threates" (198). As she approaches the field full of folk who are doing homage to Lady

I iffe, she reaches for her weapons and slaughters thousands of them, much in the manner of the Triumphs and Dances of Death that were becoming popular at the time:

> In the roughest of the rout shee reacheth forth darts;
> There shee fell att the first fflappe fiftene hundred
> Of comelye queenes with crowne, & kings full noble;
> Proud princes in the presse prestlye she quellethe;
> Of dukes that were doughtye shee dang out the braynes;
> Merry maydens on the mold shee mightilye killethe;
> There might no weapon them warrant nor no walled towne;
> Crism-children in their cradle shee craddantly dighteth.
>
> (200–07)[5]

A debate ensues between Death and Life, during which Death claims to have vanquished all the great figures of the past, including Christ himself. Life replies that Death has not won but has, rather, brought about Christ's resurrection, the Harrowing of Hell, and Death's own damnation. Life then raises the slain, tells them that they need fear Death no more, and flies away with them.

Such a poem seems curiously out of place among the invincible Deaths of the period, not only because its shows a female personification, but because it has an unrealistic ending for the time. The people of the late-fourteenth-century England were in the midst of watching Death's darts strike down fifteen hundred "att a fflappe," but no Lady Liffe was stepping in to raise them up. These were the plague years, and they seemed to stretch on and on with no relief; proud princes and chrism-children in their cradles lay strewn about the countryside, rotting.

It may very well be, then, that these all too visible signs of death—the ever present rotting corpses—determined the course that death literature and art were to take for the next two centuries. The materials had been available earlier, of course; tomb inscriptions as early as the twelfth century had admonished passers-by to think of the body within because they too would one day be dust (Ariès, 218–20), and folklore spoke of revenants from the grave who summoned the living to death or warned them to reform. Furthermore, the growing worldly attachments of medieval society had called forth *de contemptu mundi* treatises in the twelfth and thirteenth centuries, and the new orders of friars did indeed find the theme useful in reminding their flocks that there was another world to prepare for, and that death spares no one. In many of these sermons, according to Robert Potter, "death [was] actually depicted as the sergeant or bailiff of God, come to arrest an errant mankind."[6] Motivation by fear, yes; but ironically, it was this fearful personification that the later Middle Ages seized upon for comfort.

The first indication of the course that the image would take comes in the earliest known versions of the Legend of the Three Living and Three Dead, a series of French poems written toward the end of the thirteenth century.[7] In these poems, three proud young men encounter three skeletons or corpses who warn them about the vanities of the world. After a brief dialogue, the young men depart, determined to amend their lives. The whole episode appears to be rather perfunctory and perhaps was modeled on the tomb inscriptions of the time, but in its later development in art and literature the theme acquires more symbolism, and much more drama.

In the fourteenth century, the Three Dead were often more differentiated from each other, particularly in their progress from corpse to skeleton. Part of the fresco in the Campo Santo shows three young men on horseback who have come upon three coffins lying in their path. In the first lies a body still bloated after a recent death; in the second, a partially decomposed corpse; and in the third, a skeleton. Over all three coffins are crawling long worms almost as large as snakes.[8] In other such pictures of the time, the remnants of clothing on the corpses may indicate that the living are confronting themselves as they will someday be, the theme of the relentless passing of time being intensified by the progressive decay of the different corpses.

If these fourteenth-century depictions of the Legend owe much to the old warnings on the tombstones, the fifteenth-century versions generally come closer to the Dance of Death, which was then becoming popular. The corpses no longer lie quietly by the roadside; they walk or run after the living, sometimes to warn, but more often (in the later depictions) to kill. One early picture is still symbolically balanced: the Three Dead are, as usual, in progressive stages of decay, but the Three Living are now differentiated in time as well. The youngest, a prince, holds a scepter; the middle-aged man, an emperor, is dressed for battle; and the eldest, a pope, has his hands clasped in prayer. The Dead wear the same headgear as the Living whom they face, and the most decomposed corpse faces the youngest of the Living. Oddly enough, the Dead, naked except for their crowns, do not hold weapons, but keep their hands crossed modestly over their genitals (Tristram, pl. 25).

Several things have happened to the Legend from the time of its first appearance to these latest ones. First, the figures of death take more and more initiative in confronting the Living. Second, the Dead progress from tomb warnings on someone else's grave, through a still life of the individual's own recognizable progress to dust, to an impersonal force rushing to capture the individual. Third, and perhaps most important, the figure changes from a warning about the future to an immediate danger in the present.

By this time, of course, the Dance of Death had become popular as well, and the two motifs no doubt influenced each other as they developed. According to Florence Warren, the earliest painted Dance of Death, at Klingenthal, Little Basel, may date from 1312;[9] but the most famous, and probably the most influential, was the one at the Church of Holy Innocents in Paris. This elaborately rendered Dance, encompassing all classes and ages of society, is generally thought to have been painted around 1420-24, although Warren points out that there seem to be references to it as early as the reign of Charles V, who died in 1380.

The origins of the Dance are obscure—not in their paucity but in their superabundance. The influence of the friars' sermons is immediately evident in the idea of death as a bailiff of God, with its hand on every person's shoulder; the Legend, too, casts its shadow, particularly since early versions of the Dance make it clear that the corpse who comes for each person is that person as he or she will be. The concept of a progress or pilgrimage, a movement away to the grave, may also owe something to the medieval *vado mori* lyric, in which representatives of different classes announce that they are "traveling to death" in stanzas that begin and end with the chilling words, *vado mori*, or, in the English versions, "I wende to dede":

> I wende to ded, knight stithe in stoure,
> thurghe fyght in felde i wane the flour;
> Na fightis me taght the dede to quell—
> i weend to dede, soth i yow tell.
>
> I weende to dede, a kynge I-wisse;
> What helpis honor or werldis blysse?
> Dede is to mane the kynde wai—
> i wende to be clad in clay.
>
> I wende to dede, clerk ful of skill,
> that couth with worde men mare & dill.
> Sone has me made the dede ane ende—
> bees ware with me! to dede i wende.[10]

But most significant of all is the evidence that the Dance may have originated in dramatic form, only later being translated into the media of paint and verse. The old Mummers' Plays, indeed, generally contained some form of death-dance, probably based on pagan fertility rituals, during which a member of the company would be ritually "beheaded" and then resurrected, either with or without an intervening dance of mourning. Later, during the first decades of the great plagues that swept across Europe (ca. 1340–80), folk dances called "The Death Dance" or "Dance of the Dead" became popular throughout Europe. In these dances, one member of the dance would act as corpse while the others danced round him or her, pretending to mourn but actually taking liberties with the "corpse's" person. In some cases, naturally, the dance was used as an occasion for horseplay and practical jokes; in other cases, even more naturally, it was used as an excuse for kissing and fondling the "deceased" (Warren, xiv–xv). Such dances lasted well into the seventeenth century, although ecclesiastics frowned on the custom and tried to stop it—mostly, one imagines, because of the ribaldry of the action, but also because of the pagan associations of witchcraft, demon lovers, and fairy rings, to which the dances no doubt owed a good deal.

But the churchmen themselves had a dramatized version of the Dance. There are indications that sermons on death, so popular with the friars, may have been accompanied by pageants of antiphonal processions, much in the manner of the famous *Quem quaeritis*; and by the fifteenth century, the pageants seem to have grown into full-scale processions in fancy dress, just as the *Quem quaeritis* itself grew into the elaborate cycles of Mystery Plays. In 1449, a "danse Macabre" was performed at Bruges by a full company of players before Duke Philippe le Bon of Burgundy; and the cathedral records at Besançon for July 1453 show a payment of "four measures of wine" to players who performed the Dance of Death after Mass (Warren, xi).

It is interesting to speculate on how these players may have been costumed. Although we have descriptions of some skeleton costumes for use in the later Mystery and Morality Plays, Death in the early painted Dances was not always an impersonal skeleton, but more often "le Mort," the dead person himself, come to claim the living. The paintings that survive show desiccated mummies, with the flesh rotted away but the skin still taut over the remaining bones and sometimes split open at the abdomen. In some pictures, the mummies are holding musical instruments; in others, they carry the many weapons associated with death; spears, arrows, spades, rakes, scythes, and maces. In some, they wear tatters of winding-sheets; in others, bits of costume appropriate to the living whom they have come to summon. In all the pictures, the dead seem to have more energy than the living; the mummies caper and cavort along the walls, while most of the living either stand rooted to the spot or hang back with sorrowful looks on their faces. There is little doubt as to who has the advantage in these Dances, and it is certainly not Lady Liffe.

The most telling evidence that the Dance was conceived of in dramatic terms lies in the nature of the verses that accompany the paintings. These are highly individualized addresses by Death to the living, each address directed to the estate or profession of the victim; and usually there is a reply in kind from the living to Death. In the great Dance at Holy Innocents, the individual dramas are made more pointed—and more poignant—by the almost infinitely varied responses of the characters: one is frightened, another puzzled, a third resigned, still another indignant, and so on. The impact of such individualized responses on the development of tragedy can hardly be stressed enough.

John Lydgate, who composed the verses for the famous Dance of Death in St. Paul's, actually translated them from the verses at Holy Innocents, probably sometime before 1433. They are a remarkably accurate rendering, despite the modest disclaimer given in "Lenvoye de translatoure" at the end:

> Owte of the frensshe / I drowe hit of entent
> Not worde be worde / but folwyng the substaunce
> And fro Paris / to Inglond hit sent
> Oneli of purpose / yow to do plesaunce
> Rude of language / y was not borne yn fraunce
> Haue me excused / my name is Jon Lidgate
> Of her tunge / I haue no suffisaunce
> Her corious metris / in Inglissh to translate.[11]

Although Lydgate's verses remained in manuscript until 1554 (twelve manuscripts in all), they must have been quite well known to the many who were familiar with the Dance at St. Paul's; and that many were in fact familiar with this Dance is indicated by Sir Thomas More's casual reference, shortly before his death, to "the Daunce of Death pictured in Poules."[12] Tottel later printed the verses in his edition of Lydgate's *Fall of Princes* (1554), during the vast popularity of such *de casibus* collections of the time, from which many dramatists drew material for their histories and tragedies.

The overriding theme of the Dance of Death is death's leveling quality: *all* humankind will be taken, young and old, rich and poor, high and low degree. To people accustomed to seeing rich and poor tumbled together into vast burial pits during the rich and poor tumbled together into vast burial pits during the plague, this must have seemed real enough—and, Theodore Spencer adds, the element of satire implicit in such enforced equality must have been "one which the rising bourgeois class could contemplate with considerable pleasure."[13]

Death, in Lydgate's verses, alters his tone according to the person addressed. To the lawyer, he speaks in legal jargon; to the wealthy man, he issues an order to leave his riches; to the powerful, he speaks of the power of death; to the pious, he offers compliments on their preparation to receive him; to the gamester, he says "check-mat"; and to the laborer he offers rest. His words to the "amerous Squyere" are as lovely as the delights of love, and as poignant as all the poetic laments for youth that sing through the lyrics of Chaucer, Shakespeare, and Marvell:

> Ye that be Jentel / so fresshe & amerous
> Of yeres yonge / floweryng in yowre grene age
> Lusti fre of herte / and eke desyrous
> Ful of deuyses / and chaunge yn yowre corage
> Pleasaunt of porte / of loke & [of] of visage
> But al shal turne / in to asshes dede
> For al beaute / is but a feynte ymage
> Which steleth a-wai / or folkes can take hede.
>
> (433–40)

To the Constable, Death speaks like an arresting officer: "Hit is my right / to reste & yow constrayn // With vs to daunce / my maiester Constable" (137–38). And to the Canon he utters the phrase later made famous by Everyman: "Dethe cometh ai / when men leste on hym thenke" (320).

The replies are as varied as the summonses. Some bid rueful adieux to their worldly pleasures, some realize that they have wasted their lives, others are frustrated at being interrupted in mid-career, and the Sergeant—like all such officials through the ages—is downright indignant:

> How dar this dethe / sette on me a-reste
> That am the kynges / chosen officere

Which yesterdai / bothe este & weste
Myn office dede / ful surquedous of chere. . . .

(369-72)

The Juror, too, refuses to give in with good grace; as he is dragged
off, he consoles himself with the thought that he has made men
so miserable, they will be glad to see him go.

The Carthusian is more amenable to the summons, although,
as he admits, no matter how good the preparation, every man
"Dredeth to dye / be kyndeli mocioun // After his flessheli /
Inclynacioun" (356-57). Still, he prays that God will accept his
soul and his poor efforts, and closes with the audience-directed
observation that "Somme ben to dai / that shul not be to
morowe" (360). His ambivalence is echoed by the Laborer, who
is not quite sure whether he really wants what he has prayed
for:

I haue wisshed / after dethe ful ofte
Al-be that I wolde / haue fled hym nowe
I had leuere / to haue leyne vnsofte
In wynde & reyne / & haue gon att plowe
With spade & pikeys / and labored for my prowe
Dolue and diched / & atte Carte goon
For I mai sey / & telle playnli howe
In this worlde / here ther is reste noon.

(553-60)

The Child, too, allows himself a plaintive, inarticulate cry before
he resigns himself to the "wille of god":

A a a / a worde I can not speke
I am so yonge / I was bore yisterdai. . . .
I cam but now / and now I go my wai. . . .

(585-86, 589)

But it is the Monk whose voice will ring through the dark
tragedies of the Jacobean age. He will try to repent, he says, but
even if he cannot, he will put a good face on things—and perhaps
he is not the only one doing so:

God of his merci / graunte me repentaunce
Be chere owtewarde / hard to deuyce
Al ben not meri / which that men seen daunce.

(390–92)

These lines, it must be noted, are a dramatic improvement on
the French, which conclude only, "Chascun nest pas joyeux qui
danse."[14] Although Lydgate may have added "that men seen"
only to fill out his English meter, he has added a new note of
isolation to the idea of the joyless dance. Now the soul is alone
among a crowd of spectators who cannot apprehend his grief—a
motif that will reach its apex in Calantha, dancing as her heart-
strings crack in *The Broken Heart*.

Lydgate's Dance concludes with a set piece: "The kynge
liggyng dede & eten with wormes" (LXXX, marg. note). And
indeed it is the sense of bodily corruption that pervades the death-
images of fourteenth- and fifteenth-century art. It is in the fifteenth
century, for example, that the popularity of the double tomb-
monument became most popular: above, the recumbent figure
of the man as he appeared in life, and below, a rotting corpse
crawling with worms. Even the ghostly revenant of the folk-ballad
seems to have taken pleasure in showing off its worm-eaten
remains, as in this variation of one of the countless "Sweet
William" ballads:

"Gin ye be Clerk Saunders, my true-love
    This meikle marvels me;
Oh wherein is your bonny arms
    That wont to embrace me?"

"By worms they're eaten, in mools they're rotten,
    Behold, Margaret, and see,
And mind, for a' your mickle pride,
    Sae will become o' thee."[15]

Through painting and prayer book the corpse dances or
hunts, waving its rotted arms and displaying its split-open belly.
In the early Legends and Dances, it is an image of the self to
come—almost, one may say, an image of the self after selfhood

has departed. It shows up in the hunt, it hovers over the grave, and, as in the *Hours of Rohan* (1420), it may even enter the sickroom with a coffin on its shoulder.[16] In almost all these cases, there is a one-on-one relationship: the individual facing his own end.

But there was another face of death as well. In the many Triumphs of Death that were pictured at this time, the old idea of Death as Conqueror, the Horseman of the Apocalypse, rides through towns on ox-drawn triumphal carts, mowing down everyone in his path, and apparently unstoppable. In some depictions, such as the one in the *Très Riches Heures de Duc de Berry* he leads vast armies of corpses against a town, and peasant and king alike fall before the invasion. Here, as Phillippe Ariès remarks, "Death is a symbol of blind fate, very different, apparently, from the individualism of . . . danses macabres. . . . The Death of the Triumphs comes without warning."[17]

There is a subtle but important distinction between these two types of portrayals. In the Legends and Dances, death is an individual confrontation between the self and its end; the individual has time, even as death lays its icy hand on his arm, to make preparation and resign himself to necessity. If there is fear involved in the encounter, there is also the comfort of the breathing-space and of the chance to reply to the summons, to utter a last affirmation of selfhood. For the audience, too, there is a distancing effect of watching the encounter and participating vicariously in the exchange, perhaps even of being able to approve or disapprove of a soul's response to the summons.

But in the Triumphs of Death, there is no chance to participate actively or vicariously; the thousands overthrown by the armed and crowned corpse have no chance to talk back, no selection of possibilities open to them even at the moment of death. They are not even individuals any more; they are crowds. In a way, the piles of corpses that strew the ground in the wake of Death's Triumph are like the damned in the Last Judgment paintings whose moment of judgment is past, leaving them no hope and no recourse.

And in this sense, another image of death, the "Drery Deth" who stands crowned and alone, grinning out of the frame or manuscript at the viewer, is a logical extension of the Triumph. The Legend is a warning, the Dance a summons, and the Triumph a final judgment; but they are all happening to other people. The Dreary Death puts the viewer into the picture, making him one of the Living in the Legend, who must now give his own answer to the warning or summons.

Certainly, the prevalence of so many faces of Death would seem to argue for the "obsession" that so many historians have seen in the late Middle Ages. And yet, was it really an obsession? Or was it rather an understandable attempt to deal with a very present danger: the inexplicable epidemics that entered a town and slew hundreds in the midst of their revelry; the corpses piled up along the streets; the uncertainty, as one put on one's finest clothes in the morning, as to whether one would die in them before sundown?

When the human mind is faced with the incomprehensible, with chaos or destruction on too vast a scale to be absorbed, the natural impulse is to make the concept more familiar so that it can be dealt with; paradoxically, the closer a thing can be brought, the more it can be distanced. And much as Johan Huizinga has added to our knowledge of the late Middle Ages, his failure to recognize this impulse that lies behind the death art of the period has led him into misconceptions—even condemnations—of the societies with which he deals:

> The dominant thought, as expressed in the literature, both ecclesiastical and lay, of the period, hardly knew anything with regard to death but these two extremes: lamentation about the briefness of all earthly glory, and jubilation over the salvation of the soul. All that lay between—pity, resignation, longing, consolation—remained unexpressed and was, so to say, absorbed by the too much accentuated and too vivid representation of Death hideous and threatening (135).

Nothing shows better the primitive character of the hyper-idealist mentality, called realism in the Middle Ages, than the tendency to ascribe a sort of substantiality to abstract concepts (199).

The key to Huizinga's conception of the age, of course, lies in his use of the word *primitive*, a word he uses frequently about people of the period, along with *savage, barbaric,* and *childish.* Such condescension indicates that the speaker has not thought of his subjects in fully human terms or has insisted that the only proper terms are his own.[18] But each age, Huizinga notwithstanding, develops its own mental shorthand to deal with its own problems, and this shorthand, for the people who use it, implies all the things that "lie between."

In reality, the "pity, resignation, longing, consolation" were *not* "unexpressed"; we have seen them expressed in the words and attitudes of the participants in Lydgate's Dance of Death and the varied reactions of the Living in the Legend. Even the lyrics that seem to have been based on iconographic representations are remarkably complex in their simplicity:

> This lyfe, I see, is but a cherye feyre;
> All thyngis passene and so most I algate.
> To-day I sat full ryall in a cheyere,
> Tyll sotell deth knokyd at my gate,
> And on-avysed he seyd to me, chek-mat!
> lo! how sotell he maketh a devors—
> and wormys to fede, he hath here leyd my cors.[19]

There is a certain universality in such a rueful confrontation with one's own end, and even the image of death knocking at the door seems to be a timeless one. To this day, many Orthodox Jews, during the week of solemn mourning after a funeral, do not knock at the door of the bereaved when paying condolence visits because the knock is associated with the Angel of Death who has taken the deceased.

The adaptations of the *vado mori* lyric are similarly imbued with the wistfulness of passing, as are the many versions of the *Timor mortis conturbat me,* a lyric originally describing the reconciliation to one's own death, but combined by Dunbar with the *ubi sunt* and Dance of Death traditions into broader terms:

> The stait of man dois change and vary,
> Now sound, now seik, now blith, now sary,
> Now dansand mery, now like to dee;
>   *Timor mortis conturbat me.*
>
> . . . .
>
> On to the ded gois all Estatis,
> Princis, Prelotis, and Potestatis,
> Baith riche and pur of al degre;
>   *Timor mortis conturbat me.*[20]

The insistent depiction, then, of death as a concrete object to be faced, and even faced down, is a method of seeking to define the unknown, to order chaos, and, by giving to airy nothing a local habitation and a name, to find comfort in familiar things, no matter how ugly. As Philippa Tristram has so keenly observed: "[I]t is sometimes more helpful to know that a nightmare is shared, than to be told that it does not exist. They were haunted by images of physical corruption, but by animating and confronting these figures, they brought themselves face to face with their own fears, and learnt what they could from them" (183).

In this regard, it is interesting to reexamine Chaucer's *Pardoner's Tale,* one of the most chilling in the annals of death literature. The three young men gladly run off in pursuit of a Death whom they hear personified as a "theef,"[21] because a defined figure is easy to deal with. The Pardoner's audience, however—and Chaucer's—would no doubt have been horrified at this evidence of pride in the young men, since Death is always pictured as invincible by all except Christ, and the listeners would have expected to hear a description of the usual grisly figure cutting the young men down in their tracks. Instead, the young men meet an old man who complains that he cannot die, and who directs them to a tree where he has just seen Death. Under the tree, the young men find gold, and in their avarice kill each other; they have found death after all—but in themselves.

We who are unused to taking fourteenth-century iconography seriously may absorb the moral correctly but miss the implications of the encounter with the old man. Chaucer's audience would most likely have recognized this encounter as a modified version of the Legend, in which the Living are called to repentance by a vision of what they will become; and the old man, as a symbol of age, is also a symbol of mutability. In some pictures of the time, Age is indeed used as a substitute for the mummies of the Legend, or may be seen as a figure revolving to the bottom of Fortune's wheel,[22] while in *Piers Plowman*, Elde is the messenger of Dethe. Furthermore, the fact that the old man is immortal (much as he bemoans the fact) hints at a supernatural presence—and it must be remembered that Death was considered the one earthly being who could not die, at least until the Last Judgment. So the fourteenth-century audience would have seen a good deal more of the supernatural in the tale than we do today, and would have recognized the young men's response as one of the many variants in the Legend. And, unlike the young men, they would have "learnt from" the encounter.

But symbols, as we have noted, are mental shorthand for accepted communal ideas, and when those ideas change, the symbols must change as well. Fourteenth- and fifteenth-century symbolic representations of death were built onto a particular theological framework, without which they lose much of their meaning. When theologians of the sixteenth century began restructuring that framework, new symbols had to be found to replace what now seemed like mere decoration, or as Huizinga called it too early, "the abused imagery of skeletons and worms" (135). A detailed analysis of what that framework was, and how it changed, will be given in chapter 2; meanwhile, let us examine the change in the symbol itself.

At the turn of the sixteenth century, two particularly significant changes became evident in representations of Death: first, the corpse or mummy virtually disappears, giving way almost entirely to the skeleton; and second, the skeleton begins to hide from its victims far more often than it did in earlier representations. It is possible, of course, that the change from decayed flesh to bare bones is simply a manifestation of increased Renaissance knowledge of anatomy, with a concomitant desire to show off this new knowledge, but the effect is to divorce the symbol one step further from the human, and to make the figure more impersonal. And by having the figure lurk in the background—behind trees, under tables, behind the subjects' backs—early sixteenth-century artists diminished the medieval idea of confrontation and warning at the moment of death, substituting for it a sense of pervasive death—the intangible threat lurking in every corner.

The works of Dürer and Holbein may serve as examples of the symbol in transition. Dürer, in particular, shows Death in both medieval and Renaissance guises, as though he and his society had not yet come to terms with the new philosophy. His Fourth Horseman of the Apocalypse (ca. 1498) is an emaciated old man with a long beard and wild, rolling eyes, who rides an equally emaciated horse and wields a trident or rake. He and his companions gallop across the bodies of peasants and citizens much in the manner of the Triumphs of Death.[23] In "The Promenade," another early engraving, Death is a skeletonic mummy with an hourglass, who hides behind a tree in the background, laughing at two lovers.[24] In a sketch made during the plague year of 1505, Death becomes a crowned skeleton with a scythe, riding a skeletonic horse; but unlike the usual Dreary Death, which faces out at the viewer, this skeleton rides off at right angles to the viewer, paying him no attention whatsoever (92). And finally, in "Knight, Death, and Devil" (ca. 1513), although Death retains his medieval trappings—the crowned and bearded mummy with hourglass and full complement of worms—now it is the Knight who pays no attention (114). The significant point about this variation on the Legend is that the Knight is implicitly commended for ignoring Death; his faith has entitled him, not to meet it philosophically, but to pretend that it is not there. In the old Legend, it will be remembered, the Living who ignored Death's message were the wastrels, like Chaucer's three young men.

Holbein, too, puts the old symbols to new uses. His *Dance of Death* (ca. 1525) echoes the medieval form in showing all classes of people subject to Death, and in varying the responses of the victims to his summons. The monk, abbot, merchant, and abbess scream and try to break free of Death's grip; the bishop is resigned but not happy; the rich man is frantic over the loss of his wealth (Death is scooping up his gold); the child is puzzled; and the pedlar, frankly irritated at being interrupted in his journey. A singularly comforting Death, however, helps the old man into his grave, while a more questionably helpful Death drives the ploughman's horses quickly through the last furrow toward a setting sun.[25]

All these representations contain the subtle medieval nuances of the soul's confontation with death. But in many of the other pictures in the series, Death (an impersonal skeleton) is invisible to the subject of his summons. The judge, advocate, and councillor go on taking bribes without noticing him; the countess continues to pick out clothing, unaware that Death has put a necklace of bones around her neck; the noblewoman smiles at her husband, apparently oblivious to the drumroll that Death is performing on a tabor hung somewhat obscenely between his legs; and the nun, turning from her prayers to look at a young man with a lute, does not notice Death dressed as a chambermaid, putting out the candles.

This fading of Death into the background, which paradoxically made it more frightening, became a common motif of sixteenth-century portrait painting. Holbein himself did some of these portraits with the subject gazing into space while a skeleton with scythe and hourglass grins behind his shoulder;[26] and in the famous "The Ambassadors," even the viewer is tricked into overlooking Death from any but a certain angle. At the bottom of the picture, there is what looks like an off-white diagonal smudge, but when the viewer stands directly below and slightly to the left of the canvas, looking up, the "smudge" resolves itself into a skull.[27]

After Holbein, only a few attempts at the Dance of Death survive, and the change in viewpoint becomes more evident as they progress. A 1569 broadside, "The Daunce and Song of Death,"[28] shows the traditional circle of dancers, three skeletons and six people: a king, a beggar, an old man, a child, a wise man, and a fool. Oddly enough, the wise man and the old man seem the most reluctant to join the dance, while the king smiles bravely and the beggar, child, and fool kick up their heels. In the four corners of the sheet, tableaux show skeletons arresting a miser, a justice, a prisoner, and a pair of lovers, of whom only the prisoner looks Death in the face. The reluctance of the old man and the wise man to go with Death are novelties in themselves, but the most significant change in this Dance is that the Summons itself is issued not by Death but by a new figure: "Sycknes Deathes minstrel," a figure with a skull's head but fully fleshed body covered with sores, who sits on a chair made of bones, propped on a pick and shovel over an open grave. He plays a tabor and sings an invitation to the Dance—but except for their physical attitudes, no one answers.

Another broadside, published in 1580 and beginning, "Marke well the effect purtreyed here," seems in many ways closer to the old tradition but also takes a new turn.[29] In the background, gentlemen and ladies are feasting in an arbor, while Death (a skeleton) runs up to them with spear poised to throw. This is close enough to the hunting versions of the Legend to have the old flavor. Again, in the foreground, stand five figures: a bishop, a king, a harlot, a lawyer, and a "country clown." Although an odd assortment of folk, it is representative of the variety featured in the Dance. The difference is that none of the five notices that Death has entered the picture from the right, one hand grasping a spear and the other reaching out toward the clown's shoulder. The verses printed below the woodcut indicated that the five Living are thinking only of power politics in this world, while Death's speech in the verses tells the reader that his power will soon destroy that of the other figures. The verses are summarized in mottoes printed under the six figures; those under the five Living clearly show that they do not realize that they have been joined by a sixth personage:

> *Bishop:* I praye for yov fower.
> *King:* I defende yov fower.
> *Harlot:* I vanqvesh yov fower.
> *Lawyer:* I helpe yov IIII to yovr
>   right.
> *Cowln:* I feede yov fower.
> *Death:* I kill yov all.

This is the hidden death that offers no warning at the moment of arrest, and as will be seen in chapter 2, it is a logical outcome of the change in deathbed literature, which has turned from the moment of death and focused instead on the "death in the midst of life," the entire life span viewed as a preparation for death.

By this time, in fact, both the Dance and the Legend have lost much of their medieval quality of warning, retaining only the satiric note. As early as 1604, Samuel Rowlands's *Looke To It: For, Ile Stabbe Ye*, while ostensibly an address by Death to wrongdoers, is little more than a satire on those wrongdoers, with a refrain of "Ile stabbe ye" following each verse "character."[30] Death, here, is almost an afterthought, and the giving of the warning only to malefactors makes death seem like a specific punishment for evil; the universal summons of death—and its occasional comfort—is no longer a part of the message.

Rowlands approaches the traditional Dance more closely in *A Terrible Battell Betweene Time and Death* (ca. 1606). Here, Time and Death discuss the people whom they have just taken, and although much of their discussion is given to satire against social types, they do present a "good" death as well as all the retributive ones: a divine who has lived a good life and can therefore accept death gracefully. However, Time and Death soon fall out over questions of each other's importance, and the ensuing slapstick and name-calling give the remainder of the poem an untraditional air of the comic grotesque, which will be discussed at greater length in chapter 10.

By the 1630s, the new satiric tradition was firmly in place. A 1631 ballad entitled "Deaths Daunce. To be sung to a pleasant new tune call'd Oh no, no, no, not yet or, the meddow brow,"[31] despite its woodcuts of skeletons, is not a Dance at all;

it is, rather, a satirical attack on roguery, much in the manner of Rowlands but in the conditional mood—as though there were a choice:

> If Death would go to Westminster,
>   to walke about the Hall,
> And make himself a Counsellor,
>   in pleas amongst them all,
> I thinke the Court of Conscience,
>   would have a great regard,
> When Death should come with diligence,
>   to have their matter heard.

(st.5)

And finally, Walter Colman's *La Dance Machabre, or Deaths Duell* (1633), although a frequently moving poem, is neither dance nor duel but a combination of social satire and *ubi sunt*.[32] The title page, to be sure, looks promising: eight scenes of daily life in varied classes of society line both sides of the page, four panels to a side. At the top of the center section sits Death, a skeleton armed with a spear; and at the bottom, Time, a bearded and winged old man with hourglass and scythe, kneels on a globe that represents the world. On the frontispiece, a skeleton holds a spade and leans on a broken column in a graveyard (looking a little bored), and beneath him is the traditional motto: "Behould fonde man I am what thou shalt be / And as thou art soe was I once like thee."

Colman has obviously tried hard to recapture the atmosphere of the allegorical memento mori, but although the trappings are traditional, the flavor is modern. His theme is primarily the vanity of human wishes; he sees man as food for worms, and worms as gluttons of the graveyard, but the emphasis of the meditation is on the body; the afterlife of the soul is not addressed. The final effect, then, is an implication that death is the end of everything. Unlike both the medieval preachers and the Renaissance preachers and essayists, Colman does not see the other side of this "quintessence of dust": the soul that is an image of God or that can redeem its own death by meeting death bravely.

So the Dance of Death has turned comic, or has gone back to the ubi sunt whence it came; but meanwhile, what has become of the memento mori? From the beginning of the sixteenth century, it almost seems as though the skeleton, in order to retain its meaning, had to be taken to pieces, and the skull alone, that age-old symbol of mortality, still holds its own as the dreadful warning—for a while.

Skelton, early in the century, was still able to abstract an old moral from the "deedmans hed" that a friend had sent him:

I haue well espyde
No man may hym hyde
From Deth holow eyed,
With synnews wyderyd,
With bonys shyderyd,
With his worme etyn maw,
And his gastly jaw
Gaspyng asyde,
Nakyd of hyde,
Neyther flesh nor fell.[33]

But in Holbein's "The Ambassadors," already discussed as perhaps the best memento mori device of the century, one of the ambassadors wears a death's-head amulet; and in this amulet are the seeds of change.

During the latter half of the sixteenth century, while the animated skeleton behind the subject's shoulder disappears in portraits, the skull begins showing up more often at the subject's elbow or in his hand. It is difficult to account for this distinction between what must be hidden and what may be displayed or regarded, except to note that the skull is immobile. It has no legs on which to approach the subject, no hands with which to seize him; it is an end product, safely dead, that may aid contemplation but poses a warning only, not a threat.

By the end of the sixteenth century, the inanimate skull was so common that it had become first an item of fashion and then an object of derision. All classes of society began wearing death's-head rings, much in the manner that people today wear religious symbols: some as a genuine aid to prayer; some as an outward show of faith; and some, no doubt, as a matter of fashion, because everyone else had one. As the fashion spread, prostitutes began wearing the rings as well, probably as an effort to appear "respectable"; but as the sign became almost universal among members of the profession, it eventually came to be regarded as an advertisement of the wearer's trade.[34] And over the years, the symbol thus became not a manifestation of the thing it was meant to symbolize but rather an object in itself—not a reminder of death but a protection against it, a lucky charm that would allow the wearer to forget about death.

In spite of this, however, one would think that the growing vogue of emblem books, at least, would maintain the old iconography of death, since they were based on story-through-symbol like the Legend and the Dance. But Geffrey Whitney's *A Choice of Emblems* (1586) presents only one emblem of death, and that one is a female Mors with wings, who is part of a classical joke: Death and Love accidentally exchange arrows, with the result that young people die and old people love.[35] Death reappears in George Wither's *A Collection of Emblemes, Ancient and Moderne*, published in 1635 but probably written much earlier. The pictures were first printed at Utrecht in 1611 or 1613, in *Nucleus emblematum selectissimorum*, and Wither, who thought the verses clumsy, composed his own verses but did not tamper with the pictures themselves.[36] In this collection of two hundred emblems, Death as a pictorial symbol occurs eleven times, once as an animated skeleton, once as a partial skeleton, and nine times as a skull. Oddly enough, the animated skeleton is used only as an advertisement for learning; the motto is, "By *Knowledge* onely, *Life* wee gaine, / All other things to *Death* pertaine" (1). The picture shows a scientist happily engaged in his studies, with the skeleton off to one side, playing with a tableful of jewels. This theme occurs again in a picture of a scholar climbing out of a skull-strewn grave toward sun and moon; the motto here is, "To *Learning* I a love should have, / Although one foot were in the *Grave*" (87). One can hardly quarrel with the sentiment, but the tradition seems to have gone astray.

Indeed, of the remaining nine skull emblems in Wither, only five represent a traditional memento mori. Of the other four, one skull is only a stage property lying near Vice, who is struggling with Virtue over a living young man (22); one is being spurned under the heel of a cherub rising to heaven (152); one has wheat growing out of its apertures to symbolize rebirth and eternal life (21); and the last is gnashing its teeth (one supposes) over two clasped hands whose motto is, "*Death*, is unable to divide / their Hearts, whose Hands *True-Love* hath tyde" (99). And four sets of verses on death have no skulls at all in their emblems.

It is possible that death's traditional image began to disappear from emblems and be parodied in broadsides as it became more vulgarized in the ubiquitous death's-head jewelry. But it is also true that the whole iconography of death was beginning to change as new symbols and ideas became current. By the 1570s, a new poetry had become popular in England: the Petrarchan conventions of the love sonneteers. Although death poems continued to appear for a while in such popular miscellanies as *The Paradise of Dainty Devices* and the *Gorgeous Gallery of Gallant Inventions* (1578), speaking of death's "launce,"[37] and "The daunce of death, which all must runne on rowe,"[38] by the 1580s they were rapidly being overshadowed by poems in which death was to be suffered only through darts from a lady's eyes; and by the 1590s, the traditional death poem had vanished from the miscellanies altogether.

But hiding from death, mocking death, and wearing death's face as an amulet against death will not make death go away, and the human mind always needs symbols through which it can comprehend and grapple with the feared object. So as the corpse, skeleton, and skull ceased to be useful, poets were forced to seek new symbols.

One logical symbol for an event, of course, is the process that leads to it. And during a literary period of concern with love, youth, and beauty, Time as process is, logically, Time the destroyer. Throughout the poetry of the late sixteenth century, then, it is not Death but Time who carries the scythe, Time who places his hand on living flesh. In Spenser's *Faerie Queene*, he is the enemy in the Garden of Adonis, the destroyer whom not even the gods can halt:

> Great enimy to it, and to all the rest,
> That in the Gardin of Adonis springs,
> Is wicked Tyme, who, with his scythe addrest,
> Does mow the flowring herbes and goodly things,
> And all their glory to the ground downe flings,
> Where they do wither and are fowly mard;
> He flies about, and with his flaggy winges
> Beates downe both leaves and buds without regard,
> Ne ever pitty may relent his malice hard.
>
> . . . .
>
> For all that lives is subject to the law:
> Al things decay in time, and to their end do draw.[39]

As a personification, Death still has his "grisly" face in *The Faerie Queene*, but he has become less substantial and, rather than an all-conquering force, only one to the actors that Mutabilitie calls forth in her pageant of the changing seasons:

> And after all came Life, and lastly Death;
> Death with most grim and griesly visage seene,
> Yet is he nought but parting of the breath;
> Ne ought to see, but like a shade to weene,
> Unbodied, unsoul'd, unheard, unseene. . . . .

(VII.vii.46)

Further, in the great religious poetry of the late sixteenth and early seventeenth centuries, this is largely how death will appear: when invisible, as a mighty force struggling within the poet's soul, but when given a shape or personification, as an ineffectual figure who is invoked only to be dismissed or patronized:

> [Shakespeare:]
> So shalt thou feed on Death, that feeds on men,
> And Death once dead, there's no more dying then.[40]

> [Donne:]
> One short sleepe past, we wake eternally,
> And death shall be no more, Death thou shalt die.[41]

[Herbert:]
Death thou wast once an uncouth hideous thing,
    Nothing but bones,
    The sad effect of sadder grones,
Thy mouth was open but thou couldst not sing. . . .

. . . But since our Saviours Death did put some blood
    Into thy face;
    Thou art growne fair and full of grace,
Much in request, much sought for as a good.[42]

Death as an event, then, is no longer symbolized by the moment of arrest, the hand on the shoulder. The new symbols are the process leading to the event and, as in the late Middle Ages, one of the event's end products. But the end product has taken a new form. There is no inherently logical reason, after all, for a corpse or skeleton to symbolize the moment of death; the decayed body is only an aftermath, retrospective evidence that death has come and gone. If the artists of the fourteenth and fifteenth centuries seized upon this particular image because it was the most familiar sight in the plague-strewn streets of Europe, there was no reason for a later age to continue mimicking them. As the corpse began to be hidden, and Time gained ascendancy as a process-symbol for the event, it was more logical to choose an end product more appropriate to the process. And with Time so often depicted as a mower-down of fields, a changer of seasons and destroyer of earthly beauty, what better end product could there be than the withered flower?

It is perhaps better to delay a discussion of the faded or withered flower until we have traced the progress of philosophical and religious views on death through the seventeenth century. For my purposes now, it is sufficient to observe how the moment of death—the event itself—was realigned into symbols of process and end product in Renaissance art and poetry. Only on the stage did the Summons of Death—the moment of arrest—continued for a time; and even on stage, symbol was to give way to sensationalism by the Caroline years.

II

Answering the Summons

The Art of Dying

AS WE HAVE SEEN, the inconography of Death in the later Middle Ages tends to be centered on the idea of confrontation: Death calls and the living respond. What is important to note in this tradition is that the confrontation itself is based on a paradox: the end of things is actually an opportunity to begin again, a last chance to reorder an entire lifetime before being called to account for it. Such a view is compatible, of course, with a system of belief that interposed between the soul and its destruction a series of second chances. At the bedside of the dying, the last sacraments prepared the soul to make its final choice; saints and angels might be called on for assistance; the very pains of dying might be offered as penance for sins; and even if the final repentance was ragged, and the atonement barely sufficient, there was always Purgatory, where the process might be completed. When the event of death is viewed in this manner—as a last chance on earth—the event itself takes on a great deal of importance, and one prays, not for a sudden and "easy" death, but for a death that allows some breathing space.

As even Catholic theologians noted, however, the idea of the breathing space may itself become a danger, in that the living may put all the reordering off until the last minute. As early as the the thirteenth century, the church had begun encouraging annual sacramental confession, and by the early sixteenth century Catholic theologians (including the early Christian humanists) were putting more and more emphasis on the entire life as a preparation for death. To the early Protestants, too, deathbed conversion was suspect; faith and assurance of salvation, if genuine, should come early in life; a truly holy death was thus a manifestation of rather than a means of salvation; and fear of damnation not only was an unsuitable substitute for assurance of salvation but probably indicated a reprobate in the first place. Although these reactions to the old tradition were in turn modified during the seventeenth century, we can probably best trace the development of ideas through the changing nature of deathbed counseling: the Art of Dying in its many permutations.

Even with the breathing space allowed, late medieval theologians and artists seldom pretended that death as an event was pleasant. Rather, they stressed the agony of separation between body and soul, the devils that hovered about the dying person to tempt him to Hell, and the terrors of the judgment that awaited the soul. As early as the thirteenth century, death lyrics began enumerating not just the horrors of the grave (end product) but also the horrors of the deathbed (event):

> When the hede quakyth
> And the lyppis blakyth
> And the nose sharpyth
> And the senow starkyth
> And the brest pantyth
> And the brethe wantyth
> And the tethe ratelyt
> And the throte roteleth.[1]

Here we do not have the later intellectualization of death but a physical confrontation with the reality of dying, the event in all its ugliness. Still, we remember Philippa Tristram's observation: "it is sometimes more helpful to know that a nightmare is shared than to be told that it does not exist" (183); and once the nightmare of death was documented, it could be dealt with point by point.

An Indication of how fourteenth- and fifteenth-century society dealt with the nightmare may be seen in the transformation of the Death Signs lyric quoted above, which became, in the fifteenth century, an instructional book in little:

When thy hede quakyth:	Memento.
Then thy lyppys blakyth:	Confessio.
When thy nose sharpyth:	Contricio.
Then thy lymmys starkyth:	Satisfaccio.
When thy brest pantyth:	Nosce teipsum.
Then thy wynde wantyth:	Miserere.
When thy nyen hollyth:	Libera me domine.
The deth folowyth:	Veni ad judicum.[2]

To the nightmare has been added on ordering agent: a step-by-step plan of what to do at each point in the process. And it is this need to order chaos, to give the human creature something that it can *do* in a frightening situation, that marks, not only the Legends and Dances of the period, but also the flood of treatises setting forth rules on how to die.

The *ars moriendi* of the late Middle Ages is basically an instructional manual. It guides the dying, and the friends of the dying, through the crucial event in such a way as to use most effectively the last chance now provided to the soul. As Sister Mary Catherine O'Connor has so accurately characterized it, "The *Ars moriendi* is not a book of remote preparation for [death] —except for one or two perfunctory sentences in praise of a virtuous life, no *ars vivendi*. It is a complete and intelligible guide to the business of dying . . . no more intended to frighten and depress than is any medieval book on hunting or hawking or on table manners for children."[3]

During the fourteenth century, the instructional manual on dying began to take shape in compendia of religious teachings, particularly in sections based on Henry Suso's *Horologium sapientiae* (ca. 1328), which contained sample deathbed meditations and a frightening description of a soul going unprepared to death. By the end of the century, or sometime before 1408, the orderly procedure of dying was formalized in Jean Charlier de Gerson's

De arte moriendi, part of his *Opusculum tripartitum*. In this seminal work, which depended heavily on church liturgy, Gerson attempted to provide a ritual that could be followed at the dying
person's bedside when the services of a priest were not available—a
useful tool when there were so few clergy left in the plague years.
The ritual contained exhortations to the dying, sample meditations, prayers, last duties for the dying to perform, and a series
of interrogations through which the dying could affirm their faith,
indicate repentance, and commend their souls to God.[4]

Shortly after Gerson's *Opusculum*, a long series of tracts on
the art of dying began to appear all over Europe. Apparently deriving from one original treatise, the *Tractatus artis bene moriendi*,
they took many forms: long manuscripts, "blockbook" versions
(picture books for the illiterate), printed copies with and without
illustrations, and versions that varied the numbers and sources
of quotations from scripture, liturgy, pagan philosophers, and
church fathers. Despite all these variations, however, the *ars
moriendi* of the fifteenth century is essentially one document, and
allowing for the variations, we may well use one of the latest in
the series as an illustration of the handbook's method: Caxton's
1490 printing "The arte & crafte to know well to dye."[5]

The treatise is divided into six parts: (1) reasons why "one
oughte to deye gladly"; (2) temptations at the moment of death;
(3) questions to be put to the dying; (4) instructions to be given
to them; (5) meditations on the sufferings of Christ; and (6) prayers
to be said by the dying or by those assisting at their deathbeds
(A1r). The first section opens with the apparently granted assumption that the death of the body is the most fearful thing imaginable
but hastens to assure the reader that, once the pain is over, the
soul will have escaped an unsatisfactory world to live in a perfect
one with God—that is, if the soul has made adequate preparation by living a good life or at least being contrite for a bad one:
"And therefore euery good crysten man and also euerych syn-
ner verily contryte oughte not to be sorowfulle ne trouble hym
of the temporall or bodyly deth, ne he oughte not to fere ne
doubte hit, for what some euer mater or cause be layd to hym
but he oughte to suffre and receyue it pacyently and in thanks"

(A1v). Assuming that one has made this preparation, death is only "the goynge oute of pryson" and a laying down of the heavy weight of a body (A1v). Even the pagans have said that one "ought sonner to chose the bodily deth" than to do anything contrary to virtue, so surely a death that is so universally praised cannot be totally bad (A1r).

There is something a little spurious about this reasoning, and indeed it is contradicted by the carefully outlined procedures in the other sections for escaping all the dangers surrounding death. But the first sections of all these treatises are meant to proffer comfort before the battle against temptation begins, and the basic effect is to direct the mind toward death as a threshold to be crossed rather than as a pain to be undergone.

And at this threshold the temptations are mighty, as the devils gather for their last assault on the soul. According to all the *ars moreindi* treatises, those "in thartycle of death haue many greuous & strong temptacions vereli suche that in their lyf they neuer had lyke" (A2r), and these are five in number:

1. The temptation "of the fayth," when the devil will try to deceive Moriens (the dying person) into falling away from Christ, through "errours superstycions and heresie." Moriens must remember that a Christian is required to stand firm in his faith, and he may take comfort in knowing that "the deuyll maye not ouercome the persone as longe as he shall haue the usage of his free wyll well dysposed, if by his owne agrement he wyll not consent to the deuil." As an aid to resistance against this temptation, Moriens or those attending him should repeat the Creed "wyth an hye voys," and call to mind the constancy of all the saints, martyrs, apostles, and even good pagans as encouragement to steadfastness (A2r–v).

2. The temptation "ayenste hope by dyspayre," when the devil takes advantage of Moriens's weakened condition to make him grieve so much over his sins that he will despair of being forgiven. But Moriens must remember that God's capacity for mercy is infinitely greater than man's capacity for sin, and that "though that he had commited as many murthers and theftes as there ben dropes of water and small grauell in the see," though he may

never have confessed his sins before, even though he may be too ill to confess them aloud now—still, if he repents in his mind at this last moment, God will accept his contrition: "for god dyspyseth neuer a contryte herte and humble." As an exercise, Moriens should contemplate Christ on the cross: "For he hath the hede inclyned and bowed to kysse us, the armes stratched abrode for tembrace us, the handes perced & opened for to gyue to us, the syde open for to loue us, and all his body stratched for to gyue hym selfe all to us." And for encouragement, Moriens should call to mind other sinners who were forgiven: Peter, Paul Matthew, Mary Magdalene, the woman taken in adultery, the Good Thief, and "many moo other whyche were grete synners & horryble" (A2v–A3v).

3. The temptation "by impacyence: that is ayenste charite." In the great sorrow and pain of dying, Moriens may be tempted to "murmure or grutche" against God, and to act as though he were mad, tormenting not only himself but the people around him. He must remember, in this sore temptation, that charity and patience will bring him closer to God, and that, furthermore, the pain against which he is railing was sent him on purpose to help him atone for his sins: "Infyrmte tofore deth is lyke as a purgatore, soo that it be suffred . . . pacyently, gladly, & agreably. And it cometh by dyuyne dyspensacion that to the lengest vyce & synne is gyuen the lengest malady" (A3v–A4r).

4. The temptation to "spirituell pryde, by the whiche the deuylle assayleth most theym that be duoute." Since the devil cannot make the devout lose faith, hope, or charity, he rather inflates them with vainglory about their ability to withstand the other temptations. "O how thou art ferme & stedfaste in the faythe," says the devil in Moriens's heart; "o how thou art sure in hope, o how thou art stronge & pacyent, o how thou haste doon many good dedes." It is an easy step from such thoughts to the sin of presumption, and when Moriens finds himself thinking such thoughts, he must try to humble himself, particularly by remembering his sins, but not so much that he will despair; rather, he must keep in mind that "none is certayn, yf he be dygne

or worthy to haue deserued the loue of god, or the hate of god"
(A4r–v)

5. The temptation "that most troubleth the seculers and
wordly [*sic*] men, . . . the ouer grete ocupacyon of outwarde
thinges and temporall . . . which he hath moost loued in his
lyf." Moriens must put all such temporal thoughts from his mind
and renounce the things of the world that he is about to leave,
strengthening his resolve with the thought that the renunciation
itself is a form of penance that may atone for at least the venial
sins, and so spare him some of the pains of Purgatory. Above
all, Moriens must loose his hold on life itself, because hoping to
escape from death "is a thinge ryght peryllous & moche dysordred
in euery crysten man and that ofte cometh by intyncyon of the
deuyl" (A4v).

During all these temptations, Moriens may comfort himself
with the knowledge that God does not permit us to be tempted
more than we can bear. Further, we have been given the use of
reason to combat temptation, and so long as we continue to fight,
the devil cannot conquer us against our will.

In the illustrated versions of the treatise, there are two woodcuts for each temptation: one showing the devils swarming about
Moriens's bed, and one showing Moriens resisting their temptations, often with so many saints and angels on hand to help that
the room seems jammed to the very doors and windows. This approach to the temptations, to risk overusing Tristram's phrase, is
the comfort of the shared nightmare. By enumerating all the symptoms, the treatise makes deathbed fear into a known and therefore
treatable malady. Moriens is given a set of mental exercise to do,
is provided the company of others who have suffered through
the same pains before him, and is assured at each step that the
very effort, no matter how unsuccessful or discouraging, not only
is sufficient in God's eyes, but may reduce the time spent in Purgatory. When effort is made useful like this, it becomes less painful.[6]

In the third section of the treatise, attendants at Moriens's
bedside are required to ask him questions about his faith, his willingness to repent, and his readiness to die. The interrogations are

stock questions, based on Saint Anselm, on Gerson's *Ars*, and on professions of faith used in church liturgy, and are posed in such a way that Moriens may answer with a simple "ye." If there are no friends present, Moriens may ask the questions silently of himself, but it is expected that the deathbed will be a communal affair, and that the friends present are morally obligated to help Moriens turn his mind to heaven. By no means is anyone to delude the dying person into hoping for a longer life, because such a vain hope will turn his mind earthward and endanger his soul.[7]

The remaining sections are given to meditations on the life and death of Christ (in which Moriens is reminded that Christ, too, moaned and wept at His death); prayers for different stages in the dying process; and admonitions to attendants at the deathbed that they not only help Moriens to a good death but learn from the procedure how to make a good death themselves when the time comes. Throughout the whole treatise, the emphasis is on comfort, a comfort reached, one may say, by staying busy.

Before we consider the different forms taken by the *ars moriendi* in the sixteenth century, it may be interesting to note how the fifteenth-century emphasis on comfort and active participation transformed even the traditional Debate of the Body and Soul. The early medieval version of the debate had emphasized the polarity between the two, sometimes with Body and Soul ending in armed warfare, and usually with the devil carrying off Soul to torment, Soul meanwhile hurling fearful imprecations back at Body. But in *The Dyenge Creature*, a popular dialogue printed in 1507 and reprinted many times thereafter,[8] the debate takes a gentler form.

The Dyenge Creature is a dialogue—or perhaps one should call it a drama—somewhat in the manner of *Everyman* and obviously dependent on the temptations, remedies, and exhortations of the *Ars moriendi*. It is, in effect, a deathbed repentance taking place at the very last moment. In his death agony, the Creature complains to his Good Angel, to Reason, to Dread, to Conscience, and to Five Wits that they have not helped him meet this fearful moment. They reply that they have always tried, but that he has not listened to them. Creature then turns to Faith and Hope for assistance, and they introduce him to Charity, whom he has sadly neglected but who can help him if he will accept her teachings. At this point, Soul complains that it has been neglected and wasted by Creature, and laments the fact that it must now undergo eternal suffering because of him. Creature is conscience-stricken, never having thought about Soul before, and in an agony of remorse apologizes and promises to seek help. He goes back to Faith, Hope, and Charity, who now tell him about Christ's sacrifice, bid him repent of his sins, and encourage him to be of good cheer. Creature returns again to Soul, relates what he has heard, tries to make Soul comfortable, and asks whether he can do anything to help Soul through the coming time of sorrow, which has now been commuted to less than eternity. "Pray for me," replies Soul, and Creature obediently prays to the Virgin Mary, who in turn petitions her Son for Soul's salvation.

Retold baldly like this, the story sounds naive and simplistic, and perhaps even incomplete, since we never see the results of Creature's prayers. But in dialogue, Creature is indeed Everyman, his surprised dismay at every turn representing the confusion of the accidental sinner—not the hardened criminal who has "commited as many murthers and theftes as there ben dropes of water and smal grauell in the see" (Ars, A3r), but the ordinary person who has followed the line of least resistance, not realizing how he has besmirched his soul. For him, and for the 1507 reader, the result of his spiritual awakening is completion of the story; he has followed the steps of the Ars moriendi, albeit at the last moment, and has gained Heaven, if only through the indirect route of Purgatory.

But The Dyenge Creature is almost the last tract of its kind. Just as the iconography of death begins to change at the beginning of the sixteenth century, and the skeleton to hide its potential victim, so the treatises on dying begin to retreat from the moment of death and to diffuse themselves into religious controversy and the ars vivendi.

It was the whole framework of ideas that began to change during this period. Christian humanists in England, now allowed wider scope for their studies by the comparative stability of the Tudor reign, rejected the formalism of Scholastic thinking and, while always insisting that Christ was the ultimate ideal, and that therefore the "good pagans" of antiquity had unconsciously sought that ideal, looked more and more to the classics for their models of right behavior.[9] Meanwhile, the Protestant Reformation was sweeping across Europe, insisting on the utter depravity of man, preaching salvation by faith alone, casting doubt on the efficacy of deathbed repentance, and rejecting the doctrine of Purgatory. Interestingly enough, although the early humanists were Catholic, and the Protestants to a great extent distrustful of those early humanists, both groups began following their separate paths to the same end.

The most immediately evident change in the treatise on dying is the new attitude toward fear. Fifteenth-century writers had begun with the assumption that fear at the moment of death is both natural and reasonable. Lydgate's Carthusian in the *Dance of Death*, it will be remembered, remarks that no matter how well one prepares for death, the event is still frightening; and in the same author's *Assembly of Gods*, both Sensuality and Reason agree that anyone who does not fear Death is "an ydiote," an opinion that Doctryne finds amusing but does not contradict.[10] Dunbar, too, sees death as an evil that must be carefully prepared for by mental exercise:

Sen for the deid remeid is none,
Best is that we for dede dispone,
Eftir our deid that lif may we;
    Timor mortis conturbat me.[11]

And the *Ars moriendi*, while urging Moriens to "Deye gladly," treats the moment of death as fraught with very real dangers, dangers that require strong remedies.

But sixteenth-century Catholic and Protestant alike—particularly those Protestants leaning toward the Calvinist view—rejected the idea of fear, making it, like the skeleton, something to be hidden. For the Calvinist theologians especially, fear was a sign of doubt, and doubt a sign of damnation; for the new scholar of any persuasion, fear often seems to be a sign of something even worse: cowardice.

Thomas Lupset, who studied under Erasmus, More, Colet, and others of the great early Renaissance humanists, is one of the first to promulgate this new approach to—or retreat from—the fear of death. In *A compendious treatise, teachynge the waie of dieyng well* (1530), his overriding thesis is that, although "there is a meane measure of fere in deathe, that may be rekened honest and iuste, bycause nature maketh it necessary,"[12] human reason is capable of going beyond nature and of eliminating a fear that is demonstrably foolish.

Unlike the medieval *Ars*, which quoted pagan philosophers only to bolster arguments based on Christian revelation, Lupset's treatise turns to the pagans themselves to see how they were able to die fearlessly *without* benefit of revelation. His conclusion is that the human mind, vastly superior to that of an animal, can see beyond immediate sensation to the idea of life and death, and once having done so, can reason that life and death are the same, and that dying well is therefore only an extension of living well.

It is all very logical: "Reason saythe, we shoulde not feare that thynge the whiche we know not, & only yuel is worthy to be feared" (273). Now, while death cannot be good, since the giving of death to others has always been considered evil, neither can it be bad, since Christ and the holy martyrs embraced it, and even "good pagans" faced it willingly in order to combat tyranny. And since death is not of itself evil, therefore it is not to be feared.

Furthermore, death is not really unknown to us. We see it every day, and in fact we undergo it every day. Each moment of our lives passes into the past, which is dead; youth fades into age and age fades into death. Therefore, since we live every day in a state of dying, our daily conduct is also our deathbed conduct, and in order to die well, we must live well. Death itself, then, ceases to matter to one who has lived a good life.

As for the pain of dying, "it shulde be a comforte to remembre, that after the peyne of deathe, there shall be no more peyne" (279). And for the leaving of this world, why do we mourn that we will not be here tomorrow, when we do not mourn our absence from the world before we were born? By leaving the world gladly, we show that it has no dominion over us, that our minds are free of the bonds of temporality.

But beyond these rational arguments, Lupset returns again and again to the emotional claim on courage. Since death is inevitable, he says, "Let vs then take a lusty courage of this desperation, seinge there is no remedy: lette vs manfully go to it" (280). And again:

> There is no hope of remedy. Al this people that you se, howe longe thynke you shall be. It shall not be longe, but all shall by the course of Nature be called hens to dethe, and there hydde. . . . What nowe John [John Walker, to whom the treatise is addressed]? dothe not he seeme vnto you a shamefull cowarde, and a fearful wretche, a playn kikkes without an harte, that with moche intercession, with many prayers desyrethe a lytelle delay of deathe?. . . Lifte vp therfore your hart onely bycause there is no remedy, desyre not to flie when there is no place to runne to, lette necessite gyue you a courage, if al other strength decayith. (281)

These are stirring words, and almost make one want to march off to death for the sheer heroism of the thing. Indeed, "heroism" is the note that rings constantly through all of Lupset's treatise, a note that continually reemphasizes the capacity of the human spirit. And although the treatise is essentially and solidly Christian, the dangers that Lupset posits to the good life (and therefore the good death) are not the temptations of the old *Ars* but rather cowardice, idleness, and love of earthly things—all temptations that inhibit the flowering of the spirit.

Given Lupset's emphasis, in which every moment is seen as a form of death, the act of dying itself loses its importance as an event or a second chance. The whole lifetime becomes a test, indeed a campaign, and the individual's disposition at the instant of death passes judgment on his whole life: "for by the maner of hym that dyeth, we coniecture the state and condition of the soule" (177). Thus, a sudden death or a prolonged one makes no difference when life is seen as an eternal now, and deathbed repentance becomes suspect because "the yuell lyuer . . . hathe nothynge to laye before the mercy of god wherevppon he maye take hope and truste to be made worthy of the sure lyfe, in which deathe medleth not" (272).

An important change of focus has occurred between the fifteenth- and sixteenth-century *Artes*. Lydgate's Reason thought any man "an ydiote" who did not fear death; Lupset's thinks the same of any man who does fear death. The Morientes of the *Artes* and the Dances of Death acknowledged fear at death and sought ways to work through the fear to acceptance or atonement; the *Waie of Dieyng Well* demands a denial of fear once the original reasoning has taken place. Ministrations of the church give way to the activity of the human mind, and the grace of God assumes significance primarily as it is reflected in the inviolability of the human spirit. Above all, heroic dying becomes not only a spiritual victory but a temporal one as well; it can foil tyrants as well as devils when men die cheerfully in the teeth of unjust persecution. The Christian humanist *Waie of Dieyng Well*, then, opens the way for the great drama of the Renaissance, whose protagonists must face annihilation heroically without the comfort of handbooks or attendants around the deathbed.

Among the more specifically religious treatises of the sixteenth century, we may well examine that of Thomas Becon, whose Protestant *Sicke Mannes Salve* became one of the most popular devotional books of its age.[13] The book is set in a dialogue between the dying Epaphroditus and his three friends, following Epaphroditus step-by-step through his last hours of illness; and if it seems incredible that a dying man can both talk and be talked to at such length (four hundred pages in the 1561 octavo edition), we must remember that we are no longer dealing simply with a practical handbook but also with a preaching tract during the formation of the Anglican settlement, in which Roman Catholic doctrine must be specifically rejected, potentially aberrant

Protestants called back into line, and even the Christian humanists' references to "good pagans" carefully skirted.

Becon's work does retain some of the medieval characteristics.
The friends around the deathbed are reinstated; Epaphroditus
is given three temptations, impatience, despair, and excess love
of earthly companions; he is interrogated by his friends about
his faith; and the scriptural quotations of his friends offer him
the same spiritual guidance that the angels and saints provided
in the longer versions of the *Ars moriendi*. But only the framework
of the old treatise remains; a new methodology of dying must
be established for the Protestant theology.

Epaphroditus and his friends distrust the ministrations of the
church, repudiate the doctrine of good works, and place their reliance entirely on Christ's redeeming sacrifice and on salvation by
faith alone. Thus, the dying man is called upon to confess not
his individual sins but rather his Sin, the utter depravity of the
human creature, and to show by his unshakable faith that he has
been plucked from his depravity and numbered among Christ's
elect—not through his own merit but through Christ's. It is important that Epaphroditus be totally confirmed in his faith, because
after death his soul must go immediately to Heaven or Hell; there
will be no Purgatory in which to scrub away the last blemishes of
infidelity. Paradoxically, in spite of the inefficacy of good works, this
insistence on total purification before death throws Epaphroditus
back onto the need to *show* his membership among the elect; as in
Lupset, his disposition at death indicates his destination afterward.

What makes the struggle more difficult for Epaphroditus is
that the "heresies" against which all Morientes, both Catholic
and Protestant, must protest have become more visible and
tendentious than they were in the more homogeneous medieval
era. Therefore, whereas the old Moriens was required only to give
a "ye" or "nay" to the elements of the Creed, Epaphroditus must
enunciate his own creed—which he does for nearly thirty pages—
carefully rejecting Catholic interpretations of scripture, denounc-
ing popish superstition, and setting forth a detailed outline of
what a Christian must believe in order to be saved.[14] It is good,

solid, doctrinal preaching, and actually provides the reader with the same opportunity given to Moriens in the medieval *Ars*: that of saying "ye" or "nay" to an already formulated creed. Unfortunately, however, Epaphroditus is caught in what might be called the double bind that will affect much of the religious writing, as well as the treatment of despair on stage, in the next hundred years: when salvation depends on complete faith and nothing else, but when that faith is hedged around with numerous heresies that must be carefully avoided, when "simple" faith is no longer possible because of the promulgation of doctrinal traps, how can one be certain that one's faith is complete? And if one is not certain, how can one be saved?

Ironically, a belief originally based on trust in the mercy of God and distrust in human works has led to a fear of fear itself, as an indication that one's trust is not complete enough for salvation. Out of this insecurity now grows a need to give signs of faith so that one can be reassured of one's salvation. Accordingly, once Epaphroditus has recited his creed, Philemon responds with praise for Epaphroditus's holiness: "I greatly [thank] the Lord my God, good neighbor Epaphrodite, to se you in so good a mind, and to hear so goodly wordes procede out of your mouthe. These thinges are euident testimonies of your good conscience toward God. Feare you not, the Lord hath sealed you with his holy spirit, & made you through his mercy, a vessell unto honor" (198–99). Indeed, this increasing need for "signs" of election appears to give tacit approval to worldly concerns. Epaphroditus's wealth is seen as a sign of God's approval, so he is called upon not to regret his lifelong concern for worldly goods but only to make practical disposition of them as he is dying. Furthermore, since his dying disposition must be taken as an indication of his election throughout life, he is very much concerned that his friends "be witnesses before God & the worlde, that I die a Christian man" (226). What began as an inward-directed faith, contemptuous of ritual and works, has become an outward-directed concern with approval and reassurance, a concern that will be reflected in many of the Tudor moral interludes.

As Nancy Lee Beaty observes, Becon's treatise is comforting only to those who are already comforted.[15] Other Protestant treatises, however, were not so grim; many, while continuing to rail against papistry, often returned to the comfort-in-struggle propounded in the medieval *Ars*. Even Myles Coverdale, whom we now see as the leading edge of the Puritan movement within the English church, offers more consolation than Becon. In his *Treatise on Death* (1579)[16] he describes at great length the temptations of the devil at death, citing in particular those of infidelity, despair, impatience, and love of earthly companions (vainglory is omitted). But for each temptation he supplies remedial meditations, stressing God's mercy and—most important—God's willingness to accept the struggle for perfection in lieu of perfection itself.

Coverdale is strictly Protestant in his views on predestination, salvation by faith, and the evils of papistry. But as O'Connor has noted, he "would be greatly pained to know how much resemblance there was between his *Treatise* and the Catholic books of which he thought so poorly" (198). Like the medieval *Ars*, he sees life not as a single moment but as a series of moments, each providing a second chance; we will undoubtedly fall into sin every day, but each time we do, we must repent again and call on God for help. True, a bad life separates the soul from God (the "bad life" seen here in terms of faith), but it is never too late to repent (101—02).

As an aid to the dying person, Coverdale empahsizes the obligation of friends to strengthen his resolve and turn his thoughts heavenward. The friends are sternly admonished not to wear the patient out with excess talk, but to ask him simple questions about his faith and his intent, to which he is to answer "yes," much as in the *Ars moriendi*. When the patient indicates trouble of mind, however, the friends may pray with him or read him appropriate passages from the Bible to allay his fears and combat his temptations. And as the patient begins to lapse into insensibility, his friends should have him make some last sign of faith, and then encourage him to the end with these words: "Fight valiantly, as a worthy Christian, and despair not; be not afraid of the rigorous judgment of God; hold thee fast to the comfortable promise of Christ. . . . Christ thy Saviour shall never forsake thee. . . . Speak from thy heart-root with Christ thy brother upon the cross: 'Father, into thy hands, into thy protection and defence, I commit my spirit'" (107—08).

Two popular deathbed treatises of the seventeenth century follow this same plan: Christopher Sutton's *Disce Mori* (1600)[17] and Lewis Bayly's *Practise of Piety* (1612).[18] Both stress the need for struggle against the devil's last temptations (Sutton identifies these as attachment, impatience, and despair; Bayly, as infidelity and despair); both provide interrogations for the dying to respond to; and both are inclined to accept a struggle for the right disposition as meeting God's requirements. Bayly, in particular, urges the dying person not to worry if he cannot feel joy while dying, because "the truest faith hath oftentimes the *least feeling*, and *greatest doubts*" (697; author's emphasis); doubts are of the flesh and will disappear when the soul parts from the body; God will give us holy joy when the time is right. Later, Henry Montagu, in his *Contemplatio Mortis et Immortalitatis* (1631), will even protest against judging a person harshly if he *shows* a lack of joy while dying: "They take their marke amisse who iudge a man by his outward behauiour in his death. If you know the goodnesse of a mans life, iudge him not by the strangenesse of his death. When a man comes to bee iudged, his life, and not the manner of his death, shall giue the euidence with him, or against him. Many that liue wickedly, would seeme to die holily, more for feare to be damned, then for any loue to goodnesse" (115—16).[19]

But these acknowledgments of deathbed confusion are rare in the sixteenth century; writers increasingly picture life as the single moment and deathbed repentance as a contradiction in terms. So pervasive has this focus become by the end of the sixteenth century, that it is no longer a conscious doctrinal division but rather a sign of the times. Even the Jesuit Robert Southwell does not escape its influence; in *A Fovre-Fold Meditation of the Foure Last Thinges*,[20] although Southwell follows the medieval *Quattuor novissima* tradition (meditations on death, judgment, Heaven, and Hell), two new elements seem to have crept in. First, amid the traditional death signs, there is evidence of

increasing revulsion on the part of the living at the sight of the
dead or dying:

> Thy nostrils fall, and gasping thou dost lie,
> Thy loathsome sight, thy friends begin to flie.
>
> > (B1v)

> Thy carcase now, like carrion men do shunne,
> Thy friends do hast, thy buriall to procure,
> Thy servants seeks, away from thee to runne,
> Thy loathsome stench, no creature can endure;
> > And they which tooke, in thee their most delight,
> > Do hate thee most, and most abhorre thy sight.
>
> > (B3v)

And second, the deathbed attempt at repentance is called into
serious question:

> What booteth it, thy lewdness to lament,
> And leaue off sinne, when sinne forsaketh thee,
> What canst thou do, when all thy force is spent,
> Or will our Lord, with this appeased be?
> > Thy life thou ledst, in service of his fo,
> > And seruest him, when life thou must forgo.
>
> > (B3r)

This seems to be the standard form that most treatises take
from now on: the futility of deathbed remorse, the fear of death
as a sign of damnation, and a consequent emphasis on cheerful
dying and the ineffectuality of death. We have noted before the
growing comicality of the skeleton in art, and the ineffectual figure
that Death assumes in poetry; now it becomes the Triumph of
Christ rather than the Triumph of Death that the religious writers
stress. An interesting broadside printed in 1604 illustrates this
point. The *Map of Mortalitie*[21] retains two of the traditional woodcuts—the shrouded body and the skull—but its main thrust is
toward life. Three woodcuts at the top portray Jesus and symbols of the Trinity and the Mysteries of God, with verses that
proclaim Christ's victory over death. Directly below, there is a
set of words and pictures meant to be read as an acrostic: on one

side, a rooster symbolizing the awakening from sin; on the other side, a swan symbolizing the pure conscience singing "to last howre"; and, between them, these verses:

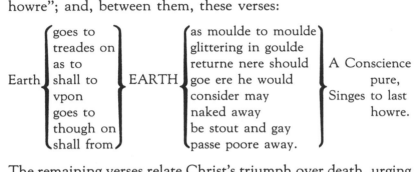

The remaining verses relate Christ's triumph over death, urging the Christian to die cheerfully, and concluding on this note: "And feare not death: pale oughlie though he be. / Thou art in thrall, he comes to set thee free."

John More's 1596 treatise, *A Liuely Anatomie of Death*,[22] pursues the point of victory over death almost as far as it will go, stopping just short of claiming that there is no such thing as death at all. Death was born of the devil, More says, but man by his fallen nature creates death in himself by sin. What we speak of as "death" is really only a passing out of the body into God; the true death lies within: "Whereby we haue to learne, that the life of sinners is no life (indeed) but a death being estranged from the life of God, & all remaine as dead, which lack beliefe in Christ" (C2v–C3r). It is true that we will be tempted at the time of passing over; the devil will tempt us to despair, the world to love of possessions, and the flesh to love of companions. But if we have believed, eschewed sin, and lived a "godly" and "upright" life, we can easily turn these tempters away, despite their insidious whispers uring us to live: "And wilt thou die (O man) . . . ?" (E1v–E3v). Only the evil will want to avoid death; in the words of the now familiar formula, "A greater token (next faith in Christ) there is not for our election, then not to stand in feare of Death" (E6v).

George Strode, too, in his *Anatomie of Mortalitie* (1618),[23] continues to stress the death-in-life motif, going beyond even Bayly and Southwell in his contempt for the flesh: "We are now in our best estate, but as a dunghill covered with snowe, which when Death shall dissolve, there shall nothing be seene of all our pompe and glory, but dust, rottennesse, and corruption" (72–73). If this sounds like the early medieval *de contemptu mundi*, it may also be overlaid with the *nausée* of Webster. And Strode has further absorbed much of the comic grotesque surrounding the corpse and skeleton during this time:

> And how loftie soever men looke, death only shewes how little their bodies are, which so small a peice [*sic*] of earth will containe whom before nothing would content; and therein the dead carcasse is content to dwell, whome at his coming the wormes doe welcome; and the bones of other dead men are constrained to give place. And in this house of oblivion and silence the carcasse being wound in a sheete, and bound hand and foote, is shut up though it neede not to have so great labour bestowed upon it, for it would not run away out of that prison, though the hands and feete were loose. (71–72)

This is not to suggest that only the negative strain survived into the seventeenth-century treatises on death; as we have seen, the thread of religious consolation remains very strong. And the humanist tradition begun in Lupset continues as well, not discarding religious themes by any means, but subordinating them to appeals to human reason—perhaps now as a means of reaching all people regardless of their more and more divergent religious views even within the Church of England. Bacon, for example, points out that "It is as natural to die as to be born; and to a little infant, perhaps, the one is as painful as the other."[24] Although contemplation of death may be "holy and religious," he says, "the fear of it, as a tribute due unto nature, is weak" (8).

J. Guillemand's *A Combat Betwixt Man and Death*, translated from the French by Edward Grimestone in 1621,[25] continues this line of thought, comparing the cries of the coward at death to the cries of the infant at birth—both are ignorant and misguided about the world into which they are being born. Like Lupset, Guillemand addresses "infidels" as well as Christians and speaks throughout in Senecan terms: since death is inevitable, we must meet it courageously. Like Lupset, too, he reminds the reader that we die a little each day, and adds that the last death must then be considered the best one, because it ends all deaths forever. In fact, death may even be viewed as a desirable step in the acquisition of knowledge; once the mind is freed of bodily and temporal constraints, how much greater will be its activity in immortality! Surely, this is a scholar's paradise that has not yet been suggested even by Bacon.

There is another interesting departure from the norm in Guillemand's treatise, although one should probably not emphasize it unduly, since it seems to be a matter of translation rather than intent: in the *Combat*, death is female. Other than Whitney's classical Mors in the 1586 *Emblemes*, we have not seen a female Death since Dame Death of the fourteenth-century *Death and Liffe*. However, what has probably happened is that Grimestone has simply translated the French too literally; abstract "death" in French is *"la mort,"* and only the dead man is *"le mort."* Still, considering Guillemand's enthusiasm for heroic dying, the feminine gender leads to some rather disconcerting and even necrophiliac images, particularly when Guillemand urges his reader (presumably male) to run to Death, to woo her, and to "imbrace" her (15). It would perhaps be rash to relate a mere literalness in translation to the growing sadomasochistic nature of death on the stage at this time—but one cannot help wondering.

It cannot be denied, however, that by this time the fear of death had become an object of contempt to worldlings and churchmen alike; to the former, it was cowardice, and to the latter, a sign of damnation. Like the Monk in Lydgate's *Dance of Death*, everyone now felt compelled to show "chere outeward / hard to deuyce," but, unlike the Monk, no one would admit that "Al ben not merie / which that men seen daunce" (391–92).

When we are forced to repress a fear instead of facing it and working it through, there arises a need to transfer the fear into a related expression, one that *can* be worked through. Aided, no doubt, by the continuous emphasis on life as one long preparation for death, or one long series of deaths, and fortified by the new poetic convention of beauty worship, the late sixteenth century began to transfer its anxiety to the passage of time, to Time the Destroyer. Rather than lamenting one's own end, one could now lament the end of all beautiful things—and the more beautiful and fragile, the better. The classical *ubi sunt* theme returned in full force, and the withered flower became an emblem of all mortality.

It is a healthy transference to mourn the passing of oneself in the passing of all things; it is the bitter made bittersweet, the nightmare shared, the company around the deathbed, the feeling that even in one's passing one is part of an eternal process. But the theme of eternal change that brings stability because it *is* eternal may lead to something less comforting as well: the questionable nature of a moment that is simultaneously the only reality and no reality at all. What this may develop into is perhaps most evident in the "Arithmetike" of Richard Greenham, whose collected *Works* yield such a cavalier tossing away of time that the whole reasoning process is worth reproducing in full:

> Well, in the numbring of our yeeres we neede take no great paine, for *Moses* hath set it downe to be 70 yeeres. If our life last but so long, a little Arithmetike will cypher it out, and we know it is a matter of no great arte to number our yeeres, euen from our first father to this ages. A worldly man in this businesse would begin to adde and to multiply, putting still to the times past that which is to come, and withdrawing from time to come, times past: But we must know that all that is past, is to be subtracted, and to be counted nothing, and the daies to come are not to be added, for an addition must be of a thing existent, but the time to come is not. But let vs make a supposition of that to be which is not, that a man may write of 70 yeeres, let vs, I say, set that downe as the grosse summe. Halfe that time is spent they say in sleepe, which then we may detract from the great number, & then there remaines but 35 yeeres. From these we may deduct 14 yeeres in our youth, wherein we are vnfit to glorifie God, or doe good to man, and so there remaines sixteene yeeres, and of these sixteene, to set downe the dayes of sicknesse, or those times which we sinfully spend in yeelding to anger, to our lustes, or to worldlinesse, wherein we are as vnprofitably occupied, asthough we were not, halfe of the

number would be cut off, and so we should leaue but seuen or eight yeeres. But now we haue the summe, from whence we might take out, but not that time out, which is past we know, seeing now it is nothing; what is to come, we know not, and it cannot be added, time is but short, and therefore great neede we haue of God his spirit to teach vs. To this we know, how suddenly death doth take from vs time to come. . . . The best way then to recken aright, is to make the number, which we may take out, and that which we should subtract, all one, and that is none. If in the way we haply finde something, we may take it for our aduantage, and see that we vse it to God his glory. For this being set downe, that our daies past are none, and the daies to come none neither: so that no daies past or to come can be counted part of our life, and consequently haue none but the present time, which is very little.[26]

I have used the term *cavalier* to describe Greenham's juggling with time, and indeed if we isolate the last few sentences of his reasoning (eliminating only the phrase "to God his glory"), we may realize with a shock that we are hearing the carpe diem philosphy of the Cavalier poets. It is one of the many ironies of the turbulent early seventeenth century that Christian homiletics should come to inform Cavalier hedonism; if the one could say, "This moment called Life is nothing," the other could reply, "It is the only thing; by your own arithmetic, nothing else exists." And both would be correct, given their first principles.

The answer to this paradox, of course, is that none of the arithmetic is to be taken any more literally than the corpse, the skeleton, or the skull; it is merely another mask that living creatures have fashioned for death because one cannot face the faceless, a clever response made to the summons because silence is unthinkable. And on the stage, where all reality wears a mask, more than three centuries of drama wrestled in the same way with death, trying to find the mask that would make it acceptable, the response that would send it away.

III

Death Takes to the Stage

The Mystery Cycles and Early Moralities

IN DEALING WITH THE SUMMONS OF DEATH onstage, it is always tempting to begin with *Everyman* (ca. 1490–1500). Certainly, this play is not only the greatest Morality Play of its time, but a drama of the human soul for all time, one that has often been performed successfully in the twentieth century and has been awarded the modern accolade of being recorded.[1] But it is not the first play in which Death has had a leading role, nor does it have the last word on how the role is to be played.

To trace the dramatic steps that led to *Everyman* and beyond is difficult at best. Many old plays have been irretrievably lost, while others are almost impossible to date, since their oral transmission so obviously preceded the earliest known manuscripts, and since even the extant manuscripts show signs of composition by diverse hands at diverse times. It is common, for example, to think of the Mystery cycles as having come first and the Moralities later—but one of the earliest Moralities *(The Pride of Life,* ca. 1390) precedes the estimated date of some of the Wakefield and N-Town Mysteries. Furthermore, modern research has called into question the old doctrine that the Mysteries descended in a direct line from the liturgical *Quem quaeritis* alone, and the Moralities directly from sermons;[2] we have also to take into account the influence of folk drama, vestiges of classical drama, and fancy-dress pageants of all varieties, including, as we have seen, pageants of the Dance of Death.

Given the dangers, then, of trying to trace the figure of Death chronologically through plays whose chronology is uncertain, we may do better to deal with it by type of play, assuming for the sake of discussion that where there are no dates available, we are dealing at large with the vast canvas of the fourteenth and fifteenth centuries.

As a personage, Death appears only once in the four surviving Mystery cycles: the Mors who comes for Herod in the N-Town *Death of Herod*. But in others of the Mysteries, we find many of the themes that are associated with Death elsewhere: consolation and the Dreary Death in the *Lazarus* plays, and repentance and the Dance of Death in the *Last Judgments*.

The Judgment plays themselves are obviously allied with pictorial representations of this second of the Four Last Things: a central figure of Christ and the saved and damned souls herded to opposite sides of the stage by angels and devils, respectively.[3] Indeed the York *Judgment* varies little from such a static display; the two saved and two damned souls are barely differentiated from each other and have no individual character traits. Christ monopolizes most of the dialogue, accusing the damned of not having performed the corporal works of mercy, in a set piece drawn from the Sermon on the Mount. The Chester *Judgment* seems to be more closely allied with the Legends and Dances. Here, the saved and damned are made into types of earthly rulers: pope, emperor, king, and queen (some apparently later hand has added a damned justice and a damned merchant). It is significant that neither group claims to have lived a sinless life, and that, in fact, all the souls enumerate their sins, each according to the temptations of his or her estate: avarice, lechery, injustice, cheating the poor, and so on. But all the saved souls have apparently repented and done penance before their deaths and have suffered in Purgatory before being found fit for Heaven:

Imperator Salvatus:
In pugatorye my soule hath binne
a thosand yeares in woe and teene. . . .

> Though that I to synne were bayne and bowne
> and coveted riches and renowne,
> yett at the last contrytion
> Hath made mee on of thyne.[4]

But the saved do not yet presume; they admit freely that there may be more sins clinging to them than they are aware of, and so they continue to ask Christ for mercy.

The damned souls, on the other hand, have already despaired. Having made no effort to repent in life, all they can do now is lament their fate, wish that they had never been born, and even, in one particularly petulant outburst from the Merchant, try to throw the blame for their wickedness onto God:

> Why made thou me, lord, of nought? Whye?
> To worch in world so wickedlye
> and nowe burne in the dyvelles bellye?
> Alas, that ever I was borne!

(333-36)

The most obvious contrast between the saved and damned, then, is not the degree of sin but the willingness to use free will for repentance—a lesson taught very strongly in the *Ars moriendi*.[5] And because differentiated individuals have enunciated the doctrine, the audience is more likely to absorb the different possibilities of response to deathbed repentance, just as in the Dances of Death.

The Wakefield and N-Town *Judgments* (or, as the play is called at N-Town, *Doomsday*) carry individualization of response even further. At N-Town, the visual presentation of the souls is more dramatic, as the souls apparently fit their actions to their words; the saved announce, "On kne we crepe, we gon, we glyde / to wurchepp oure lorde that mercyfull is," and the damned cry, "A mercy, mercy, we rubbe, we rave"—all obviously moving about the stage in appropriate postures of reverence or frenzy.[6] When all are positioned on the stage, the devils address the damned individually as types of the seven deadly sins, each soul apparently having a specific sin lettered visibly on his or her head:

And that on their forehed wyttnes I take
For ther is wretyn with letteris blake
Opynly all there synne.

(76–78)

Since the souls are not mighty figures like Pope, Emperor, King, and Queen, the misdeeds of which they are accused can be closer to the audience's own, as in the cases of wrath and lust:

In wratth thi neybore to backbyte
them for to angere was thi delyte
thou were evyr redy them to endyte
On the seke man rewyst thou nought.

(101–04)

Sybile slutte, thou salte sewe,
All your lyff was leccherous lay,
to all your neyborys ye wore a shrewe;
all your plesauns was leccherous play.

(118–21)

From what follows—a plea by the damned for mercy—it appears that there was originally a speech on repentance, perhaps from the devils, perhaps from Christ; but the remainder of the manuscript is missing. Still, the fragment that we do have indicates that the N-Town *Doomsday* may have been written at a time when the static Legends had given way to the more personalized Legends and the Dances, which demanded a more individualized response to the warning of Death than was possible with simple emblems of kings and popes.

The Wakefield *Judgment*, perhaps the most literary of the four plays,[7] is also the most evocative of the death literature of the day. Here the damned are not necessarily singled out as types of sins but are, rather, described by Tutivillus and the demons in a boisterous catalogue of sinners that often sounds like Langland's description of the field full of folk in *Piers Plowman*. To give examples of these descriptions here is fruitless; much of their effect depends on accumulation of detail that goes on for pages at a time, sometimes in long satires on particular social types, sometimes in stanzas that jumble a dozen types together. The net

effect is not only the kind of social satire that was becoming prevalent in contemporary poetry and the Dances themselves, but a
more audience-directed warning; here, the devils seem to say, are
the creatures who will be damned, and if the shoe fits wear it.

But the Wakefield *Judgment* is no simple satire or *ars vivendi*.
As Tutivillus and his demons berate the damned, we begin to
hear themes from the early versions of the *Ars moriendi*, particularly in the demons' hellish parodies of the *ubi sunt*:

> Where is the gold and the good that ye gedred togedir?
> The mery menee that yode hider and thedir?
> Gay gyrdyls, iaggid hode, prankyd gownes, whedir?
> haue ye wit or ye wode, ye broght not hider
>   Bot sorowe. . . .
>
> For all that ye spard and dyd extorcyon,
> For youre childer ye card, youre heyre and youre son,
> Now is all in oure ward, your yeeres ar ron. . . .[8]

This is the *ubi sunt* with a difference—not a lament for the passing of beautiful things, but an acknowledgment of the futility of
worldly goods at the moment of death. The same theme appears
in the Dances of Death, the treatises on dying, and the Morality
plays that lead to and include *Everyman*. The audience may, therefore, very well start and draw backward when the demons finally
herd the souls away; their summons to the damned sounds sus-
piciously like Death's to the Dancers:

> . . . com now with fendys
>   To youre angre;
> your dedys you dam;
> Com, go we now sam,
> It is commen youre gam,
>   Com, tarry no langer.
>
> (607–12)

The *Judgments*, of course, deal with the aftermath of death,
the time of no second chances, even though they are meant as
warnings about death. Closer to the actual Summons in life are
two of the *Lazarus* plays: those at N-Town and Wakefield.

The N-Town *Lazarus* is especially concerned with consolation of both the living and the dying, and is a very human drama
that goes beyond the simple biblical narrative of the other plays.
Martha and Magdalen are not merely bystanders or foils for a
miracle in this play; they are true mourners who are all too
humanly subject to irritation in the midst of their grief. When
the four Consolers become too garrulous and sanctimonious for
Magdalen, who has, after all, just lost a dear brother, she is quite
capable of telling them, none too subtly, to go away and leave
her alone:

> I thanke yow frendys for your good chere;
> myn hed doth ake as it shulde brest;
> I pray yow therfore while ye ben here
> A lytil whyle that I may rest.
>
> (281–84)

The Consolers, in fact, at first seem to do everything wrong,
according to the *Artes* and *Doctrynalls*. They are persistently cheerful, persistently hopeful, and persistently insensitive to the emotional needs of the dying man and his family. When they first
enter, although they have been told that Lazarus is near death,
they insist on trying to "jolly" him back to health, even implying that if he does not get well it is his own fault. Lazarus is thus
put in the position of defending his right to die, a defense that
the Consolers will not accept:

> 4 *Consolator:* Ye shall haue hele and leue in qwart
>   If ye wol take to yow good chere.
> *Lazarus:* Whan deth on me hath shet his dart
>   I shal haue hele and ly on bere.
> 1 *Consolator:* Be of good comfort and thynke not so;
>   put out of herte that idyl thought;
>   Youre owyn mys-demynge may werke yow wo
>   and cause yow sonere to deth be brought.
>
> (61–68)

And the Consolers continue in this vein, refusing to accept the
inevitable or help Lazarus accept it, until Lazarus, perhaps to gain
some respite from their exhausting joviality, does what his sister

will do later—sends them away on an errand. There follows a touching little death scene. Martha pitifully tries to interest Lazarus in small bodily comforts ("What wele you ete? what wele ye drynk?" [102]), but he is beyond eating and drinking and, now rid of his troublesome Consolers, peacefully commends his soul to God and dies on the last words of the *vado mori:*

> My wynde is stoppyd, gon is my breth,
> And deth is come to make myn ende;
> to god in hevyn my sowle I qweth;
> Farewell, systeryn, for hens I wende.

(105–08)

The sisters now try to console each other in a paroxysm of grief, the immediate response to the death of a loved one. Magdalen, more given to emotional excess than Martha, wishes that someone might kill them, too, so that they could rejoin their brother; but the Consolers, not understanding the sisters' need for catharsis at this moment of bereavement, take their cue from Martha's rhetorical question ("A, hoo shal comforte our carefulness?" [116]) and offer the wrong kind of comfort, as usual:

> Be of good comforte and thank god of al
> For deth is dew to every man;
> What tyme that deth on us shal fal
> non erthely wyght the oure telle can.

(129–32)

They are rebuked, gently enough, by Martha:

> We all shul dye, that is sertan,
> but yit the blood of kynde nature
> When deth the brother awey hath tan
> must nedys murne that sepulture.

(133–36)

Undaunted, the Consolers briskly go about the business of preparing Lazarus's body for interment, meanwhile driving Magdalen to the verge of hysteria by refusing to let her mourn: "Thus for to grugge ageyns godys myght / Ayens hygh god ye do offens" (175–76). Poor Magdalen hardly stands a chance against the officious Consolers; when Martha goes out to meet Jesus, they eagerly stay behind to "comforte" her sister, significantly giving their comfort in the very words of the *vado mori* that Lazarus had used:

> Mary Mawdelyn be of good herte
> And wel be-thynke yow in your mynde
> Eche creature hens must depart;
> ther is no man but hens must wende.

> (273–76)

It is at this point that Magdalen pleads a headache and sends them away.

The Consolers, of course, are absolutely correct in everything they say, but they have said it at the wrong time and to the wrong person. This is the advice that they should have given to Lazarus on his deathbed; it is the preparation for the dying, not the solace for the living.

It may be argued that the Consolers are deliberately acting obtusely in order to force their auditors to contradict them with a more acceptable response. Indeed, this is the argument that has sometimes been advanced to prove that the Dreamer in Chaucer's *Book of the Duchess* is a psychologically perceptive consoler; by pretending ignorance of the Knight's bereavement and wonder at his grief, the Dreamer forces the Knight to console himself.[9] But this argument about the Dreamer has been called into question,[10] and we may well question it in respect to the Consolers of the N-Town *Lazarus*.

The first thing to note about the Consolers is that they do not console. Lazarus has to send them away before he can compose himself for death; Martha gently reproves them for their insensitivity; Magdalen pleads a headache and wishes that someone would cut her throat (143); and in general the Consolers, like those in the Book of Job, seem to do more harm than good. It is only Jesus, once he arrives, who both understands the sisters' need to mourn and helps them to the true consolation; and in this regard, it is significant that the Consolers do not understand even Jesus' tears, asking why such a mighty prophet should weep

(376–77). Even after the miracle, they continue to misunderstand, thinking that Jesus has promised not a heavenly consolation but eternal life on earth: "oure deth ye may A-slake and kepe us stylle on lyve" (448).

It is the "helpful" group of Consolers, then, rather than the nearly hysterical Magdalen, who presents the horrible example of misplaced consolation. In contrast, Jesus shows the way to true consolation: acceptance of God's will, yes—but with the humane allowance for a time of mourning before looking forward to reunion with the loved one in Heaven. It is only after the catharsis of tears that Jesus raises Lazarus from the dead; and only after the same catharsis that Martha and Madgalen are ready both to receive and to give consolation themselves.

The Wakefield *Lazarus* does not deal with consolation but proceeds almost immediately to the miracle. Lazarus, in this play, serves as a figure of Dreary Death proclaiming his memento mori in the manner of the Legend or the Death-figures of *Herod* and the Moralities:

> youre dede is Wormes coke,
> youre myrroure here ye loke,
> and let me be your boke,
>   youre sampill take by me;
> fro dede you cleke in cloke,   [seize in claw]
>   sich shall ye all be.
>
> (119–24)

And for ninety-two grisly lines, he tells both the onstage and the offstage audience what will happen to them. Despite all their gay clothing, he says, they will rot away in the grave, where worms and toads will devour their flesh. Their great hall will be a narrow grave, and their clothing a winding sheet. Stinking like "dog in dike" they will lie, while their executors rob their wives and children of all the wealth that they have acquired in life, and, after a while, even their wives and children will forget them. Do not, therefore, put your trust in the earthly life, Lazarus warns his audience, but heap up riches for Heaven: the good deeds that alone will accompany you to the grave and thence to salvation.

I have been in Hell, he adds, and have seen what the damned must suffer. Take warning, then, amend your lives, and put your trust in God.

Lazarus's speech is an impressive one, very close in substance to the warnings on tombstones and in the Legends. The use of varying stanzaic patterns in the speech also suggests that it may have been augmented over the years as the storehouse of death literature increased. And outside of the last three stanzas, in which Lazarus describes his own sufferings in Hell, the whole speech might have been delivered by the Death who comes for Herod, Humanum Genus, and Everyman.

In the N-Town *Death of Herod*, Death enters much like the Vice of the Moralities; unseen by his victim, he addresses the audience and informs them of who he is and how he will destroy the man who now seems so happy and secure:

> Ow I herde a page make preysyng of price,
> all prynces he passeth he wenyth of powste. . . .
> I am deth goddys masangere;
> All myghty god hath sent me here
> Yon lordeyn to Sle with-owtyn dwere
>   for his wykkyd werkynge.
>
> (168–69, 177–80)

Like Dame Death of *Death and Liffe*, he wields power not just over humanity but over all living things:

> All thynge that is on grownd I welde at my wylle:
> both man and beste and byrdys wylde and tame
> Whan that I come them to, with deth I do them kylle,
> Erbes, gres, and tres stronge, tak them all in same,
> Ya, the grete myghty Okys with my dent I spylle.
>
> (182–86)

And, he cautions the audience, once he has struck, there are no more chances: "For aftere my strook man hath no space / to make amendys for his trespace" (191–92).

Now Mors invites the audience to watch with him for a while as Herod gives free rein to his prideful boasting, and then to see

Herod struck down without warning. The scene is very effective: Herod and his soldiers laugh and drink; Herod brags that he is now the unchallenged ruler of the world, "for now my fo [Jesus] is dede" (219); the soldiers remember with glee how they killed all the children; Herod calls to his minstrels to "blowe up a mery fytt" (232)—and suddenly the music turns to discord, as Mors strikes Herod down and a devil leaps up, crying: "All oure! all oure! this catel is myn!" (233). And when all has quieted down, Mors steps forward and stands before the audience, not just a Dreary Death but a figure from the Legend:

> Thow I be nakyd and pore of array
> and wurmys knawe me al a-bowte,
> yit loke ye drede me nyth and day,
> For whan deth comyth, ye stande indowte.
> Evyn like to me, as I yow say,
> shull all ye be here in his rowte.
>
> (272–77)

That Death should be both actor and acted upon seems strange, until we remember that in the early Legends and Dances it was the dead who proclaimed the warning. This Mors, then, is apparently a transitional figure composed of many of the conventions of the time and designed to pull out all the stops in order to shock. As God's messenger, he brings a punitive death for pride and wickedness; as an element of nature, he mows down all living things; and as a worm-eaten corpse, he is a mirror of the self as it will be. But the one truly unusual thing about him—for the time—is the fact that he allows no breathing space.

It is difficult to explain this anomaly. Even if we assume a late composition date for the *Death of Herod* (the earliest manuscript appears to be of the mid-fifteenth century), the hidden death does not become really widespread for another sixty or seventy years. The most probable explanation is simply that the audience wanted a happy ending for the play. The sudden death, it will be remembered, was considered the most horrible way to die, solely *because* the soul has no opportunity to confront death and gain a breathing space for repentance. Therefore, an audience having seen Herod's mass murder of the innocents would most likely consider sudden death a just punishment, the worst possible thing that could be done to such an evil man. The emergence, then, of the worm-eaten corpse from the omnipotent slayer might have been the only way to force the audience into seeing Mors as their own death as well as Herod's, to turn them from jubilation to the requisite dread.

One of the interesting ironies in the *Death of Herod* is the juxtaposition of Mors's claims to omnipotence with those of Herod; the audience knows that one figure speaks truly and the other falsely, and that the pride of the human King will fall before the stroke of Death. This type of irony is developed to its fullest extent in *The Pride of Life,* an early Morality that makes the prideful creature not just a wicked king but a symbol of life itself—in fact, the King of Life. And far from being ignorant of a Death who waits behind his chair, the King of Life is so confident of his power that, like the revelers in the *Pardoner's Tale,* he challenges Death to a duel.

Unfortunately, although the Prologue gives a summary of the fight between Life and Death, the fight itself is missing from the surviving manuscript facsimile.[11] What remains is the King's boasting, and his refusal to listen to the Queen and Bishop when they warn him that he must die. The King, who is almost lovable in his childish pomposity, is supported in his folly by Strength and Health, two braggart soldiers who form his retinue, and by Mirth, his court jester and messenger. And although I have chided Huizinga for his use of the word *childish* when referring to a society, I am tempted to continue using it about the King of Life, if only because his Queen and Bishop seem to share my temptation. The King, although he is boastful like Herod, and flies into tantrums like that evil king, has none of Herod's malice; he is rather a silly human creature, easily wounded in his vanity, easily goaded into foolish extravagances, and just as easily pleased with trifles. When he and his knights brag about what they will do to Death, they sound not like soldiers but like boys playing at soldiers:

Rex: Streinth and Hele, qwhat say ye,
    My kinde korlin knightis?
  Schal Deth be lord over me
    And reve me of mightis?

1 Miles: Mi lord, so brouke I my bronde,
    God that me forbede
  that Deth schould do thee wronge
    Qwhile I am in thi thede.

  I wol withstonde him with strife
    And make his sides blede,
  And tel him that thou art King of Life
    And lorde of londe and lede.

2 Miles: May I him onis mete
    With this longe launce,
  In felde other in strete,
    I wol him yive mischaunce.[12]

The Queen, indeed, treats these foolish creatures like children. She is very patient with her husband, explaining to him in careful, logical steps that since he had a beginning, he must have an end; that "Holy writ and prophecye" say so (244); and that his own observation should tell him that no man lives forever. The king immediately flies into a tantrum:

Rex: Woldistow that I were dede
    That thou might have a new?
  Hore, the devil gird off thi hede
    Bot that worde schal thee rewe.

                           (195–98)

Although such an outburst might have grave repercussions in a later play such as *Edward II*, *Othello*, or *Lear*, here the Queen patiently ignores the insult (and illogic) and continues to try to talk sense to the King. But he will not listen; he soothes himself with the thought that all this is only a "women tale" meant to spoil his fun and "mak myn hert sore" (215). The Queen insists that she is only trying to help him see his duty to his kingdom and the church so that he will act more responsibly—but this is the wrong thing to tell a headstrong child; the King takes it as a slur on his manhood and decides to challenge Death to a duel:

> *Rex:* Qwhat prechistou of Dethis might
> And of his maisterye?
> He ne durst onis with me fight
> For his bothe eye.
>
> (239–42)

Throughout this part of the play, the King of Life is more silly than wicked. He listens to flatterers, insults the Queen and Bishop who are trying to help him, and makes absurd boasts that he cannot live up to. But in spite of the insupportable things that he says to his wife and the Bishop, he never harms them in any way, and it is obvious that the Queen loves him in spite of his petulant outbursts; when she sends for the Bishop, she says only that her husband has fallen into error, not that he is evil, and indeed her message may be loosely translated as "Come and talk some sense into his silly head."

Because the King of Life is such a mixture of good and bad, of cruelty and kindness, of vanity and insecurity, the audience is led to identify with him even while it is censuring him, and to fear for him in what is so obviously a foolhardy excursion to his own doom. His pitiful stature is even more marked by his unconscious echoes of lines normally associated with Death: he calls for "Mirth my messenger" (263) as God calls for Death; his knights brandish their spears like the Death in the Legends and Dances; and he announces himself to the audience in words like those of Mors in the N-Town *Herod:*

> King ic am, kinde of kingis ikorre,   [chosen]
> Al the worlde wide to welde at my wil;
> Nas ther never no man of woman iborre
> Oyein me withstonde that I nold him spille.
>
> (121–24)

What Death replies to the King of Life we do not know. But according to the Prologue, after laying waste Life's kingdom, Death confronts Life himself and "delith him depe dethis wounde" (91).

There follows a scene with which we are now familiar, the separation of body and soul, and the soul's rescue by the prayers of the Virgin Mary:

> Qwhen the body is down ibrought
>   The soule sorow awakith;
> The bodyis pride is dere abought,
>   The soule the fendis takith.
>
> And throgh priere of Oure Lady mylde
>   The soule and body schul dispyte;
> Sche wol prey her son so mylde,
>   Al godenisse sche wol qwyte.
>
> The cors that nere knewe of care,
>   No more than stone in weye,
> Schal wit of sorow and sor care
>   And thrawe betwene ham tweye.   [suffer]
>
> The soule theron schal be weye
>   That the fendis have ikaghte;
> And Our Lady schal therfor preye
>   So that with her he schal be lafte.

(93–108)

From this we may gather that there was originally a breathing space at the moment of death, during which the King of Life's body and soul engaged in the traditional Debate, and Life gained self-knowledge, repented of his pride, and threw himself on the mercy of God, here represented (as in *The Dyenge Creature*) by the intercession of the Blessed Virgin.[13]

The final figure to look at before we turn our attention to *Everyman* is Humanum Genus of the *Castle of Perseverance* (ca. 1400–25). By the time Death enters in this very long play, the audience has seen Humanum Genus grow from infancy to old age, beleaguered by the World, the Flesh, and the Devil. He has been first tempted to join the Seven Deadly Sins, has then been recovered by the Virtues, and finally won back to Sin by Covetous, the World's most persuasive henchman. Now, as an old man, Humanum Genus is totally devoted to Covetous, the only sin of which he is still capable. Unlike Herod and the King of Life, he does not claim that he will never die—but he says that there will be time enough to think about death later, and meanwhile he will try to grow richer and richer. In his case, Death enters not when the hero is claiming to be immortal but when he seems prepared to damn his own soul to Hell:

> *Humanum Genus:* On Covetise is all my lay,
>   And shall till Death me overthrow.
>   "More and more," this is my stevene.　　　[dream]
>   If I might always dwellen in prosperity,
>   Lord God, then well were me!
>   I would, the medys, forsake Thee,
>   And never to comen in heaven.[14]

As in *Herod* and *Pride of Life*, then, Death enters as an agent of retribution just as the victim has reached his worldly peak and spiritual nadir. But lest the audience feel exempt from the summons, Death turns and announces himself with the traditional warning:

> Ye shall me dread, everyone;
> When I come, ye shall groan;
> My name in land is left alone:
>   I hatte "Drery Deth."
>
> 　　　　　　　　　　　　　　(2801–04)

Interestingly enough, one of Death's rueful comments seems to date the play sometime after the worst onslaughts of plague, or at least between epidemics:

> In the great pestilence
>   Then was I well know.
> But now almost am I foryete;
>   Men, of Death, hold no tale.
> In Covetous their good they get;
>   The great fishes eat the small.[15]

After the usual sermon on the inevitability of dying, Death crosses to Humanum Genus and strikes him with a lance. But Humanum Genus does not die immediately; although he is not as sympathetic as the King of Life, neither is he as hateful as Herod, and so he must be allowed time to repent. He first calls on the World to save him, but World casts him off and begins giving his riches away to Garcio, a young man who obligingly tells Humanum Genus to hurry up and die; Humanum Genus already stinks anyway, he points out, and it is now someone else's turn to use his riches. Utterly wretched, Humanum Genus realizes that he has stored up the wrong goods for the wrong kingdom. "God keep me from despair!" he cries (3005), and although he knows he deserves Hell, with his last breath he throws himself upon the mercy of God:

> Now my life I have lore.
> Mine heart breaketh sore.
> A word may I speak no more.
>   I put me in God's mercy.   [Mankind dies.]
>   (3019–22)

That last word, *mercy*, becomes the key word in the remainder of the play. Humanum Genus's soul pleads it in his own defense, and Mercy herself—one of the Four Daughters of God—continues to remind Justice and Truth of God's promise to redeem anyone who has called on her. Justice and Truth reply, reasonably enough, that God has also promised to judge people by their works, and that this man's works have been almost uniformly bad. With Peace, they carry the debate before God, who finally decides in favor of Mercy and calls Humanum Genus out of Hell to sit at His right hand. But as the play ends, God warns the audience not to presume on His mercy; all will be judged on how they perform the corporal works of mercy on earth. This is the same warning, of course, that is given in the Judgment plays.

The repentance of Humanum Genus, then, is a chancy one. It succeeds because it is heartfelt and based on self-knowledge, but it almost fails because it comes at the very last moment. A question is also raised, during the Debate of the Four Daughters of God, as to whether Humanum Genus has made a perfect act of contrition; that is, has he really felt sorrow for his sins, or is he only afraid of Hell? We remember that this is the line of demarcation between the saved and the damned in the N-Town and Chester Judgments: both call for mercy, but the saved base their plea on contrition, the damned on fear without it.

This question of last-minute contrition was to become more and more important in years to come. Protestant and Catholic would debate it; Doctor Faustus was to reject it; and the great human figures of *Measure for Measure* to explore it in all its heavenly and earthly forms. But for the late medieval mind, it was the classic anagnorisis, the *nosce teipsum* demanded by the *Artes moriendi*, and, as such, the gateway to redemption. Once a person has said in his heart, "Now I see," he has performed the first step of penance, the acknowledgment of guilt—and guilt itself implies the working of free will to choose between good and evil. Because contrition in this sense is dependent upon realization and choice, Death in the Mysteries and early Moralities became not merely a punitive measure but an educational process. Lazarus learns the lesson in spite of his comfortless comforters; the poor silly King of Life learns it is his debate between body and soul; and Humanum Genus learns it when the World deserts him and leaves him face to face with Death and himself. But it is in *Everyman*, the greatest of the Morality plays, that the educational process of Death is most fully elaborated and the first stirrings of Renaissance drama begin.

IV

Death as Educator

Everyman

IN ITS DAY, *EVERYMAN* MUST HAVE caused a sensation. Because we are now so familiar with the play, we tend to take its conventions for granted, seeing in it the beginnings of the great themes of isolation and self-knowledge treated in *King Lear* and *Hamlet*, and perhaps even judging the older Moralities by what we admire in *Everyman*. But the key to *Everyman's* power is that it turns Morality conventions upside down. This is not to suggest that the play preaches a new moral; it is as firmly orthodox in its doctrine as it is heterodox in its methods, and in fact, as Lawrence V. Ryan points out, "the doctrinal content is *Everyman's* reason for being."[1] What differs is the method of instruction—a method that not only teaches doctrine in a new way but forces the audience to develop a new way of viewing drama.

In the Mysteries and earlier Moralities, Death is a coda to the piece; the audience watches the linear development of a figure's life and then sees Death strike him down. At the moment of arrest, furthermore, Death becomes a sort of guest lecturer, announcing himself to the audience, explaining his purpose, delivering a homily on good works and repentance, and reminding members of the audience that they, too, will come to dust. The audience is thus given all the information that it needs and is prepared to evaluate the response of Death's victim in terms of what it has learned from the onstage Death and what it knows of the Dances, Legends, and *Artes moriendi*. The victim himself then becomes an exemplum of, more than a participant in, the discourse between audience and Death.

Such generalizations, of course, must always be modified for individual plays. The *Judgments* and the Wakefield *Lazarus* are after- rather than before-the-fact pronouncements; the battle scene in *Pride of Life* must have included a discourse between Death and Life; and Humanum Genus, in the *Castle*, begins to learn about eternal verities at the moment of death. But as a rule, the audience knows more than Death's victim does, and Death represents the end of a linear progression, the last event in a chain.

In *Everyman*, Death begins the chain of events. Everyman enters as a fully developed human creature, and only as he is learning to die does the audience learn about his life. This retrospective development of plot and character onstage is an innovation in medieval drama, a method of exposition that points backward to Greek and Senecan tragedy and ahead to the powerful tragedies of the Renaissance but does not seem to be allied with the medieval stage. Or does it? The *Judgments*, we recall, are similarly based on explanation by means of past events, and they themselves appear to have their roots in the Dances of Death, which expand the moment of death into a recapitulation of life and an adjustment to the act of dying.

It is insufficient, then, to say, as Jim Corder does, that *Everyman* represents not a Summons of Death but an *Ars vivendi*, a linear description of the creature's journey from youth to old age and death.[2] It is true that Everyman does not die immediately after the Summons, but neither does he put together a life; rather, he watches with increasing trepidation as his life falls apart—twice.

This dual structure of Everyman's moment of death teaches the audience to learn in a new way. There are two definitions of self-reliance (actually a form of self-knowledge), and two forms of death. During the first half of the play, the audience knows more about Death than Everyman does but must learn from Everyman about his life. The hero, on the other hand, may instruct the audience piecemeal about the facts of his life but must learn through questioning about the meaning of his life and death alike. By the midpoint of the play, the hero and audience begin to learn at the same pace; but at this point, both must reevaluate many assumptions formed in the first half of the play. Learning, then, becomes not merely a receiving of information but a development of the ability to formulate questions.[3]

Death is the first of Everyman's instructors, although Everyman is still so ignorant of the lesson that he cannot formulate the correct questions and therefore cannot understand the instruction. The very opening of the play makes it clear that this "messenger" of God's is an agent of correction rather than of punishment; God tells the audience that he is sending Death, not to slay evildoers, as in *Herod* and the *Castle*, but rather to call people to a "reckoning," an explanation of what they have done with the lives lent to them. If people are not called to account periodically, says God, they will fall away not only from grace but from their own human nature:

> For, and I leave the people thus alone
> In their life and wicked tempests,
> Verily they will become much worse than beasts;
> For now one would by envy another up eat;
> Charity they all do clean forget.[4]
>
> (47–51)

Death appears at God's summons and pauses only for a brief address to the audience before going in search of Everyman. It is significant, in the context of what will follow, that his address contains only hints; although given a headstart, the audience is not taken entirely into Death's confidence:

> Every man will I beset that liveth beastly
> Out of God's laws, and dreadeth not folly.
> He that loveth riches I will strike with my dart,
> His sight to blind, and from heaven to depart,
> Except that alms be his good friend. . . .
>
> (74–78)

Everyman then enters, and what follows is unique in the annals of death drama so far: Everyman does not recognize Death when they are face to face. One of two things may be happening here. First, Death may be costumed as an ordinary messenger, with none of the traditional signs of death, such as skulls, worms, scythe, or spear. This seems unlikely, however; Death mentions that he has a "dart" with him, and the frontispieces of the sixteenth-century printed versions show Death as a skeleton, indicating that people were accustomed to seeing him in this guise. We are left, then, with something almost revolutionary in drama of the time: a skeleton (or mummy) has appeared to Everyman, and Everyman does not notice.

The progress of Everyman's self-deception may be discerned in his response to Death's initial summons. At first, he merely echoes Death's words, a classic method of stalling for time:

> *Death:* In great haste I am sent to thee
>   From God out of his Majesty.
> *Everyman:* What, sent to me?
>
> (90–92)

Next, ignoring Death's hint that they are about to "depart" (96), he asks a question whose answer he should already know but does not wish to face: "What desireth God of me?" (97). Death mentions a "reckoning," and Everyman now falls back on evasion and a pretense not to understand: "To give a reckoning longer leisure I crave; / This blind matter troubleth my wit" (101–02). But the problem with pretended ignorance is that it forces the messenger's hand; an attempt at evasion, it ironically becomes a demand for further explanation. And Death obligingly repeats his message in more concrete terms, so that Everyman can no longer ignore it. Now that Everyman must deal with a direct but unwelcome statement of fact, his demeanor changes to one of hostility and denial, although his form of denial again serves only to force the messenger's hand: "Full unready I am such reckoning to give. / I know thee not. What messenger art thou?" (113–14).

To this point, Everyman's method of learning has been through various stages of denial. By refusing more and more pointedly to accept the message, and by rejecting in turn each of Death's attempts to explain, he has backed himself into a mental corner where he is bombarded over and over again with the very message that he is trying to avoid. And because he has finally expressed his rejection in the form of hostility, he has placed himself in a mental framework within which he can no longer formulate questions that will bring him useful answers. The only path out of hostility is through escalated hostility or pacification; there are no grounds for cooperation.

The audience witnessing Everyman's retreat has meanwhile been subjected to a new kind of dramatic irony—suspense. Knowing the messenger to be Death, and wondering why Everyman does not recognize him, it has watched in fascinated horror this unexpected attempt to escape from the inescapable, much as twentieth-century filmgoers watch in growing dread as the hero wanders closer and closer to a hidden murderer or a monster— except that here the monster is in Everyman's mind. Everyman is systematically cutting off one escape route after another as he backs toward the corner, and his "I know thee not" is the last fatal step that ushers in the drumroll cadences of Death's fearful pronouncement, and the crumbling of Everyman's defenses:

> *Death:* I am Death, that no man dreadeth.
>   For every man I 'rest, and no man spareth. . . .
> *Everyman:* O Death! thou comest when I had thee least
>   in mind!
>
> (115–16; 119)

From the arrogant creature who audaciously insulted God's own messenger, Everyman changes to a pitiful bargainer. First he attempts to bribe Death:

> In thy power it lieth me to save,
> Yet of my goods I give thee, if thou will be kind;
> Yea, a thousand pound shalt thou have,
> If thou defer this matter to another day.
>
> (120–23)

When this plea fails, Everyman asks for a reprieve of twelve years so that he can amend his "book of reckoning" and make himself ready for judgment. Death will have none of this. Now becoming frantic, Everyman grasps at any straw that will make his journey easier to contemplate. Will he come back again if his reckoning is acceptable? Death says no. Will he be able to take his friends along? Death says only if he can find any who are willing to go. Finally, Death impatiently tells Everyman that he is being "mad," and Everyman, who had earlier tried to bargain—first for a reprieve until some indefinite "other day" and then for a respite of "twelve years"—is now reduced to begging for just one more day:

> O wretched caitiff! whither shall I flee
> That I might 'scape endless sorrow?
> Now, gentle Death, spare me till tomorrow,
> That I may amend me
> With good advisement.
>
> (171–75)

Death refuses to bargain any longer and leaves Everyman alone to begin his journey. Everyman is now in that state of despair that is often brought on by misplaced hope. Still unwilling to accept the inevitable but terrified of what he cannot accept, he cries out against his own existence in words that echo those of the damned souls a century earlier, and that will be echoed by another damned soul—Doctor Faustus—nearly a century later:

> Now have I no manner of company
> To help me in my journey and me to keep;
> And also my writing is full unready.
> How shall I do now for to excuse me?
> I would to God I had never been gete! . . .
> The time passeth; Lord, help, that all wrought.
> For though I mourn it availeth naught.
> The day passeth, and is almost a-go;
> I wot not well what for to do.
>
> (186–90; 193–96)

To this point, in what might be called the first act of the play, Everyman has shown all the symptoms of a person confronted by the idea of his own death: shock, disbelief, resentment, attempts to bargain for smaller and smaller reprieves, and finally a frenzy of quasi despair that is no despair at all but rather a desperate hope that there must be *something* one can do to prevent this calamity, if only one had time to think of it. And having rejected the inevitable, Everyman is of course unequipped to deal with it.

Theologically, Everyman is rejecting salvation by rejecting God's message. His attempts at bribery, and his pitiful questions about what happens after death, show that he is still thinking in terms of this world rather than of God's kingdom. The irony of his two questions—will he come back and will he have company?—is that, in heavenly terms, the answers are "yes": he will come back to life in Heaven, and he will have the company of the angels and saints. But in rejecting the lesson that Death brings him, Everyman makes it impossible for Death to tell him what he needs to know. It is a vicious cycle: In order to ask a question, one must already know part of the answer, and because Everyman asks the questions in terms of this world, he cannot receive an answer in terms of the next world.

Further ironies in the play develop from the fact that Death, in his own way, has actually told Everyman many of the things that he will find out through experience during the rest of the play: that only a very "hardy" friend will go with him; that his worldly goods have been only lent to him and will be passed on to someone else when he is gone; and that it is within himself and his "five wits" that he must look for the power to amend his life and find salvation. This, of course, is what Everyman has been told all his life; but he has apparently rejected all of God's messengers during his life, and now having rejected the idea of Death as well, he must struggle through his deathbed suffering to the truth that has always been available to him. Once again, it is not the correct answer that he must find, but rather the correct question.

Psychologically, Everyman has followed a pattern of response to death that is virtually timeless. As Allen D. Goldhammer has pointed out, his interview with Death follows the three preliminary stages of the dying process as defined by modern psychologists: denial, anger, and bargaining.[5] Goldhammer, to be sure, excepts the stage of anger, which, he says, "does not appear until later encounters" (91), but Everyman's original audience would most likely have seen the anger as well. Death, after all, has announced himself as God's messenger, and Everyman's rudeness to him is a violation of the laws of feudal diplomacy, by which a lord's messenger was to be treated with the same courtesy due to the lord himself. There can be no question about Everyman's hostility at this stage, and it is at the height of denial and anger that the bargaining process begins.

What might be called the second act of *Everyman* focuses on Everyman's growing isolation as he is deserted in turn by Fellowship, Kindred, Cousin, and Goods. As the "betrayals" occur, Everyman is forced further and further toward acceptance of Death and reliance upon himself. The growing hostility that Fellowship, Kindred, and Cousin show as Everyman presses them for a commitment to join him is, as Goldhammer notes, representative of "the inability of friends to accept one's terminal state" (92). But it is more than this; it is another method of instruction. Everyman's stock response throughout the departure of the things of the world is "I was deceived." In other words, he is in the process of being *un*deceived, of seeing his own rejection of Death as an error once he sees the error manifested in others.

Everyman is also developing a theologically healthy distrust: the things of the world lie. Fellowship offers to accompany him to Hell, but when taken up on the offer, he glibly explains that he meant the offer in terms of bawdry and murder. Kindred and Cousin have also sworn eternal allegiance, but now Kindred has other things to do, and Cousin cannot make the journey because of a cramp in his toe. Significantly, these scenes are the closest thing to comic relief in all of *Everyman*. Indeed, in other circumstances the scenes would be quite funny, but their juxtaposition with Everyman's impending death makes them shocking instead, not only to Everyman but to the audience.

It is tempting, at this point in the play, for hero and audience alike to reject Fellowship, Kindred, and Cousin utterly; to view them in the light of the traditional comic devil or Vice and to cast them off as betrayers of the soul. And at this point in the play, it is a reasonable response. But hero and audience will later have to reevaluate the response in terms of the second set of false friends, and will find that what is to be rejected is the attachment to worldly connections, not the connections themselves. And here lies the reason for the abortive comicality of the scenes. The audience is being led to reject the frivolity on stage as something inappropriate to the action; it is being directed into forming a scale of values about what is most important in the universe; and, like Everyman, it is being prepared for the next set of lessons.

Goods is the last of the earthly betrayers, and the most malicious of the four. Closely allied to Covetousness, the Vice of the *Castle*, he has been deliberately lying to Everyman all along and has led him into avarice only to damn him. His mockery of Everyman sounds curiously like Garcio's mockery of Humanum Genus; and in a crushing irony, it is also a recapitulation of Death's warning to Everyman:

> *Death:* What! weenest thou thy life is given thee,
>   And thy worldly goods also?
> *Everyman:* I had weened so, verily.
> *Death:* Nay, nay; it was but lent thee;
>   For, as soon as thou art gone,
>   Another a while shall have it, and then go therefrom
>   Even as thou has done.
>
> (161–67)

> *Goods:* As for a while I was lent thee,
>   A season thou hast had me in prosperity. . . .
>   Therefore to the soul Goods is a thief;
>   For when thou art dead, this is my guise—
>   Another to deceive in the same wise
>   As I have done thee, and all to his soul's reprief.
>
> (440–41; 447–50)

Goods' apparent viciousness is a last step in dramatic misdirection; just as the audience has been led to reject earthly companions for their inappropriate frivolity, so it will now despise earthly goods for their inherent evil. Not until the second half of the play will the audience have to revise its judgment and see all the rejected earthly things in their proper context. But while the audience is rejecting, Everyman is being rejected, and both are approaching the midpoint at which they will begin to learn together.

The order of these rejections, furthermore, is not only dramatically effective but doctrinally sound and psychologically accurate. Ryan has noted that the false friends "appear in a climactic order according to the increasing danger of each as a distraction from one's maker,"[6] and indeed the attachment to worldly companions and goods is seen as one of the major temptations of the devil in the *Ars moriendi*. In Lydgate's *Dance of Death*, it is difficult to part with loved ones, but even more difficult, as the Burgess says, to part with "Howses rentes / tresoure & substauns":

> There-fore / wise is no creature
> That sette his herte / on gode that mote disseuere
> The worlde hit lente / & he will hit recure
> And who moste hathe / lothest dieth euer.
>
> (308–12)

The Empress, too, in Lydgate's poem, sees the temptations in this order, although in her summary of vanities she lists them in descending order of importance:

> All worldy power / now may me nat availe
> Raunsoun kyndrede / frenship nor worthynesse
> Syn deth is come / myn hih estat tassaile.
>
> (78–80)

Such hierarchic ranking of theological dangers is grounded in the psychology of relationships between the self and things outside the self. Each false friend in *Everyman* is closer to Everyman's self: Fellowship is a peripheral thing that is often changed with time, locality, or mood; Kindred is something closer to the self, something that is always there and can be drawn on at will; Cousin is the specific manifestation of Kindred that seems to mirror the self; and Goods is a mistaken image of the self—personal objects that one has gathered outside oneself as an identity for the self. It is this increasing degree of identification with the self that makes each attachment increasingly dangerous to the soul, and increasingly shattering to the psyche when the objects are removed.

As each betrayal comes closer to what Everyman perceives as his own identity, then, he feels his identity being stripped away layer by layer until, in worldly terms, he is a nonentity. But by this process he has also been forced to discard the worldly terms with which he previously bolstered his rejection of Death; and now that he is reduced to his real self, he is ready to find terms in which to ask the right questions.

It is at this moment of spiritual and emotional nakedness that the third act may be said to begin. For the first time, Everyman accepts the fact of his isolation and, in doing so, also accepts the fact that what he is and does is more important than what he has. His earlier wish that he had never been born now gives way to a healthier kind of self-hate, one based on self-realization and a desire to change:

> Then of myself I was ashamed,
> And so I am worthy to be blamed;
> Thus may I well myself hate.
> Of whom shall I now counsel take?
> I think that I shall never speed
> Till that I go to my Good Deeds.
> But alas! she is so weak
> That she can neither go nor speak.
>
> (476–83)

Doctrinally, he has gone through the first steps of repentance: acknowledgment of sins, sorrow for the sins, and resolution to sin no more. And psychologically, he is learning to see things as they are instead of as he wishes them to be, to accept the fact of his imperfections, and to work through his difficulties instead of denying them or blaming them on others. This is the emotional state that leads to health, and the spiritual state that leads to salvation. By turning to Good Deeds for counsel, he is not only reaffirming the doctrine of salvation through good works, but is asserting his own integrity as a person responsible for his own actions. Later in the play, he will carry this self-reliance too far, trusting in his physical properties rather than in his soul, but now it is a healthy sign that he is ready to stand alone without worldly props.

When Good Deeds introduces Everyman to Knowledge, then, she is actually showing him something that he has gained through his own efforts: the *nosce teipsum* of the *Artes moriendi*. In this sense, Knowledge is not the end product of learning, as we think of it today, but rather the process itself, the insight that enables one to learn. And theologically it is the acknowledgment of sin that is the first step toward repentance, the opening of the soul to grace.

Confession, the first of the sacraments that Everyman will go to on his journey to death, is quite clear about the relationship between thoughts and deeds on the path to salvation. He says to Everyman:

> Because with Knowledge ye come to me,
> I will you comfort as well as I can,
> And precious jewel I will give thee,
> Called penance, voider of adversity. . . .
> Ask God mercy, and He will grant truly;
> When with the scourge of penance man doth him bind,
> The oil forgiveness then shall he find.
>
> (558–61; 570–72)

As in the earlier *Ars moriendi*, penance is viewed not only as a punishment for sin but as a form of prepayment that diminishes the time in Purgatory:

> *Everyman:* In the name of the Holy Trinity,
> My body sore punished shall be.
> Take this, body, for the sin of the flesh. . . .
> Now of penance I will wade the water clear,
> To save me from purgatory, that sharp fire.
>
> (611–13; 617–18)

The intent to undergo punishment, and the active working out of the intent, are in themselves good deeds that add to

Everyman's store. Thus, his penance strengthens his previously meager Good Deeds, who is finally able to rise from the floor and accompany Everyman to his reckoning.

It is interesting, in this context, to look ahead a century to Claudius's abortive repentance scene in *Hamlet*. Claudius's rueful "Words without thoughts never to Heaven go" (3.3.98) appears at first glance to be a properly Protestant remark on the inefficacy of verbal formula unaccompanied by faith; but if we look more closely at the scene, we can see Everyman's dilemma without Everyman's solution. Claudius has earlier mused:

> But oh, what form of prayer
> Can serve my turn? "Forgive me my foul murder"?
> That cannot be, since I am still possessed
> Of those effects for which I did the murder—
> My crown, mine own ambition, and my Queen.
> May one be pardoned and retain the offense?
>
> (3.3.51–56)

The answer, of course, is no. Claudius has balked after the first step—acknowledgment of sin—and will not go on to confession and amendment. The will to action is missing; what Claudius has really said is, "Thoughts without deeds never to Heaven go."

In contrast, Everyman has taken the next, active step. Good Deeds now clothes him in the symbolic garment of contrition and readies his book of reckoning, and Everyman seems almost eager to begin his journey:

> *Everyman:* Now blessed be Jesu, Mary's Son,
>   For now have I on true contrition.
>   And let us go now without tarrying;
>   Good Deeds, have we clear our reckoning?
> *Good Deeds:* Yea, indeed I have it here.
> *Everyman:* Then I trust we need not fear.
>   Now, friends, let us not part in twain.
>
> (649–55)

In a lesser play, this would be the resolution and happy ending, with Everyman striding off triumphantly to salvation. Surely the contemporary audience would have thought it so—but, like

Everyman, the audience would have been mistaken. It is at this point that the play begins again.

Before Everyman can go to his reckoning, he is given four new companions: Strength, Discretion, Beauty, and Five Wits. Since they are introduced by the steadfast guides Knowledge and Good Deeds, and since Everyman is in a state of grace, it is easy to accept the new companions as true friends, in contrast to the false friends of the early scenes. Everyman, we may assume, has now learned his lesson and will rely on his own properties rather than on things outside himself. And has not Death earlier counseled him that his Five Wits will show him the way to salvation (168)? But these companions, like the others, will desert him.

All starts well, certainly. The new friends promise to stay with Everyman "unto death's hour" (688)—a promise that has ominous overtones only in retrospect—and Five Wits delivers a theologically correct homily to Everyman on the efficacy of the sacraments. It is only after Everyman leaves the stage to receive the last two sacraments (the eucharist and extreme unction) that the more alert members of the audience may begin to see some limitations in even these new friends. Five Wits has praised the priesthood as the highest guide for humankind; but after Everyman's departure, Knowledge adds that the office of the priesthood is sometimes betrayed by sinful priests, and delivers a satire in little on such bad shepherds. Five Wits seems curiously obtuse about Knowledge's point:

> *Five Wits:* I trust to God no such may we find.
>   Therefore let us priesthood honor,
>   And follow their doctrine for our souls' succor.
>
> (764–66)

Such an overly sanguine view of reality begins to be called into question almost as soon as Everyman reenters. Suddenly, for the first time since the Summons of Death, Everyman begins to feel the death signs physically: "Alas! I am so faint I may not stand, / My limbs under me do fold" (788–89). And the physical properties on which he has relied perhaps too much begin to fail him. First his Beauty goes, then his Strength, with Discretion following shortly thereafter; and finally even his Five Wits desert him. Moreover, despite his earlier experience with the things of the world, he is no more able to accept the second set of betrayals than he was the first. Even more to the point, the more querulously he accuses them of treachery, the more hostile they become, much in the manner of the first false friends:

> *Everyman:* Strength, you to displease I am to blame;
>   Yet promise is debt, this ye well wot.
> *Strength:* In faith, I care not!
>   Thou art but a fool to complain.
>   You spend your speech and waste your brain;
>   Go, thrust thee into the ground.
>
> (820–25)

What has happened? Surely Everyman's state of grace, bolstered by Knowledge and the sacraments, should have prepared him to bid a more even-minded farewell to the world, or at least to expect less of it. And yet this last set of departures calls forth his most agonized response: "O Jesu, help! All hath forsaken me!" (851).

Theologically, Everyman has been attacked by the most insidious temptation described in the *Ars moriendi:* the temptation to vainglory. Having given up his attachment to things outside himself, he has come to rely too much *on* himself; having cast off despair and watched his Good Deeds grow, he has wandered too close to the sin of presumption. Like Moriens in the *Ars,* he has heard the devil's whisper: "O how thou art ferme & stedfaste in the faythe, o how thou art sure in hope, o how thou art stronge & pacyent, o how thou haste doon many good dedes."[7]

The key to this double temptation of Everyman's—first to despair and then to vainglory—lies in what he and the audience have been learning about the uses of earthly things. Just as Five Wits has proved an insufficient companion, even after having been recommended as a guide by both Death and Knowledge, so Goods has reappeared as a help to salvation, even after having lured Everyman to the edge of damnation:

Everyman: In alms half my goods I will give with my
   hands twain
   In the way of charity, with good intent,
   And the other half still shall remain;
   I it bequeath to be returned there it ought to be.
   This I do in despite of the fiend of hell,
   To go quite out of his peril
   Ever after and this day.

(699–705)

And in fact Goods has earlier hinted to Everyman how riches
may be used either for good or for evil:

Goods: But if thou had me loved moderately during,
   As to the poor to give part of me,
   Then shouldst thou not in this dolor be,
   Nor in this great sorrow and care.

(431–34)

The things of the world, in other words, have a neutral capa-
bility and are good or evil only as the human creature uses them.
The first companions—even Goods—were never evil in themselves; they betrayed Everyman only because he had used them
to betray himself. And the new companions were not good in
themselves; Everyman had obviously turned Beauty and Strength
into bawdry and riot with Fellowship (271–82) and had used his
Five Wits to seek out pleasure rather than Knowledge.

Everyman, in fact, has made the same mistake twice, relying
on temporal answers instead of eternal questions. And in this
second form of the same error, the audience has been led to join
him, by being lulled into the expectation of a happy ending too
soon, only to be even more bitterly disappointed than Everyman
himself. Whereas the audience was able to feel smug in its fore-
knowledge during the first betrayal, it has now been tricked by
the reversal of a dramatic convention into identifying more closely
with the tricked Everyman, and will instinctively echo his an-
guished cry: "O Jesu, help! All hath forsaken me!"

But as always in *Everyman*, it is not only the theology or the
dramaturgy that persuades. Psychologically, Everyman has

reached the last and most profound depth in the process of dying: the point at which the dying person begins to lose control of his faculties. As Beauty departs, he must learn to accept the repulsiveness of his own person, so graphically described in the death-signs lyrics; as Strength and Discretion go, he must deal with the frustration of not being able to move or think as he wishes; and as his Five Wits leave him, he must watch helplessly the final flickering out of what has been his only universe.

It is this very helplessness that makes Everyman's descent into the grave so poignant—and so victorious. It is the letting go of the self that we all fear the most, the recognition that there is nothing further to be done, that we have lost control, that our solipsistic assumptions about our own importance are dissolving before our eyes. It is Nothing encroaching upon Everything. It is the end.

At this moment, the self is stripped, not only of the accretions of the world, but of its very selfhood. And at this moment of apparent annihilation, who would not be tempted to cry with Everyman, "All hath forsaken me"? The answer, of course, as Conrad Aiken has pointed out, is the Christ himself "cried his 'forsaken' . . . on the darkening hilltop."[8] And Everyman, in his final letting go, is joining Christ in his final agony.

The *Ars moriendi*, we remember, encouraged meditations on the Passion as a way of uniting the soul with Christ crucified. Although Everyman has perhaps unconsciously echoed Christ's words in his last shock of self-realization, his doing so rescues him from vainglory, forces him to turn back to his Good Deeds for help (instead of to his earthly personhood), and locates him on the correct road to Heaven: that state of healthy uncertainty prescribed by the *Ars*, in which the soul will not presume to say "yf he be dygne or worthy to haue deserued the loue of god, or the hate of god." Having seen, as Lydgate's Bishop put it, that "al shal passe / safe oneli owre merite,"[9] Everyman puts his trust in Good Deeds, whom he now recognizes as his only "true friend" (855), asks God for mercy, and commends his spirit to God in Christ's words from the cross: "*In manus tuas*—of might's most / Forever—*commendo spiritum meum*" (886–87).

It is ended. After Everyman and Good Deeds go into the grave together, Knowledge announces that Everyman's soul has indeed made a good reckoning, and an Angel appears to call Everyman's soul to bliss. Everything has happened with lightning speed—one hundred and fifty lines from Knowledge's dispute with Five Wits to Everyman's death and salvation, as compared with seven hundred lines from Death's announcement to Everyman's penance. There has been no gradual winding down in debate, as in the *Castle* and *Pride of Life*; no lengthy explanation, as in *Herod* and *Lazarus*. We go to the grave with Everyman, and the play is over. This type of whirlwind ending that deliberately leaves the audience shaken was to culminate in the great tragedies of the Renaissance, the shattering last scenes of *Hamlet* and *King Lear* that leave the audience stunned, drained, and finally ready to ask the correct questions.

The Doctor's epilogue, then, like the last words of Fortinbras and Albany, are meant more to ease the tension than to instruct. As spectators, we have already experienced the lesson: we have been shuttled between the expected and the unexpected in dramatic convention; we have been knowing observers of the playwright's irony and smug dupes of our own expectations; and, having been thrown off balance by the dual nature of our response, we are at last left in the same healthy state of doubt as Everyman's—a doubt that turns to anagnorisis only with the last-minute announcement of Everyman's salvation. As we gather up our coats and trail out into the street, we too may be looking cautiously over our shoulders, wondering, like Everyman, whether we "be dygne or worthy to haue deserued the loue of god, or the hate of god."

V

Death Takes an Alias

The Late Moralities and the Secular Mode

PERSONIFIED DEATH RARELY makes an appearance under his own name on the English stage of the sixteenth and early seventeenth centuries, and it is tempting to attribute the figure's disappearance to a simple cause: as the Mystery and Morality Plays gave way to "real-life" drama, allegorical personages become inappropriate. But this standard explanation not only oversimplifies the case but ignores what actually happened to the drama of the period. The Morality play itself continued well into the last decades of the sixteenth century and was then permuted into the masque, in which deities, spirits, virtues, and vices still paraded in fancy dress. Even "real-life" plays continued to feature allegorical figures, if only in plays within the plays or in prologues or debates between the acts. And ghosts and devils haunted the stage until the closing of the theaters in 1642. If Tragedy and Comedy, Fortune and Fame, and Hecate and Mephisophilis could walk the stage, why then was Death absent from their company?

Paradoxically, beginning in the latter half of the sixteenth century, death as an event became far more common on the stage than it had been during the previous two centuries. Seneca-influenced, multiple-murder plays like *Selimus* and *Soliman and Perseda* often yielded in excess of a dozen corpses onstage and another half-dozen offstage, while even the great tragedies like

Hamlet and *The Duchess of Malfi* left the stage littered with bodies in their last scenes. The bony sergeant, strict in his arrest, might well complain, like the devils of the Wakefield *Judgment*, that his increased workload in these latter days was driving him to exhaustion. Absent from the stage?–no, but he appeared under a series of aliases, becoming a symbol rather than an allegory.[1]

To speak of Death's "alias," however, is to invite another common misconception about his role. Scholars have been almost unanimous in seeing a symbolized Death in any figure of punishment or retribution in sixteenth-century Moralities. But this member of a "series of allegorical figures who signify judgment and punishment in this life"[2] is not necessarily our skeletonic friend of the N-Town *Herod*; in fact, given the theology of the day, he is more often a preacher of conversion. Of the twelve "aliases" listed by Peter J. Houle in *The English Morality and Related Drama*, for example, only one is an actual summons of and to death (God's Plague in *Enough Is as Good as a Feast*); the others are figures of temporal punishment or political reform.[3] It is easy to understand how scholars and critics have come to make this error; the fault is not theirs but the rise of a new system of reward and punishment in the late Morality. Simply stated, in these plays the good do not die.

It may be helpful, in this regard, to digress for a moment on the nature of the Morality hero. In the Middle Ages, the old Mankind figure was a mixture of good and evil. As in the *Castle*, he might backslide any number of times after being won over to virtue, or, as in *Everyman*, he might do a few good deeds among his bad ones. But generally, at the moment of death, he would achieve anagnorisis and be granted a second chance for salvation —either through penance or through the intercession of the Blessed Virgin—and, if necessary, could complete his penance in Purgatory. Almost all these properties of the Catholic Mankind were refuted by early Protestant theology, and, as one might expect, the characters in the plays changed accordingly.

Again, those critics who note the growing division between good and bad morality figures, the tendency of the protagonist to become almost a Vice or a Virtue himself, may be reasoning backward about dramatic development.[4] The all-good or all-bad protagonist is certainly no closer to the realism of later drama than is the lovable, ruffianlike King of Life or the poor, bewildered Everyman; if anything, the new types are less convincing as humans than their predecessors. Rather, the Protestant (and particularly the Calvinist) theology of predestination, the classification of all souls as unchangeably either elect or reprobate, may have given rise to onstage souls of the same order.

Although Lutherans and early Calvinists disputed the exact nature and consequences of predestination, and although the developing Anglican theology eventually rejected the Calvinist doctrine of perseverance in grace (see chapter 7), most of the Protestant Morality Plays that we shall consider here show the influence of ideas held by the Calvinist party within the English church; and these ideas almost naturally call for such a bifurcation of humanity. Since a creature's destiny is sealed before birth, there can be no last-minute change; in fact, there can be no change at all. True, the elect experience a "conversion," a "turning again" to God; but the reprobate are doomed to evil all their lives. Backsliding and subsequent recovery are out of the question, because the elect are given the gift of perseverance, and any soul which does not perserve in faith and holiness is ipso facto reprobate.[5] A Calvinist Humanum Genus would not be accepted into the Castle of Perseverance a second time, nor would his prayer for mercy be answered once he left.

Furthermore, as I have noted in chapter 2, in a system predicated upon justification by faith alone, the anagnorisis—in this case, the conversion or attaining of faith—must come well before the moment of death; as a gift from God, it must be complete from the start; and as a sign of salvation, it must remain unshaken to the end. According to Calvin: "wherever this faith is alive, it must have along with it the hope of eternal salvation as its inseparable companion. Or rather, it engenders and brings forth hope from itself. When this hope is taken away, however eloquently or elegantly we discourse concerning faith, we are convicted of having none" (*Institutes*, III.iii.42). The fearful Everyman and confused Dying Creature, learning about faith at the last moment and trembling in terror of Judgment, would stand convicted as charged.

In a Protestant Morality, then, the souls to be saved must evince their election throughout the play; but, unfortunately, unmitigated goodness and surety of salvation make for singularly dull drama. We must have villains to boo as well as heroes to cheer, and if the villains are ineffectual from the beginning, we are deprived of the suspense that lends savor to our booing. We must also have the horrible example to show us what might have happened instead; but in a theological system that denies free will and damns backsliding, the horrible example must come from outside the good hero. And since vice itself cannot die,[6] the bad character must be a reprobate human creature rather than a vice.

Like all such generalizations, of course, these must allow for exceptions. Not all the new Moralities are strictly Calvinist, nor even are all the Calvinist plays totally consistent. The two "bad" children in *Nice Wanton*, for example, repent at the hour of death; and it is never quite clear in *Trial of Treasure* whether Lust is a reprobate soul or simply one of Just's temptations (the good do not have vices). In addition, as with the drama of the preceding two centuries, we must generalize only from fragments that have survived, without ever being sure of what has been lost or why. And we must also remember that, concurrently with the new drama, the old continued to play, both in private performance and on the pageant wagons in public streets.

That much of the old drama persisted is evident from town records, at least as far as the Mystery pageants are concerned. The Catholic Morality plays may have died an earlier death, perhaps out of irrelevancy to the new religion, perhaps out of fear. The 1520s through 1550s were indeed frightening times for some. One of the hallmarks of the English Reformation was the close association of religious belief with loyalty to the ruling monarch, who was not only temporal but spiritual ruler. Proponents of the old religion, therefore, became not only heretics but traitors and, as such, were liable to the terrible penalties for treason. Their position was complicated by uncertainty as to what the "old" and "new" religions were; during Henry VIII's reign, at least, articles of faith seemed to change every few years. One year there might be three sacraments, the next year, seven; praying for the dead might be encouraged today and taboo tomorrow. Considering the Treasonable Utterances Act passed under the aegis of Thomas Cromwell in 1534, by which even idle conversation became as actionable as a printed pamphlet, it may have been safer not to produce any of the plays that contained questionable doctrine.[7]

As we have seen in Epaphroditus's deathbed confession of faith,[8] such spiritual and doctrinal confusion tends to lead more often to doctrinal polemics than to the simple faith originally propounded by the Reformation itself; and for the soul's solace under such conditions, it becomes easier to decry a common spiritual enemy than to flounder among one's own uncertainties. Consequently, as Rainer Pineas has pointed out, "where the old play warned its audience against errors of conduct, the new play, for the most part, warned its audience against errors of theology—namely, Catholicism."[9] And because the new drama was given over to propaganda and controversy, attention was necessarily drawn away from the individual soul. Whole systems were now on trial, not the poor dying creature within the system.

And yet the Mystery cycles survived well into the reign of Elizabeth I, although her proclamation of 16 May 1559 prohibited the performance of plays "wherein either matters of religion or of the gouernance of the estate of the common weale shalbe handled or treated," unless such plays were approved and licensed by local authorities.[10] Gradually, however, the licensing restrictions and popular aversion to the old religion took their toll. In some townships, the authorities simply denied licenses; in others, where the populace still clung to old ideas or traditions, a little bureaucratic neglect shuffled the applications to the bottom of a growing pile of business, where they were conveniently lost. Throughout the 1560s, the popular cycles gradually starved to death or strangled in red tape, and by 1570, the York cycle—the last of the great pageants—breathed its last.[11]

Perhaps coincidentally, but more likely not, the 1560s and 1570s have given us the largest surviving bulk of new drama since the Mystery cycles themselves. It was in these two decades that the translations of Seneca's plays began coming off English presses; and it was in these two decades, too, that Protestant Moralities, secular tragedies, English chronicle plays, and classic and domestic comedies and farces virtually jostled each other off the stage in their bid for public favor. Despite the licensing requirements that were probably meant to clear the boards of Roman Catholics on the right and Anabaptists on the left, the Elizabethan settlement opened up a far wider middle ground of allowable religious content in the drama of the day. To be sure, it was still good policy to attack Romanism on stage; this was not dealing with "matters of religion" but rather deriding a foreign power. And as long as God could be kept off the stage, even the most blatant preaching might pass for ethical instruction—as long, too, as it did not contradict the growing list of articles of faith, which were now primarily Calvinist, though with enough latitude for many interpretations short of Rome or Anabaptism. With the extremes effectively closed off, the middle road lay open on the stage, and hordes of new playwrights rushed to catch the nearest way.

Of the new Morality playwrights, one of the most interesting is W[illiam?] Wager, whose *The Longer Thou Livest, The More Fool Thou Art* (ca. 1567) and *Enough Is as Good as a Feast* (ca. 1570) show both the development of the all-good or all-bad protagonist and the return of Death to the stage. Moros, the "fool" of *The Longer Thou Livest*, is a descendant of the earlier youth-play heroes, who are seduced into vice until they are brought back to the fold by a combination of grace, the Virtues, illness, self-knowledge, and the hanging of their evil companions.[12] But Moros, like the reprobate sons in another youth-play of the time, *Misogonus*, never does return to the fold, despite the urging and instructions of Discipline, Piety, and Exercitation. A fool at the beginning, he remains a fool at the end, ignoring, like the revelers in the *Pardoner's Tale*, the warning of the Legend.

Although Houle, as I have noted, cites God's Judgment as the Death-figure in *The Longer Thou Livest*, he is so only in the sense that he warns Moros of the end and administers a temporal judgment along with Moros's sudden illness:

> *God's Judgment:* With this sword of vengence I strike thee.
>   [Strike Moros and let him fall down.]
> Thy wicked household shall be dispersed,
> Thy children shall be rooted out to the fourth degree
> Like as the mouth of God hath rehearsed.
>
>   (ll. 1791–94)[13]

Moros seems dazed and ignorant of what has happened; speaking to himself rather than to God's Judgment, he muses on his sudden discomfort as being perhaps the "falling sickness" or the "palsy" (1795–98). And when God's Judgment urges him, "If thou hast grace for mercy now call," Moros seems not to hear him. The days of the *Castle* are gone, and Moros, as a reprobate Protestant, does *not* have the grace to call for mercy. Instead, he dismisses his uneasiness as a fit of indigestion, and God's Judgment fairly snorts in disgust, pronouncing a Calvinist judgment on the oblivious Moros:

> *Moros:* It was but a qualm came over my heart;
> I lack nothing but a cup of good wine.
> *God's Judgment:* Indurate wretches can not convert
> But die in their filthiness like swine.
>
>   (1803–06)

Confusion, the actual Summons, then enters to bear Moros to Hell, but before they go, both Confusion and God's Judgment point out to Moros for fifty lines that all the world will now scorn him. Only at the end of this diatribe does Confusion refer to Moros's punishment in the afterworld:

> *God's Judgment:* To all the world shall appear thy abusion,
> Thy wickedness, and false belief to great and small.
>
>   (1809–10)

> *Confusion:* But thou art now a peasant of all peasants,
> A derision and mock to man and woman.
> Come forth of thy folly to receive thy hire,
> Confusion, poverty, sickness and punishment;
> And after this life, eternal fire
> Due for fools that be impenitent.
>
>   (1845–50)

What we have here is the converse of the faithful man's deathbed in the *Sicke Mannes Salve*. Epaphroditus, we remember, was concerned with his good fame as an elect Christian soul; and his friends hastened to assure him that they would tell everyone about his dying demeanor and the tangible signs of God's favor that surrounded him—that is, his worldly success. Moros, on the other hand, is punished with bad fame and worldly failure, damnation coming almost as an afterthought. It is not merely, as some critics have suggested, that "the distinction between heaven and earth . . . becomes less acute" in these plays,[14] or that the afterworld loses its significance; rather, with the Judgment having occurred before birth, Heaven and Hell become foregone conclusions, and the soul, in trying to determine whether it is saved or damned, looks more and more toward outward signs of grace. That these signs should come to include worldly comfort or pain is almost an inevitable result, and since death is the ultimate worldly pain, we should not be surprised to find, as I have noted earlier, that in these plays only the bad souls die.

This is not to suggest that the good never suffer any pain at all in the Protestant Moralities, but they do so only infrequently, and usually offstage. One of the few instances of this holy suffering occurs in the *Trial of Treasure* (ca. 1567), an anonymous play obviously meant more as exhortation than as entertainment; it is prefaced by Saint Paul's stricture to "Do all things to edify the congregation,"[15] and has as its good hero a figure much given to preaching to both his on- and offstage audience. Just, the elect soul, indeed often tends toward a Malvolio-like, gloomy brand of Puritanism; to his counterpart, Lust, whom he has caught singing, he declares:

> *Just:* But remember ye not the wise man's sentence?
> It is better in the house of mourning to be
> Than in the house of laughter, where folly hath residence,
> For lightness with wisdom cannot agree.

(Dodsley, 3:264)

Preachers such as William Perkins were later to exhort their con-
gregations in the same way, putting laughter only one step below
dancing in sinfulness:

> Againe, if we must give an account of every idle word, then also
> of every idle gesture and pace: and what account can be given of
> these paces backward & forward, of caprings, jumpes, gambols,
> turning, with many other friskes of lightnesse and vanitie, more
> beseeming goats and apes, of whom they are commonly used, then
> men. Whereas Salomon esteemed laughter as madnesse, he would
> (no doubt) have condemned our common lascivious dauncing much
> more for madnesse, laughter being but the least part of it.[16]

We may be inclined to agree with Lust when he tells Just: "I think
thou hast drunk of Morpheus seed. / Thou goest like a drom-
edary, dreamy and drowsy" (3:264). But that is beside the point.

Although Lust's wrestling match with Just, and Just's declaration that "Inordinate lust with the just may not dwell" (3:266),
would seem to make Lust one of Just's tempters, Lust is obviously
the reprobate soul in this play. He himself is tempted by "Inclination the Vice," is drawn to his damnation by Lady Treasure
and her brother, Pleasure, and is taken away by an interesting
Death-figure: Time the Destroyer, whom I shall discuss shortly.
But before Lust dies, he is "vexed with pain" by God's Visitation, not a punisher in this play, but an even-handed giver of
pain to just and unjust alike, sent to try men's souls.

Theologians such as Richard Greenham did indeed speak of
the "crosses" that the elect were given in order to humble them
before God and thus bring about their regeneration; under such
crosses, the elect would feel the strengthening power of God's
grace, and, having come through the trial, would be comforted
both spiritually and—Greenham hints—materially.[17] The reprobate, denied this grace, would sink under the tribulation. So God's
Visitation, although he refers to himself as "God's minister,"
makes it plain that he is a trial for the soul rather than God's
"mighty messenger," Death:

God's Visitation: Even now I am come from visiting the Just,
  Because God beginneth first with his elect;
  But he is so associated and comforted with Trust,
  That no kind of impatience his soul can infect.

(3:294–95)

We may begin to recognize, here, the deathbed temptation to impatience, to which even the medieval Moriens was subjected. Moriens was supported in his trial by the saints and angels; Just is supported by Trust (that is, in God). But Moriens died; Just is given his Consolation in this world, and lives:

Consolation: Consolation is my name, even as Trust hath said,
  Which is joy or comfort in this life transitory. . . .
Trust: Receive this crown of felicity now at this space,
  Which shall be made richer at the celestial place. . . .
Just: Now praised be God for this riches of renown;
  Felicity, in this world, the just doth enjoy.

(3:298)

This, of course, is the crucial point of divergence in the new moralities. We never see Just struggling through his deathbed temptations; we do not see him emerging triumphant in Heaven; nor do we see Lust and Just confronting each other at the Last Judgment. In fact, the medieval *Ars* and *Doctrynall* would most likely have considered *Trial of Treasure* a dangerous play, in that it might encourage the sick to hope for life as a reward for their patience. Everyman, we remember, was rebuked by Death for hoping to "come again shortly" to life if his reckoning was accounted good (146–52).

Part of the departure from tradition may be theological; that is, Just's recuperation is actually the process of regeneration, the dying of the old man and the rebirth of the new, helped by the visitation of humbling tribulation (although Just has seemed quite regenerate enough during the earlier scenes). Perhaps we are also witnessing an allegorization of the injunction that he who would gain his life must be willing to lose it, here to be interpreted (ironically enough) in earthly terms. And in addition, we may be dealing with a sense of community among an increasingly alienated group of believers. That is, when one sees oneself as a member of God's elect among a nation of reprobates, it is tempting also to project oneself as being lovingly protected from the evils that beset the rest of erring mankind. Therefore, although we (as the elect) know that all must die, to preserve our elect image we may want to posit a greater longevity for ourselves in which to enjoy God's blessings as an example to the evil. The Just, in other words, will inherit the earth—if only on stage.

All these considerations, undoubtedly, came into play in shaping the survival of the good on stage during the 1560s and 1570s. But as explanations they cry for explanations themselves. Above all, what we are seeing is the same shift of emphasis that we noticed in the death literature of the century: the truncation of the stages of dying. When fear of death is forbidden as a sign of damnation (or of cowardice), the human creature is expected to proceed immediately to the psychological stage of acceptance, bypassing denial, anger, bargaining, and despair completely.[18] And yet, such immediate acceptance is dramatically unrecognizable as death; and unless it is accompanied by a heroic gesture such as martyrdom, battle, or death-before-dishonor, it is especially unrecognizable as a victorious death. The simple, uncomplaining death of the innocent, in fact, gives the audience a sense not of triumph but of pathos; and to achieve a dramatic contrast between the all-good and the all-bad we cannot afford to present the good as pathetic.

In effect, the denial of death here has been transferred to the audience as well as to the villain. And we should not be surprised; we have seen the beginnings of this trend in Dürer's Knight riding confidently past Death and the Devil, in the transformations of the Dance of Death into the Hidden Death, in the broadsides and ballads threatening only malefactors with Death, in the substitution of the Triumph of Christ for the Triumph of Death, and in the growing use of the memento mori as a lucky charm to ward off death. Nor should we condemn the new practice of dealing with death anxiety any more than we condemned the ubiquitous skeleton of the Middle Ages; every society, as we have seen, has its own mental shorthand about its fears, and the prevalence of this particular convention at its time indicates that, *for* its time, it assuaged its inventors' fears. In the 1580s it would come to be rejected, but by then it had served its moral purpose and could afford to give way to a new, dramatic one.

And yet the anonymous playwright of *Trial of Treasure* seems to have had trouble with his shorthand at the end of the play. Just survives his tribulation conventionally, but Lust's demise is almost in the nature of a retreat from the hypothesis of the play, transforming as it does the reprobate into a cast-off property of the elect. Lust has been struck down by God's Visitation, and we expect to see him lose his Pleasure and Treasure and be carried off to Hell—but something goes awry. God's Visitation does take Pleasure away, but only because the godly deserve Pleasure whereas the ungodly have forfeited it. And Treasure? Unlike the Goods who forsook Everyman, Treasure refuses to leave Lust, even when Time enters and declares that they both must perish:

> *Time:* I am ent'red in presently for a certain purpose—
> Even to turn Treasure to rust and slime,
> And Lust, which hath long disdained the Just,
> Ensuing his filthy and vile inclination,
> Shall immediately be turned to dust,
> To the example of all the whole congregation.
>
> (Dodsley, 3:296)

It appears, oddly enough, that Lust *can* take his Treasure with him, and the two go off hand in hand with Time, who returns shortly "with a similitude of dust and rust" (S.D. 3:299). Although Time still speaks of Lust as one of the ungodly—that is, a personage in his own right—Just's question, "What foolish man in them [Lust and Treasure] will put trust / If this be the final end of their bliss?" (3:299), suggests that either he or the playwright is beginning to confuse Lust with one of the Vices of the play. What we finally have, at the end of *Trial of Treasure*, then, is the same warning that Everyman, Humanum Genus, and all their kind once received—that worldly things will pass away. Time and

Just, in spite of their original roles, emerge in their last speeches as our old friend the Dreary Death, the audience-directed warning; and Time himself gives voice to the words that we will hear again in *The Faerie Queene* and all the laments for faded flowers:

> *Time:* You know that all such things are subject to time;
> Therefore me to withstand is no reason or rhyme;
> For like as all things in time their beginning had,
> So must all things in time vanish and fade.
>
> (3:296–97)

Although we are quickly reassured that "Just, possessing Trust, remaineth constantly" (3:300), the formula has already begun to slip, and Time the Destroyer takes Death's place on the stage, as he will do in the poetry of the next hundred years.[19]

For W. Wager, on the other hand, the formula does not slip. Heavenly Man and Worldly Man, in *Enough Is as Good as a Feast*, remain human to the end, and Worldly Man's death is exactly what it should be: panicky, angry, sniveling, and damned. Worldly Man, indeed, may be considered either as a direct descendant of the medieval Humanum Genus or as a forerunner of the tragic heroes of the next several decades, in that he is presented with a series of choices that determine his fate. But his tragic flaw is here construed as his predestined nature, so that his choices are seen not as free will but as the fruits of his pre-birth damnation. As Enough, the Virtue of the play, says:

> *Enough:* But it is an old saying and true certainly:
> It will not out of the flesh that is bred in the bone verily.
> The worldly man will needs be a worldly man still.
>
> (861–63)

One of the marks of Worldly Man's reprobacy is the fact that he does undergo a seeming conversion at the beginning of the play but is then lured back to sin by Covetous, the same Vice who once caused Humanum Genus to backslide in the *Castle*. Humanum Genus was given his second chance; but for Wager's audience, there could be no second chance: Calvinist doctrine taught that any falling away from faith or godliness showed that no conversion had existed in the first place. Furthermore, those who had been so attracted to the truth of God's ways that they could make even a temporary show of conversion were doubly convicted when they fell away from it: "I say, therefore, that they sin against the Holy Spirit who, with evil intention, resist God's truth, although by its brightness they are so touched that they cannot claim ignorance. Such resistance alone constitutes this sin."[20] Or, as God's Plague tells Worldly Man before his death:

> God's Plague: [Thou] once on the plow had'st taken hold,
>   But willingly again thou rannest in the dike;
>   Therefore, thy plague shall be doubled sevenfold.
>
> (1248–50)

Before Worldly Man is struck down, he is given fair warning by a Prophet, a figure who begins speaking offstage in the manner of the Hidden Death. Unlike the oblivious Moros, Worldly Man hears and trembles at the warning, uttered in "the words of the prophet Jeremy" and also in those of the Legend and of Time the Destroyer:

> Prophet: O thou earth, earth, earth! hear the word of
>   the Lord;
>   Know thyself to be no better than clay or dust.
>   [Let the Worldly Man look suddenly about him.]
>   See that thy life to God's truth do always accord:
>   For from earth thou camest and to earth thou must.
>
> (1185–88)

Worldly Man is frightened by the warning, but he demonstrates his lack of grace and inability to repent by the quality of help that he summons in his confusion. His chaplain, whom he knows as Devotion, is actually Ignorance, a Roman Catholic priest who speaks in country-clown dialect and macaronic Latin, and who enters the scene boasting about how he has confounded the "Genevians" with his brilliant Latin tags. As Pineas has noted, Ignorance is one of the many anti-Catholic figures used in the polemical Moralities of the day (169), but he is more than that in *Enough*; he is also an allegory of the deathbed temptation to infidelity, a temptation into which Worldly Man readily falls.[21]

While Worldly Man's henchman, Covetous, is offstage summoning Ignorance, Worldly Man begins to feel the death signs, and as he lies down to sleep, God's Plague enters and stands over him in the threatening posture of the Hidden Death: "[Enter God's Plague and stand behind him awhile before he speak]" (S.D. 1220). Worldly Man remains asleep throughout this scene, but when Covetous and Ignorance wake him, we are told that he has heard every word as in a nightmare—an early instance of the warning dreams attributed to later Renaissance stage figures such as Clarence and Richard III. The message that God's Plague brings is in part a traditional one, the same that Death gave to Humanum Genus and Everyman:

> *God's Plague:* Thy life thou shalt lose even out of hand,
>   And after death thy just reward receive.
>   Thy ill-gotten goods shall not thee deliver,
>   Thine costly buildings nothing shall prevail,
>   Thy odors, thy sweet smells and thou shalt perish together,
>   Thy rings, thy bracelets, and gold chains shall fall.
>   Strangers and those whom thou didst never know
>   Shall possess that which by fraud thou hast got.
>
> (1229–36)

Indeed, the specificity with which God's Plague lists the things of the world that must pass away at death may remind us of the picturesque language of Lydgate's *Dance of Death*. But God's Plague is Death with a difference, the late sixteenth-century Death who, although he moves through walled cities like the invincible Triumph, strikes down only the evil:

> *God's Plague:* I am the plague of God properly called
>   Which cometh on the wicked suddenly;
>   I go through all towns and cities strongly walled,
>   Striking to death, and that without all mercy.
>
> (1243–46)

There is no question, in this play, of contrasting Worldly Man's behavior in tribulation with Heavenly Man's, with all the ensuing complications; Worldly Man is simply coming to a deservedly bad end, and we are asked to watch (with terror if not with pity) as he and his friends do everything wrong around the deathbed.

In his illness, Worldly Man calls for a physician, and although contemporary tracts on dying could not agree on the propriety of summoning physical comfort before spiritual, this Master Physician also turns out to be a preacher.[22] But Worldly Man does not like the news the Physician brings—that he must die—and not only refuses to repent (which would mean accepting the fact of his impending death) but refuses to pay the bill. It is difficult to know which refusal piques the Physician more; at any rate, he departs with the standard predestinarian observation that "Belike it is too late to amend; / In wickedness thou hast lived, even so thou wilt end" (1375–76).

Covetous knows better (he thinks) how to comfort Worldly Man. Against all the injunctions of the deathbed manuals, he tries to convince his friend that he will live:

> *Worldly Man:* O Policy, sick, never so sick. O, hold my head.
> O sirrah, what shall become of my goods when I am dead?
> *Covetous:* Dead? body of me, do you reckon to die this year?
> Hold your peace, I warrant you, you need not to fear.
>
> (1319–22)

But Worldly Man continues to sicken, and with intermittent cries of "O must I needs die?" and "Is there no remedy?" he decides to make his will. His original audience must have been chilled by the legal words that he almost speaks as he begins to dictate the will, words that also open prayer:

> *Worldly Man:* In the name, first of all do thou indite.
> *Ignorance:* In the name—in, in, in—in the name what more?
> *Worldly Man:* Of—   [Fall down.]
>
> (1401–03)

Having failed to turn his mind to death, Worldly Man is unable to turn his voice to God and dies on the verge of uttering His name. Covetous and Ignorance laugh over Worldly Man's end, bid farewell to the audience, and leave. And onto the empty stage

capers Satan, rejoicing like the fiends of the Mystery cycles and
warning the audience about its own doom in the very words of
those fiends:

> *Satan:* O, O, O, O—all is mine, all is mine! . . .
>   Spare not, nor care not, what mischief you frequent,
>   Use drunkenness, deceit, take other men's wives,
>   Pass of nothing—one hour is enough to repent
>   Of all the wickedness you have done in your lives.
>   [Bear him out upon his back.]
>   (1428; 1456–59; S.D. 1471)

To see the Devil carrying away a soul to Hell is nothing new;
the convention looks backward to the *Castle, Herod,* and *Pride
of Life,* and ahead to *Friar Bacon and Friar Bungay, Doctor Faustus,*
and *The Devil's Charter.* Even the Vice of *Like Will to Like,* Nichol
Newfangle, is carried off by Lucifer, and Confusion performs the
office for Moros in *The Longer Thou Livest.* But Worldly Man's
passage is a particularly effective one, in that the portage to Hell
comes after a humanly physical death and occurs when the dead
hero is alone on stage, abandoned by his earthly companions.
We have here the isolation theme that pervades medieval death
literature, a theme that will be recaptured in Marlowe's *Doctor
Faustus* and the great tragedies of the Elizabethan and Jacobean
stage.

It is evident, too, that even the Protestant Morality playwrights could hardly help going to the old Mystery cycles for
inspiration when they wished to make a particularly telling effect
on their audiences. Wager's Satan leaps out at the up-to-date
Worldly Man with words that are as old as the N-Town *Herod;*
and Courage, the Vice of *The Tide Tarrieth No Man* (ca. 1567),
tells the audience about his hell-bound "Barge" of fools in a one-
hundred-and-two-line catalogue quite obviously indebted to the
Wakefield Master's demons of the *Judgment:*

> *Courage:* Crafty cutpurses,
>   Maidens, milknurses,
>   Wives of the stamp
>   Who love more than one,

For lying alone
Is ill for the cramp.
Husbands as good
As wigs made of wood
We have there also,
With servants so sure
As packthread most pure
Which men away throw. . . .[23]

The *Tide*, it must be noted, is structured almost entirely on the theme of Time, and specifically on the "strange arithmetike" later calculated with such excruciating detail by Richard Greenham. Throughout the play, the good and bad characters live out their opposing interpretations of the proverb that gives the play its name; the good stress the old *contemptus mundi* and the shortness of time for repentance, while the bad or flighty ring changes on the *carpe diem:*

Wantonness: Yea, but husband I say consider in your mind
    That now we are young, and pliant to play,
    But age, approaching, makes us lame and blind,
    And lusty courage doth them draw away.

                                                        (1163–66)

But *Tide* has already begun to follow the more moderate theology of the developing Anglican church. Although it retains the standard anti-Rome polemics and gives the regenerate consolation in this life instead of the next, it does not insist on a strict predestinarianism. Wastefulness, the husband of Wantonness, is allowed to live a sinful life, to be subject to despair, and then to repent and live.

In this sense, Wastefulness may be considered the obverse of Lust, who was also struck by tribulation. Wastefulness enters "poorly," bemoaning his fate; and, realizing (as Lust did not) that he has wasted his life's "arithmetike," he falls prey to Despair, who enters "in some ugly shape" (S.D. 1582). There follows a long dialogue between the two, much in the manner of the deathbed temptation scenes in the arts of dying, and finally Despair persuades Wastefulness to commit suicide. But Faithful Few

arrives in the nick of time and saves Wastefulness from this
desperate act by reminding him of Christ's promises. The two
kneel and pray, and Despair, now overpowered by Wastefulness's
faith, flees the stage.[24]

This scene may be a sign of the discomfort that some playwrights were beginning to feel with the approved formula for the
stage: the all-good (elect) and all-bad (reprobate) figures whose
knowledge of their eternal destination is neither presumption nor
despair but rather an acknowledgment of God's foreordained plan.
True, both Luther and Calvin had spoken of a grief resembling
despair that even the elect must go through before regeneration,
but on the stage a conflict arose between showing the elect regen-
erated and demonstrating the fruits of election. That is, if the
elect are upheld by grace, how can they be shown as sinners?
And if the reprobate are doomed to sin and perdition, how can
they be shown as overcoming Despair and becoming regenerate?
Furthermore, as the writers of the older Moralities had discovered,
if we really wish to reclaim sinners in the audience, how can we
do so without showing them one of their own kind reclaimed?

The problem would later be solved by the reintroduction of
the complete human creature on stage—the man or woman composed of both good and bad, whose salvation could be worked
out with fear and trembling by actor and audience alike. With
the whole person reassembled, it would then also become possible to show a "good" death without giving scandal or inducing
the wrong emotion in the audience; as in the older plays, the
sinful part of man could earn its death, while the regenerate part
could earn its reward in heaven.

One of the early indications of the changing trend—if only
in the audience's demands—is Nathaniel Woodes's *Conflict of Conscience* (ca. 1581), a play important for the influence that it seems
to have had on *Doctor Faustus*,[25] but also for the fact that Woodes
felt it necessary to change his play's ending almost as soon as the
pages were off the press. Originally, the play was based on the
life, apostasy, and suicide of Francesco Spira, who had succumbed
to the blandishments (or threats) of Rome and had fallen away
from his Protestant faith. Afterward, convinced that he had

forfeited Heaven by his apostasy, and equally convinced that the apostasy itself was the unpardonable sin, he fell into a state of despair and killed himself. The first version of Woodes's play follows the historical pattern fairly closely, although he adds for the public delectation a set of comic priests and Vices, as well as the serious Vice, Horror, who leads "Spera" into despair. But almost before the first version had been printed, Woodes changed the prologue and conclusion of his play to rename Spera "Philologus," in order to advise the audience that this was a play about every man rather than a historical figure and—most important of all—to allow Philologus to repent, die a good death, and be saved.

Philologus's condition is indeed a serious one. Having fallen away from his faith into the clutches of Rome, he cannot expect, by the very terms of his abjured faith, to be accepted back into the "Christian" community, that is, salvation according to Calvin, who had said that "return to the communion of Christ is not open to those who knowingly and willingly have rejected it" (*Institutes*, III.iii.23). His friends, Theologus and Eusebius, try to reason him out of his despair by speaking of God's infinite mercy and the salvation of others in his plight, but Philologus is too firmly convinced of his damnation to listen, insisting that all the others were special exceptions: "King David always was elect, but I am reprobate."[26]

Eusebius and Theologus, in the manner of the arts of dying, attempt to help Philologus overcome temptation by having him recite first the Lord's Prayer and then the Creed, but Philologus insists that even while he is speaking the words, his heart is blaspheming, a sign that he is "secluded clean from grace" and that he is damning himself even further by mouthing words that he does not feel in his heart. Calvin would have agreed with Philologus: "[I]t is fully evident that unless voice and song, if interposed in prayer, spring from deep feeling of heart, neither has any value or profit in the least with God. But they arouse his wrath against us if they come only from the tip of the lips and from the throat, seeing that this is to abuse his most holy name and to hold his majesty in derision."[27]

Interestingly enough, while Philologus continues to insist that his faith is gone, he preaches a strict predestinarian interpretation of Calvinist doctrine and truly believes it, so much so that when his friends point out that he *has* returned to faith, he uses the familiar double bind of his faith to deny it: if he did have faith, he says, he would not be in despair of having faith. At their wits' end, Eusebius and Theologus finally let him go, assuring him that they will pray for him, and with the equivalent of "Don't bother" Philologus runs off to—what? In the first version, to "hang himself with cord" (2078); but in the second version, to repent and to die "exhorting foe and friend / That do possess the faith of Christ to be constant to the end" (2082-83). This is rescue at the last moment, the likes of which we have not seen since Humanum Genus's cry for mercy in the *Castle*.

I shall examine the dynamics of such despair more fully in my discussion of *Doctor Faustus*; what concerns us here is the radical change in Philologus's end between the first edition and the second of *The Conflict of Conscience*. It can hardly be that Woodes himself underwent such a drastic change of heart in the space of a few days. We must probably look more to his audience for explanations, an audience that had been undergoing a change both of heart and of taste over the space of two decades.

During the 1560s and 1570s, despite the political and religious questions that remained unanswered, England was experiencing the same (perhaps illusory) return to normality that it had experienced after the Wars of the Roses. Moderation and stability were the order of the day as Elizabeth attempted to bind together a country torn by two successive religious revolutions, and the atmosphere (if not the actuality) of greater tolerance encouraged the same explosion of intellectual and cultural inquiry that had accompanied the early years of the Tudor dynasty. Among the many "Englishings" of classic and contemporary continental authors in this new renascence of the arts, Euripides, Seneca, Plautus, and Terence came out of the classrooms and onto the public stages, which were well prepared for them by the increasingly limited selection of licensable plays dealing with "matters of religion or of the gouernance of the estate of the common weale." Although, as we have seen, the Protestant plays about "matters of religion" did obtain their licenses and continued for many years, audiences were becoming more and more accustomed to the sight and sound on stage of "real" people, violent action, and—perhaps most insidious of all—the political and religious beliefs of cultures other than their own.

Meanwhile, the Elizabethan religious compromise was having an equal and opposite reaction on the increasingly alienated extreme Calvinists, who were gradually forming what we now know as the Puritan party. Although their beliefs had been given space in the Articles of Faith, it was not an exclusive space, allowing as it did those loopholes for less strict interpretation of Calvin's doctrines. And organizationally, the Church of England remained obdurately opposed to the reforms in church structure that the Puritans demanded. Consequently, a rift began to widen between Puritan and Anglican, and since Puritans were, for the time, a minority party, we should not be surprised that they began showing their disapproval by withdrawing from the mainstream of English society—not just in worship but in dress and daily life.[28] And one of the societal customs from which they withdrew was playgoing.

In the snowball effect of rejection and counterrejection that should be familiar to us in the twentieth century, the rejected playhouse audience came more and more to reject "Puritan" (that is, extreme Calvinist) sentiments on stage, until the Puritan himself, by the turn of the seventeenth century, became a stock figure of fun or, in plays like *Measure for Measure*, as great a potential evil as the Catholics of old.

In 1581, mutual aversion had not yet progressed so far, but Nathaniel Woodes was already faced with an audience less open than before to the rigidly Calvinist formula for damnation. Which version of his play was closer to his own beliefs we shall never know—although Theologus and Eusebius seem, to our modern sensibilities, to have the best of the argument—but it is quite likely that between one printing and another Woodes came to the realization that audiences would no longer pay to see a man brought so close to the edge of redemption and then cast into the pit of damnation. In fact, since Theologus and Eusebius do argue so well—better even than the consolers in *Doctor Faustus*—and since the play can be so easily changed by a simple alteration of prologue and epilogue, it is my own opinion that Woodes first wrote almost against his will for an audience that he thought still existed and was relieved to discover his miscalculation.

There are several indications in the text itself of Woodes's preference for the new style. First, the *Conflict* is written in fourteeners, those ungainly heptameter couplets popular among Seneca's translators and imitators, and more common to the transitional plays like *Horestes* and *Appius and Virginia* (both about "real" life but retaining the Morality Vices) than to the outright Moralities. Second, Philologus is a "mixed" rather than a predestined character. Unlike Worldly Man, he does not start off bad, have an illusory conversion, and then relapse into his true evil nature; rather, he begins as a stalwart defender of faith and truth, and then falls because of human weakness: fear for his family and a temporary infatuation with worldly goods. And finally, in the new version, Philologus does not survive his repentance, as the Protestant Morality heroes are wont to do, but dies in a state of acceptance, giving good counsel from his deathbed and redeeming his evil life through his holy death.

This type of redemptive death will become a hallmark of the great tragedies of 1590–1610, when the classic, medieval, and Renaissance ideas of anagnorisis all combine to make the deathbed experience a last splendid chance for the dying creature to reclaim his own lost worth and to give meaning to the seemingly meaningless destruction that has followed in the wake of his *hamartia*. It is an earthly reward, to be sure, often associated with the Renaissance ideal of fame;[29] but the religious hope for salvation beyond the earth is usually hinted at as well, if only by the onlookers.[30]

Of course, not all the deaths on the late sixteenth-century stage were redemptive ones. Bloody potboilers such as *Soliman and Perseda* or *Selimus* often seem to have been created for the sole purpose of eliciting a lively curiosity as to who would be killed next, or how many at one blow. Indeed, Soliman sometimes seems to order executions for want of other sport; and Abraham, the physician in *Selimus*, poisons himself in addition to his two victims for no discernible reason except (we may say from our modern sense of superiority) that it seems like a good idea at the moment:

> *Abraham:* Faith, I am old as well as Bajazet
> And have not many months to live on earth;
> I care not much to end my life with him.[31]

But before we indulge our sense of superiority, we should remember the hundreds who die in *Tamburlaine*, the stage strewn with corpses in *Hamlet*, and our own western and war films, in which men drop like flies. For the Elizabethans, as for us, Theodore Spencer observes, "death was a fascinating subject for reflection" (180).

Thomas Kyd (if he was indeed the author of *Soliman and Perseda*) may unwittingly have given the best explanation for the impetus behind the revived dramatic interest in death. At the end of this gruesome tragedy, Love, Fortune, and Death (who have been acting as Chorus to the play) step forward and vie for credit for what has happened. And Death silences the other two by pointing out that although they have taken part in the action, it is he who has resolved everything:

> *Fortune:* I give world's happiness and woe's increase.
> *Love:* By joining persons, I increase the world.
> *Death:* By wasting all I conquer all the world;
>   And now, to end our difference at last,
>   In this last act note but the deeds of Death. . . .[32]
>   Pack, Love and Fortune! play in comedies:
>   For powerful Death best fitteth tragedies.
>
>   (Dodsley, 5:372–73)

We may recognize here the 1580 broadside, one of many variations on its theme, in which men and women boast of their roles in life until Death tops them with his "I kill you all."

If Death best fitteth tragedies, it is because true tragedy must deal with the universal; and the only thing universal to poor fragmented humankind is death. Or as Henry W. Wells has put it so cogently: "Ideal tragedy evokes sadness rather than hate, sympathy rather than unmixed horror. Such art becomes universal in that it brings home to the spectators tragic elements ever present in their own lives."[33] The difference between *Soliman and Perseda* and *The Duchess of Malfi* is a difference of degree rather than of kind, the difference between a bid for popularity and a quest for universality. And when the great tragedians of the Elizabethan and Jacobean stages went in quest of universality, they found themselves back in the fullest of the fields full of folk—the crowded field across which moved the Dance of Death.

As we have seen, the Dance itself is the most nearly perfect drama; by its nature, it shows the strengths and weaknesses of each dancer who responds to the common Summons, each in a necessarily individualized way. But the literal Dance, with grinning skeletons and souls in tow, had outlived its original shock effect by the 1590s and was reduced to the commonplace: friezes that one saw every day in churches and broadsides that needed continually new gimmickry in order to work. What the late Elizabethan dramatists had to do, then, was take the familiar literality and translate it into a new metaphor, one that would unfailingly bring the old to mind but dress it in new clothes.

To be sure, the bones showed through the clothing; but that was part of the effect. In many ways, the death imagery of late Elizabethan drama is far more emblematic than has been credited. Each time a character uses the old conventions to describe death, he or she in effect presents a picture to the audience, one that will then be interpreted in the "real" language and action of the play. *Richard II* may serve as an example. Observe how the different pictorial conventions are laid before the audience in Richard's most famous speech:

> For God's sake, let us sit upon the ground
> And tell sad stories of the death of kings—
> How some have been deposed, some slain in war,
> Some haunted by the ghosts they have deposed,
> Some poisoned by their wives, some sleeping killed,
> All murdered.

> (3.2.155–60)

This is a panorama in brief of one of the Dances, done in the manner of the *de casibus* tradition: the fall of princes. But Richard's overview has glossed over some of the individual vignettes: his dancers have all been murdered; there is not one of them who has died the natural death that comes to all princes and commoners alike. What Richard has left out is as telling as what he has included, and by his omission he shows the weaknesses of his own character and his inability to see himself as a mortal human creature responsible for his own actions. For those in the audience who have missed the point, however, Shakespeare allows Richard to zoom in, as it were, on a detail of the panorama; and in this detail the ubiquitous Death of the Dances appears in his sixteenth-century shape, hiding in disguise until the moment for the Summons arrives:

> K. Rich: . . . For within the hollow crown
>   That rounds the mortal temples of a king
>   Keeps Death his Court, and there the antic sits,
>   Scoffing his state and grinning at his pomp,
>   Allowing him a breath, a little scene,
>   To monarchize, be feared, and kill with looks,
>   Infusing him with self and vain conceit,
>   As if this flesh which walls about our life
>   Were brass impregnable, and humored thus
>   Comes at the last and with a little pin
>   Bores through his castle wall, and farewell King!
>   (3.2.160–70)

The contradictory pictures presented to an audience who could be expected to know them both are indications of Richard's vacillating mind. The first picture, with its omissions, is a denial of universal mortality; the second is an acceptance of it, made even more commonly human by the touch of folklore in the image of the "little pin," a fairy-tale motif representing the triumph of seemingly humble things over the seemingly powerful.[34] And when Richard later rejects the second picture to concentrate on the first—"all murdered"—the audience knows that he cannot come to good.

It is not the purpose of this discussion to summarize all the metaphors used by Renaissance stage figures in *speaking* of Death: the cold hand, the empty eye-sockets, Death the bridegroom, the fell sergeant strict in his arrest, and so on. Indeed, Theodore Spencer has covered that field so comprehensively that even to recapitulate his work would be to diminish it. Rather, I should like to examine briefly the aliases under which Death himself appeared onstage to issue the Summons, and then, in subsequent chapters, to examine in depth Death's leading role in representative plays.

In some early attempts to give Death a role of his own, he is allowed to act as Chorus. He appears, as we have seen, with Love and Fortune as Chorus in *Soliman and Perseda*; and he reappears as Homicide (with Avarice and Truth) in *Two Lamentable Tragedies*. But in the latter, he is the truncated Death that Richard II imagined—"all murdered"—and is more an emblem of the Vices loose in the world than a reminder of mortality. As Tragedy (with Comedy and History) in *A Warning for Fair Women*, he focuses more on critical theory than on death itself, and as Revenge in *The Spanish Tragedy*, he (or, rather, she) summons to judgment after death, to Elysium or Tartarus rather than to the grave. In all these plays, Death stands apart from the action, the most hidden of Hidden Deaths, and by his association with and commentary on only murder, serves to distance himself from the audience instead of bringing home to them their common lot. It is only when he steps inside the play and puts on the costume of someone else that he becomes most like himself.

Not all Death's costumes are realistic ones, however. In Dekker's *Old Fortunatus*, for example, Fortune becomes the Summoner. An unabashedly allegorical figure in this quasi folktale, she offers Fortunatus a choice of gifts: wisdom, strength, health, beauty, long life, or riches.[35] The audience that knows its old Moralities will immediately be alerted to the trap here: except for wisdom, all the proffered gifts are illusory and transitory. And indeed, Fortunatus seems to remember his Moralities as he muses on the offer:

Fortunatus: I will be strong; then I refuse long life,
And though mine arm should conquer twenty worlds,
There's a lean fellow beats all conquerors;
The greatest strength expires with loss of breath.
The mightiest, in one moment, stoop to death. . . .
Beauty is but a painting, and long life
Is a long journey in December gone,
Tedious and full of tribulation.

(1.1.268–72; 282–84)

But unfortunately, Fortunatus mistakes wisdom for one of the transitory gifts, not recognizing it as our old friend Knowledge, the only true conductor to temporal and eternal happiness. He chooses, instead, riches (our old enemy Goods), and in the manner of the King of Life, issues his defiance to Death—not realizing that she is standing, listening, in the wings in the guise of Fortune:

Fortunatus: If that lean, tawny-face Tobacconist death, that
turns all into smoke, must turn me so quickly into ashes,
yet I will not mourn in ashes, but in music—hey, old lad,
be merry! Here's riches, wisdom, and strength, health,
beauty, and long life. (If I die not quickly.) Sweet purse,
I kiss thee; Fortune, I adore thee; care, I despise thee;
death, I defy thee.

(1.1.336–41)

It would be interesting to know how this was staged; Fortune might have frowned behind Fortunatus's back—or, more ominously, she might have glanced back over her shoulder at him, given him a ghastly smile, and plucked back part of her costume to show the audience a skeleton.[36] But even without such a palpable hammering home of the point, the audience should have recognized Fortunatus's "asking for it" in issuing such a challenge. And, indeed, his good son, Ampedo, tries to give his father the warning of the Legend, the message of Elde:

Ampedo: The frosty hand of age now nips your blood,
And strews her snowy flowers upon your head,
And gives you warning that within few years
Death needs must marry you. . . .

Could you survey ten worlds, yet you must die;
And bitter is the sweet that's reaped thereby.

(2.2.138-45)

Fortunatus, however, pays no attention, and, as we might expect, Fortune later returns to strike him down in the midst of plenty. He cries out the last desperate plea of all his kind—"Oh, let me live but till I can redeem!" (2.2.244)—but receives the implacable "too late" of the Judgment, and a moral not on how he might have escaped death but how he might have met it bravely: "Hadst thou chosen wisdom. . . / . . . death's stern brow could not thy soul affright" (2.2.248-49). Interestingly enough, of the two sons to whom he leaves his ever-filled purse and wishing hat, Ampedo—the good son who destroys the hat in an attempt to exorcise from the sons the sins of the father— dies an undeserved but stoically accepting death, and with his last breath utters the familiar Greek tag, "No man before his death is truly blessed" (5.2.154). Andelocia, on the other hand—the bad son who, like his father, puts his trust in riches—remains a coward to the end.[37]

Such direct allegory as *Old Fortunatus*, however, became increasingly rare on the stage after 1600; meanwhile, Death was establishing other aliases. One of these was a direct descendant of the Dance of Death: the masque or play that culminates in death or death-tidings. Hieronomo's revenge in *The Spanish Tragedy* is based on such a Dance, in which the audience becomes a participant; and Calantha, dancing on and on in *The Broken Heart* as people bring her word of her loved ones' deaths, is herself learning to die in the rounds of the Dance.

A variant on the convention is the final masque in Marston's *The Malcontent*; although Altofronto/Malevole's masque is meant to unmask, to bring himself and his court back to life instead of to death, the treat of revenge hangs over the revels (at least for the audience) until Altofronto dispels it. And, as both W. E. Slights and Brownell Salomon point out, Altofronto's masque is the last step in his attempt to bring the wicked to anagnorisis—a step, we may say, that is dependent on the threat of impending death, a chance at deathbed repentance.[38]

But the masques of death are seldom this benevolent. The revelers in Tourneur's *The Revenger's Tragedy*, Middleton's *Women Beware Women*, and Shirley's *The Cardinal* are bent on murder and accomplish it. The masque in *Women Beware Women*, in fact, represents another of the guises of Death: the seemingly random or accidental death that kills without looking at its victim; a variation on the Triumph, or on Dame Death who killed fifteen hundred "at a flap." In Middleton's play, during the masque, Isabella wafts poisoned incense toward Livia, who at the same time showers flaming gold on Isabella; Guardiano falls through the trapdoor that he has prepared for Hippolito; Hippolito is fatally wounded by the arrows fired by the "Cupids" of the masque, hired by Livia; and Hebe and Ganymede, unexpected additions to the masque who have been hired by Bianca to poison the Cardinal, accidentally mix up the goblets and poison Bianca's lover, the Duke, instead. Confusion reigns, and although there cannot be said to be any innocent bystanders among the heaps of corpses (in Middleton, there is little unblemished innocence), the sheer haphazardness and rapidity of the carnage emphasize the confusion in the moral life of the Duke's court.

Too often, however, innocent (or nearly innocent) bystanders *are* included in the carnage. In *The Duchess of Malfi*, Antonio, who is on a perhaps ill-advised mission to be reconciled with Ferdinand and the Cardinal, is accidentally cut down in the dark by Bosola, who has arrived on the scene to kill Ferdinand. In *Hamlet*, Gertrude, who for all her incestuous activity has had no hand in Claudius's murder plots, accidentally drinks from the poisoned cup meant for Hamlet.[39] In many historical plays, fathers accidentally kill sons, or sons fathers, to dramatize the senselessness of war (see especially *3 Henry VI*. 2.4), or innocent children may be slain to show a tyrant's brutality. In most of these accidents, the meaningless death is meant to point a moral about the corruption of specific lives; Hippolito, noting significantly before he dies that "man's understanding / Is riper at his fall than all his lifetime,"[40] states the moral for *Women Beware Women*:

> *Hippolito:* Lust and forgetfulness have been amongst us,
>   And we are brought to nothing. . . .
>   . . . vengeance met vengeance
>   Like a set match, as if the plagues of sin
>   Had been agreed to meet here all together.
>   (5.2.146–47; 157–59)

But, as we shall see, by the end of the Caroline years, the mean-inglessness of death will come to exemplify the meaninglessness of life itself.

Closely allied to the accidental or wholesale death that builds on the emblem of the Triumph is the death by the least likely suspect (to borrow a term from detective fiction).[41] Two examples from Shakespeare should suffice. Macduff, although perhaps more accurately termed a revenger (another alias of Death's, after all), brings death much in the manner of the old Death who never failed to answer a personal challenge, whether laid down by Herod, Humanum Genus, the King of Life, or the revelers in the *Pardoner's Tale:*

> *Macbeth:* I bear a charmed life, which must not yield
>   To one of woman born.
> *Macduff:*   Despair thy charm,
>   And let the angel whom thou still has served
>   Tell thee Macduff was from his mother's womb
>   Untimely ripped.
>   (5.8.12–16)

The effect of this entrance of Death depends upon taking both the victim and the audience by surprise; it is not to be confused with murders committed from ambush or in disguise, where the audience knows what the victim does not. The audience must be made to feel the same shock of fear as the victim, as though the victim had cried (like Fortunatus), "Death, I defy thee!" and some familiar figure already on stage had thrown back his hood to reveal skeletonic features and replied, "You called?"

In *King Lear*, too, this least likely suspect appears, this time in the person of one who is given no name but "1 Servant." Here, as Cornwall is putting out Gloucester's eyes and is seemingly in control of other men's lives, the lowliest of the faceless intervenes, and Cornwall's servant controls the life of his master:

> 1 *Servant:*   Hold your hand, my lord.
> I have served you ever since I was a child,
> But better service have I never done you
> Than now to bid you hold.
>   [They draw and fight. Cornwall is wounded.]
>   (3.7.72–75; S.D. 78)

But not all Death's aliases are earthly ones. Ghosts of the already dead also bring threats of vengeance or warnings of impending doom. Although at first a Senecan chorus (much like the Death, Homicide, and Tragedy that we have discussed), the ghost began a gradual infiltration into the play itself, occasionally, as in *Locrine*, taking rather more active measures than necessary to bring about the death that it had come to predict.[42] At times, indeed, the ghost may be a protective one, like Charlemont's father in *The Atheist's Tragedy*, the echo in *The Duchess of Malfi*, or the Friar in *Bussy d'Ambois*: it may even be a spurious "ghost," like the lady who masquerades both as her own ghost and as the medium who has raised it, in *The Lost Lady*. But more often it is a ghost who brings ominous tidings: a command to revenge or a command to die. Andrugio's ghost in *Antonio's Revenge* not only calls for the revenge but also becomes an unnamed co-conspirator in it. Brutus, visited by Caesar's ghost, knows that he will die. And the series of eleven ghosts who visit Richard III in a dream bid him not only to die, but to "Despair and die" (5.3).

Devils, too, retain their foothold on the stage, bearing away souls already contracted to them (as in *Friar Bacon and Friar Bungay, Doctor Faustus,* and *The Devil's Charter*), but also tempting living creatures to suicide, and thus to damnation. Elizabethan experts on ghostlore indeed saw this temptation to despair as one of the signs that an apparition might be the devil in "a pleasing shape," and King James himself, before his accession to the English throne, warned about the danger in his *Daemonologie:* "It is [the devil's purpose] to obtaine . . . the tinsell of their life, by inducing them to perrilous places at such time as he either followes or possesses them which may procure the same."⁴³ It is just this possiblity of the Summons to suicide that Horatio fears when the Ghost beckons to Hamlet:

> *Horatio:* What if it tempt you toward the flood, my lord,
> Or to the dreadful summit of the cliff
> That beetles o'er his base into the sea,
> And there assume some other horrible form
> Which might deprive your sovereignty of reason
> And draw you into madness?
>
> (1.4.69–74)

And in the Dover Cliff scene of *King Lear*, Edgar tries to show Gloucester the better way of life and death alike by describing in devilish terms the companion who has led Gloucester to the "cliff":

> *Edgar:* As I stood here below, methought his eyes
> Were two full moons, he had a thousand noses,
> Horns whelked and waved like the enridged sea.
> It was some fiend. . . .
>
> (4.6.69–72)

Interestingly enough, there is at least one devil who trapped his prey not through despair but through presumption. In Barnabe Barnes's *The Devil's Charter* (ca. 1607), Pope Alexander has relied too much on his assurance of salvation to believe that the devil can ever claim his soul; but in the conventional "undeceiving" scene, just before Alexander is dragged off to Hell, the devil disabuses him of such notions:

> *Alexander:* My soul is substance of the living God,
> Stamp'd with the seal of heaven, whose character
> Is his eternal word, at which hell trembles.
> *Devil:* And what of that? Thou therein hast no part.
> I do confess thy soul was first ordain'd
> To good; but by free will to sin thou, slave,
> Hast sold that soul from happiness to hell.⁴⁴

Alexander then points out that God must have created the soul for salvation, because He has given it so much power, and has added to it a "mind intelligent," something that the animals cannot claim (M1r). The devil admits part of the point: yes, the soul began "lily white," and yes, man is more than an animal because of his mind; but he is supposed to use that mind to seek the higher things, not to debase it to the level of an animal's by thinking only about the trivia of the present moment (M1r–v).

Even allowing for the absurdities of plot in this multiple-murder play (which owes more to *The Jew of Malta* than, as has been claimed, to *Doctor Faustus*), it is a fascinating document in what has happened, dramatically, to the soul's response to itself and to death. Unlike the Calvinist assumptions that the soul is created from a "corrupt mass," that the will is not free but depends on God's plan for it, and that the mind is an obstacle rather than an aid to attaining salvation, Barnes's devil (who, in the convention of the "undeceiving" scene, must be understood as finally telling the truth) points a moral that would have been accepted by medieval Catholic and seventeenth-century Anglican alike. In fact, the only reason Pope Alexander cannot repent appears to be simply that he has fallen out of the habit of thinking, and too much into the habit of giving orders:

> *Alexander:* Mercy, mercy, mercy; arise, arise; up, up; fie, fie;
>   no, no? Stir, stubborn, stony, stiff, indurate heart! Not yet
>   up? Why, what? Wilt thou not, foul traitor to my soul?
>   Not yet?
>   [The Devil laugheth.]
>   Help, help, help, above; stir, stir, stupidity!   (M1v)

We should not be deceived by Pope Alexander's use of the word *indurate*; Barnes by no means wishes to show that death-bed repentance is impossible or that a bad life figures forth pre-destined reprobacy. Earlier in the play, the wicked Lucrezia Borgia, poisoned by her brother/lover Caesar, has undergone a death-bed repentance so sincere and so convincing that her handmaid is drawn to repentance as well:

> *Lucretia:* Ah, Moticilla, whom I trained up
>   In cunning sleights and snares of filthiness,
>   Forgive me for that sin; live and repent.

Moticilla: Oh, God forgive me, for my sins are great,
And if his goodness lend my life some space,
I will with penance call on him for grace,[45]
And spend the remnant of my life in prayer.

(H2v)

The Devil's Charter, of course, can hardly be counted as one of the "great" tragedies of the period, but the bad that imitates the good may show the thought and character of a time better than the good alone can do; the greats of any age, after all, may be exceptions. And in the two and a half decades surrounding the turn of the seventeenth century, the hallmark of tragedy (and often of comedy and tragicomedy as well) was this varied response to the Summons of Death.

What makes the response to death so much more expressive than a response to love, honor, or any other part of life is not only that death is universal (some may say that love, too, is universal), but that, as Samuel Johnson observed, "Depend upon it, Sir, when a man knows he is to be hanged in a fortnight, it concentrates his mind wonderfully."[46] If it is true that at the moment of death a person's whole life flashes before his eyes, it is true, too, that in the Dance of Death his whole life flashes before the audience's eyes. This sharing of Everything at the moment when it is about to become Nothing unites actor and audience, so that, paradoxically, only the moment of death unlocks the secret of life.

It is, in fact, this knowledge of the community of death that makes us recoil in horror from the deathbed of one whose secret does *not* unlock. Critics since Coleridge, for example, have puzzled over Iago's "motiveless malignity," trying to find a motive for the malignity or to explain Iago's actions in terms of dramatic types: the Vice, the Devil, the complicating factor. But Iago's motives are not that impenetrable; any spectator who has military experience will recognize in him a certain type of shifty career man who has advanced so far and can advance no further, who blames everyone else for his own failures and hardly cares in the end what becomes of himself, so long as he can ruin the ones who have what he does not. It is not Iago's life, with all its deception and self-deception, that finally puzzles us; it is his death. "Demand me nothing," he says; "What you know, you know. / From this time forth I never will speak word" (5.2.303–04). And in spite of all that he has already told us, we feel that he is taking some dreadful secret to the grave, something so dreadful that neither he nor Shakespeare can share it with us.

But in the main, we do come to know the figures who die before our eyes on the Renaissance stage. We see the good in all their human weakness: the mild Henry VI venting his first and last outburst of anger; the heroic Byron, before he composes himself, screaming in fear. We see the bad redeeming their lives at death: Edmund trying to countermand his order for Cordelia's death; Laertes asking forgiveness not only of God but of Hamlet. We see regret for what might have been: Tamburlaine, arrested in mid-career, agonizing over the map of lands that he has not yet conquered; Hamlet appointing others to do what he cannot do tomorrow for Denmark. We see Death turning the mighty wretched and the wretched mighty: Edward II and Richard II ennobled in death, not because they have suddenly turned good, but because in their suffering they have rejoined pitiful, suffering, noble humanity. Even the monster Richard III stands forth at the end as a poor, tortured creature crying out, in the isolation of his death, at the isolation of his life:

> K. Rich: I shall despair. There is no creature loves me,
> And if I die, no soul shall pity me.
> Nay, wherefore should they, since that I myself
> Find in myself no pity to myself?
>
> (5.3.100–03)

At the communal moment of the deathbed, actor and audience may speak to each other in the words of the dying Summer to his good steward, Solstitium, in Thomas Nashe's *Summer's Last Will and Testament*:

> I grieve no more regard was had of thee;
> A little sooner hadst thou spoke to me,
> Thou hadst been heard, but now the time is past.

Death waiteth at the door for thee and me;
Let us go measure out our beds in clay:
Nought but good deeds hence shall we bear away.[47]

From Nashe's play, too—part masque, part lament, part satire, part sermon, itself performed before a frightened private audience during the plague year—comes one of the most poignant and most often quoted death lyrics of English literature:

Beauty is but a flower
Which wrinkles will devour,
Brightness falls from the air,
Queens have died young and fair,
Dust hath closed Helen's eye.
I am sick, I must die:
    Lord, have mercy on us.

Strength stoops unto the grave,
Worms feed on Hector brave,
Swords may not fight with fate,
Earth still holds ope her gate.
Come, come, the bells do cry.
I am sick, I must die:
    Lord, have mercy on us.

(283)

Like the infinitely varied Dance of Death on which it (perhaps unconsciously) modeled itself, the late Elizabethan and early Jacobean stage bodied forth the infinitely varied elements of the human soul and ranged them before the onslaught of the common enemy, Death. And, as in the Dance, among the infinite variety and the universality we are sure to recognize the most important of individuals—ourselves.

Medieval Summons, Renaissance Response

Tamburlaine, Parts I and II

HAVING SEEN THE PERSISTENCE of medieval patterns in the secular drama of the Renaissance, we should not be surprised to find a distinctly medieval tinge to the plays of Christopher Marlowe. And yet Marlowe's own life was so controversial, so downright violent in its storms of fortune, that it has always been tempting to view him as an arch-rebel mocking the old beliefs and exposing the old traditions as shams. Indeed, the temptation is a valid one; but in order to mock a belief, one must first take it seriously.

It is not the purpose of this discussion to try to settle the question of whether Marlowe intended his plays to encourage the "aspiring mind"[1] or to warn against the dangers of "self-conceit";[2] such arguments have been developed elsewhere without any two critics' ever coming to an agreement.[3] Rather, for our purposes, it will be sufficient to examine the ways in which Marlowe used an old form for new purposes, the medieval Summons and Judgment in the "modern" context of *Tamburlaine* and *Doctor Faustus*.

There can be no doubt that Tamburlaine, even in *Part I* of the two-part play, is meant to appear audacious in the highest degree; a major portion of the first play is concerned with world-daring and god-daring boasts, with implied blasphemies and charges of blasphemy. But there is actually very little explicit blasphemy until act 5, and that little is usually spoken by Tamburlaine's enemies, either while bemoaning their own fate or while attributing blasphemous sentiments to Tamburlaine:[4]

> *Bajazeth*: Ah, villains, dare ye touch my sacred arms?
>   O Mahomet! O sleepy Mahomet!
> *Zabina*: O cursed Mahomet, that makest us thus
>   The slaves to Scythians rude and barbarous!
>
> (I: 3.3.268–71)

> *Cosroe*: What means this devilish shepherd to aspire
>   With such a giantly presumption,
>   To cast up hills against the face of heaven,
>   And dare the force of angry Jupiter?
>
> (I: 2.6.1–4)

Bajazeth's and Zabina's exclamations against Mahomet, of course, hardly carry the force that Tamburlaine's will carry in *Part II*; the Turkish rulers have not yet become the pitiful suicides of act 5, and Elizabethan audiences would have been delighted to see the false god of Islam mocked and disthroned. As for Cosroe's accusation, Tamburlaine has not yet "dared" Jupiter verbally but has, rather, claimed him as a model of behavior:

> *Tamburlaine*: The thirst of reign and sweetness of a crown,
>   That caus'd the eldest son of heavenly Ops
>   To thrust his doting father from his chair
>   And place himself in the empyreal heaven,
>   Mov'd me to manage arms against thy state.
>   What better precedent than mighty Jove?
>
> (2.6.12–17)

Tamburlaine's own role, as he sees it in most of *Part I*, is not as a darer of gods but the beloved of God, "the scourge and wrath of God" who has been sent to overthrow the Turk (3.3.44–47) and conquer earthly princes. Although he rapidly forgets his holy mission, subordinating it to his own dreams of earthly glory, he continues to perceive himself as God's anointed, for whom the heavens themselves will be turned in their courses:

Tamburlaine: The chiefest God, first mover of that sphere
   Enchas'd with thousands ever-shining lamps,
   Will sooner burn the glorious frame of heaven
   Than it should so conspire my overthrow.

                 (4.2.8–11)

But that Tamburlaine was indeed seen as an atheist is evident from the spate of imitation Tamburlaines who appeared on the Elizabethan stage. Selimus, in particular—the eponymous hero of the 1594 play now attributed to Robert Greene—adds outspoken defiance of all gods to his echoes of Tamburlaine's boasting. And Selimus is obviously meant to be a successor to Marlowe's world-conqueror; if his actions alone do not make the message clear, references to Tamburlaine throughout the play,[5] and the appearance of "Tonombey, Usan-Cassano's son" (l. 2419), most definitely tell the audience where to look for precedents. Selimus's aspirations certainly sound like echoes of Tamburlaine's:

Selimus: But we, whose mind in heavenly thoughts is clad,
   Whose body doth a glorious spirit bear,
   That hath no bounds, but flieth everywhere,
   Why should we seek to make that soul a slave,
   To which dame Nature so large freedom gave?

             (*Selimus*, ll. 349–53)

Tamburlaine: Nature that fram'd us of four elements,
   Warring within our breasts for regiment,
   Doth teach us all to have aspiring minds.
   Our souls, whose faculties can comprehend
   The wondrous architecture of the world
   And measure every wand'ring planet's course,
   Still climbing after knowledge infinite,
   And always moving as the restless spheres,
   Wills us to wear ourselves and never rest. . . .

             (*Tamb.*, I: 2.7.18–26)

Unlike Tamburlaine's, however, Selimus's words follow closely upon what may be one of the boldest statements of atheism on the Renaissance stage:

> *Selimus:* Then some sage man, above the vulgar wise,
>   Knowing that laws could not in quiet dwell
>   Unless they were observed, did first devise
>   The names of Gods, religion, heaven, and hell,
>   And 'gan of pains and feign'd reward to tell. . . .
>   Whereas indeed they were mere fictions,
>   And if they were not, Selim thinks they were:
>   And these religious observations
>   Only bugbears to keep the world in fear.
>
>   (326–36)

But this is Tamburlaine's imitator speaking, not Tamburlaine himself. For Marlowe's audience, Tamburlaine's "atheism" must have been an impression gained more from his actions than from his words. Much of the impression, to be sure, may be attributed to his rise from obscure birth to become a challenger of the established order, a disrupter of the hierarchy of kind given by God; even more may be attributed to his successful defiance of the rule of Fortune, that medieval quasi deity who herself had come to seem a Scourge of God in the Renaissance *de casibus* collections like *Mirror for Magistrates*. But most of all, it may spring from the ways in which Tamburlaine, either consciously or unconsciously, assumes the role of God in sending Death and Judgment.

Tamburlaine is frequently described physically as an emblem of Death. Menaphon, for example, tells Cosroe that "His lofty brows in folds do figure death" (I: 2.1.21)[6] and Agydas turns this "figure" into a more literal emblem after he has received one of Tamburlaine's death-dealing frowns:

> *Agydas:* Upon his brows was portray'd ugly death,
>   And in his eyes the fury of his heart,
>   That shine as comets, menacing revenge,
>   And casts a pale complexion on his cheeks.
>
>   (I: 3.2.72–75)

The glowing eye-sockets and pale countenance described here are reminiscent of descriptions of our old friend, the Dreary Death, just as Tamburlaine's king-drawn chariot of *Part II* will evoke memories of the Triumph of Death.

It soon becomes clear, however, that Tamburlaine himself is not Death but rather the sender of Death. The dying Cosroe refers to Death first as Tamburlaine's henchman and then as his "harpy":

> Cosroe: An uncouth pain torments my grieved soul,
>   And Death arrests the organ of my voice,
>   Who, ent'ring at the breach thy sword hath made,
>   Sacks every vein and artier of my heart.
>   Bloody and insatiate Tamburlaine! . . .
>   . . . and now doth ghastly Death
>   With greedy talents gripe my bleeding heart
>   And like a harpy tires on my life.
>
> (I: 2.7.7–11, 48–50)

And Tamburlaine himself refers to Death as his "servant" (I: 5.1.117), later boasting of the trouble to which he puts this servant: "Where'er I come the Fatal Sisters sweat, / And grisly Death, by running to and fro / To do their ceaseless homage to my sword" (I: 5.1.454–56).

A generation of playgoers whose memories include both the moral interludes of Elizabeth's reign and tales of the banned morality and mystery plays—playgoers whose churches were decorated with the Dance of Death and whose very hands displayed memento mori rings—could hardly fail to recognize, if only subliminally, the godhead that Tamburlaine assumes when he sends forth Death, his mighty messenger.

Agydas's suicide in 3.2 of *Part I*, then, becomes an inversion of both the Summons and the *Ars moriendi*. After he has tried to dissuade Zenocrate from marrying Tamburlaine, not realizing until too late that Tamburlaine has been listening (a ubiquitous and omniscient God?), Agydas sees the frown on Tamburlaine's face and immediately interprets it as his "soul's overthrow" (3.2.87), in the death-emblem terms we have already noted. His interpretation is correct. Techelles and Usumcasane enter with a dagger, and Techelles says, "See you, Agydas, how the king salutes you. / He bids you prophesy what it imports" (3.2.88–89).

"The King" has indeed sent mighty messengers, and the "naked dagger" (S.D. 3.2.88) may as well have been a dart.

What follows is even more noteworthy. Agydas, upon receiving the Summons, makes no attempt to fight or fly; he recognizes its inevitability, greets it with the resigned fatalism of a character in the Dance, and implements the Summons by stabbing himself with the dagger. But his self-slaughter is not viewed as an act of cowardice or despair; Usumcasane refers to it, rather, as "manly," and declares that Agydas will now be given a "triple-worthy burial" (3.2.109–12), one of the few decent burials afforded to any of Tamburlaine's victims.[7]

Why is Agydas's suicide "honorable," and the later suicides of Bajazeth and Zabina merely pitiable? Perhaps because Agydas has shown the proper behavior according to the humanist *Treatise of Dieyng Well*. Lupset, we remember, emphasized the need for courage in the face of inevitable death: "Let vs then take a lusty courage of this desperation, seinge there is no remedy: lette vs manfully go to it" (280). And Lupset, too, praised the exemplary pagan, Canius, who: "playde with deathe, and shortely his quiete harte gaue a foule checke mate to the tyrantes crueltie: he shewed hym selfe to be in spirite as farre aboue all kynges violente power, as these myghtye princes thynke to haue a strong dominion ouer all theyr subiectes" (267–68). Agydas in like manner rejoices in his ability to stay "the torments he [Tamburlaine] and heaven have sworn," and to "wander free from fear of tyrant's rage" (3.2.99; 102), showing his "lusty courage" in the "manly" act of suicide. He does not rage or beg like Bajazeth; he does not wait until desperation overrides his love of life; like Canius, he manfully goes to it.

By itself, of course, this scene does not create the echoes of death literature that give Tamburlaine his aura of godhead. Nor do the deathlike descriptions of Tamburlaine alone suffice, or his own boasting of his power over death; both, after all, may be considered part of the tradition of the heroic *beot*—or even, as in the case of the King of Life, a sign of weakness. But the tents of Tamburlaine, and the emblematic properties that he assigns to them, may very well raise him to the Judgment throne that he has not yet explicitly claimed for himself.

On the first day of a siege, when Tamburlaine pitches his white tents, mercy and forgiveness are offered to all who will repent. On the second day, when the tents are red, noncombatants receive mercy, but those who have offered resistance to Tamburlaine are slain. And on the last and fatal day, when the tents are black and Tamburlaine rides forth in his black clothing, the time of mercy is over; all will perish. John P. Cutts has speculated that the progression of colors—white, red, black—may be reminiscent of the sequence of the horses sent out in Revelation, a prelude to the sending forth of Death.[8] Charles G. Masinton notes further that Elizabethan audiences associated black not merely with a progression toward death but with death and evil themselves.[9] But there is more, emblematically, to the tents of Tamburlaine than a progression of color or a progression toward death; there is also a progression of damnation.

In this context, the white tents carry the warning of the Legend: although you have sinned, it is not too late; repent, amend your lives, and you will be saved and cherished by the mercy of God. The red tents, too, may be viewed as a second chance in either the Catholic or the Protestant sense: the evil that you have done must be purged away (whether in Purgatory or through the death of the sinful body), but the soul that has placed its faith in Christ will be rescued from eternal death. In this sense, the "guilty" civic leaders and "innocent" citizens may represent the deathbed debate between body and soul, in which the body (Governor) "dyes gladlye" to release the soul (governed) from earthly prison or eternal torment. And the black tents? To a generation steeped in traditions of the Four Last Things, those black tents could suggest nothing less than the moment after Divine Judgment.

That Tamburlaine himself sees his black tents in this light is evident from his famous speech to the virgins of Damascus:

Tamburlaine: Behold my sword; what see you at the point?
1 Virgin: Nothing but fear and fatal steel, my lord.

> *Tamburlaine*: Your fearful minds are thick and misty, then,
> For there sits Death, there sits imperious Death,
> Keeping his circuit by the slicing edge.
> But I am pleas'd you shall not see him there.
> He now is seated on my horsemen's spears,
> And on their points his fleshless body feeds.
> Techelles, straight go charge a few of them
> To charge these dames and show my servant, Death,
> Sitting in scarlet on their armed spears.

(I: 5.1.108–18)

The first image of Death that he presents to his victims is that of a judge "keeping his circuit." But, he adds, he is "pleas'd" (like a "predestinating" monarch or deity) to turn the judgment over to his "horsemen"—and here, in the image of the charging horsemen with death on their spears, it is easy to envision the four horsemen of Revelation to whom Cutts alludes in his note on the progression of tent colors. We remember, surely, the charging horsemen in Dürer's *Apocalypse*, and the bodies falling beneath their horses' hooves. There hardly seems to be a doubt in Tamburlaine's mind about his right to send forth the apocalyptic horsemen, or about whose "mighty messenger" Death has become. The Summons to Judgment has been sounded, and Tamburlaine has spoken.

Indeed, the refrain of the *Last Judgment* plays—"too late!"—echoes through all the talk about Tamburlaine's black tents. The virgins of Damascus, before they make what they know to be an ineffective plea for mercy, have remonstrated with their Governor in these terms:

> *1 Virgin*: If humble suits or imprecations . . .
> Might have entreated your obdurate breasts
> To entertain some care of our securities
> Whiles only danger beat upon our walls,
> These more than dangerous warrants of our death
> Had never been erected as they be. . . .

(5.1.24–32)

We might easily be listening, here, to the cries of the damned—or to the bitter complaint of Soul to Body. And Tamburlaine himself answers the virgins' plea with a contrast between the "sweet mercy" of his "milk-white flags" and the "terror" of his "coal-black tents," explaining to them, as though their fate were a thing predestined by God, that their entreaties are now "too late" (5.1.67–73).[10]

I do not mean to suggest that Marlowe shaped his whole play around an analogy with the *Creation* and *Last Judgment* plays of the Mystery cycles; had he wished to do so, there were precedents enough to make a convincing Devil of Tamburlaine, precedents more obviously used by the author of *Selimus*. But the echoes of Judgment remain in sufficient quantity to have shocked Elizabethan audiences, and it is small wonder that these audiences demanded a sequel to the play; they could hardly leave Tamburlaine on the throne of God without wanting to know "what happened next."

What happened next was the fall of Tamburlaine, the translation of a sender of Death into a receiver of Death.

Tamburlaine does not "dye gladlye" in *Part II*. In fact, his death is a travesty on the counsels of dying well given by medieval Catholic, Renaissance Christian humanist, and Calvinist alike. Unlike Everyman, he never progresses beyond the stages of denial, anger, and bargaining; and unlike Lupset's Canius or Strode's dying Christian, he never develops a sense of nonchalance or humor. If anything, his conquering spirit creates a new kind of double bind for the dying man: there is one "lean conqueror" whom no mortal can defeat, and the more one tries, the more ineffectual the battle appears.

The seeds of Tamburlaine's ways of dying have been planted as early as 2.4 of *Part II*, in which Tamburlaine rages against the death of Zenocrate. According to the traditions of the deathbed, everything that he does here is not only wrong but backward. Like the Consolers in the N-Town *Lazarus*, rather than comforting Zenocrate he rages so that she must comfort him, and she must also give him the required deathbed instructions that he should be giving her:

> *Zenocrate:* I fare, my lord, as other empresses,
>   That, when this frail and transitory flesh
>   Hath suck'd the measure of that vital air
>   That feeds the body with his dated health,
>   Wanes with enforc'd and necessary change.
>   . . . .
>   For, should I but suspect your death by mine,
>   The comfort of my future happiness
>   And hope to meet your highness in the heavens,
>   Turn'd to despair, would break my wretched breast,
>   And fury would confound my present rest.
>   But let me die, my love, yet let me die;
>   With love and patience let your true love die.
>   Your grief and fury hurts my second life.
>
>   (2.4.42–46; 61–68)

But while Zenocrate is composing herself to die, and trying to compose her husband, Tamburlaine continues to rage in a manner that suggests that he is afflicted more by the affront to his own honor than by sorrow for the dying Zenocrate. When he speaks of "pale and ghastly death" now, it is of the "darts [that] pierce the center of *my* soul" (2.4.83–84; emphasis added), not Zenocrate's; and after Zenocrate has died, he rails at the Fates whom he formerly termed his servants:

> *Tamburlaine:* What, is she dead? Techelles, draw thy sword
>   And wound the earth, that it may cleave in twain
>   And we descend into th' infernal vaults
>   To hale the Fatal Sisters by the hair
>   And throw them in the triple moat of hell
>   For taking hence my fair Zenocrate.
>
>   (2.4.96–101)

His rage grows worse and worse, as he threatens to make war on heaven, reviles the "amorous Jove" who is cuckolding him by stealing Zenocrate to be "queen of heaven" (2.4.107–08), and, in a rush of fetishistic or sympathetic magic, orders that the town where Zenocrate died be burnt to the ground. Marlowe's audience would hardly expect, as their Catholic ancestors would have done, Tamburlaine to offer up prayers and good works for Zenocrate's soul; such practices were by now looked upon as papist superstition. But they would certainly expect him to erect a noble monument, in Renaissance style: a human work of beauty in stone, paint, or poetry to keep Zenocrate's fame immortal before the eyes of the world. Instead, Tamburlaine gives the world dust and ashes, mortality rather than immortality. And Zenocrate's "stature" (2.4.140), placed in the wreckage, will make her a hated symbol of the devastation, an ironic memento mori in her own right.

The truly noble monument, which he keeps only for his own viewing, is itself a misuse of the traditional symbol. Zenocrate is to be embalmed and placed in a gold coffin, which Tamburlaine will take with him everywhere, and which, in fact, he will demand to have near him as he himself is dying. She thus becomes for him a perverted memento mori of another kind: one that will cause him, not to remember death, but to forget it: "Though she be dead, yet let me think she lives" (2.4.127). To be sure, he may have been provoked into this excess, originally, by Theridamas's premature counsel that does not allow for normal grieving: "Ah, good my lord, be patient. She is dead, / And all this raging cannot make her live" (2.4.119–20). But his subsequent actions— the portage of the coffin and his addresses to it—show that in fact he does continue to deny the separation that death entails.

We who have inherited both the Jacobean and the Caroline versions of this raging, and the modern Romantic's injunction to "Rage, rage against the dying of the light,"[11] may applaud Tamburlaine's violence in the face of death. Certainly, George Chapman, who so obviously modeled his ultraheroic protagonists on Marlowe's mighty line, applauded it; Byron, for example, goes raging to his own death for nearly two hundred and fifty lines, meanwhile bargaining, railing against injustice, and threatening to slaughter the executioner and bystanders alike:

> *Byron:* Out, ugly image of my cruel injustice!
>   Yet wilt thou be before me? Stay my will,
>   Or by the will of Heaven, I'll strangle thee!
> *Vitry:* My lord, you make too much of your own body,
>   Which is no more your own.

Byron: Nor is it yours;
    I'll take my death with all the horrid rites
    And representments of the death it merits;
    Let tame nobility and numbed fools
    That apprehend not what they undergo,
    Be such exemplary and formal sheep.[12]

We may assume, then, that the Jacobean transformation indicates approbation of Tamburlaine's behavior. But did Marlowe himself feel such unqualified approbation? The sources and structure of *Part II* suggest that he did not.

Both Eugene M. Waith and Douglas Cole have likened Tamburlaine to Seneca's Hercules and have seen his raging in the light of Senecan convention.[13] But Cole further points out that such excess of emotion is generally a mark of weakness in Seneca, and that "Tamburlaine's companions . . . are related to the Senecan line of rational confidantes [*sic*] who try to calm an impassioned sufferer" (110). And the fact that Marlowe gives Tamburlaine an extra opportunity to rage against death—Zenocrate's death does not appear in Marlowe's sources[14]—may be an indication that there is meant to be a note of ironic warning in the first opportunity: a variation, misapplied by Tamburlaine, of the old Legend.

The contrast, too, of other deaths with Tamburlaine's in *Part II* points up a failing in the heroic posture. As we have noted, Zenocrate herself, a model of right, makes a "good" death. She accepts the inevitability of mortality ("I fare, my lord, as other empresses"), cautions Tamburlaine against the deathbed temptations, counsels her children, and turns with hope to heaven. Although hers is not an explicitly religious death, it would have satisfied Renaissance Christians; she is an exemplum of faith, patience, hope, and courage. Since there is no remedy, she bravely (one is tempted to say "manfully") goes to it, and dies during the playing of music, that Renaissance symbol of harmony.

Olympia and her young son also provide patterns of dying against which Tamburlaine's may be measured. Like Agydas in *Part I*, Olympia chooses death before dishonor; to prevent capture and torture by Tamburlaine's men, she resolves to kill her son "gently . . . and quickly" (3.4.24–25) and then commit suicide. Her son "manfully" agrees:

> Son: Give me your knife, good mother, or strike home;
> The Scythians shall not tyrannize on me.
> Sweet mother, strike, that I may meet my father.
>
> (3.4.28–30)

The resolution shown by both Olympia and her son, who are at this moment standing over the body of Olympia's dead husband, is particularly interesting when it is compared with the reaction of Zabina in *Part I*, who goes mad when she discovers her husband dead. Olympia allows herself only four lines of mourning (an apostrophe to "ugly Death" in 3.4.11–14) before she turns her attention to what must be done next, so that her decision to die seems a result, not of an excess of grief, but of a rational process of thought.

This is not to suggest that Olympia is totally cold in her response to death. Her four-line apostrophe to the personified figure is almost as emotional as Tamburlaine's longer one:

> Olympia: Death, whither art thou gone that we both live?
> Come back again, sweet Death, and strike us both!
> One minute end our days, and one sepulcher
> Contain our bodies! Death, why com'st thou not?
>
> (3.4.11–14)

But this emotion, like Magdalen's in the N-Town *Lazarus*, is catharsis rather than despair or denial. And Olympia's attempted suicide is obviously not meant to be mistaken for despair, because before she turns the knife on herself, she calls upon her god for pardon almost in the manner of the medieval Moriens:

> Olympia: Ah, sacred Mahomet, if this be sin,
> Entreat a pardon of the God of heaven
> And purge my soul before it comes to thee.
>
> (3.4.31–33)

Although Olympia's attempt is interrupted and she does not die until she later tricks Theridamas into killing her, she receives

the same accolade for her attempt as Agydas did for his success—
Techelles's exclamation that " 'Twas bravely done" (3.4.37). Interestingly enough, when Theridamas and Techelles lead her away
to Tamburlaine, from what they think death to what they think
life, Theridamas's words suggest that they are preparing her for
death-in-life. Like the grim summoner in the Dance of Death,
he tells her, "you must go with us—no remedy" (3.4.79), and she
responds in kind:

> *Olympia:* Then carry me, I care not, where you will,
>   And let the end of this my fatal journey
>   Be likewise end to my accursed life.
>
> (3.4.80–82)

It is tempting to claim Sigismund, along with Zenocrate and
Olympia, as another "good" death, but I cannot agree entirely
with Douglas Cole, who takes Sigismund's dying speech at face
value: "Sigismond [sic] looks upon his affliction not only as a punishment, but as a way of spiritual purgation; his prayer is that
the physical pain of his wounds and death will be accepted by
God, along with his personal contribution, as satisfaction for his
sin of perjury."[15] It is true that Sigismund says all the correct things
at the moment of death; he appears to have acknowledged his
sins, repented, done penance, and asked God for mercy:

> *Sigismund:* O just and dreadful punisher of sin,
>   Let the dishonor of the pains I feel
>   In this my mortal well-deserved wound
>   End all my penance in my sudden death;
>   And let this death, wherein to sin I die,
>   Conceive a second life in endless mercy.
>
> (2.3.3–9)

But when Orcanes enters afterward, not having heard this deathbed repentance, Marlowe creates a set of dramatic ironies that
must be absorbed either by Orcanes or by Sigismund. Sigismund
is now dead and cannot speak for himself or make restitution
to the living. Orcanes, unaware of Sigismund's "state of grace,"
if such it be, consigns Sigismund's soul to Hell and his body to

beasts of prey, denying him a decent burial. And perhaps most significant of all, Orcanes takes what he assumes to be Sigismund's damnation as a sign of Christ's power, becoming, if not a convert to Christianity, at least a respecter of Christ who defends His power against the doubts of a skeptic:

> *Orcanes:* What sayest thou yet, Gazellus, to his foil,
>   Which we referr'd to justice of his Christ
>   And to His power, which here appears as full
>   As rays of Cynthia to the clearest sight?
> *Gazellus:* 'Tis but the fortune of the wars, my lord,
>   Whose power is often prov'd a miracle.
> *Orcanes:* Yet in my thoughts shall Christ be honored,
>   Not doing Mahomet an injury,
>   Whose power had share in this our victory.
>
>   (2.3.27–35)

There is certainly a good deal of ambiguity in this scene. If Sigismund is saved and Orcanes mistaken, then Orcanes's quasi conversion is based on error and Christ is made to look ineffectual. On the other hand, if Christ has manifested Himself in the defeat of Sigismund, and Orcanes is correct about his damnation, then Sigismund's repentance is as dubious as all such deathbed repentances had become in the current treatises on dying. Furthermore, Gazellus's skepticism about such cause-and-effect "miracles" will later add to the ambiguity of Tamburlaine's burning of the Koran and subsequent illness. Is Tamburlaine's death a form of retribution from heaven? Or merely a "fortune of the wars" and his own choleric nature? And is it really blasphemy to repudiate a false god in what seems to be a tentative quest for the Almighty? Tamburlaine says:

> Well, soldiers, Mahomet remains in hell;
> He cannot hear the voice of Tamburlaine.
> Seek out another godhead to adore—
> The God that sits in heaven, if any god,
> For He is God alone, and none but He.
>
>   (5.1.196–200)

Surely such a test (and failure) of a false god would be familiar to Marlowe's audience, who had biblical examples before them of the prophets who had challenged the false gods in similar ways.[16]

But only fifteen lines later Tamburlaine is struck by a sudden illness, which later proves fatal. Roy W. Battenhouse has pointed out that theological tracts of the time viewed acts of sacrilege against even false gods as comprising religious impiety, and that "Calvin had said that if idolaters lift themselves up against their own forged gods they thereby show themselves contemners of *all* divine power."[17] Cole, however, sees the scene with the Koran as Marlowe's way of satisfying Elizabethan audiences both ways:

> Given the terms of this challenge. . . . it would be unreasonable to expect lightning to strike at this precise point, for that would "prove" Mahomet a deity. By introducing the first traces of Tamburlaine's affliction some lines later . . . Marlowe has perhaps solved the problem of showing some kind of retribution for Tamburlaine's overreaching pride and inhumanity while avoiding the implication that Mahomet is responsible for it.[18]

But neither of these viewpoints explains the shock effect of the scene, or, for that matter, the incongruity of the contrast between Sigismund's retributive death and Tamburlaine's. In the first, the true God's hand is believed to be present in the visible world of battle but absent in the invisible world of the soul. In the second, the false god's hand is believed to be absent in the visible world of the burning of the Koran but present in the invisible world of Tamburlaine's malady.

Ambiguity heaped upon ambiguity—it is small wonder that so much scholarly ink has been spilled in an effort to understand Tamburlaine's death. Even the Governor of Babylon adds to the confusion. When first confronted by his own death, he hurls a very Tamburlaine-like defiance at his captors:

Governor: Vile monster, born of some infernal hag
    And sent from hell to tyrannize on earth,
    Do all thy worst! Nor death, nor Tamburlaine,
    Torture, or pain can daunt my dreadless mind.

(5.1.11–13)

But the moment Tamburlaine (like Mephistophilis) threatens to tear his flesh ("up with him, then! His body shall be scarr'd" [5.1.114]), the Governor begins to bargain for his life, much in the manner of Everyman, Doctor Faustus, Chapman's Byron, and Tamburlaine himself. And like all his fellow bargainers, he finds his bargaining to be in vain.

To enumerate all the ways of dying in *Tamburlaine, Part II*, would be both tedious and virtually endless; even Susan Richards, in her excellent study of the subject, has had to select and summarize more than I have done here.[19] Like a Renaissance Dance of Death, Marlowe's play takes an almost infinite variety of personalities through their mortal paces to the grave, ending with Tamburlaine, the "kynge liggying dede & eten with wormes."[20]

And Tamburlaine, for all his boasting, makes almost as bad a death—given the standards established in the rest of the play—as does the Governor of Babylon. Although he has earlier claimed that "Sickness or death can never conquer me" (5.1.220), his deathbed raging is a form of denial and bargaining that violates the standards for a courageous death set forth in the death literature of the Middle Ages and Renaissance alike. Theridamas, like the religious treatises on dying, must counsel him to "leave these impatient words" (5.3.54), to stop denying and "grudging against" the word of God and the lot of humankind. Techelles, next, must remind him of Lupset's counsel on the stoical acceptance of pain: "Sit still, my gracious Lord; this grief will cease / And cannot last, it is so violent" (5.3.64–65).[21] But Tamburlaine pays no attention to either of them.

Toward the end, Tamburlaine attempts to find immortality both in heaven and on earth, but his hope of heavenly immortality is vested in the gods whom he has already repudiated, and the earthly, in sons whom he must pretend to be parts of himself:

> *Tamburlaine:* In vain I strive and rail against those powers
> That mean t' invest me in a higher throne,
> As much too high for this disdainful earth. . . .
> My flesh, divided in your precious shapes,
> Shall still retain my spirit, though I die,
> And live in all your seeds immortally.
>
> (5.3.120–22; 170–72)

Unfortunately, much of this equivocal acceptance sounds a bit like "make-do," coming as it does so closely on the heels of the most convincing part of his raging: his diatribe to Death, a speech made directly to the familiar, personified "ugly monster" of the Dances:

> *Tamburlaine:* See where my slave, the ugly monster, Death,
> Shaking and quivering, pale and wan with fear,
> Stands aiming at me with his murdering dart,
> Who flies away at every glance I give,
> And, when I look away, comes stealing on.
> Villain, away, and hie thee to the field!
> I and mine army come to load thy bark
> With souls of thousand mangled carcasses.
> Look, where he goes! But see, he comes again
> Because I stay. Techelles, let us march
> And weary Death with bearing souls to hell.
>
> (5.3.67–77)

Medieval audiences would undoubtedly have seen a great deal of futility in such a speech, reminiscent as it is of the "bad" responses of the Legends and the Dances. Had Everyman, Humanum Genus, or the King of Life responded in this way, his soul would have been damned to Hell; denial of death admits of no repentance. But that was in another century; and besides, the age was dead.

Tamburlaine's duel with the medieval skeleton is, in fact, symptomatic of the feverish duel of contrasts in the Elizabethan age. The very bravado that typifies such figures as Sidney, Ralegh, and Gloriana herself may be called—if the anachronism will be forgiven—a form of future shock, in which human society must run as fast as it can simply to stay in the same place, and twice as fast to get anywhere. In such a promising young age, one can either fulfill the promise or stay young; Time the Destroyer keeps one from doing both. Defeat is inevitable; but one cannot admit to defeat.

We have seen, in earlier chapters, how the figure of Death gave way to the figure of Time toward the end of the sixteenth century, while Death as a personage became an artistic figure of fun. Tamburlaine's own mockery of the "ugly monster" is part of this tradition—but there is something more dreadful than the skeleton that is overtaking Tamburlaine, something that he has been fighting throughout both parts of the play: mutability. And "fighting" is the operative word.

By assuming the role of Death-sender, Tamburlaine has denied the inevitable from the first scene of *Part I*. He has translated his own fear, and the fears of his audience, into a role of action in which he is always sending death *away* from himself; and only in such carnage can he be safe. As G. K. Chesterton's Guthrum, the great leader of the Danes in The *Ballad of the White Horse*, was to explain it centuries later,

> "The heart of the locked battle
>   Is the happiest place for men;
> When shrieking souls as shafts go by
> And many have died and all may die;
> Though this word be a mystery,
>   Death is most distant then.

> "Death blazes bright above the cup,
>   And clear above the crown;
> But in that dream of battle
>   We seem to beat it down.

> "Wherefore I am a great king
>   And waste the world in vain,
> Because man hath not other power,
> Save that in dealing death for dower,
> He may forget it for an hour
>   To remember it again."[22]

Like Guthrum, Tamburlaine is happiest when he is wading in blood "up to the chin" or instilling in his sons the joy of doing so (II: 1.3.69–101; 3.2.95–129). His response to the death of Zenocrate is to burn and pillage; and his response to his own impending death is to threaten men and gods alike with bloody wars. But despite his half-believed declaration that the last battle with Callapine will "recure" him (5.3.105–06), when he returns from the field his condition worsens and he remembers death again. At the last, like Guthrum whose "heart fail[ed] thereat" (229), he must "read what is written / So plain in clouds and clods" (230); and with his last breath he utters the moral of the Legends and the Dances: "For Tamburlaine, the scourge of God, must die" (5.3.238).

Is Tamburlaine's death, then, cautionary or exemplary? Probably both. Marlowe himself seems to have delighted in eliciting horrified gasps from his countrymen, whether he believed his own bold statements or not; and he also seems to have discovered that part of the horrified gasp is grounded in a perverse admiration: humankind's repressed wish to "get away with murder" even while it condemns the murderer. Such a gasp had certainly made the comic Vice popular in the old Moralities; and such a gasp was enough to make the outrageous Tamburlaine outrageously popular. There may indeed be a moral implicit in the death of Tamburlaine. But it can easily be drowned out by the gasp.

VII

The Summons to Hell

Doctor Faustus

AFTER THE AMBIGUITIES in *Tamburlaine*, the moral of *Doctor Faustus* seems painfully clear: "Regard his hellish fall" (Epi.4: 2005). But even here, Marlowe's use of the medieval convention is colored by his time; Faustus falls prey not only to the devil or to his own self-conceit but also to a distinctly post-Reformation despair. And the nature of that despair may be as ambiguous as Tamburlaine's presumption.

To view all of Marlowe's flawed protagonists as Renaissance "overreachers," men whose aspiring minds are to be admired even as their human limitations defeat them, may be valid, but Faustus's reach so far exceeds his grasp that even his aspirations seem equivocal. As I have shown elsewhere,[1] he is not only a bad Christian but a bad scholar; he is more concerned with publishable information than with widsom, seldom fulfills his heroic boasts, and allows himself to be fobbed off with empty spectacle and practical jokes when he should be delving into questions about the nature of the universe—the reason, after all, that he gave for selling his soul in the first place. Even his celebrated paean to Helen is an exercise in self-deceit; having earlier explained that all such apparitions are "but shadows, not substantial" (xii.55: 1259), he surely knows that the answer to his famous question, "Was this the face that launch'd a thousand ships?" (xviii.99: 1768), is very simply "No."

But Faustus's scholarship (or lack of it) is not at issue here; it is rather his death that concerns us, and his death is unequivocally a bad one. In psychological terms, Faustus never emerges from the bargaining stage of dying; his final soliloquy is filled with impassioned pleas to the heavens, to Christ, to the earth, stars, and clouds, to his own body, and finally to death itself in the person of Lucifer. Like Everyman before him, he begs for progressively decreasing parcels of time in which to repent:

> *Faustus:* Stand still, you ever-moving spheres of heaven,
>   That time may cease, and midnight never come;
>   Fair nature's eye, rise, rise again, and make
>   Perpetual day; or let this hour be but
>   A year, a month, a week, a natural day,
>   That Faustus may repent and save his soul.
>   (xix.136–41: 1929–34)

And, like Everyman, he feels the relentlessly crushing weight of inexorable Time: "The stars move still, time runs, the clock will strike, / The devil will come, and Faustus must be damn'd" (xix.143–44: 1936–37).

But even Faustus's bargaining is a form of self-deceit. After all his pleading for "a month, a week, a . . . day," he is given the better part of an hour, and instead of using it to repent, he uses it only to continue bargaining. His offers to endure horrible physical pain for the salvation of his soul are also false bargains; before asking the mountains to fall on him, the earth to swallow him, and the clouds to absorb him and then vomit him forth, he has already shown his fear of pain and his readiness to give up repentance after the first or second pang:

> *Faustus:* See, see where Christ's blood streams in the firmament!
>   One drop would save my soul, half a drop. Ah, my Christ!—
>   Rend not my heart for naming of my Christ;
>   Yet will I call on him. O, spare me, Lucifer!
>   Where is it now? 'Tis gone. . . .
>   (xix.146–50: 1939–43)

His final plea to God, then, to "Let Faustus live in hell a thousand years, / A hundred thousand, and at last be sav'd" (xix. 169–70:

1961–62) is patently worthless. From the beginning of the play to the end, Faustus has shown that he cannot bear even a moment of physical pain, let alone a hundred thousand years of it.

The Old Man shows a better way of dying. Although, as we shall see, he may represent the warning of the Legend, the Good Counsel of the moralities and *Artes*, or simply the elect soul, in a sense he is also an example of the courageous stoic, the man who "manfully goes to it." Mephistophilis, at least, seems to recognize in him not only the elect soul but the imperturbable soul; when Faustus asks that the Old Man be tortured, Mephistophilis replies:

> His faith is great; I cannot touch his soul;
> But what I may afflict his body with
> I will attempt, which is but little worth.
>
> (xviii.87–89: 1756–58)

The phrase "which is but little worth" is exactly the note of offhand contempt for afflictions of the body that runs through the new treatises on dying. We have seen it before in Lupset and shall see it again in Guillemand; we shall see it, too, in Hamlet, who goes manfully to meet the Ghost:

> *Hamlet:* Why, what should be the fear?
>   I do not set my life at a pin's fee,
>   And for my soul, what can it do to that,
>   Being a thing immortal as itself?
>
> (1.4.40–47)

And like the courageous men of the new tracts, the Old Man throws a parting shot at tyrants, although in this case he is taunting the tyranny of Hell:

> *Old Man:* Satan begins to sift me with his pride:
>   As in this furnace God shall try my faith,
>   My faith, vile hell, shall triumph over thee.
>   Ambitious fiends, see how the heavens smiles
>   At your repulse and laughs your state to scorn!
>   Hence, hell! for hence I fly unto my God.
>
> (xviii.122–27: 1791–96)

This is not to suggest that the Old Man is a purely secular figure; he is as much a religious emblem as the Seven Deadly Sins, the Good and Bad Angels, and Mephistophilis himself. But even the heterodox in Marlowe's audience can see that the Old Man's death has in it all the good things that Faustus's has not: courage, laughter, and victory.

As for those critics who see Faustus's death and damnation as a sort of unjust justice, a striking down of the aspiring human creature who will not give up his aspirations or his "self-sufficiency,"[2] it may be interesting to inspect more closely Faustus's final attempts at bargaining. This "self-sufficient" martyr for the scholarly cause, in order to escape a painful death, offers, in turn, to be turned into a "brutish beast," that is, to be less than a man (xix.176: 1968); to dissolve his body into air and his spirit into water, that is, to undergo annihilation of the self (xix.183–87: 1975–78); and finally, in perhaps the greatest irony of all, to burn his books—a scholar's nightmare (xix.190: 1982).

The books that he offers so desperately to the holocaust at this last moment are, of course, his books of magic. But in the context of the play, they are more than books of magic; they are the accumulations of knowledge that he has substituted for wisdom throughout his life. During his opening soliloquy, he has systematically and symbolically discarded books of philosophy, medicine, law, and religion, claiming to have mastered their contents and to have found them insufficient. Later, when he has sold his soul for knowledge and power, Mephistophilis gives him—books! And again, Faustus confuses knowledge with wisdom; for him, as Edward A. Snow points out, "One art follows directly upon another, each beginning precisely where the last left off, each neatly condensed, predigested, and encapsulated within the covers of its own book."[3] The fault lies not in Faustus's books, but in himself, that he misuses them. Consequently, his final pleas become, for the scholar, the last in a long series of abuses to which Faustus has subjected learning, here pitifully mixed with another appeal for more time:

> *Faustus:* Adders and serpents, let me breathe awhile!
>   Ugly hell, gape not! Come not, Lucifer;
>   I'll burn my books!—Ah, Mephistophilis!
>
> (xix.188-90: 1980-82)

And yet *Doctor Faustus* is more than a tract on the abuse of learning, just as it is far more than a tract on the perils of overreaching. As Leo Kirschbaum has so aptly noted: "It does not matter what *you* think of Hell or what Marlowe thought of Hell. What does matter is that in terms of the play, Faustus is a wretched creature who for lower values gives up higher values— that the devil and Hell are omnipresent, potent, and terrifying realities."[4] Essentially, *Doctor Faustus* is a morality play that looks back to the pattern of the medieval Moralities: a soul strays into evil practices, is counseled by forces of good and evil, and finally dies, going either to Heaven or to Hell, depending on the choices that it has made. The fact that Faustus, in his weakness, either vacillates in his choices or chooses not to choose does not change the play's emphasis on choice and free will—at least for the mainstream Anglicans in Marlowe's audience.[5]

To the very end, Faustus is reminded over and over again that he may still make the correct choice, may still repent and be saved. Even after his Good Angel leaves him and his last hour begins, he is granted the vision of "Christ's blood stream[ing] in the firmament," a symbol of both the Eucharist and Christ's redeeming mercy. In the older Moralities, Faustus might at this moment have cried out for that mercy, and like Humanum Genus, or like the King of Life and the Dyenge Creature, might have been granted it.

In this context, the Old Man and the scholars of the final scenes may be seen as the warning of the Legends and the deathbed companions of the treatises on dying. The Old Man, in particular, is a deliberately enigmatic figure in *Doctor Faustus*. In Marlowe's source, *The Historie of the Damnable Life, and Deserued Death of Doctor Iohn Faustus*, he is identified as "A good Christian an honest and vertuous olde man, a louer of the holy scriptures, who was neighbour vnto Doctor Faustus,"[6] a mundane figure well known to Faustus. This old man counsels Faustus over a long period of time, and Faustus's enmity toward him grows only gradually, as the old man becomes a constant reminder of his guilty conscience. But in Marlowe's play, the Old Man appears out of nowhere, is almost immediately rejected, and disappears from the play as rapidly as he came into it. Although he does not have the supernatural characteristics of Chaucer's Old Man in *The Pardoner's Tale*, he is a similarly emblematic figure rather than a real person—the Elde of the Legend who prefigures Death.

The scholars who leave Faustus to his doom are also familiar figures. They are the friends about the deathbed who must help the dying soul in his struggle, and if they are somewhat ineffective in their ministrations, they at least know what *should* be done at this moment. "Look up to heaven and remember God's mercy is infinite," says the Second Scholar (xix.39–40: 1835–36); and "Call on God," insists the Third Scholar (xix.54: 1848), even after Faustus has told them that he is deep in deadly sin. And, most significantly of all, the scholars do not reject Faustus as damned when he tells them that he has abjured God and given his soul to the devil; in fact, upon receiving this news, they become more insistent that he pray to God, and now offer to join their prayers with his. Obviously, they have not lost confidence in deathbed repentance, or in the power of communal prayer. Weak they may be, and failures in their duty to stay with the dying man until the end, but they do not accept Faustus's despairing evaluation of his destiny. It is Faustus who sends them away:

> 2 *Scholar:* O, what may we do to save Faustus?
> *Faustus:* Talk not of me, but save yourselves and depart.
> 3 *Scholar:* God will strengthen me. I will stay with Faustus.
> 1 *Scholar:* Tempt not God, sweet friend; but let us into the next room and pray for him.
> *Faustus:* Ay, pray for me, pray for me; and what noise soever ye hear, come not unto me, for nothing can rescue me.
> 2 *Scholar:* Pray thou, and we will pray, that God may have mercy on thee.
> *Faustus:* Gentlemen, farewell. If I live till morning, I'll visit you; if not, Faustus is gone to hell.
>
> (xix.75–84: 1868–79)

It is not entirely true, then, as Pauline Honderich suggests, that "the old dispensation . . . no longer has its old efficacy" in the world of *Doctor Faustus*.[7] The "old dispensation" is offered time and time again to Faustus: by the Good Angel, by the Old Man, by the (admittedly weak) scholars, and finally by the vision of Christ's redeeming blood—the last of which, we must remember, appears to Faustus while the scholars are praying for him in the next room. And that most of Marlowe's audience would have been happy to see Faustus accept the offer is evident from the way in which a similar audience had demanded a "happy" new ending to *The Conflict of Conscience*, an ending based on repentance at the very last moment. It is Doctor Faustus the character, not *Doctor Faustus* the play, that refuses all these offers of the old dispensation; it is Faustus, not his world, that is the fatalist.

To be sure, Faustus claims that his damnation proceeds from his blasphemy against God; and the Old Man, in contrast, says that his own faith will save him. But to contend, as David Kaula does, that the play is therefore a "distinctly post-Reformation play because the hero's destiny hinges entirely on the question of faith, a question which does not enter into *Everyman*,"[8] is to ignore, first, both Everyman's second set of temptations and the fact that the medieval *Ars* gives infidelity as the first deathbed temptation; and second, that repentance was considered, even after the Reformation, as an act of will. Even Lily B. Campbell, in an otherwise brilliant analysis of Faustus's despair, states that Protestants of the time would have seen his sin as final and irredeemable by any "good works."[9] In fact, "good works" are not in question in *Doctor Faustus*; it is Faustus's repentance that matters. And Faustus will not repent.

The Anglican view of repentance is clearly laid out in the book of homilies designated for reading in Elizabethan churches. The penitent must take four steps: contrition of heart, confession of sins "unto GOD," faith in God's promises of salvation, and amendment of life.[10] Even at the last moment, when amendment has become an academic question, it may still be possible to substitute the intent for the deed. Myles Coverdale, we recall, insisted on the soul's obligation to struggle toward salvation no matter how bleak the prospect might seem,[11] and Lewis Bayly was to add that the dying man's emotional state is not to be taken as a sign of his spiritual state, that "the truest faith hath oftentimes the least feeling, and greatest doubts."[12]

By Marlowe's time, such encouragement was being preached weekly from the pulpits of the Church of England:

> Whereby it followeth necessarily, that although we doe, after we bee once come to GOD and grafted in his Sonne Jesus Christ, fall into great sinnes (for there is no righteous man vpon the earth that sinneth not, and if wee say wee haue no sinne, we deceiue our selues, and the trueth is not in vs) yet if wee rise againe by repentaunce, and with a full purpose of amendment of life doe flee vnto the mercie of GOD, taking sure holde thereupon, through faith in his Sonne Jesus Christ, there is an assured and infallible hope of pardon and remission of the same, and that wee shall bee receiued againe into the fauour of our heauenly Father. (2: 262)

Marlowe's audiences must have heard this passage ringing in their ears when they listened to Faustus misquoting—or, rather, half-quoting—the Scriptures in his opening soliloquy:

> *Faustus:* Jerome's Bible, Faustus, view it well. *Stipendium peccati mors est.* Ha! *Stipendium,* etc. The reward of sin is death: that's hard. *Si pecasse negamus, fallimur, et nulla est in nobis veritas.* If we say that we have no sin, we deceive ourselves, and there's no truth in us. Why then, belike we must sin, and so consequently die.
>
> Ay, we must die an everlasting death.
>
> (i.38–45: 65–73)

Faustus has quoted the well-known homily almost verbatim up to the point at which it contradicts him, and Elizabethan audiences would have been arrested by his omission as one is shocked by the absence of an expected sound. Indeed, there can be little doubt that here Marlowe was employing the rhetorical trope of aposiopesis: the deliberate omission of an expected phrase or word in order to force the audience into both completing the thought and noting its lack of completion.[13] Faustus, the audience knows, is very simply wrong.

The *Homilies* caution against such misreading of the Scriptures, and in no uncertain terms:

> Whereupon we doe not without a just cause detest and abhorre the damnable opinion of them which doe most wickedly goe about to perswade the simple and ignorant people, that if wee chance after wee be once come to GOD, and grafted in his Sonne Jesus Christ, to fall into some horrible sinne, shall be unprofitable to vs, there is no more hope of reconciliation, or to be receiued againe into the fauour and mercy of GOD. (2: 261)

A "damnable opinion," indeed—one that Mephistophilis constantly reiterates to Faustus, who in this context may be considered one of the "simple and ignorant people" who believe it. The result is one that the *Homilies* had predicted:

> For as in all other things mens hearts doe quaile and faint, if they once perceiue that they trauell in vaine: Euen so most specially in this matter, must we take heede and be ware that we suffer not our selues to bee perswaded that all wee doe is but labour lost: For thereof either sudden desperation doeth arise, or a licencious boldnesse to sinne, which at length bringeth unto desperation. (2: 260)[14]

As we have noted, the Protestant insistence on man's utter depravity seems to have encouraged such dangerous temptations to despair. True, Martin Luther had denounced such misconceptions as Faustus's in terms similar to those of the *Homilies*: "[The Devil] can fashion the strangest syllogisms: 'You have sinned: God is wrathful toward sinners; therefore despair.' "[15] But he had also insisted that the soul must experience a sort of despair in order to attain salvation; that is, man must recognize that he is utterly sinful, capable of no good, and deserving of damnation, before he can accept his dependence on God and cry wholeheartedly for mercy. So far, so good; Faustus certainly has many moments when he is persuaded that he is worthy of damnation. But why can he not proceed from this conviction to an equal conviction of God's redeeming mercy? The Protestant doctrine was certainly adamant about man's "assured and infallible hope of pardon" (*Homilies*, 2: 262), and in fact maintained it steadfastly against the Catholic insistence that "none is certayn, yf he be dygne or worthy to haue deserued the loue of god, or the hate of god":[16]

> Certentie of faith, is whereby any thing is certenly beleeved: and it is either generall or speciall. Generall certentie, is to beleeue assuredly that the word of God is truth it selfe, and this both we and Papists allow. Speciall certentie, is by faith to apply the promise of salvation to our selves, and to beleeve without doubt, that remission of sinnes by Christ and live ever lasting belong to us. This kind of certentie we hold and maintaine, and Papists with one consent deny it; acknowledging no assurance but by hope.[17]

The problem with such assurance is, of course, the double bind that we have seen before, a double bind exacerbated by Calvin's doctrine of perseverance in grace, and by the new position given to good works—as not a means to salvation but a sign of salvation. Calvin had agreed that despair is necessary before the soul can turn to God; but, he added, once the soul has turned to God, any recurrence of despair is a sign that the turn was never made in the first place, that the soul is not among the elect. Doubt, therefore, is a sign of damnation. Futhermore, since the elect demonstrate their status by manifesting the will of God (that is, by performing good works), the more sins a man commits, the more he may assume that he is damned. True, he may repent of his sin; but recurrence of sin, like recurrence of despair, is a sign that the repentance was not genuine in the first place.

Calvinist writers of Marlowe's day seized upon the potential in Calivn's doctrine to create a circular argument whose circularity was almost unbreakable. Among these writers was Richard Greenham, whose teachings, described in chapter 2, were prevalent at Cambridge when Marlowe was attending. Arthur Dent, too, in *The Way to Euerlasting Life* (1583), having made election dependent on repentance, next made repentance dependent on election:

> *Reason:* But haue the children of God any assurance in this world of their election?
> *Religion:* Yea, verily, for from whence commeth Repentance and the fruits thereof, but from the Regeneration by the faith of Christ,

but this faith is giuen to the elect onely: *Ergo* onely the elect do repent and giue themselues to obey the commandement of God, the rest haue not the will to thinke a good thought, much lesse to doe any good.[18]

According to this view of repentance, in order to repent one must have been saved in the first place; but if one thinks, as Faustus does, that one has been damned, one is constrained to believe that repentance is impossible. For someone already in the state of despair, which both Luther and Calvin had posited as the first step toward repentance, there is in fact very little way *into* that repentance except through an act of faith of which the despairing are usually incapable—an emotional surge of assurance, or, in other words, a cessation of despair.

Furthermore, even the sense of assurance, said many Calvinist divines, may be deceptive. According to William Perkins, "many persuade themselves of Gods mercie & yet are deceived; neverthelesse all such as doe truly beleeve are not deceived" (*Discourse*, 62). How, then, is a person to know that he has truly repented and is truly of the elect? The mass of sixteenth-century treatises on the subject seem to agree on three signs of election: first, the repentance must be accompanied by a grief that very closely resembles despair itself: "So that it is not enough to saie I haue sinned, but to say I haue most traiterously sinned, I haue most obstinatly, carelessly, and rebelliously sinned, I haue monstrously offended in such a place, in suche a house, in suche company, in such a daie."[19] Second, in the midst of this grief, there must come a sudden sense of comfort, an unquestioning faith in God's mercy accompanied by a conviction that one is personally, definitely, and irreversibly saved. No "guiltie sinner," says Perkins, can feel this "confidence and bouldness" in his heart (*Discourse*, 52). And third, the repentance (or conversion, as it is now called) must lead to a complete change in the person; no matter how upright he has seemed before, he must become a completely new person living a completely new life. If he is not conscious of this marked change in himself, he has not repented and is damned. Perkins further explains that the act of doubting is itself sin:

"[N]ow it is the will of God to which he hath bound us in conscience, to beleeve the remission of our owne sinnes: and therefore rather not to doe it, is presumptuous disobedience" (*Discourse*, 21). Just as Everyman's penance itself was a good deed, so the Calvinist's doubt about his salvation adds to his store of sins.

If Marlowe was indeed reacting against these doctrines, to which he had been so constantly exposed at Cambridge, what better rebuttal could he find than to demonstrate that the doctrines themselves carried the seeds of Faustus's failure to repent—or, rather, to persevere in repentance? According to Calvinist doctrine, the elect will be comforted when they call on God; but Faustus, when he calls on God, is mocked or threatened by Mephistophilis, Lucifer, and the Bad Angel. The fact that the Good Angel always accompanies and contradicts the Bad Angel is almost irrelevant; the presence of the Bad Angel is in itself a sign to the Calvinist that his faith is not complete.

Significantly, the only time that Faustus seems to feel even a touch of the necessary assurance is in his meeting with the Old Man, who does appear to draw Faustus through the first stages of repentance. The Old Man begins with motivation by fear: a warning that deathbed repentance is not to be trusted:

> Old Man: Yet, yet, thou hast an amiable soul,
>   If sin by custom grow not into nature:
>   Then, Faustus, will repentance come too late,
>   Then thou art banish'd from the sight of heaven.
>   (xviii.43–46: 1712–15)

The refrain "too late!" we have heard before, in the *Judgment* plays; and in this medieval sense, the Old Man is warning Faustus about the moment after Judgment. But in the Calvinist sense, the Old Man may be echoing the doctrine of predestination: that there is a type of soul that cannot repent, and the longer the soul waits to attempt repentance, the more it is confirmed in its damnation. According to Perkins: "Neither will it alwaies boote a man after many yeares to say at the last cast, Lord be mercifull to me, I have sinned. Though some be received to mercy in the time of death, yet farre more perish in desperation, that live in their sins wittingly and willingly against their owne conscience" (*Discourse*, 77).

Faustus responds to the Old Man's first plea by entering that state of despair in which the soul is convinced that it has merited damnation: "Where are thou, Faustus? wretch, what hast thou done? / Damn'd art thou, Faustus, damn'd; despair and die!" (xviii.55–56: 1724–25). It is at this point that Mephistophilis, like the Vice Despair of the moralities, hands him a dagger; and it is at this point that the Old Man stays Faustus's hand from suicide and offers him assurance of salvation. The Old Man's assurance, it must be noted, is given in the indicative mood—not "if you repent you will be saved" but "salvation is at hand"—and is presented in the visual terms that the forces of evil have hitherto used to tempt Faustus to sin:

> Old Man: I see an angel hovers o'er thy head
>   And with a vial full of precious grace
>   Offers to pour the same into thy soul:
>   Then call for mercy, and avoid despair.
>
>   (xviii.61–64: 1730–33)

For the first time, Faustus does feel "comfort" of a sort:

> Faustus: O friend, I feel
>   Thy words to comfort my distressed soul.
>   Leave me awhile to ponder on my sins.
>
>   (xviii.65–67: 1734–36)

It is significant that, in feeling this comfort, Faustus now speaks of his sins in the plural; up to now, he has spoken only of his "sin," the sin of trafficking with the Devil. This is the moment of proof; if Faustus will acknowledge his sins to God, will say, "I haue monstrously offended in such a place, in suche a house, in suche company, in such a daie," he may yet repent and be saved. But in sending away the Old Man, he has sent away his comforter, and left alone with Mephistophilis, he immediately relapses into doubt:

> Faustus: Accursed Faustus, where is mercy now?
>   I do repent, and yet I do despair;

> Hell strives with grace for conquest in my breast.
> What shall I do to shun the snares of death?
>
> (xviii.70–74: 1739–42)

This last question is the same one that Everyman asked in his first throes of denial and bargaining, ignoring the fact that he had already been told what he must do. And at the mention of the word *death*, Mephistophilis steps forward and addresses Faustus *like* Death—the Death of the Dances, of *Herod*, of the *Castle*, and of *Everyman* itself: "Thou traitor, Faustus, I arrest thy soul / For disobedience to my sovereign lord" (xviii.75–76: 1743–44).

To the Calvinist mind, this is an almost unquestionable sign of damnation. Not only has Faustus begun to doubt after what he thought was assurance but, according to Calvinist divines, he must now assume that his "assurance" was in fact presumption, and therefore yet another sin. "Presumption wil give a man the slippe in the time of sickenesse and in the houre of death; and the testimonie of good conscience stickes by him to the end."[20] He is indeed caught in a double bind; since he is afraid of damnation he must be damned, and since he must be damned he is afraid of damnation.

If most audiences of Marlowe's day and our own deplore Faustus's error and, with the scholars, hope to the very end that he will still manage to repent like Philologus or Humanum Genus, Puritans (of Marlowe's day and our own) would long ago have given Faustus up for lost and would have taken this "arrest" by Mephistophilis as merely one more sign of his predestined end. Has he not from the beginning shown an unregenerate conscience and a lack of that "speciall certentie" of his own salvation that every elect soul must feel? Is not the Old Man, in contrast, an example of how the elect bear witness to their faith? Why, as early as Faustus's first pact with the Devil, he has blasphemed the words of God by using them to speak of Hell: "*Consummatum est*: this bill is ended, / And Faustus hath bequeath'd his soul to Lucifer" (v.74–75: 463–64). Again and again he refers to his traffic in necromancy as "resolution," one of the terms used by theologians to signify perseverance in grace:

Valdes, as resolute am I in this [magic]
As thou to live; therefore object it not.

(i.133–34: 161–62)

Then fear not, Faustus, to be resolute
And try the uttermost magic can perform.

(iii.14–15: 242–43)

Now go not backward; no, Faustus be resolute;
Why waver'st thou? O, something soundeth in mine ears,
"Abjure this magic, turn to God again!"
Ay, and Faustus will turn to God again.
To God? He loves thee not. . . .

(v.6–10: 394–98)

Even Wagner, Faustus's comic foil throughout the play, un-wittingly points up his master's unregeneracy at the end. Com-menting on Faustus's preparations for death, Wagner says:

I think my master means to die shortly:
He has made his will and given me his wealth,
His house, his goods, and store of golden plate,
Besides two thousand ducats ready coin'd.
I wonder what he means. If death were nigh,
He would not banquet and carouse and swill
Amongst the students, as even now he doth,
Who are at supper with such belly-cheer
As Wagner ne'er beheld in all his life.[21]

(xviii.1–9: 1674–80)

The making of wills, although encouraged by the new treatises on dying, was not to be substituted for spiritual preparations for death, and yet Wagner makes it clear that Faustus's will is his only preparation. Marlowe's audience would no doubt have re-membered the Protestant Morality *Enough Is as Good as a Feast*, in which the unregenerate Worldly Man's last act is to reject the physician's call to repentance and to begin making a will instead. As Ignorance says of him after his death, "All his study was who should have his goods when he died" (1413).[22]

According to the extreme Calvinist position, then, and especially the Puritan position, Faustus has demonstrated his unregeneracy over and over. And if these signs were not enough, he shows yet another sign of being reprobate: he delights in watching plays.

Mephistophilis, indeed, is a hellish impresario in *Doctor Faustus*. He presents an almost endless series of pageants and shows for Faustus—not the least among which is the Pageant of the Seven Deadly Sins—with all the roles played by devils. Calvinists like William Perkins were most adamant about the noxious effects of such shows, and included "Playes and Enterludes" among the "sundrie kindes of recreations [that] are to be neglected": "Playes and Enterludes, that stand in the representation of the Vices, unless it be in the way of dislike, . . . much lesse is it warrantable to gesture and represent vice in the way of recreations & delight" (*Discourse*, 46). Mephistophilis specifically tells first the audience and then Faustus that the first show (containing, by the way, a dance—another recreation that Perkins condemns) is meant to "delight" Faustus's mind (v.82–84: 471–73); and Faustus declares that the Pageant of the Seven Deadly Sins "doth delight my soul" (vi.170: 712). He is obviously in a bad way, spiritually speaking, and can be expected to come to no good.

Arieh Sachs has speculated, from the printed editions of *Doctor Faustus*, that Puritans of the seventeenth century were not averse to reading the play, and most likely did read it, as an exemplum of the reprobate's fate.[23] But these readers were not part of Marlowe's sixteenth-century audience, and Faustus's conformity to Puritan ideas of reprobacy may have served quite a different dramatic purpose for the Anglican who watched him despair and die.

The disputed ending to *Doctor Faustus* may cast some further light on that purpose. Whether Marlowe wrote the scholars' final speeches, outlined them for others to write, or would heartily have wished the speeches to perdition, their inclusion indicates that playgoers of the time demanded such an ending. And it is therefore interesting to note that the scholars are determined to give Faustus an honorable burial in spite of the evidence they have of his wrongdoing:

> 2 *Scholar:* Well, gentlemen, though Faustus' end be such
> As every Christian heart laments to think on,
> Yet, for he was a scholar, once admir'd
> For wondrous knowledge in our German schools,
> We'll give his mangled limbs due burial;
> And all the students, cloth'd in mourning black,
> Shall wait upon his heavy funeral.
>
> (xx.13–19: 1995–2001)

This "due burial," so often a mark of approval in Marlowe's work, does not necessarily mean that we must agree with the scholars and accept Faustus as scholar par excellence, any more than we necessarily agreed with Orcanes about the state of Sigismund's soul when Orcanes refused Sigismund "due burial." We have seen, as their deathbed attendants have not, both Sigismund's repentance and Faustus's lack of genuine scholarship. It is the scholars' response itself, rather than the response's validity, that must interest us.

As before, the scholars are correct in theory, if infirm of purpose. Most Anglican theologians insisted that although the state at death might very likely signify the state of salvation, no person was to presume to judge another person's state of salvation from his manner of dying. Indeed, John Donne was later to point out that Christ himself had died a violent and shameful death, and that therefore: "Still pray we for a peaceable life, against violent deaths, and for time of repentance against sudden deaths, and for sober and modest assurance against distempered deaths, but never make ill conclusions upon persons overtaken with such deaths."[24] And in *2 Henry VI*, which may have run concurrently with *Doctor Faustus*, Shakespeare surrounds the deathbed of Cardinal Beaufort with the right and wrong sorts of visitors:

> *King Henry:* Lord Cardinal, if thou think'st on Heaven's bliss,
> Hold up thy hand, make signal of thy hope.
> He dies, and makes no sign. O God, forgive him!
> *Warwick:* So bad a death argues a monstrous life.

King Henry: Forbear to judge, for we are sinners all.

(3.3.27–31)

Warwick, we know, is correct in his estimation of the Cardinal's life;[25] but Warwick, who is given the Puritan moral to speak, will himself prove a conspirator and murderer. King Henry, on the other hand, is a fool; but he is a holy fool who follows (anachronistically) the Book of Common Prayer and the Arts of Dying at the dying man's bedside. We must assume, therefore, that Henry's is the morally correct response, even as we pity his naiveté.

What then of Faustus's death? He has sinned, has died, and has been carried off to Hell, still denying and bargaining with Death at his last hour. In reality, he has not changed very much from his opening scene, when he bade "*on kai me on* farewell" (refusing to consider "being and not being") and with fitting irony prophesied his own doom along with that of humankind:

> *Faustus:* Yet art thou still but Faustus, and a man.
>   Couldst thou make men to live eternally
>   Or being dead raise them to life again,
>   Then this profession were to be esteem'd.
>   Physic, farewell!
>
> (i.23–27: 51–55)

In both Christian and classical tragedy, the most important question is "Who am I?" Faustus unwittingly answers this question—and then discards the answer—in his farewell to physic: he is "but Faustus, and a man." It is God who can "make men to live eternally / Or being dead raise them to life again." In turning away from self-knowledge, Faustus has turned away from the ability to repent and be saved; he has denied his relationship to God, and has thus closed down communication between himself and God's grace. As Mephistophilis tells him, he was always "in danger to be damn'd" (iii.53: 279).

But this does not mean that Faustus was always incapable of being saved. Mephistophilis, it is important to notice, does not say "damn'd," but rather "*in danger* to be damn'd," implying a free choice on the part of Faustus as to what he will do. Indeed, when Mephistophilis admits that it was he who threw temptations in Faustus's path even before the conjuration (xix.90–96: 1885–89), he is begging the question. Even to Calvinists, temptations were not sins unless the mind entertained them. Faustus was always "in danger," but he also always had the option of escaping the danger by saying no.

A strict Calvinist might say the *I* am now begging the question, that the soul predestined to damnation cannot say no. But as I have shown, Marlowe could hardly have expected the strictest Calvinists to attend his play, as their own beliefs would have kept them from the theater. We must assume, then, that he was writing for an audience that was inclined to see Faustus's despair, not as a natural function of his predestined state, but as a headstrong refusal to acknowledge his sin, turn to God, and amend his life.

In this sense, Mephistophilis's famous, "Why, this is hell, nor am I out of it" (iii.77: 304) may stand as Faustus's motto during life. His is a self-created hell, one in which he is never satisfied, because his refusal to accept his own limitations forces him, ironically, to accept the paltry rather than continue grappling unsuccessfully with the important. He will watch a pageant rather than explore *on kai me on*; and he will go to perdition rather than ask for help of God or man. He has been sinful and boastful; he has even been vindictive; but, above all, like so many tragic heroes before him, he has been colossally wasteful and catastrophically blind.

Faustus, who has scrambled away from self-knowledge throughout the play, is, like Everyman in his early stages, unequipped to ask the right questions, and is therefore, like Everyman, unequipped to face death. Still scrambling at his last hour, he dies screaming his denial of Death, and yet we can harldy imagine a Hell worse than the one that he has created for himself on earth. His self-imposed despair and all such double binds, Marlowe seems to suggest, lead not only to a denial of death, but to a denial of life itself. Only in this sense is Warwick's observation valid: "So bad a death argues a monstrous life"—and so bad a life argues a monstrous death.

VIII

The Kindly Summons

Measure for Measure

IN MANY WAYS, Shakespeare's *Measure for Measure* may be considered a culmination of the Morality tradition that extends from *Pride of Life* to *Doctor Faustus*—a tradition that poses the moment of death as an understanding of life, offers the soul a last chance on earth to choose salvation or damnation, and dispatches the soul accordingly. But in *Measure for Measure*, the soul is not dispatched. And in this respect, Shakespeare's "problem" play mirrors the "problem" of life itself: that even though death offers the perfection of salvation to an imperfect world, we are often afraid to accept the terms of the offer; and that when we have overcome our fear and are ready to embrace death as a release, the kindly offer may be withdrawn.[1]

This is not to suggest that *Measure for Measure* is a grim forerunner of the twentieth-century pessimistic school, or that we are meant to leave the theater shaking our heads in pity over the bad fortune that has inflicted life upon the characters of the play. Claudio, Isabella, and Angelo, we feel—yes, even Lucio and Pompey—will be as moderately happy with their lots as any human creatures can hope to be. But there *are* some grim sets of images that dominate the action of the play, of which the primary and most pervasive is that of the prison, both the literal prison of Vienna and the figurative prison of life.

The pivot of the action in *Measure for Measure* is, of course, Claudio's death sentence, and throughout all but the first and last scenes of the play, Claudio remains in prison. To this prison come the Duke, Isabella, Lucio, and Pompey; in this prison reside the Provost and Abhorson the executioner; and ordering its affairs are Angelo and Escalus. Outside the prison walls are more walls: Isabella's convent, Mariana's moated grange, and Angelo's double-locked garden and chamber. By the end of the play, although some of the characters will elect to remain in their enclosures, or will exchange one enclosure for another, most of the doors will be opened, and the inmates allowed to leave. What is interesting, however, is that each character will first come to realize that there are more ways out of prison than the one that he or she has planned, and that one of the doors is death.

In several of the possible sources of Shakespeare's play, this alternate exit is indeed made the subject of a grim joke. Juriste, the Angelo-counterpart of Cinthio's *Epitia* (1582), also promises to free Epitia's brother from prison if she will go to bed with him; but after she has done so, Juriste sends her the dead body of her brother with a messenger who explains: "This . . . is your brother whom my lord Governor sends you freed from prison."[2] In the play that Cinthio himself created from this story in the *Hecatommithi*, the joke becomes more elaborate; the messenger is made to deliver the message twice—once to the Maid and once to Epitia—and Juriste's sister, Angela, explains the irony to the audience, who may have missed the point:

> *Angela:* My brother I have cursed. . . .
> He answered, that he promised Epitia
> To give her Vico freed from prison, true,
> But never promised to release him living;
> So that she has exactly what he promised.
>
> (3.2; Bullough, 436)

In George Whetstone's *Promos and Cassandra* (1578), another promiser fulfills his promise ironically. With the head sent to Cassandra, Promos sends a message: "To Cassandra, as Promos promised thee, / From prison, lo, he sends thy brother free"

(4.2; Bullough, 469). And in Thomas Lupton's *Too Good to Be True* (1581), although no such ghastly message is carried to the Gentlewoman with her husband's body, the Judge speaks in what appear to be deliberately equivocal terms: "and whereas your husband should have been executed tomorrow in the morning, I will dispatch him and send him home tomorrow unto you before noon at the furthest, if it be not before. . . . The time is not long; tomorrow you shall have him safe and sound with you" (Bullough, 520). The Gentlewoman's husband is, of course, "dispatched" by the hangman.

Shakespeare omits this sadistic joke from his play—perhaps to spare the audience some horror, but more likely to make Angelo less evil and more forgivable.[3] But the underlying irony of the joke is inherent to a more serious tradition: the *de contemptu mundi* view of life itself as a prison and death as a release. A motif running through both Catholic and Protestant Arts of Dying, it is most forcefully stated by Pope Innocent III in *De Miseria Condicionis Humane*:

> "Infelix homo, quis me liberabit de corpore mortis huius?" Certe non vult exire de carcere qui non vult exire de corpore, nam carcer anime corpus est.

> ["Unhappy man that I am, who will release me from the body of this death?" Surely, no man wishes to escape from prison who does not wish to escape from the body, for the body is a prison to the soul.][4]

And again, of the just man Innocent says: "Sustinet seculum tanquam exilium, clausus in corpore tanquam in carcare" ["He endures the world as though he were in exile, locked up in his body as in a prison"] (2: 18). The 1576 translator of Innocent's treatise, H. Kirton, indeed editorializes further on the theme: "Beholde the lamentation of the silly soule, which would faync bc discharged out of prison. Whereof the Psalmist sayth thus. O lorde bring my soule out of captiuitie. There is no rest nor quietnesse in anye place heere in this world."[5] And the translator of Petrus Luccensis's *Dialogue of Dying Well* (trans. 1603) carries the analogy still closer to Claudio's own case: "When an imprisoned malefactor hath receaued sentence of death and knoweth he cannot escape, oh how many waylings, and how many lamentings maketh the wretche in that time, seeing that assuredly he must foorthwith be put to death. In this case are all men liuing found to bee, against whome as soone as euer they be borne, in this miserable and transitorie lyfe, the seuere sentence of death is pronounced."[6]

That such a motif had become almost a commonplace by the time of *Measure for Measure* is evident not only from its appearance in treatises, poems, and broadsides,[7] but also from the sardonic remark made by Sir Charles Mountford on his release from prison in Thomas Heywood's *A Woman Killed with Kindness* (ca. 1603), a play whose subplot also requires that a sister sacrifice her honor for her brother's well-being:

> *Keeper:* Knight, be of comfort, for I bring thee freedom
>   From all thy troubles.
> *Sir Charles:*   Then I am doom'd to die;
>   Death is th' end of all calamity.[8]

And in this sense of death as a release from prison, the famous act 3 prison scene of *Measure for Measure* may be considered as a series of attempts by the Duke and Isabella to offer Claudio every possible escape route out of his prison, while Claudio obdurately refuses them all.

Shakespeare's audience would certainly have understood the Duke's "Be absolute for death" speech (3.1.5–41) as a compendium of many traditional Christian exhortations on the vanities of life; and if, as some critics have maintained, the speech contains allusions to pagan philosophers such as Lucretius,[9] it is Lucretius filtered through Christian homiletics. Pope Innocent himself had used many of the figures and analogies that the Duke uses: the baseness of the flesh; the revolt of the organs of the body; and the afflictions that torment all living creatures regardless of age, class, or virtue. Treatise after treatise had echoed Innocent in employing these figures, and had echoed as well his comparison of death to a welcome sleep, just as does the Duke:

Duke: Thy best of rest is sleep,
    And that thou oft provokest, yet grossly fear'st
    Thy death, which is no more.

(3.1.17–19)

But in order to welcome sleep, one must first be weary, and Claudio is by no means weary of his life. Consequently, the Duke, like the preachers before him, must first evoke in Claudio a sense of the frustrations of life:

Duke: Reason thus with life:
    If I do lose thee, I do lose a thing
    That none but fools would keep. A breath thou art,
    Servile to all the skyey influences
    That dost this habitation where thou keep'st
    Hourly afflict. . . .
                    Thou art not certain,
    For thy complexion shifts to strange effects,
    After the moon.

(3.1.6–11; 23–25)

This idea of the insubstantiality of human existence is certainly not contrary to Christian belief, as J. W. Lever has claimed;[10] it does not deny the divine origin of the soul, but rather contrasts the soul's heavenly importance with the laughably frail earthly shell in which the soul resides. E. Hutchins, in his popular religious handbook, *David's Sling Against Goliath* (1598), had made many such comparisons about human life on earth:

> Now therefore reason with me. Shal we feare death for the losse of a shadow: shall wee by sighs and sobs storme againste the Lorde for the losse of a vapour? . . . So y^t our life is like a ruinous house, alwayes readie to fall: like a thin thred, alwaies readie to rotte: like a running cloude, whereof we are vncertaine, where and when it falleth.[11]

Considering the downfall of Claudio's expectations, he should certainly be receptive to such preaching.

But unfortunately, weak mortal creatures seldom respond as they should and, when subjected to uncertainties in life, usually assume that they can find compensating certainties in that same life. Such was Everyman's assumption; such is Claudio's. At first, it is true, he seems to have resigned himself to death, and to be giving the theologically proper response: "To sue to live, I find I seek to die, / And, seeking death, find life. Let it come on" (3.1.42–43). Sutton's *Disce Mori* had said much the same thing: "That which we call life, is a kinde of death, because it makes us to die: but that which we count death, is in the sequele a very life: for that in deede it makes us to live."[12] Or, in Kirton's translation of *De Miseria:* "We then are dying whiles we liue, and then doe we cease from dying, when we cease to liue. Therefore it is better to dye, alwayes to liue, than to liue to dye euer. For the mortall lyfe of man is but a liuing death."[13] For Claudio, so far, so good. But he and the audience know something that the Duke does not know: Isabella has been to see Angelo about Claudio's pardon, and is even now on her way to the prison—to open, as Claudio thinks, an exit for him other than Death. As long as he retains this hope for another escape, he cannot "be absolute for death."

There is, furthermore, another element missing from Claudio's apparent preparation for death: repentance. The *de contemptu mundi* sermon that the Duke has given him was traditionally only the first step toward readying the dying man; it forms the first of three parts in Innocent's *De Miseria,* the other two of which deal with the deadly sins and the pains of hell; and it serves primarily as an introduction to the serious business of death in all the Arts of Dying. But the Duke does not have a chance to proceed to the second step of his deathbed counseling; he is interrupted by the arrival of Isabella.[14] And from the moment Isabella enters, we know that Claudio has not really accepted the fact of death.

Claudio's first question—"Now, sister, what's the comfort?" (3.1.53)—is much like Everyman's questioning, in that it is posed in temporal rather than eternal terms; his "comfort," at this point, should be the ghostly comfort that the Duke has given, but Claudio speaks only in terms of life on earth. Isabella apparently senses his weakness and his excessive attachment to life at any cost; although she has earlier assured herself that her brother would gladly die "On twenty bloody blocks" to save his soul and hers (2.4.176–82), his plea for "comfort" seems to frighten her into a circumlocution. Instead of blurting out Angelo's perfidy and the choice that Claudio must make, she spins an elaborate conceit on Claudio's coming journey to heaven, where he will be an "everlasting lieger," an ambassador in the court of God (3.1.56–60). It is noteworthy that she omits any mention of the words *die* and *death*, and inverts the traditional figure of the Summons as messenger, making Claudio the messenger instead.

But Claudio, like Everyman, is still looking for a way out and, like Everyman, by a series of more and more insistent questions forces his sister into telling him what he does not want to know:

> *Claudio:*   Is there no remedy?
> *Isabella:* None but such remedy as, to save a head,
>   To cleave a heart in twain.
> *Claudio:*   But is there any?
>
>   (3.1.60–62)

The audience may be reminded, at this point, of parts of the first debate between Angelo and Isabella, in which earthly and heavenly "remedies" were compared:

> *Isabella:* Must he needs die?
> *Angelo:* Maiden, no remedy.
>
> . . . .
>
> *Angelo:* Your brother is a forfeit of the law,
>   And you but waste your words.
> *Isabella:*   Alas, alas!
>   Why, all the souls that were were forfeit once,
>   And He that might the vantage best have took
>   Found out the remedy.
>
>   (2.4.48; 71–75)

Why does Isabella not point out this heavenly "remedy" to Claudio? Perhaps because his mode of questioning has already indicated to her, as it has to us, that he is not open to heavenly comfort yet, that he is still too concerned with earthly comforts.

Isabella, then, becomes a shrewder comforter than the Duke has been—although she, too, will temporarily fail. Taking her cue from Claudio's questions, she turns not to the *de contemptu mundi* (which her brother will not believe) but to the Christian humanist's approach to death: the appeal to heroism and the integrity of the human spirit. She begins in the negative vein, evincing doubt about Claudio's courage—perhaps as a natural expression of her new fear, but also as a plea for Claudio to prove her wrong:

> *Isabella:* Oh, I do fear thee, Claudio, and I quake
> Lest thou a feverous life shouldst entertain,
> And six or seven winters more respect
> Than a perpetual honor. Darest thou die?
> The sense of death is most in apprehension,
> And the poor beetle that we tread upon
> In corporal sufferance finds a pang as great
> As when a giant dies.
>
> (3.1.73–80)

This is much like two of the arguments used by Lupset: first, that it is just as foolish to haggle over a few years of life as it would be for a condemned felon to demand to approach the scaffold last in line; and second, that the pain of dying is of necessity a short one, feared more by beasts than by men (*Dieyng Well*, 280–81). Lupset, too, had described with scorn the shameful death of a contemporary malefactor, in order to draw his readers into rejecting such a manner of dying. And this ploy, for the moment, seems to work on Claudio. Flushed with resentment, he demands hotly, "Why give you me this shame?" (3.1.80). And just as he has echoed the religious tone of the *de contemptu mundi* in his reply to the Duke, so he echoes the heroic tone of Lupset's valorous man in reply to Isabella: "If I must die, / I will encounter darkenss as a bride, / And hug it in mine arms" (3.1.82–84).

Alas, alas, as Isabella would say. The sexual imagery and conditional "if" bode no good. But since Claudio has apparently responded to the call to honor, Isabella reinforces her appeal in the positive vein, congratulating him on his nobility and adding a confirmatory appeal to family as well as to individual honor: "There spake my brother, there my father's grave / Did utter forth a voice" (3.1.85–86). Claudio, after all, as the eldest male in the family, *should* be willing to lay down his life to protect his sister's honor. But can there be some subliminal warning bell that causes her, even in the midst of her approving speech, to answer Claudio's *if* with such a positive *yes*? "Yes," she says, "you must die" (3.1.86).

Claudio is still bargaining. To be sure, he can expect more than the "six or seven winters" that Isabella has predicted for him, and for a man still too firmly attached to this world to see things in terms of the next, even six or seven years seem better than six or seven hours. Perhaps he may even find a way, during those years, to redeem his honor—and his soul. But he is in the position, now, of Lupset's convict, merely dropping back a place in line each time the line moves toward the hangman; and every time he drops back, he makes death harder for himself.

Both the Duke and Isabella may indeed have misjudged the nature of Claudio's fear, or at least the nature of his worldly attachment. He is not merely clinging to the outward trappings of fashion, as the Duke has imagined; nor is he merely flying from the fear of corporal pain, as Isabella has thought. Claudio is more pagan than either of his comforters realizes; he fears and half believes in the total annihilation of self. The first words of his last desperate appeal for life are a cry of horror at self-disintegration, a cry couched solely in terms of the body, the only self he knows:

> *Claudio:* Aye, but to die, and go we know not where,
>   To lie in cold obstruction and to rot,
>   This sensible warm motion to become
>   A kneaded clod. . . .

$$(3.1.117–20)$$

The very words of the Legend have become, for Claudio, not a reason to prepare for death but a reason to dread it.

When Claudio turns his mind to the possibility of an afterlife, he is perhaps not quite pagan, but not quite an ideal Christian either. He gives no thought to Heaven, but pictures in turn the fires of the preachers' Hell and the torments of Dante's Inferno: the "thick-ribb'd ice" of the traitors and the windblown, eternal motion of the uncommitted and the lustful. All his thoughts are of dissolution, agony, and damnation; he has succumbed at once to the deathbed temptations of infidelity, impatience, and despair.

In such a state of mind, Claudio may well cry out, with Lydgate's ploughman—and with Hamlet—that the suffering of life may be preferable to the sleep of death, that "the dread of something after death" (in Claudio's case, perhaps, the dread of Nothing after death) "makes us rather bear the ills we have / Than fly to others that we know not of" (*Hamlet*, 3.1.78–82):

> *Claudio:* The weariest and most loathed worldly life
> That age, ache, penury, and imprisonment
> Can lay on nature, is a paradise
> To what we fear of death.
>
> (3.1.128–31)

He cannot, now, believe the preachers who have tried to tell him the opposite: "Yea, this case of the soule is such a cage of filth, as a man of God hath said, that no Bocardo, no dungeon, no sinke, no puddle, no pitte is in any respect so evil a prison for this bodie, as the bodie is of the soule."[15]

This is not to suggest that Claudio is wrong to fear death; no preacher or poet would have claimed that such fear is un-natural. But all would have remarked upon Claudio's failure to overcome his fear, whether by faith or by reason, and would especially have pointed out that to bargain for life at the expense of one's soul is a grievous sin: "Saynt Austyn sayth: More greate is the dommage of one soule the which is loste and deed by damp-nacyon than it is of ye dethe of a thousande bodyes deed of the dethe corporall and by putryfaccyon."[16] How much worse, then, to bargain for life at the expense of someone else: a deed that will encompass the "dampnacyon" of not one, but two immortal souls.

Claudio, however, is beyond the reach of traditional appeals. He is a Worldly Man in a sense undreamed of by Wager and the other sixteenth-century moralists: the man who sees nothing beyond the limits of his own consciousness, the quasi solipsist who in his own demise sees the disappearance of the universe. Both the medieval and the Renaissance Christian formulas are therefore meaningless to him, since both posit a universe independent of his own being; for him to accept death, he must be convinced of the existence of things outside himself, of a continuity of Being once he is gone. And Isabella, whose impulsiveness so often bursts forth in wild and whirling words, in her own desperation hits upon the right cure for her brother:

> *Isabella:*   O you beast!
>   O faithless coward! O dishonest wretch!
>   Wilt thou be made a man out of my vice? . . .
>   . . . Take my defiance!
>   Die, perish! Might but my bending down
>   Reprieve thee from thy fate, it should proceed.
>   I'll pray a thousand prayers for thy death,
>   No word to save thee.
>
>   (3.1.135–37; 142–46)

It is an angry speech, a furious speech, a violent rush of words from a young woman at the end of her rope. And almost from the earliest performances of *Measure for Measure*, critics have either denounced the speech or made tortuous excuses for it.[17] But, ironically, the one thing that both Isabella's detractors and her champions have glossed over too quickly in their analyses of her words is the most important thing about them: they work where all else has failed.

Up to now, Claudio has managed to control his universe, despite the sentence of death, and has thus managed to maintain his sense of being the universe. He has sent for his sister, and his sister has arrived. He has tossed off the correct response to the Duke's sermons, and the Duke has been satisfied. He has juggled with the seven deadly sins to make Angelo's proposition seem sinless, and he has convinced himself and fully expects to convince his sister. Even the apparent coincidence that the "precise" Angelo should suddenly act out of character in a way that may save Claudio's life is proof that Claudio's will makes and remakes the universe. How, then, should he die?

The only answer is Isabella's. Her defiance, her thrusting of death in his face when he has it least in mind, her very refusal to listen to his repeated cries of "Oh, hear me, Isabella!" are all concrete evidences of a world outside Claudio's control. And Claudio, who has delcared himself unafraid of "age, ache, penury, and imprisonment," is shocked back to reality by something far worse than any of them: a sister's contempt.

To be sure, his immediate response to Isabella's outburst is no more promising than was his response to the Duke's sermon or Isabella's first appeal: "I am so out of love with life that I will sue to be rid of it" (3.1.170–71). We have heard these words before, and then have heard Claudio retract them. But his preface to them, this time, *is* promising: "Let me ask my sister pardon." Theologically, he has taken the first step toward repentance, and psychologically, he has taken the first step toward acceptance; he has admitted that there is Being outside himself, and at least one human being, if not a divine one, more important than himself.

The results of Isabella's shock treatment become most evident later in the play, when Claudio and Barnardine are served their death warrants. Claudio now evinces a calm acceptance of his mortality, and when asked about Barnardine, uses a simile that links his past with Barnardine's present: "As fast locked up in sleep as guiltless labor / When it lies starkly in the traveler's bones" (4.2.64–65). Despite the implicit irony of the word *guiltless* (Claudio is not above a bit of sarcasm himself), this is not the traditional metaphor of sleep as a type of corporeal death, but rather a metaphor that the Duke has introduced earlier: sleep as a type of spiritual death—an insensibility to the meanings of life and death alike: "Thou hast nor youth nor age, / But, as it were, an after-dinner's sleep, / Dreaming on both" (3.1.32–34). The Provost himself sees Barnardine in these terms; "A man that apprehends death no more dreadfully but as a drunken sleep"

(4.2.140–41). And when Barnardine receives the Summons, he flatly refuses to die.

In the old Morality plays, and even in the new secular tragedies, Barnardine would have no choice. The King of Life and Everyman at first refused to die; Moros, Worldly Man, and Fortunatus refused to die; Tamburlaine and Macbeth refused to die; and all of them died. Why Barnardine is allowed his refusal we shall see later; but the refusal itself, at this point, serves as an almost allegorized extension of Claudio's previous denial and bargaining, and thus throws his present acceptance into sharper relief. Indeed, the connection between the two men is reinforced by the nature of Barnardine's imprisonment, a form of transitional half-life similar to his "drunken sleep." He is the prisoner who cannot and will not be released to life or death; he has gained stay after stay of execution, and, the Provost says, if he were offered a chance to escape, he would not go. Like Claudio, he prefers the circumscribed prison of his own ordering, where, by denying the power of forces outside himself, he may maintain the semblance of control. Does he not have "the liberty of the prison" (4.2.145–46)? But it is a prison after all.

The Duke's evaluation of Barnardine's insensibility—"Unfit to live or die. O gravel heart!" (4.3.63)—is, then, a commentary on Claudio's earlier behavior as well. But as always in this play where people say much more than they think they mean, the Duke is speaking not just of Barnardine and Claudio, but of all the major figures who move around him in prisons of their own making—including himself.

Like Claudio in his physical and mental prison, Angelo, Isabella, and the Duke begin by thinking that they can order the universe to their own requirements. Angelo, in particular, is the Puritan mind carried to its coldest extremes; he is a man who has mentally segregated humankind into the all-good and the all-bad, with no room in his world for the mixed creature who can sin, repent, and sin and repent again. But although—or perhaps because—he so easily sends the reprobate to a literal prison, he does not see that he is creating a separate but equal figurative prison for the elect.

Raymond Southall has postulated Angelo as an extreme type of post-Reformation Catholic who relies too much on outward signs of grace, and Isabella as an extreme Protestant who relies too much on inward, individual signs; both, says Southall, must recombine into "Medieval Christianity."[18] But such an interpretation seems curiously perverse—or, at least, makes Shakespeare seem curiously perverse in his methods. Why, after all, clothe a symbol of radical Protestantism in a nun's habit unless to confuse the audience needlessly? And why refer to a Catholic as "precise" (1.3.50), a term used almost exclusively of Puritans in Shakespeare's day? Indeed, Shakespeare's audience might have recognized Angelo as a Puritan even without references to his "precision," and would certainly have recognized the dangerous nature of his Puritanism: the frighteningly sincere distinction between good and evil that allows for no compromise and will make no exceptions, even for oneself.

To speak of Angelo's sincerity may sound as contradictory as to speak of Iago's honesty. But Isabella is only partly correct, during the judgment scene, when she says, "I partly think / A due sincerity govern'd his deeds / Till he did look on me" (5.1.443–45). A due, if warped, sincerity has governed Angelo's deeds even after he has looked on Isabella; he is as sincere in his sin as he was in his virtue. It is especially interesting to watch him chart his moral regression throughout the play, and to match the chart against William Perkins's outline of the progress of sin:

> Actuall sinne in the first degree of *tentation*, is, when the mind upon some sudden motion, is drawne away to thinke evill, and withall is tickled with some delight thereof. For a bad motion cast into the mind, by the flesh and the devill, is like unto the baite cast into the water, that allureth and delighteth the fish, and causeth it to bite. Sinne in *conception*, is when with the delight of the mind, there goes consent of the will to do the evill thought on. Sinne in *birth*, is when it comes forth into an action or execution. Sinne in *perfection*, is when men are growne to a custome and habite in sinne, upon long practice. . . . And sinne thus made perfect, brings foorth death.[19]

In Angelo's first stage, temptation, he does indeed use the image of the bait and fish: "O cunning enemy, that to catch a saint / With saints dost bait thy hook!" (2.2.180–81). And when he has failed to master his temptation, he speaks of his "conception":

> *Angelo:*   Heaven in my mouth,
>   As if I did but only chew His name,
>   And in my heart the strong and swelling evil
>   Of my conception.
>
>   (2.4.4–7)

Even his shocking double entendre to Isabella, "Plainly conceive, I love you" (2.4.140), may carry more than double meaning in this sense; he is inviting Isabella to give consent of her will to sin. And by the time he tells her, in no uncertain terms, "Fit thy consent to my sharp appetite" (2.4.160), he has looked ahead to the next stages of his sin: "I have begun, / And now I give my sensual race the rein" (2.4.158–59). He is predicting, here, not merely the birth, or action, of the sin of fornication, but perfection in sin, the next sin that he will "perform in the necke of" the first[20]—lying to cover his tracks: "Say what you can, my false o'erweighs your true" (2.4.169).

Having charted his course so accurately, he must now expect that his "sinne thus made perfect, brings foorth death." And indeed, when we next see him alone, he explains in soliloquy that his reason for ordering Claudio's execution, in violation of his promise, was not gratuitous villainy, but an attempt to stave off retribution for a while:[21]

> *Angelo:*   He should have liv'd,
>   Save that his riotous youth, with dangerous sense,
>   Might in the times to come have ta'en revenge
>   By so receiving a dishonor'd life
>   With ransom of such shame. Would yet he had liv'd.
>
>   (4.4.26–30)

That last phrase is a telling one. Angelo, knowing that he deserves death, half craves the punishment but fears the consequences. For him, in his state of sin, death means hell.

From the beginning of the play, Angelo has served as his own prosecutor, judge, and jury. He sincerely believes what he tells Escalus:

> *Angelo:* When I that censure him do so offend,
>   Let mine own judgment pattern out my death,
>   And nothing come in partial.
>
> (2.1.29-31)

When he does "so offend," he convicts himself utterly, leaving no room for a repentance that he, as a reprobate, cannot expect to be granted. Consequently, although he dreads the damnation that he knows will follow death, when his sins are exposed during the judgment scene he twice demands his right to die—almost, we feel, with a touch of relief that the flight from death is over:

> *Angelo:* Immediate sentence then, and sequent death
>   Is all the grace I beg.
>   . . . .
>   I am sorry that such sorrow I procure.
>   And so deep sticks it in my penitent heart
>   That I crave death more willingly than mercy.
>   'Tis my deserving, and I do entreat it.
>
> (5.1.371-72; 472-75)

Before we applaud Angelo's self-judgment, however, we must remember that a "penitent heart" does not refuse grace, mercy, or a chance to amend. This is not acceptance of death, but something uglier, something that we have seen many times before— despair. Isabella may forgive him; Mariana may forgive him; the Duke and all the laws of man and God may forgive him; but unless something drastic happens, Angelo will never forgive himself. Like Barnardine refusing to escape from jail, Angelo is locked into the prison of his rigid Puritan belief: once a sinner, forever damned.

Isabella herself, who stands in opposition to Angelo throughout the play, opposes him only in the sense that a mirror-image
opposes the thing that it reflects. She, too, wants to order the
universe. Her idea of order, however, leans more toward an ideal
of neatness than a system of rectitude; she is far more willing than
Angelo to make moral exceptions for other people, and is not
above a bit of special pleading for a cause that she does not wholeheartedly espouse. It is especially noteworthy that when she learns
that her brother has impregnated Juliet, her immediate response
is not moral revulsion but commonsense practicality: "Oh, let
him marry her" (1.4.49). But although she grants human society
its right to go to hell happily on the road of its own choosing
(something that Angelo cannot allow), she herself wants a divorce
from that society, and would choose for herself, instead, a martyr's
crown—and a martyr's isolation.

There is no need to condemn the whole system of monasti-
cism, or to assume, as Darryl F. Gless has recently done, that
Shakespeare is condemning it,[22] in order to see the self-imprisoning
nature of Isabella's choices. She is not content with the already
severe restrictions placed on the Poor Clares, whom she seeks
to join, but would have the whole order translated into an ideal
society of martyrs, one that probably cannot exist among fallible human creatures:

> *Isabella:* And have you nuns no farther privileges?
> *Francisca:* Are not these large enough?
> *Isabella:* Yes, truly. I speak not as desiring more,
>   But rather wishing a more strict restraint
>   Upon the [sisterhood], the votarists of Saint Clare.[23]
>   (1.4.1–5)

Whether Lucio is indeed "mocking" her when he calls her "a thing
enskied and sainted" (1.4.34) is a moot point; the important point
is that Isabella would like to see her chosen world in these terms,
and that she finds it difficult to accept the existence of her own
noble thoughts in the mind—or on the lips—of an ignoble creature
from outside her world.

There is no reason, then, to doubt Isabella's word when she twice offers to lay down her life for her brother; it is the heroic thing to do, and Isabella yearns to be a saintly hero. The very words she uses about her voluntary martyrdom show that she has adopted her ideas about sacrifice from the luridly detailed martyrologies of the time, as well as from the combined sensual and spiritual imagery of Loyolan meditation and the new poetry:

> *Isabella:* [W]ere I under the terms of death,
>   Th' impression of keen whips I'd wear as rubies,
>   And strip myself to death, as to a bed
>   That longing have been sick for, ere I'd yield
>   My body up to shame.
>
> (2.4.100–05)

But Isabella is not at this moment in the ideal world of the martyrologies, and her imagery only whets Angelo's sensual appetite. Furthermore, not even the audience is allowed to retain Isabella's romantic view; we are made too vividly aware of the fact that those "keen whips" are in the hands of the rough-hewn Abhorson and the bumbling Pompey, an ex-pimp.

Nothing goes the way Isabella expects. Angelo turns her brilliant logic-chopping against her; the noble Law makes illicit propositions; her glorious martyrdom must be traded for a sordid tumble; and her valiant brother, who should rush to her protection, turns out to be a sniveling coward. It is small wonder that when the Duke greets her, after her disastrous interview with Claudio, she can hardly wait to get back to her nice, safe convent. "I have no superfluous leisure," she says. "My stay must be stolen out of other affairs, but I will attend you awhile" (3.1.156–58). This is no mere social excuse; Isabella has found the world too disappointing—yes, even too messy—and wants only to return as soon as possible to her ideal world where there are (she thinks) no loose ends and no human frailties.

It is exactly at this point that the Duke steps in and begins arranging the "happy" denouement. As Rosalind Miles, who perhaps unconsciously uses the prison metaphor in her analysis, points out: "With this structure of character and plot involving

Isabella, Angelo, and Claudio, the audience comes to realize that there is no help for these three from each other. Shakespeare has closed the trap of the plot upon them, and it is a trap which can only be opened from the outside. They must have external help, and that help must be the Duke's" (*Problem*, 260). It is true; we do feel that there is, at this point, no way out but a guilty life or death for the three. But the "trap" of which Miles speaks is Shakespeare's only at second remove, and each of the characters has come to the trap through the mental trap that each has built for himself or herself. Furthermore, the Duke's "external help" is itself a product of his own mental prison.

Miles's observation that the Duke's "outside intervention is bound to be artificial and unreal" (260) is a good one; but again it focuses too much on Shakespeare's plot-making at the expense of the Duke's.[24] The Duke, after all, could just as easily have revealed himself at this point and saved the three in a more straightforward manner. But he, too, is circumscribed by a need to order the universe—a need that combines the active meddling impulse of Angelo with the passive withdrawal impulse of Isabella. From such a mixture can come only disaster.

From the beginning of the play, it is obvious that the Duke has been an anti-Machiavel, a ruler who wants to be loved more than feared by his subjects, and who has consequently been both too removed from and too permissive toward the people of Vienna. He has "ever loved the life removed," he tells Friar Thomas (1.3.8), but his failure to become more involved with the punitive aspects of his ducal responsibility has caused sin to run riot in Vienna. Friar Thomas's commonsense reply to this—"It rested in your Grace / To unloose this tied-up justice when you pleased" (1.3.31–32)—is not, however, to the Duke's liking. He pleads that it will seem "tyranny" in him to enforce the laws that he has previously ignored and, in a revealing bit of rationalization, explains why he has given that chore to Angelo:

> *Duke:* I have on Angelo impos'd the office,
>   Who may, in th' ambush of my name, strike home,

And yet my nature never in the fight
To do in slander.

(1.3.40–43)

We may recognize here the sentiments of every official, major or minor, down to the present day: the desire to be loved as a beneficent figure and as a source of recourse against one's own rigorous enforcement agencies.

But things do not go according to plan for the Duke any more than they do for Angelo, Isabella, or Claudio. Like the eavesdropping kings and queens of Shakespeare's history plays before him,[25] the Duke discovers that his people do not universally applaud him, and he must listen to some unpleasant truths about himself even from the most slanderous tongues. Lucio, in the midst of his calumnies, actually says what the Duke himself has been saying about the effects of his rule:

> *Lucio:* Would the Duke that is absent have done this? Ere he would have hanged a man for the getting a hundred bastards, he would have paid for the nursing a thousand. . . . The Duke yet would have dark deeds darkly answered, he would never bring them to light. Would he were returned!
>
> (3.2.123–26; 186–89)

Significantly, the next person whom the Duke asks about his "absent" self is Escalus, a man who can be depended upon to give a good report; but even so, the audience cannot help thinking for a moment that the Duke is playing with fire, and that eavesdroppers deserve what they hear.

And what of the famous bed-trick? It is indeed "artificial and unreal," as Miles has said, and so flimsy that we can hardly imagine Isabella agreeing to it if it had not been endorsed by a friar. Furthermore, at the introduction of the bed-trick, the play begins to change with an audible creaking of machinery. But there is one thing about it that has been consistently overlooked by critics who condemn it: the bed-trick does not work.[26]

In the tales and plays that used the trick before *Measure for Measure*, the ploy does what it is supposed to do: it brings about recognition, reconciliation, or revenge. Even in Shakespeare's own *All's Well That Ends Well*, Helena gets the man she wants through a bed-trick (regardless of what we think about the scoundrel that she gets). But in *Measure for Measure*, the trick makes everything worse: it hastens the order for Claudio's execution, temporarily blackens the reputations of both Isabella and Mariana, and throws Angelo into a dangerous state of despair. The Duke himself is placed in a quandary by Angelo's response to the trick; he must suddenly change all his plans, must find a new way to save Claudio's life and Barnardine's soul, must very nearly reveal himself to the Provost ahead of schedule, and must later subject himself and the two women to public scorn. What has gone wrong?

The living men and women of *Measure for Measure*, when they assemble at the judgment scene, have wrought havoc with their own lives, with the lives of others, and with the storybook ending that we expect of a comedy. There have been too many playwrights at work within the play, each working from a script that the others have not seen. Even after the final revelations and pardons, many of them seem only to have left one prison for another. Mariana has come out of her moated grange to be tied for life to the puritanical Angelo. Angelo himself is in a state of despair that leads only to hell. Isabella, after what she has undergone, is as firmly locked out of her convent as she was once locked in. The Duke must abandon his own quasi-monastic dreams to undertake marriage and resume his rule of Vienna. Pompey has moved from the whorehouse to the executioner's shed. Barnardine, in or out of prison, remains in his "drunken sleep." And Lucio is married to a prostitute. Nothing, it seems, has changed, except possibly for the worse. Or has it?

The falling-off that so many audiences have seen in the second part of Shakespeare's play is a reflection of the falling-off that his characters have seen in their ideal worlds as they learn to accept both death and life—their own and others'. And, as in many of the Arts of Dying, the central event of Claudio's death sentence has taught the lesson. Death, far from being the glorious martyrdom of Isabella's dreams, the comfortable sleep of the Duke's dreams, the nuisance of Barnardine's, the punishment of

Angelo's, or the horror of Claudio's, is in fact simply a part of life, to be accepted on its own terms and neither fled from nor sought after. The readiness, as Hamlet would say, is all; and the readiness itself casts a steadier light on life, revealing that it cannot be perfect but must not therefore be scorned. If life, in fact, is second best to heaven or whatever perfection each person imagines as his or her ideal, second best to perfection is not a lowly status after all.[27]

This, then, is why Angelo and Barnardine must not be allowed to die. Theologically, they have not achieved repentance; and, psychologically, they have not yet learned to live. In the end, what Mariana has said of Angelo is the lesson that all the great but fallible human creatures of *Measure for Measure* are in the process of learning about existence as they leave us:

> *Mariana:* They say best men are molded out of faults,
>   And, for the most, become much more the better
>   For being a little bad. So may my husband.
>
> (5.1.444–46)

Death, as Sir Charles Mountford has said, is the end of all calamity; but in the words of the old Jewish proverb, "You don't die so easy; you live with all your aches and pains."[28] The universe itself is a compromise of warring elements, and it is only through a truce with death that we may begin to negotiate with life.

The Summons of Nothingness

The Duchess of Malfi

IT MAY SEEM PERVERSE TO CLAIM John Webster's *The Duchess of Malfi* as a companion piece to *Measure for Measure*. Shakespeare's play begins with a death sentence and ends with four marriages; Webster's begins with a marriage and ends with ten deaths; in *Measure for Measure*, the characters emerge from prison into daylight (however overcast that daylight may be); in *The Duchess of Malfi*, they wander ever deeper into darkness, madness, and despair. But in both plays, the major characters—and the audience—do battle with a world that will not order itself to their demands; and in both, the action leads to and radiates from a stunning scene in which one central figure faces a nightmarelike summons of death.

Certainly, even if there were no other similarities between the two plays, the nature of the critical reaction to them should tell us something about their kinship. Both plays make critics angry, if not with the plays, then at least with each other. As with *Measure for Measure*, critical opinion on *The Duchess of Malfi* has developed into a furious quarrel over the motivation of the play's characters, the validity of its action, and the overall philosophy behind it.[1] Some have tried to make the play into a Sartrean gloss on the world as Hell; others have seen it as a Christian allegory of the road to Heaven.[2] The Duchess herself has been

described as everything ranging from a medieval saint to a modern
bitch,[3] while the question of Ferdinand's incestuous longing has
generated as much serious discussion as is usually reserved for
the personality of a historical figure.[4] Why all this controversy
over what might seem like a typical Jacobean horror play? We
may catch a glimpse of the answer if we revisit Claudio in his
prison cell for a moment.

Claudio, we remember, was tormented not by an assurance
of damnation, like Angelo's, nor even by an assurance of annihilation, but primarily by an uncertainty about both—a fear of the
unknown, that void which the human mind is so ready to fill
with horrors of its own making. "To fall into nothingness," says
Philippa Tristram, "is the expression of physical nature; a confidence that God will sustain his creation in being is the achievement of faith."[5] Given this faith, Tristram says elsewhere, "a man
may advance confidently to his reward in a future life; but when
death loses its heroism, the continuity between life and afterlife
is ruptured by the agnostic spectacle of physical mortality" (10).
Claudio, terrorized by his agnostic spectacle, was shocked into
heroism by the faith of the people around him; but in the *Duchess*,
there is no one available to administer the shock. Everyone speaks
as if he agreed with Claudio.

This is not to suggest that Webster necessarily agreed with
Claudio. It is always tempting to explain the increased horror
of Jacobean drama by pointing out the increased confusion and
disillusionment of Jacobean society; but R. W. Chambers has
shown that it would be just as easy to make a case for the confusion and disillusionment of late Elizabethan society and the
renewed stability and hope of early Jacobean society.[6] Furthermore, the *Duchess* is set in sixteenth-century Italy, which traditionally signaled to Webster's audience both a corrupt court and
a corrupt church—if an example at all, then a horrible example.
Therefore, I do not think it any safer to assume, on the evidence
of Webster's two great tragedies, that he was a despairing agnostic
than to assume, on the evidence of *Tamburlaine* and *The Jew of
Malta*, that Marlowe was a hopeful atheist. The question that
seems to govern Webster's speculation in *The Duchess of Malfi*

may be, not "What if the universe were as Claudio imagines?" but rather "What if everyone thought so?"

In such a state of uncertainty, one of the responses is to invent new systems of ordering; to take a seemingly disordered universe and catalogue, categorize, shape it into a meaningful whole. But as a paradoxical corollary to this need, externally enforced order then becomes the enemy because, being already shaped, it cannot be re-shaped to the mind's demands. Thus time, death, decay, and the stars themselves become uncontrollable nightmares. A further corollary that appears in the *Duchess* is a growing rigidity of human society and a concurrent reversal of convention. That is, as reasons for certain behavior erode, the rules of behavior become more strictly codified until the rules are ends in themselves, not to be deviated from at the risk of chaos. The insecure person, unable to control the mindless patterns of the universe, turns instead to his fellow creatures and reasserts his controlling power by manipulating others—often with the aid of those uncontrollable forces themselves. The more he fears, the more he projects his fears onto others. And gradually, all the modes of comfort generated by the old systems become not comforts but dangers to those who are being controlled by them. If it is any comfort to the manipulators—and it frequently is, as we shall see—they have turned the universe upside down.

Webster himself turns the dramatic universe upside down in his portrayal of such a society. Darkness, for example, is a literary convention often used to indicate a state of ignorance, confusion, or evil; and much of the important action of *The Duchess of Malfi* is set in physical darkness. But calling for light is no solution; when the torches are brought, they illuminate an uglier reality. In the light, the Duchess sees what she thinks to be the severed hand of her husband and the dead bodies of her husband and children (4.1).[7] Bosola sees the wounded body of Antonio, whom he has mistakenly attacked in the dark (5.4). Ferdinand, when he goes mad, chooses to retreat into world of safe darkness after his eyes have been "dazzled" by reality: "I'll go hunt the badger, by owl-light: / 'Tis a deed of darkness" (4.2.334–35). Even the steady light of the stars is not an unmixed blessing; although Antonio in his first love scene prays, "And may our sweet affections, like the spheres, / Be still in motion" (1.1.482–83), Bosola's later "Look you, the stars shine still" (4.1.100) is used not to comfort but to rebuke and torment the Duchess.

It is interesting to note that this reversal of the customary associations of light and darkness is often extended to include the audience. The Duchess is not the only one who is deceived by the wax figures of Antonio and the children. Until Ferdinand tells Bosola that "These presentations are but fram'd in wax" (4.1.112), Webster's audience would have been most likely to accept the illusions as reality, being quite inured to the use of wax stage props to represent decapitated heads, strewn limbs, and other gruesome stage business. Even the modern audience will be jolted out of a feeling of superiority toward the stage manager when it discovers that the clumsy props are really supposed to be clumsy props.[8] There is, then, a kind of horrified fascination in seeing that things really *are* what they seem, a shocking reversal when one has been led to believe the opposite.

Webster toys with his audience, too, in his use of coincidence. The three major coincidences in the play are at first unsettling in their departure from the larger-than-life realism of the action; William Archer, in fact, in his famous diatribe against Webster, found them not only unsettling but preposterous.[9] But when viewed most closely, the coincidences seem to miscarry from their purpose. Antonio's dropping of the horoscope that he has cast for his and the Duchess's first child (2.3) should, in the tradition of stage coincidence, reveal their secret to Bosola. But Bosola misunderstands the implication of the horoscope, and his assumption that Antonio is the Duchess's "bawd," rather than her husband, gains the couple two more years of spied-upon happiness. Similarly, Antonio's and Cariola's departure from the stage during the hair-brushing scene (3.2) may lead the Duchess into betraying her feelings to Ferdinand, who has stealthily entered while she is talking, but it also removes Antonio from the danger of Ferdinand's anger, and again prolongs the secret. And finally, Bosola's accidental stabbing of Antonio (5.4) does nothing to the action that has not already been made inevitable by Antonio's well-intentioned but ill-judged rush toward death. In fact, the accidental murder allows Bosola to draw Ferdinand and the Cardinal from their guard for purposes of his own revenge and the bloody denouement. The pointlessness of this last "coincidence," and a hint that Webster may indeed be toying with his audience, is suggested in the exchange between Malateste and Bosola, in which Webster reminds people that they are watching a play:

> *Malateste:* How came Antonio by his death?
> *Bosola:* In a mist: I know not how—
> Such a mistake as I have often seen
> In a play.
>
> (5.5.93–96)

The Echo scene, too (5.3), adds to the play's aura of inverted convention. Such echoes, used as oracular or ironic commentary on a protagonist's musings, had become popular both in poetry and drama, and were often used in combination with offstage utterances of ghosts. The below-stage "Swear!" of Hamlet Senior (1.5) may be part of this tradition, as is the chorus of ghosts— Andrugio, Feliche, and Pandulpho—who echo the last word of Antonio's tirade on man in Marston's *Antonio's Revenge.* "Murder!" they cry from all sides; and Marston's Antonio translates the echoed noun into an imperative verb: "Aye, I will murder" (3.1.128).[10] This resonance of ghostlore is amplified in *The Duchess of Malfi* by Antonio's insistence that the Echo is "very like my wife's voice" (5.3.26), and Webster's Antonio has been echoed in turn by modern commentators, most of whom see (as I do) the Duchess's spirit hovering over act 5.[12] But Delio, usually a voice of common sense in the play, says later that the haunting is "Your fancy, merely" (5.3.46), and the audience, not having seen the "face folded in sorrow" (5.3.45), again must decide for itself. Whereas Macbeth may muse that "This supernatural soliciting / Cannot be ill, cannot be good" (1.3.130–31), Webster's audience must determine whether the echo's soliciting is even supernatural. Just as the wax dummies were only wax dummies, so this Echo may be only an echo.

But, even here, the audience may not rest. If the Echo is not the Duchess, it is still important because it is a sound. Two scenes later, the dying Bosola will sum up what proponents of the "gloom" in Webster's universe take as Webster's own despair for humankind. Between the "mistake . . . seen in a play" passage and the pronouncement that "Womanish and fearful mankind" lives in a "shadow or deep pit of darkness" (5.5.101–02), Bosola says, "We are only like dead walls, or vaulted graves, / That ruin'd, yields [*sic*] no echo" (5.5.97–98). As a cry of despair, it is impressive; but as a simple matter of stage business, it is not true. The audience that has puzzled through the meanings of a very vocal Echo in scene 3 knows that ruins do indeed yield echoes, whether supernatural or not, and therefore that Bosola (as usual) is not to be trusted.

Bosola himself, among his many other functions in the play, is one of several travesties on the iconography of death and the arts of dying. Like the Dreary Death figures in the old mysteries and moralities, he is at once a warning of, a summoner to, and a product of the grave; but unlike the Dreary Death, he is frightened of his own role, and in fact seems to have a morbid aversion to life and death alike. His continual harping on the grotesque aspects of bodily decay goes beyond the standard rantings expected of the stage malcontent, and there is, in addition, always a question of whether his melancholy is part of his real nature or merely a pose for his own ends. Antonio thinks it genuine (1.1), but Ferdinand recognizes its ambiguity: "Be yourself," he says to Bosola; "Keep your old garb of melancholy" (1.1.277–78). And Bosola keeps his garb of melancholoy as a kind of hair shirt under all his subsequent disguises, tormenting himself with it as much as he torments those around him.

One of the more significant of Bosola's early appearances as Dreary Death is his confrontation with Castruchio and the Old Lady in act 2, scene 1. At first he is a combination of the malcontent and the Warning of the Legend, chastising social climbers and mocking the attempts of the old to appear young, the ugly to appear beautiful. But when he has finished his social commentary in prose, he rounds on the audience like the Death of the mysteries, and with an exordium of "observe my meditation now," delivers his searing moral in blank verse:

> *Bosola:* Though we are eaten up of lice and worms,
>   And though continually we bear about us
>   A rotten and dead body, we delight
>   To hide it in rich tissue: all our fear—
>   Nay, all our terror—is lest our physician
>   Should put us in the ground, to be made sweet.
>
> (2.1.55–60)

This passage is one of the critics' favorites; it is cited, not without a shiver of delighted horror, to prove either Webster's nausea at the world or Bosola's role as prophet of the world to come—in either case, with Bosola placed firmly in the *de contemptu mundi* preaching tradition. And down to the middle of line 58, it is true that Bosola echoes the words of Pope Innocent and all his imitators, including the Duke's sermon to Claudio in *Measure for Measure.* Bartholomew Chappell had pointed the moral in his dapper little quatrains, each with a sting in its tail:

> Our bodies are a cursed ground,
>   our skin is like to withered hay:
> Our humours weake and watrish found,
>   which filthie wormes shall suck away.[12]

And George Strode was to say it more graphically: "We are now in our best estate, but as a dunghill couered with snowe, which when Death shall dissolve, there shall nothing be seene of all our pompe and glory, but dust, rottennesse, and corruption."[13] Or in Robert Southwell's catalogue of horrors:

> Beholde the place, in which thou must abide,
> Is loathsome, dark, vnsweet, and very straight,
> With rotten bones, beset on euery side,
> And crawling wormes, to feed on thee do waite:
> O hard exchange, O vile and hatefull place,
> Where earth and filth, thy carcase must imbrace.[14]

Bosola's pronouncement, then, is well within the convention of seeing the living body as a walking grave, proceeding naturally out of a corrupt mass and progressing ineluctably back to corruption. As he says the words, Bosola is in fact holding the apricots that he has ripened in horse-dung, apricots that he will give to the Duchess and that will induce labor and the birth of her son. From corruption will issue corruption: a new human life, a "dunghill couered with snowe." But the point of divergence from convention in Bosola's speech is as important as the points of similarity. The body, in his imagery, does not return to dust; it is "put" there by a physician, as a kind of remedy for life. For Bosola, the worms and corruption of the traditional iconography of death exist only above the ground, and the grave itself is sweeter than the body placed in it.

Nor is this the traditional Christian allegory of salvation: Christ the physician giving "sweetness" after death to a soul that has been imprisoned in the "filth" of the body. Rather, the placing of the body in the ground is a cause of "all our fear— / Nay, all our terror"—a form of burial alive, where the irony of the word *sweet*, against the backdrop of the known corruption of the grave, casts into doubt the wisdom of any physician who should propose such a remedy.

It is a ghastly portrait of life and death alike, with apparently no acceptable escape from either. And one can hardly help seeing it as Bosola's own view, despite his pose as satiric malcontent. Significantly, he uses the pronoun "I" only when he speaks of his unrecognized and unrecompensed secular activities; when he delivers his vivid diatribes on the corruption of the body, he turns instead to the accusing "you" or poetic "we"—an effective device by which the speaker can universalize his failings while giving listeners to understand that he really refers to everyone but himself. The malcontent posture appears to be not only a fashionable pose for Bosola, not only a cloak for his espionage activities, but also a means of coping with his own fears by projecting them onto others.[15]

Nowhere more than in Bosola's famous act 4 confrontation with the Duchess does his power of rationalizing and manipulating manifest itself, and it significantly does so, there, in inversions of the Summons of Death. Entering disguised as an old man, directly after the dance of madmen—perhaps as a coda to the Dance of Death—he announces, "I am come to make thy tomb"

(4.2.116) and launches himself into what many have seen as a *de contemptu mundi* sermon:

> *Bosola:* Thou art a box of worm-seed, at best, but a salvatory of
> green mummy:—what's this flesh? a little crudded milk, fantastical
> puff-paste; our bodies are weaker than those paper prisons boys
> use to keep flies in; more contemptible, since ours is to preserve
> earthworms. Didst thou ever see a lark in a cage? such is the
> soul in the body: this world is like her little turf of grass, and
> the heaven o'er our heads, like her looking-glass, only gives us
> a miserable knowledge of the small compass of our prison.
>
> (4.2.124–33)

Taken out of context, this is standard fare: the body as food for worms, the prison of the soul. Just such an approach was used to Claudio, with the implication that he must now come to terms with death. But we cannot take the passage out of context. Claudio was a convicted felon, legally arrested and sentenced under law, however rigorous that law might have been, and was further called upon to lay down his life for his sister's honor. To die bravely, for him, was to die submissively. The Duchess, on the other hand, is about to be murdered, and it is her murderer who is preaching submission to her.

Critics who see Bosola's role in this scene as the Duchess's spiritual comforter[16] appear to have overlooked this small detail: that Bosola has come to murder her and her maid and children. True, Bosola has earlier told Ferdinand that "when you send me [to the Duchess] next, / The business shall be comfort" (4.1.136–37). But when have we ever been able to take Bosola at face value? The fact remains that before this pronouncement, he has just spent the last twenty lines goading Ferdinand into a homicidal frenzy, and is now, despite his apparent protests, ready to commit the homicide that Ferdinand demands. And just as he has used religious-sounding words to make Ferdinand squirm in 4.1 ("Send her a penitential garment to put on / Next to her delicate skin" [119–20]), so he does the same to make the Duchess squirm in 4.2. How the Duchess reacts we shall see later.

When the executioners enter to the Duchess and Bosola, he tacitly admits his deception by changing roles. He is no longer the Warning of the Legend, but "the common bellman / That usually is sent to condemn'd persons / The night before they suffer" (4.2.172–74). And the dirge that he sings to her, justly celebrated for its beauty, is again a compendium of traditions turned upside down. It is lovely, it is soothing, it is very nearly hypnotic—but it is full of contradictions and dangerous to the Duchess' sanity. Indeed, when Bosola comes to the *de contemptu mundi* section of his dirge, at first hauntingly reminiscent of the Duke's sermon, he gives himself away:

> Bosola: Of what is 't fools make such vain keeping?
>   Sin their conception, their birth weeping;
>   Their life a general mist of error,
>   Their death a hideous storm of terror.
>
> (4.2.186–89)

Death a hideous storm of terror? He has just sung that "Here your perfect peace is sign'd" (185). For someone who has come to give comfort, either he is going out of his way to inspire terror or he has let his personal fears surface accidentally again—or both. And now he issues the formal Summons:

> Bosola: Strew your hair with powders sweet,
>   Don clean linen, bathe your feet,
>   And (the foul fiend more to check)
>   A crucifix let bless your neck.
>   'Tis now full tide, 'tween night and day:
>   End your groan, and come away.
>
> (4.2.190–95)

This is certainly not Christian comfort, with its emphasis on physical rather than spiritual preparation for Death the Bridegroom. In fact, given Bosola's previous rantings about the filth of the body, this summons to cleanliness may appear to be a variation on his cloying image of the "sweet" grave. Even the crucifix that he recommends is a false note; although, as Bettie Anne Doebler points out, the crucifix was a standard accompaniment to deathbed ministration in the medieval *Artes*,[17] Webster's audience would have been more likely to see it as a papist superstition, and therefore perhaps more a temptation by than a hindrance to "the foul fiend."

What Bosola is offering is not comfort but a travesty on comfort. Indeed, we may recognize in it echoes of another false comforter, Spenser's Despayre:

> What if some little payne the passage have,
> That makes frayle flesh to feare the bitter wave?
> Is not short payne well borne, that bringes long ease,
> And layes the soule to sleepe in quiet grave?
> Sleepe after toyle, port after stormie seas,
> Ease after warre, death after life does greatly please.
>
> (FQ, I.ix.40)

As in any tempation to despair, the soul must make a subtle distinction between a willingness to die and a wish to die. The first is accession to necessity (or, for Christians, to God's will); the second is suicide, for Christians, the sin of Judas. And Bosola's appeal to the Duchess tempts her to an even more perverse variation on the second: complicity in her own murder. It is Webster's, not Bosola's irony that rings the pun on Bosola's "'Twas to bring you / By degrees to moritification" (4.2.176–77); Bosola means the Duchess to understand "mortification" as "humility," and, alas, many critics have accepted his definition at face value again. But the Duchess knows that what he really means is "humiliation," an entirely different thing; and, as we shall see, she fights back, not to save her life, but to die bravely.

It is, perhaps, Antonio rather than the Duchess who has internalized Bosola's message. If Antonio believes in a God at all, he seldom mentions it. His one extended reference to Heaven describes it as a "curious artist" that "takes in sunder / A clock or watch when it is out of frame, / To bring 't in better order" (3.5.63–65). In the next century, this watchmaker image became the deists' favorite image for the impersonal nature of God, and Antonio does not appear to have more than a deistic conception of religion. How, then, does he face the threats of death and the pains of life? By an attempt at stoic endurance, yes; by a reliance, Bosola-like, on physical action, of course; but also, like many newly irreligious people, by a transference of his search for reassurance from religion to superstition.[18] He casts horoscopes, looks for portents, and sees ghosts in echoes—but, ironically, his new form of supernatural guidance aggravates rather than assuages his fear.

Delio, as always, comments matter-of-factly on Antonio's superstition, although it is one of Webster's characteristic ironies that this commonsense refutation of prophecy is almost a prophecy itself:

> *Delio:* 'Tis but the shadow of your fear, no more:
>   How superstitiously we mind our evils!
>   The throwing down salt, or crossing of a hare,
>   Bleeding at nose, the stumbling of a horse,
>   Or singing of a cricket, are of pow'r
>   To daunt whole man in us.
>
> (2.2.74–79)

Later in the play, Ferdinand will literally attempt to wrestle with the "shadow" of his fear (5.2), and only one scene after Delio's speech, Antonio will let a nosebleed "daunt" him so much that he will display guilt before Bosola and drop the not-really-fatal horoscope.[19]

This is not to suggest that Antonio is a coward; on the contrary, he has an almost foolish disregard for his personal safety. He must be dissuaded by the Duchess from spending the night with her when Ferdinand is near (3.2), and must be directed to flee when discovery or capture is imminent (3.2; 3.5). Once the Duchess is no longer there to advise him, he determinedly sets forth on what he must know is an impossible—if not suicidal—mission: to attempt a reconciliation with her brothers. Indeed, each time he speaks to Delio of his plan, he speculates equally on his success and his failure, and almost seems to relish the failure more:

> *Antonio:*   . . . if it fail,
>   Yet it shall rid me of this infamous calling;

For better fall once, than be ever falling.

(5.1.72–74)

Come: I'll be out of this ague;
For to live thus is not indeed to live:
It is a mockery, and abuse of life—
I will not henceforth save myself by halves;
Lose all, or nothing.

(5.3.47–51)

Antonio, hunting blindly for assurance in his watchmaker universe, cannot cope with the uncertainties of life. Despite his stoic declaration that "Contempt of pain, that we may call our own" (5.3.58), he can face only physical pain, and in a world that inflicts mental pain as well he can see no remedy but death. His gratitude when Bosola brings death to him is the very reaction that Bosola has tried to elicit from the Duchess:

Antonio: Pleasure of life, what is 't? only the good hours
    Of an ague; only a preparative to rest,
    To endure vexation.

(5.4.67–69)

It is entirely possible that the sense of waste generated by Antonio's almost self-inflicted death is what has led some critics to take at face value Bosola's cry when he sees what he has done: "We are merely the stars' tennis-balls, struck and banded / Which way please them" (5.4.54–55). But Bosola himself has earlier denied that the stars have any connection with human activities:

Ferdinand: Why some
    Hold opinion all things are written [in the stars].
Bosola: Yes, if we could find spectacles to read them.

(3.1.60–62)

Duchess: I could curse the stars. . . .
    And those three smiling seasons of the year
    Into a Russian winter, nay the world
    To its first chaos.
Bosola: Look you, the stars shine still.

(4.1.97–100)

Furthermore, we must not forget that the coincidence of Antonio's death is no more coincidental than Webster's other tricks on the audience, and in fact follows logically from Bosola's and Antonio's purposes in coming to Milan: Bosola to kill, and Antonio to be reconciled or die.

What Bosola is doing, in his diatribe against the stars, is simply what he has done throughout the play: excusing his actions by claiming that he is just following orders. He has repeatedly done it with Ferdinand, accusing his employer of sole guilt for the instructions that he himself has carried out; telling himself that an act is wrong, and then performing it with sadistic embellishments of his own;[20] and even excusing his personal revenge for Ferdinand's ingratitude by claiming that the Duchess's dying look has demanded it. But, as always, Bosola gives himself away when he finally takes his revenge; temporarily forgetting the Duchess in the heat of the moment, he cries out as he kills Ferdinand, "Sink, thou main cause / Of *my* undoing!" (5.5.63–64; emphasis added). Only at the moment of his own death does Bosola come to grips with his humanity, and even then he must first deliver *sententiae* before acknowledging that they are inappropriate to his case:[21]

> *Bosola:* In what a shadow, or deep pit of darkness,
>   Doth womanish and fearful mankind live!
>   Let worthy minds ne'er stagger in distrust
>   To suffer death, or shame for what is just—
>   Mine is another voyage.
>
>   (5.5.101–05)

It is perhaps fortunate for Bosola's sanity that he dies before he has a chance to contemplate what that "voyage" is and where it leads. Until now, he has been able to goad others into fearing it, as a release from his own fears. He does not have the equanimity to face the "deep pit of darkness" without forcing others ahead of him to block the view. And, ironically, for all Bosola's description of mankind as "womanish and fearful," of the three people who refuse to block the view—the Duchess, the Cardinal, and Julia—two are women.

Julia is the "bad" woman who is meant to form a contrast with the "good" Duchess. She woos for lust rather than for love, and unlike the Duchess, who is faithful to her secret vows, she is capable of flirting almost simultaneously with her current lover (the Cardinal) and two prospective lovers (Delio and Bosola) virtually under the gaze of her husband. Does she feel guilt, or the need to transfer guilt? There is no evidence that the question has ever crossed her mind. Amoral Julia, the pawn in everyone else's games, is simply a straightforward cheat who has developed a method of making things comfortable by shrugging off what she cannot explain. Even when she has been poisoned by the Cardinal, and must face the same mysterious "voyage" that terrifies Bosola, she dies with a shrug, and in her sardonicism earns the rare distinction of having effectively silenced Bosola:

> *Bosola:* O foolish woman,
>   Couldst not thou have poison'd him?
> *Julia:*   'Tis weakness,
>   Too much to think what should have been done—I go,
>   I know not whither.
>
> (5.2.286–89)

This is an acceptance of uncertainty that Bosola cannot share or understand. Despite his villainy, he is still caught in the transition between belief and unbelief: the middle ground where Claudio's "Ay, but to die and go we know not where" is still a horrified "What if?" instead of a resigned "So what?"

But Bosola's obsessive verbalizing of his fears is simply idle conversation beside Ferdinand's. Alone of all the major characters in the play, Ferdinand finally does have a nervous breakdown under the pressure of reality. Unlike Bosola, he cannot distance his fears or pass responsibility on to others, because one of his fears is the loss of power—a fear that makes him assert ownership over everything, including his own thoughts and deeds. To lose control, for him, is to fall into nothingness; but unlike the Duchess and the Cardinal, he cannot maintain the control, cannot face his thoughts, and lets others goad him into the very extravagances that frighten him.

Ferdinand's hallmark in the play is a constant retreat from the things that he cannot face, a retreat that he tries to mask by ordering people to take the things away. He refuses to meet the Duchess's husband (3.2); he will not look at the Duchess until she is dead, and then, faced with a worse reality, orders Bosola to "Cover her face" (4.2.264); and he finally sends Bosola himself away (4.2). But above all, he will not face his own motivation. As he retreats systematically from one thing after another, he in effect withdraws from reality, but the visions that he conjures up for himself are more frightful than the reality out of which he distorts them.

Ferdinand's most obsessive ravings, of course, center on his sister. As the Cardinal notes throughout 2.5, he is already a little crazy on the subject. And since F. L. Lucas's proposal of the incest theme (noted earlier), it has generally been accepted that Ferdinand's almost insane words and actions grow out of an incestuous passion for the Duchess that he cannot indulge, cannot dissipate, and cannot face. Certainly, ungovernable rage growing out of irrational jealousy is not an uncommon device. Ferdinand's "My sister! O my sister! there's the cause on't" (5.5.71) is both a reminiscence of Othello's "It is the cause, it is the cause, my soul" (5.3.1) and a precursor of Giovanni's "My sister, O my sister!" in Ford's more explicitly incestuous *'Tis Pity She's a Whore* (5.6.21)[22] But perhaps there is more to Ferdinand's simultaneous obsession and revulsion than a simple matter of incest.

Amid the sexually promiscuous activity of the play's society, Ferdinand does not appear to have a sexual liaison, or ever to have had one. He is decidedly uncomfortable with other people's ribald joking (1.1), and his own dirty joke to his sister is not ribald but smutty, and is meant to humiliate her:

> *Ferdinand:* And women like that part which, like the lamprey,
>   Hath ne'er a bone in it.
> *Duchess:*   Fie, sir!
> *Ferdinand:*   Nay,
>   I mean the tongue: variety of courtship.
>
>   (1.1.336–38)

Perhaps it is not merely his repressed incestuous passion that frightens Ferdinand so much but sexuality in general. For him, it is one of the great unknowns, an uncontrollable force dangerously close to madness and death. He sees sex everywhere, everything he sees seems ugly, and, like Bosola, he cannot stop talking about his fear. While the Cardinal is busy lecturing the Duchess on family honor, Ferinand keeps talking about "those joys, / Those lustful pleasures" (1.1.325–26). Even the madmen whom he chooses for her torture are ones who will be sure to talk smut to her.

It is ironic—or perhaps predictable—that Bosola, who shares Ferdinand's fear of the body, should be the one who eventually drives him over the brink of madness. There is a hint of things to come even in their first encounter:

> *Ferdinand:* I would not have her marry again.
> *Bosola:* No, sir?
> *Ferdinand:* Do not you ask the reason: but be satisfied,
>   I say I would not.
>
>   (1.1.256–58)

Ferdinand's protestations about not wanting the Duchess to remarry are not entirely true, since he does later pick a second husband for her in Malateste. To be sure, Malateste is a gentleman, whereas Antonio is only the Duchess's steward. But the courtiers' description of Malateste in 3.3.10–34 indicates that he is the type of man whom the Duchess would despise, and who would cause her either to avoid sex with him or to go through with it and hate it. What is unpleasant for Ferdinand must be made unpleasant for everyone.

At any rate, there would seem to be no reason for Ferdinand to become so defensively testy with Bosola on the subject, since Bosola has not specifically asked for the reason behind Ferdinand's categorical statement. After the Duchess is killed, Ferdinand does volunteer a reason, partially, one feels, to stop Bosola from harping on the subject of her death. But Ferdinand has not learned to rationalize credibly. His reason, that he had hoped to gain his sister's fortune (4.2.283–85), is given too late and too unconvincingly; it deceives neither Bosola nor himself. And as Bosola continues to press the issue, Ferdinand, unable to face his real reasons but forced to face his fear of them, is driven into a final retreat from reality: a madness in which he can "throttle" his own shadow and act out his nightmares.

Ironically, although Ferdinand's madness may cause his deepest fears to surface, it also puts him more firmly in control of them. His lycanthropy, a descent into animality, is part of the dissolution that has obsessed him throughout the play, but now that the dissolution has begun, he seems to be able to face it with more equanimity—almost, like Antonio facing his death, with relief:

> *Ferdinand:* Look, what's that follows me?
> *Malateste:* Nothing, my lord.
> *Ferdinand:* Yes:—
> *Malateste:* 'Tis your shadow.
> *Ferdinand:* Stay it, let it not haunt me.
> *Malateste:* Impossible: if you move, and the sun shine:—
> *Ferdinand:* I will throttle it.
>   [Throws himself down on his shadow.]
> *Malateste:* O, my lord: you are angry with nothing.
> *Ferdinand:* You are a fool: how is't possible I should catch my
>   shadow unless I fall upon't?
>   (5.2.31–41)

The word *nothing*, innocent enough in Malateste's mouth, is significant in Ferdinand's mind. He has been running from Nothing all his life, and only in his madness can he turn at bay and face it. Indeed, his digging up of graves and carrying about of dead men's limbs (5.2.12–15) might almost be a gloss on the dead man's hand that he brought to the Duchess in 4.1. The difference now is that he is presenting the memento mori to himself, although, to be sure, it is still a perversion of the symbol: a limb rather than a skull.

Ferdinand has often acted as a variant of the traditional memento mori. As early as 1.1, he begins to show the Duchess her own death: "This was my father's poniard: do you see? / I'd be loth to see 't look rusty, 'cause 'twas his" (331–32). In the hair-brushing scene, he hides like the skeletonic figure in Renaissance "vanity" portraits, watching a woman regard her graying hair in a looking-glass. When she turns and sees him, he hands her the weapon that he has warned her with earlier, and bids her "Die then, quickly!" (3.2.71). And yet, in all his warnings and all his presentations of death, he is neither the warning of the Legend nor the beckoning figure of the Summons, but rather a more sinister creature that we have met before: the knife-bearing Despair. Although Bosola has told the Duchess that the figure of her "dead" husband and children are meant to bring her to resignation, the orthodox purpose of a memento mori (4.1.57–60), Ferdinand is quite clear about the real purpose of the display: "To bring her to despair" (4.1.116).

When Bosola's function is seen thus, in the light of his master's, it becomes plain why the Duchess must resist his ministrations. To accede to his terms will mean, for her, acceptance not of God's minister but of Despair's. Even in the old allegories— the Mysteries, the Moralities, and *The Faerie Queene*—Despair's voice had sounded perilously like God's; but in those allegories, the tempted souls knew that there was a God to whom they could turn instead. When the soul has lost its standard of comparison, when there is no other voice to listen for, how, then, can it conquer despair?

The answer is that of the Duchess. In fact, her death scene is such a powerful one, and has drawn so much admiration even from reluctant critics,[23] that it is easy to overlook the roots that her dying demeanor has in her past behavior.

Some critics have cited the Duchess's last scene as an example of not only a good but a specifically Christian death.[24] Much as one would like to accept this, if only for the sake of dramatic contrast with the irreligion of the other characters, the idea is called into question by the evidence in the play. It is true that she kneels to be strangled, and speaks of "heaven gates" (4.2.232), and that she tells Bosola that she is not frightened of death because: "Who would be afraid on't? / Knowing to meet such excellent company / In th' other world" (4.2.210–12). But on the other hand, her earlier conversation with Cariola indicates a less positive attitude on the subject:

> *Duchess:* Dost thou think we shall know one another,
>   In th' other world?
> *Cariola:*   Yes, out of question.
> *Duchess:* O that it were possible we might
>   But hold some two days' conference with the dead,
>   From them I should learn somewhat, I am sure
>   I never shall know here.
>
> (4.2.18–22)

This type of questioning is not an indication of strong belief, but rather a search for conviction. The scene is similar to the one between Desdemona and Emilia before Desdemona's death: the beleaguered heroine asks her confidante a question, hoping not for a reasoned answer but rather for an opportunity to talk herself into a desired frame of mind. The confidante, it must be remembered, is of a lower class than the heroine and is not expected to discuss the subject as an equal; she is merely a sounding-board for the heroine. This is not an uncommon way of dealing with one's fears, but it does indicate that a fear exists.

In the Duchess's case, the question about an afterlife occurs at a significant time. Cariola has just offered two unwanted and unasked for bits of advice and has been rebuked as a fool. Now Cariola herself has raised an uncomfortable question:

> *Duchess:* When I muse thus, I sleep.
> *Cariola:* Like a madman, with your eyes open?
>
> (4.2.16–17)

The Duchess's question follows directly upon this and effectively changes the subject until she is ready to deal with it, several lines later. In the actual death scene, as we shall see, she uses the same method of answering a question with another question in order to remain in command of the situation.

But perhaps this is just a dark night of the soul from which the Duchess will recover at her death; she has, after all, made reference to Heaven earlier in the play. At first glance, her parting

from Antonio seems to posit a personal God, or at least a purpose in the universe:

> *Duchess:* And yet, O Heaven, thy heavy hand is in't.
> I have seen my little boy oft scourge his top
> And compar'd myself to't: naught made me e'er
> Go right but heaven's scourge-stick.
>
>   (3.5.78–81)

Unfortunately, this comparison is uncomfortably close to Bosola's
talk about the "stars' tennis-balls," in which the human will is
"struck and banded" for amusement by an uncaring power. In
fact, the image of Heaven as a little boy is not very awe-inspiring,
and is similar to Bosola's description of the body as "those paper
prisons boys use to keep flies in."

The moral that the religious allegorists draw from the
Duchess's actual death can hardly be supported by the text. Consider, for example, this description of her supposed repentance:
"Despising the world, living a good life, meditating on death as
a way of self-knowledge, coming to an existential acceptance of
the necessity for mercy through facing one's sin, and finally overcoming despair through throwing oneself on the mercy of God."[25]
Although the Duchess may have "lived a good life," the other
parts of the description bear little resemblance to the actions that
make her most triumphant. In fact, there is no need to force the
Duchess into the pattern of a traditional Christian saint in order
to admire her. Her whole strength—we may say her whole self-
knowledge—lies in *rejecting* the traditional (and spurious) spiritual blandishments of Bosola and Ferdinand, and indeed in asserting her tie to this world rather than the next: "I am Duchess of
Malfi still" (4.2.142). She certainly does not "face [her] sin," either
the general sinfulness of the Christian tradition or the "sin" attributed to her by her brothers—which the audience hardly considers
a sin in the first place. And her only cry for "mercy" significantly
comes during her temporary return to life, after Bosola has told
her the lie about Antonio's reconciliation with her brothers
(4.2.350–53); it is difficult, in this context, to tell whether the

"Mercy!" is addressed to God or to Bosola, or whether it is simply the French *merci*.

And yet, there is something genuinely uplifting in the Duchess's death, something that makes one feel, as Robert Ornstein says, that "her self-possession in the face of death is a spiritual victory rather than a glorious defeat."[26] The source of this feeling need not be Christianized in order to be spiritual; it appears to lie not only in what she says about "heaven's scourge-stick," but also in her words about the madmen outside her window:

> *Duchess:*   Nothing but noise and folly
> Can keep me in my right wits, whereas reason
> And silence make me stark mad.
>
> (4.2.5–7)

It is a physical fact that when one is lost in a mist or in darkness, silence is a danger and noise the greatest aid in recovering one's sense of direction. Similarly, in human affairs, opposition is an enemy of complacency and a major spur to perseverance. The "noise and folly" surrounding the Duchess are a form of mental sonar that shows her what is to be avoided and how to avoid it; without the vision of madness held up before her, she might easily drift by degrees into a madness of her own, not recognizing it until it was too late. But the Duchess, for all her talk of going "into a wilderness" (1.1.359), thrives on danger, because danger is a direction post and a call to action.

It is not that the Duchess has Antonio's foolish recklessness; she is aware of the value of a strategic retreat, and must often force Antonio to fall back and regroup when he would rather fly into the cannon's mouth. Rather, she responds to threats with a bravado that robs her persecutors of their pleasure and so gives her a heady feeling of victory that carries her through any situation—even her own death.

The Duchess will not be dominated. Unlike Ferdinand, she will not be goaded by others into raving and self-exposure, but turns the goads on her tormentors and leads them to expose themselves. Her simple reply to her brothers' diatribe on her possible remarriage, "I think this speech between you both was studied, / It came so roundly off" (1.1.329–30), effectively strips the veneer from Ferdinand more than any impassioned speech would have done and leads to his first threat on her life, and his first dirty joke. Similarly, her one-line replies to him during the hair-brushing scene, interspersed with perfectly logical questions, drive him into a frenzy and lead to his repeated "I will never see thee more" (3.2.136; 141), one of his standard retreats from what he cannot face.

It is true that the Duchess occasionally slips in a very human way, particularly when she permits herself to seek comfort out-side herself. She allows Bosola, for example, to play upon her emotions in the pregnancy scene (2.1), when her physical condi-tion lowers her resistance both to his words and to his dubious apricots; and she comes close to breaking down after she has seen the wax figures of her husband and children. But she recovers quickly. When Bosola says, "Now, by my life, I pity you" (4.1.87), she calls him a fool, the epithet that she usually reserves for her maid. And in her last scene, her famous "I am Duchess of Malfi still" is a major turning point for her; it has been virtually forced out of her by Bosola's insults, but it seems to show her that she has been forced into a defensive position—and from then on, she turns to the attack.

One of the most effective ways that any oppressed people has of fighting back against a tyrant is to develop a sardonic sense of humor based on rigid common sense, an acceptance of the worst, and the ploy of answering a question with another question—one that the opponent cannot really answer. Lupset's good pagan, Canius, had mastered this strategy; and the Duchess has developed it to a science.

The Duchess's apparent obedience to the Summons is it-self strongly reminiscent of Canius'. According to Lupset, when Canius was sentenced to death by Caligula:

> Therat Canius turned him with lowe courtesy and sayd: My most gentill prince I hartely thanke you.

This answere came from a noble stomacke, whereby he
shewed the mad ragis of the cruell tyrant to be so ferre intolerable,
that vnder hym dethe was to be reckened for a benefit and a good
tourne. . . And great merueil men had to behold this Philosopher
howe mery he was after this tyrantes thretenynge.[27]

It is noteworthy that the Duchess, too, when she begins to resist
Bosola, says, "Let me be a little merry" (4.2.151), and that her
two *sententiae* on the welcome nature of death may carry stings
in their tails:

Duchess: I have so much obedience in my blood,
  I wish it in their [her brothers'] veins to do them good.

(4.2.169–70)

  . . . tell my brothers
That I perceive death, now I am well awake,
Best gift is they can give, or I can take.

(4.2.224–25)

The second of these is part of her long speech mocking Bosola's
attempt to frighten her. And the first? The word *obedience* is
ambiguous; it may be taken as obedience either to her brothers
or to the summons of death. But it can also mean, "I wish they
were about to die, too."

But the question is the Duchess's most powerful weapon. I
think that Ralph Berry is only partially correct when he notes
the frequency of unanswered questions in the play: "At different
times, all the characters are racked with doubt as to the meaning of life, and the rightness of their course through it. Constantly
they ask each other questions, and receive from one another
inconclusive answers" (132–33). The point is that when everyone
around us is as ignorant as we are, to be the one to formulate
a question is to place oneself in control of the situation. *We* are
the ones who are demanding information; our opponent is the
one who must admit ignorance and defeat. Furthermore, since
a question in itself is a demand, and an answer an accession to
that demand, the person who can ask the last question is the

person who is giving the orders. And when our opponent is trying to turn the argument in one direction, our question can divert the argument into other channels or expose the absurdity of the opponent's position.[28]

The Duchess, as we have seen, knows the rhetoric of questioning very well. She uses it on Ferdinand in the hair-brushing scene, uses it on Cariola when a question of madness arises. And in her death scene, she uses it to stunning effect on both Cariola and Bosola. There is something astonishingly modern—something that might almost be called "street-smart"—about her words after Cariola's hysterical "Call for help!" We might hear such a remark in a tenement apartment or a well-insulated suburban home: "To whom? to our next neighbours? they are mad-folks" (4.2.197–98). What is particularly interesting here is that the Duchess has anticipated Bosola, who should be the one to point out the hopelessness of her situation, and has thereby wrested control from him.

Bosola realizes what is happening and tries to restore his position of power by having Cariola, the Duchess's "straight man," taken away: "Remove that noise" (4.2.199). Interestingly, though, he is unconsciously echoing the words that the Duchess used about her emotional sonar: "Nothing but noise and folly / Can keep me in my right wits." And when he removes the "noise and folly" of Cariola, he himself steps into the vacuum and becomes the next straight man that the Duchess will use to keep herself sane. The ensuing give-and-take is almost in the nature of a comic "turn," and is worth reproducing at length:

> *Bosola:* Here are your executioners.
> *Duchess:* I forgive them:
>   The apoplexy, catarrh, or cough o' th' lungs
>   Would do as much as they do.
> *Bosola:* Doth not death fright you?
> *Duchess:*   Who would be afraid on't?
>   Knowing to meet such excellent company
>   In th' other world.
> *Bosola:* Yet, methinks,
>   The manner of your death should much afflict you,
>   This cord should terrify you?

Duchess: Not a whit:
  What would it pleasure me to have my throat cut
  With diamonds? or to be smothered
  With cassia? or to be shot to death with pearls?

(4.2.206–18)

By turning Bosola's words against him, the Duchess has not only prevented him from tormenting her further, has not only talked herself into accepting death, but has put her enemy of the moment on the defensive and made him look small and ineffectual. He is, in fact, so unsettled by her self-command that he lets the remainder of his power slip from him, allowing his victim to give the order for her own death: "Pull, and pull strongly, for your able strength / Must pull down heaven upon me" (4.2.230–31). And even after she is dead, the joy of the kill seems to go out of him; all he can do is brusquely dispatch Cariola and the children—with surprisingly few words, for Bosola—until Ferdinand comes in and provides a more malleable victim onto whom he can project his fears.

There is a certain delight in being able to confound an oppressor in this way. It is not simply a matter of survival, or stoical acceptance, or even belated self-discovery. There is something more to it, a "spiritual victory," celebrated in the humorous remarks attributed to all the religious and political martyrs of history, as well as to the heroes of such diverse genres as the romance, the hard-boiled detective story, and the war film. To reach the breaking point and discover that one's spirit is not broken is a thrilling experience, not only because one survives, but also because one has given "a foule checke mate to the tyrantes crueltie";[29] because somewhere in such an experience is the hint that wrong will *not* always conquer, that (as Chesterton says), "Even on earth, it may go ill / At last with the evil earls."[30]

If we could end on such a note, *The Duchess of Malfi* would stand as a highly optimistic document. But Webster did not end here; the Duchess's death is only the first in a series of ten, and (except for Julia) only one person dies on a note of self-possession like the Duchess's. Unfortunately, that person is one of her murderers.

The Cardinal is a strange figure. He does not appear to be afraid of anything; even his political maneuverings and murders seem to be done in a fit of boredom. Although he is a potentate of the church, he never mentions God or Heaven, and his two references to Hell and the Devil are defeatist and abstracted. After he has poisoned Julia, his words are curiously Faustian: "I would pray now: but the devil takes away my heart / For having any confidence in prayer" (5.4.27–28). And later, his musing on his own end is so offhand that it seems more like an academic problem than a personal concern:

> *Cardinal:* I am puzzled in a question about hell:
>   He says, in hell there's one material fire,
>   And yet it shall not burn all men alike.
>   Lay him by:—how tedious is a guilty conscience!
>   When I look into the fish-ponds, in my garden,
>   Methinks I see a thing, arm'd with a rake
>   That seems to strike at me.
>
>   (5.5.1–7)

R.W. Dent has cited a number of sources, classic and contemporary, for that chilling "thing arm'd with a rake"; these figures are portents of death, revenge, or damnation, and most often brandish a sword, although there are a few who carry rakes.[31] No doubt Webster was familiar with these passages, but he was also likely to be familiar with the iconography of death and Hell, and to have combined the verbal and pictorial images into one. In medieval and Renaissance depictions of the Judgment, the Devil drags souls into Hell with a rake; and the Cardinal's "thing," following so closely upon mention of Hell, might suggest such an image to Webster's audience. But the Devil is not the only figure who carries a rake. Dürer's Fourth Horseman of the Apocalypse swings a rake rather than a scythe, and in many pictures of the skeletonic Summons, the pursing Death often carries a rake, shovel, or pick-axe.[32]

The "thing" in the Cardinal's fish-pond, rather than being a specific figure drawn from any of Webster's sources, is more likely a deliberate compendium of all the literary and pictorial bogeys representing things beyond the world: ghosts, portents, devils, and death—all of which form the great "Ay, but to die and go we know not where" of the transitional skeptic imagination, the "agnostic spectacle" of which Tristram speaks (10). It is the very vagueness of the Cardinal's reference that makes the figure so horrifying: "Methinks I see a thing . . . / That seems. . . ." This is the nightmare, the thing at the periphery of the vision, the suspicion that even death is unreal because the universe itself is unreal, the hint that the Nothing that beckons us at the last is no different from the Nothing that already is. And the Cardinal often seems to be a representative of that Nothing.

Una Ellis-Fermor has rightly noted that the Cardinal "keeps his counsel to the end";[33] he is a kind of cosmic black hole in the universe of the play, who takes in everything and gives back nothing. If he has any fears at all, he is remarkably skilled, like Bosola, in projecting them onto others, and then, like the Duchess, in deriving a positive joy from watching his victims' discomfort. In 2.4, he deftly maneuvers the otherwise indomitable Julia this way; and similarly, he can easily stir up Ferdinand with some well-timed reticence:

> *Ferdinand:* Methinks I see her laughing—
> Excellent hyena!—talk to me somewhat, quickly,
> Or my imagination will carry me
> To see her, in the shameful act of sin.
> *Cardinal:* With whom?
>
> (2.5.38–42)

With that simple "With whom?" the Cardinal sets Ferdinand off on one of his most obsessive ravings; and when Ferdinand finally runs out of breath and invective, the Cardinal's "Are you stark mad?" (2.5.66) sets him off again. Like the Duchess, he has found the question to be the best weapon in a struggle for power.

Although the Cardinal appears, like the Duchess, to lose his composure at the end, he, too, quickly recovers. And it is Bosola, "the born loser,"[34] who, in trying to bring the Cardinal to despair, instead restores his sense of identity:

> *Bosola:*   I do glory
>   That thou, which stood'st like a huge pyramid
>   Begun upon a large and ample base,
>   Shalt end in a little point, a kind of nothing.
>
> (5.5.76–79)

What Bosola means as an insult the Cardinal takes as a compliment; he *insists* on being a "kind of nothing." For him, Claudio's fear is simply a fact, and in a hideous inversion of the neoplatonic ideal, to align himself with the meaning of the universe is to become one with the great Nothing—and to draw all others after him. Indeed, if Bosola thinks that the Cardinal will allow him to die as Something, to assert individual power over things and reap glory from the carnage on the stage, he is sadly mistaken. When Bosola has finished boasting about his revenge, the Cardinal calmly deflates him and dies with his self-possession intact:

> *Cardinal:* Look to my brother:
>   He gave us these large wounds as we were struggling
>   Here i' th' rushes:—and now, I pray, let me
>   Be laid by, and never thought of.
>
> (5.5.87–90)

"Let me be laid by." These are the same words that he used about his book on Hell: "lay him by." He has put forth as his ideal that which Bosola will (erroneously) say comes to all men, and which Delio will (piously) say comes to evil men: oblivion. In effect, the Cardinal, like the Duchess, has given the order for his own death and robbed others of their power over him. We may even say that his vices are the dark side of her virtues; that although the two characters seem to set forth for the opposite poles of Everything and Nothing, the same road serves for both.

We are left, then, with nothing certain in our own universe. If the admirable Duchess and the despicable Cardinal are so much alike, if darkness is safe and light deceiving, if everything is in fact so open to contradictory interpretations, what is the purpose of Webster's play—or, Webster might seem to ask, of life? The answer may be that the question is immaterial.

And in this way, *The Duchess of Malfi* differs from *Measure for Measure*—by leaving its characters with more questions than answers, much in the manner of the universe itself. Just as seventeenth-century essayists explore the nature of truth by enumerating types of error, so Webster has explored the nature of life by examining its dissolution. The world around the Duchess *is* disordered and chaotic; but she survives and even triumphs, not by trying to make sense out of the disordered pieces, but by building from within and not attempting to find cosmic solutions beyond her power. What Delio calls "integrity of life," and moderns might call "quality of life," is the victory. And sometimes it can be best shown in the moment of crisis, the time of "noise and folly," the hour of death.

X

Memento Mockery

The Old Iconography Begins to Slip

WHILE ALL THESE CHANGES were taking place in the dramatic representations of deathbed counseling, another tradition of death was also undergoing a transformation on the stage, sometimes in subtle, sometimes in more blatant ways. At first glance, the proliferation of skulls, skeletons, and dressed-up corpses on the Jacobean and Caroline stages might seem to indicate a return to the iconography of the Middle Ages: the Dreary Death who beckoned all to the grave. But beginning in the early Jacobean years, we can see something disturbingly different happening to the parade of bones and rotting flesh; the fearful pursuer is becoming a puppet in the hands of the living, and in many cases, a joke.

To be sure, the element of jesting was never entirely absent from the old iconography. In the Dances of Death, grinning skeletons kicked up their heels in grotesque good cheer, although their victims seldom joined in the fun; and a certain amount of badinage seems to have been expected even from devout practitioners of the memento mori exercise, the meditation on a dead man's skull. In Petrus Luccensis's *Dialogue of Dying Wel,* for example, a man addresses the skull of a dead youth in words that seem more mocking than fearful:

> Where bee thy fine yealow heares? where is thy faire white forehead? where is thy cleare shyning eyes? where is thy tongue that so well

could speak? where be all the liuelie sences of thy bodie? where is thy face so goodlie and so faire? where is thy trim delicate skin and flesh? Thow arte now without a nose, without eyes, without eares, thow haste not so much as one haire left vpon thy head: what rasor hath bene so cruel that it hath shauen away all thy haire and flesh, euen to the very bone? who hath taken away thy beautie? who hath made thee so monstrous and ill fauored? whereof cometh so great deformitie? Thow arte to vs that be liuing so horrible and vglie to beholde, that thow puttest euerie one in feare.[1]

The mockery of the old tradition, however, was a form of self-mockery. Like Chaucer's Troilus looking down from Heaven and laughing, the medieval and early Renaissance Christian laughed at the skull because he saw in it the absurdity of human pretensions before the throne of God. Such a concept cannot be stressed enough. It is not the sense that everything is ridiculous because it will one day collapse into Nothing, but rather a sense that it is absurd to care so much for an inferior product—both the skull and the flesh that clothes it—instead of the Everything that lies beyond it. In the first view, one looks into the skull's empty eye-sockets and sees only the bone at the back of the head; in the second, one looks beyond the bone into infinity.[2]

One of the last orthodox uses of the memento mori on the Renaissance stage is the famous graveyard scene in *Hamlet*. In fact, the progressive focusing of Hamlet's attention on the dead is in many ways similar to the progress of thought in *Everyman*: each time, the mode of thinking draws closer and closer to the self, and each time, it is more forcibly directed there by circumstances outside the self. Hamlet, however, begins in a more receptive frame of mind than Everyman did. Although his initial discourse is almost purely social satire on various estates—those of the politician, courtier, lady, lawyer, and landowner—in the midst of his satire he draws a moral that applies to himself, something that later, less orthodox playwrights will fail to do:

> *Hamlet:* And now my Lady Worm's chapless, and knocked about
> the mazzard with a sexton's spade. Here's fine revolution, an we

had the trick to see 't. Did these bones cost no more the breeding but to play at loggats with 'em? Mine ache to think on't.   (5.1.96–101)

And each time Hamlet tries to avoid "thinking on't," someone or something will bring the message home to him again, much like the old warning of the Legend.

First, Hamlet attempts to engage the gravedigger in a discussion of his trade: For whom is he digging this grave? How long has he been a gravedigger? "How long will a man lie i' the earth ere he rot?" (5.1.141–79). Such questioning is a means of distancing the subject of mortality; it proceeds from the current death to the living worker and finally to abstract scientific inquiry. But the gravedigger almost incidentally hands Hamlet the skull of Yorick, and Hamlet must suddenly face the mortality not of a social "type" but of someone intimately associated with his own childhood. Small wonder that his next words are more emotionally charged than his previous satire, comprising a highly personal mixture of regret, fear, laughter, and disgust:

> *Hamlet:* Alas, poor Yorick![3] I knew him, Horatio—a fellow of infinite jest, of most excellent fancy. He hath borne me on his back a thousand times, and now how abhorred in my imagination it is! My gorge rises at it. Here hung those lips that I have kissed I know not how oft. Where be your gibes now? Your gambols? Your songs? Your flashes of merriment that were wont to set the table on a roar? Not one now, to mock your grinning? Quite chopfallen? Now get you to my lady's chamber and tell her, let her paint an inch thick, to this favor she must come—make her laugh at that.   (5.1.202–14)

Forced to face the dissolution of the beautiful things that he knew in more innocent days—not merely Yorick, but his father, his mother's virtue, Ophelia's love, the courtiers' friendship, and the whole society of Denmark—Hamlet again tries to turn his meditation outward. He moralizes first on the anonymous lady of ll. 212–14, and then on Alexander the Great, a figure distanced by time and emblematic usage: "Why may not imagination trace the noble dust of Alexander till he find it stopping a bunghole?" (5.1.225–26). But again he is interrupted by mortality closer to home: Ophelia's funeral. This is a much more recent and an unexpected loss. And now all efforts at moralizing end, as Hamlet reacts with the elementary emotions of anger and grief. It is only in the next scene, after he has achieved the catharsis of looking death progressively closer in the face and evaluating his own responses to it, that Hamlet is able to reach acceptance even of his own death:

> *Hamlet:* Not a whit, we defy augury. There's special providence in the fall of a sparrow. If it be now, 'tis not to come; if it be not to come, it will be now; if it be not now, yet it will come. The readiness is all. Since no man has aught of what he leaves, what is 't to leave betimes? Let be. (5.2.230–35)

This is a reversal of Hamlet's two earlier soliloquies on death: the first, in which, although rejecting suicide as contrary to God's law, he viewed death as an escape from pain (1.2.129–59); and the second, in which he extrapolated the problem of being and not-being (the Aristotelian *on kai me on* that Faustus so cavalierly dismissed) to humanity in general, with the observance that the "dread of something after death . . . puzzles the will" and leads to an impasse where neither life nor death seems acceptable (3.1.56–88). Although we have seen Hamlet working out the solution to this problem throughout the play—that the human "will" should not presume to make decisions on life and death at all, such decisions being the jurisdiction of God—it is significant that Shakespeare has used the old iconography of the graveyard to lead to the "Let be" that echoes Horatio's observation in act 1:

"Heaven will direct it" (1.4.91). Ironically, although our own iconography often pictures Hamlet with a skull to show that he is
the "Melancholy Dane," it is through contemplating the skulls
of the graveyard that Hamlet banishes his melancholy forever.
We will seldom see such usage of the skull again in the drama
of the seventeenth century.

And yet, oddly enough, there is one graveyard scene during
this period that is, if possible, more orthodox than the one in
Hamlet; but its orthodoxy derives from a completely different tradition. Cyril Tourneur's *The Atheist's Tragedy* (ca. 1611) is essentially a revival of the Protestant Morality play of the 1560s and
1570s, in which the all-good hero is given the self-assurance not
to come to terms with death but almost to ignore it.

Although critics like Michael H. Higgins have noted the Calvinistic bifurcation of humankind in Tourneur's play, with its
ineluctably good characters on the one hand and ineluctably bad
ones on the other, these critics have for the most part overlooked
the dramatic heritage of their theme.[4] D'Amville himself, the
atheist of the play's title, often bears a striking resemblance to
the reprobate of the late Morality. At the beginning of the play,
he is a compendium of Worldly Man and Lust, propounding from
the first his disbelief in divine providence and a determination
to make his heaven in this world:

> D'Amville: Then if death casts up
>   Our total sum of joy and happiness,
>   Let me have all my senses feasted in
>   Th' abundant fullness of delight at once,
>   And with a sweet insensible increase
>   Of pleasing surfeit melt into my dust.
>   . . . .
>   Here are my sons. . . .
>   There's my eternity. My life in them
>   And their succession shall for ever live.
>   (1.1.16–21; 123–25)[5]

Like the morality reprobates, too, he is given a warning of doom,
which he chooses to explain away in quasi-scientific terms: "Dost

start at thunder? Credit my belief, / 'Tis a mere effect of Nature" (2.4.141–42). And like the Morality reprobate, he is warned again in his sleep, waking only to scoff at something so contrary to fact:

> [*Ghost of*] *Montferrers:* D'Amville, with all thy
> wisdom th'art a fool,
> Not like those fools that we term innocents,
> But a most wretched miserable fool,
> Which instantly, to the confusion of
> Thy projects, with despair thou shalt behold.
> [D'Amville starts up.]
> *D'Amville:* What foolish dream dares interrupt my rest
> To my confusion? How can that be . . . ?
> (5.1.27–32)

The echoes of *The Longer Thou Livest* are immediately apparent in this passage, both in the emphasis on blind folly and in the prediction of earthly confusion:

> *God's Judgment:* Thy wicked household shall be dispersed,
> Thy children shall be rooted out to the fourth degree. . . .
>
> *Confusion:* So at length evermore it cometh to pass
> That the folly of fools is openly blown,
> And then in this world they have confusion,
> That is, reproof, derision, and open shame.
> (*Longer*, 1792–93; 1829–32)

Even in the execution scene, D'Amville, like Moros, thinks that a cup of wine will drive away the strange sickness that he feels in the presence of death (*AT*, 5.2.201–05; *Longer*, 1803–04).

Other resemblances to the Protestant Morality are almost too numerous to mention here, but a particularly interesting one is the counseling that Languebeau Snuffe gives the ailing Montferrers. Although the bad counselor is now, significantly, a Puritan rather than a Catholic, it is almost impossible not to recognize in his speech the will-making scene in *Enough Is as Good as a Feast*:

> *Languebeau:* All men are mortal. The hour of death is uncertain. Age makes sickness the more dangerous, and grief is subject to distraction. . . . In my understanding, therefore, you shall

do well if you be sick to set your state in present order. Make
your will. (2.1.131–36)

And the execution scene itself is much like the end of *Trial of
Treasure*: Charlemont and Castabella (Just), having come through
the trial of God's Visitation with the aid of trust in God, are
given consolation in this world, while D'Amville (Lust) trembles
in fear and watches his worldly hopes crumble into rust and dust
before he himself is borne off by a providential accident.

In this context, the graveyard scene becomes a series of
emblems on the two opposed spiritual states. When Charlemont
enters, his meditation centers on the equalizing nature of death,
and the peace of the grave:

> *Charlemont:*   . . . O,
>   That man with so much labour should aspire
>   To worldly height, when in the humblest earth
>   The world's condition's at the best!
>
>   (4.2.17–20)

Later, to hide from his pursuers, he takes refuge in a charnel house,
and is even able to draw a moral from the slipping of a skull:

> *Charlemont:* I'll hide me here i'th' charnel house,
>   This convocation-house of dead men's skulls.
>
>   [To get into the charnel house
>   he takes hold of death's head;
>   it slips and staggers him.]
>   Death's head, deceiv'st my hold?
>   Such is the trust to all mortality.
>
>   (4.2.76–79)

Unfortunately, this moral, like the skull, has slipped from
Tourneur's control. In the other graveyard imagery it is life, not
death, that is uncertain. But later in the scene we return to the
comforts that the righteous find in mortality: Charlemont and
Castabella, suddenly drowsy in the midst of murder and attempted
rape, go placidly to sleep "with either of them a death's head for
a pillow" (S.D. 4.2.204). And there the two innocents remain,

upheld by trust, as Languebeau, in his amorous pursuit of Soquette, stumbles on the body of Boracchio:

> *Languebeau:* Verily thou liest in a fine premeditate readiness for the purpose. Come, kiss me, sweet Soquette.—Now purity defend me from the sin of Sodom! This is a creature of the masculine gender.—Verily the man is blasted.—Yea, cold and stiff!—Murder, murder.   [Exit.] (4.2.206–10)

There they remain, too, when D'Amville returns and "starts at the sight of a death's head" (S.D. 4.2.210):

> *D'Amville:* Why dost thou stare at me? Thou art not
> The skull of him I murder'd. What hast thou
> To do to vex my conscience? Sure thou wert
> The head of a most dogged usurer,
> Th'art so uncharitable.
>
> (4.2.211–15)

The emblematic contrasts are immediately obvious. Languebeau, the fleshly hyprocrite, finds in the corpse two sexual perversions: sodomy and necrophilia. D'Amville, the moneylender and murderer, finds in the skull an accusing nemesis and a self-portrait which he refuses to recognize. Both turn in horror from what they have seen—and the Jacobean audience might have noticed that the horrifying visions are similar to contemporary sermons on Hell, which threatened sinners with the most violent extremes of their earthly sins for all eternity, not as a reward but as a punishment. Meanwhile, Charlemont and Castabella sleep on peacefully, finding rest in death because of their blameless lives.

Although we can hardly compare *The Atheist's Tragedy* to *Hamlet* in merit, we can see in both the culmination of an older memento mori tradition: in the latter, a recognition and acceptance of one's own face in the skull; and in the former, an ability to disregard the skull altogether as a mere interruption between the good life and the good afterlife. But in the ten years between these two plays, something had already happened to make the symbols on which they relied virtually obsolete.[6]

In *Hamlet*, Horatio says of the gravedigger's occupation: "Custom hath made it in him a property of easiness" (5.1.75–76). And indeed, preachers of the memento mori exercise had warned that it was not to be overdone for this very reason. Petrus Luccensis delivers the caution along with his initial instructions:

> And the better to print this remembrance in themselues, some haue taken a dead mannes head, and kept it in a secret place, and certaine tymes in the week set it before their eyes, and verie wel and deligentlie considered it, and by way of imagination kept long talk with it, and this not euerie day but once or twise a week, because it so moueth, more our affection, then it would do yf euerie day wee should see the same: for by long custome being once made familiar vnto vs, it would moue vs nothing at all. (C3r)

It is a tribute to both Shakespeare's and Tourneur's dramatic skill that they were able to move their audiences by means of the overfamiliar, without having to add new gimmickry to do so. In fact, Shakespeare, as we have seen, was even able to capitalize on the overfamiliarity of the tradition by having his characters misuse or misunderstand, not the symbol itself, but an allusion to the symbol. Richard II exhibits his character flaws through the flaws in his description of the Dance of Death; and Falstaff, for all his jesting, brings the death's-head briefly before the audience out of the smeared countenance of Doll Tearsheet:

> *Doll:* Thou whoreson little tidy Bartholomew boar pig, when wilt thou leave fighting o' days and foining o' nights, and begin to patch up thine old body for Heaven?
> *Falstaff:* Peace, good Doll! Do not speak like a death's-head. Do not bid me remember mine own end. (*2 HIV*, 2.4.250–55)

The effect of this passage is similar to that elicited by Hal's reply, "I do. I will," to Falstaff's "Banish plump Jack and banish all the world" in *Part I* (2.4.526–27); the audience is suddenly aware that Falstaff is joking dangerously with forces beyond his control—like the old allegorical figures who declared, "Death, I defy thee!" and then died.

By the 1590s, of course, Doll Tearsheet was probably wearing a death's-head on her middle finger; and had she exhibited her ring instead of unconsciously speaking its message, Falstaff (and his audience) would most likely have dissolved into laughter. Such laughter was not uncommon in the decades to follow, when the association of bawds with death's-head rings had become standard comic fare. In Marston's *The Dutch Courtesan* (ca. 1604), Cocledemoy says of prostitutes: "As for their death, how can it be bad since their wickedness is always before their eyes, and a death's head most commonly on their middle finger?" (1.2.49–51);[7] Bellamont, in *Northward Ho* (Dekker et al., 1607), declares: "as if I were a bawd, no ring pleases me but a death's head" (4.1.157–58);[8] and in Massinger's *The Old Law* (ca. 1616), Gnotho tells his discarded wife: "Sell some of thy clothes to buy thee a death's head, and put upon thy middle finger: your least considering bawd does so much" (4.2; 583).[9] In chapters 1 and 2, I have outlined some of the causes for this raillery; now let us look at some effects.

Two of the pivotal scenes in Thomas Dekker's *The Honest Whore, Part 1* (ca. 1604) are the mock-funeral of Infelice in act 1 and Hippolito's address to a skull in act 4 (significantly, the other two are Bellafront's whorehouse and the madhouse confrontation that ends the play). In the first of these scenes, it is obvious that Dekker understands the growing obsolescence of his imagery. To open a play with a funeral had long been a way of predicting doom—a dramatic memento mori, one might say—but Dekker immediately undercuts the effect by placing traditional *sententiae* on death in the mouth of an unsympathetic character, and then by having the hero's best friend reject them:

> Duke: Na, na, be but patient:
>   For why death's hand hath sued a strict divorce
>   'Twixt her and thee: what's beauty but a corse?
>   What but fair sand-dust are earth's purest forms?
>   Queens' bodies are but trunks to put in worms.
> Matheo: Speak no more sentences, my good lord, but
>   slip hence.
>
>   (1.1.53–58)

We will later discover, too, that the Duke is uttering not only platitudes but lies; Infelice is drugged, not dead, and the whole funeral is a charade to rid the Duke of a distasteful potential son-in-law.

The ploy works temporarily. Hippolito, convinced that his Infelice is dead, rants in grief and anger over his loss and vows that he will henceforth spend every Monday—the day on which Infelice supposedly died—locked up in solitary meditation. But the order of his vow is significant:

> Hippolito: I swear to thee, Matheo, by my soul,
>   Hereafter weekly on that day I'll glue
>   Mine eyelids down, because they shall not gaze
>   On any female cheek. And being locked up
>   In my close chamber, there I'll meditate
>   On nothing but my Infelice's end,
>   Or on a dead man's skull draw out mine own.
>
>   (1.1.121–27)

The memento mori exercise, coming almost as an after-thought to what sounds perilously like a misanthropic (or, more accurately, misogynistic) sulk rather than genuine grieving, is as much of a platitude as the Duke's words. But here it is not certain whether Dekker is in complete command of his subject, whether he or Hippolito is about to skew the iconography into what Theodore Spencer sees as sensationalism rather than symbology.[10] Since Hippolito continues his rounds of worldly pleasures on days other than Monday, and in *Part II* will become a quasi villain who tries to lead Bellafront back into the sin that she has abandoned, Dekker does seem to recognize the perversities in Hippolito's frame of mind. But material to the plot of *Part I* is the fact that the skull scene does convert Bellafront from sin in the first place; so the scene remains an uneasily transitional one, its efficacy looking back to an old tradition and its perversity looking ahead to a new.

The very nature of Hippolito's meditation has begun slipping from the norm. Of its fifty-four lines, the first twenty-one are an address to Infelice's portrait, rather than to the skull. Hippolito contrasts Infelice's natural beauty with two kinds of "painting": first, the cosmetics used by "fond women," and next, the inadequate representation of true beauty in portraiture. In effect, Hippolito must make a transition from the trope of true and false beauty into that of life and death, not through the *de contemptu mundi* tradition, but through the new secular debate on *ut pictura poesis*:

> *Hippolito:* Nothing of her but this? This cannot speak;
>   It has no lap for me to rest upon,
>   No lip worth tasting: here the worms will feed,
>   As in her coffin. Hence, then, idle Art;
>   True love's best pictured in a true-love's heart.
>
> (4.1.48–52)

When Hippolito finally does turn to the skull, he turns not only from Infelice's picture but from Infelice herself. "What's here?" he exclaims. "Perhaps this shrewd pate was mine enemy's" (55–56). And for seven more lines, he points out such as enemy's inability to harm him, all the ploys of the living being "picked away! to the bare bone!" (63). Although this passage is obviously modeled on the social satire of the old tradition, it is seriously weakened by Hippolito's relish in triumphing over a fallen enemy, as well as by the absence of specific allusion to a particular type or class. Finally, thirty-one lines into his meditation, Hippolito acknowledges that all flesh will come to this; but even here, his words have grown out of a new secularity:

> *Hippolito:* What fools are men to build a garish tomb
>   Only to save the carcass whilst it rots,
>   To maintain 't long in stinking, make good carrion,

> But leave no good deeds to preserve them sound,
> For good deeds keep men sweet, long above ground.
>
> (4.1.71–75)

Note that the "good deeds" here are not Everyman's means to salvation, but Renaissance man's means to good fame.[11] The whole concept of otherworldly immortality has disappeared, and because Hippolito has specified the skull as an "enemy," he almost seems to be holding himself up as an exemplar of those good deeds.

Hippolito's meditation ends, as it began, on art: "Draw me my picture, then, thou grave neat workman, / After this fashion, not like this" (78–79)—that is, like the skull, not the picture. The colours of a portrait wear off, he explains, "But here's a fellow: that which he lays on, / Till doomsday alters not complexion. / Death's the best painter, then" (81–83). It is a clever summation, with two more rhymed couplets to come (like the Duke's remarks earlier in the play), but its very cleaverness runs contrary to the orthodox meditation on death. Instead of seeking solace, or a lesson on his own mortality, Hippolito has set himself up as Death's patron, giving an approving nod to the artistry of "the best painter" and a disparaging scowl to human portraiture. He has not accepted death; he has put himself in control of it.

The Honest Whore, then, is an uneasy compromise between the old and the new: still half-convinced that the old tradition ought to work, but no longer quite sure *how* it ought to work. There will be a few more such compromises as we go along, but they will become more infrequent and far more uneasy. Like Hippolito, a new generation of dramatic figures will make the skeleton dance to their own tune—and the music, accordingly, will jar.

Perhaps the most extensive example of this new tune can be found in a nondramatic work published some two years after *The Honest Whore*: Samuel Rowland's *A Terrible Battell Betweene Time and Death* (1606).[12] Beginning and ending as a traditional Dance of Death, the poem degenerates halfway through into a slapstick farce in which Time and Death become more ridiculous than their victims. At first, the two vow cooperation; Time reminds Death that "My Sythe cuts downe; vpon thy dart they die, / Thou hast an houre glasse, and so haue I" (5), and Death joins Time in laughing about how mortal creatures waste their time, giving their "finest corne" of youth to the devil; "And when the night of age brings painfull grones, / Then in Gods dish they cast their rotten bones" (6). Death even jokes about the way people try to use a memento mori to forget death rather than remember it:

> *Death*: Some make my picture a most common thing,
>   As if I were continual in their thought,
>   A *Deaths hed* seale vpon a great gold ring,
>   And round about *Memento Mori* wrought:
>   Which memory with gold cannot agree,
>   For he that hates the same best thinks on me.
>
> (7)

After some ten pages of social satire on their victims, however, Time and Death begin to resent each other's claims to importance. Time announces that it is he who is "Gods agent in affaires, / And hath bin so, euer since the creation" (28). He alone seats and deposes kings, and he alone orders the sun, moon, and stars. Death replies that there is no need to brag, because "At least thy selfe knowes I am full as good, / Being Gods steward, sinnes reward to pay" (29). Surely all men recognize this, he adds, because everyone fears Death, "but prethee tell me, what is he fears *Time*?" (32). Obviously, men have not the slightest respect for Time, and "euery hower neglect thee" (32). Time then gives Death the lie direct, and the battle is on:

> *Death*: What (Father gray-beard) doth your choler rise?
>   Can you so ill digest to heare your crimes?
> *Time*: Why goodman bone-face, with your vaulty eies,
>   What is't to me if men abuse their *Times*?
>   Where learnd your dry and empty pate the skil,
>   That *Time* should answere for mens doing il.
>
> (33)

It is fairly obvious what will happen from here on, and in fact the invective that follows is comical in the extreme. The following passage is particularly interesting:

Time: Thou lookest like the inside of a tombe,
  All rotten bones, with sinnews bound togither,
  Thy guts are gone, for they lack belly roome,
  And al thy flesh is lighter than a feather:
  Thy head is like an empty drie oil iarre,
  Where neather teeth, nor nose, nor eies there are.

From eare to eare thou hast a mouth vnshut,
  With armes and hands like to a Gardners rake,
  Thy ribs shew like a leather ierkin cut,
  Thy voice resembles hissing of a snake:
  Thy legs appeare a paire of Crane-stilts right,
  And al thy formes more vgly than a sprite.

Thy picture stands vpon the Ale-house wall,
  Not in the credit of an ancient story,
  But when the old wiues guests begin to braule,
  She points, and bids them read *Memento Mori:*
  Looke, looke (saies she) what fellow standeth there,
  As women do, when crying Babes they feare.

                                    (35–36)

Time has transformed all the frightening aspects of the old iconography into absurdities by comparing them to household objects
used by members of the lower or servant classes, and has thus
made not only the imagery but death itself laughable. In the third
stanza, too, Time has taken Death's previous mockery of those
who disregard the true meaning of memento mori, and has shifted
it to the memento mori itself, making it meaningless. The alewife
to whom he refers so slightingly has, after all, attempted to rec-
tify men's behavior by calling their attention to their destined
ends; but because Time heaps such scorn on her and her kind,
the reader is forced to view the whole exercise as a childish or
"womanish" thing. The tension of Shakespeare's Doll-Falstaff
scene has no place here.

Time and Death eventually make up their quarrel and go
about their business, and the poem ends with the ominous toll-
ing of a bell. But the reader is left with an impression different
from that inspired by the old Dance of Death: through laughter
at a physical image of death, he has been able to forget death's

physical pangs. Much of this effect comes from Rowland's choice of speakers. In the old literature, Death or the dead spoke seriously of their horrors, and any jesting on the subject was allowed only to a Vice, who was obviously and dangerously mistaken,[13] or to a living creature mocking human pride through the medium of a skull. Thus, *la mort*—Death itself—could be mocked only at one's peril; and *le mort*—the dead person—was a vehicle for mockery of *le vif*, the living. However, in the *Terrible Battle*, because the ridicule is placed in the mouths of Time and Death, the final effect is very like that of the battles between Morality Vices: the audience sees the quarreling figures as ineffectual rather than all-conquering.

This analogy is not altogether an empty one. Just as the medieval playwrights had made the Vices comic to show that vice is not insuperable, so seventeenth-century religious poets often ridiculed the allegorical figure of Death to point up Christ's victory over death. Both the familiarity of overuse and the religious search for new comforts, then, have seized on the comic grotesque of the skeleton, and danger now lies in two directions: first, in taking the outmoded symbol seriously without providing a serious framework that will explain it; and second, in confusing the symbol with reality—the dead body with Death—and then mocking the wrong one. Both dangers can lead to mere sensationalism; and in addition, the first carries seeds of unintentional comedy, the second, of moral schizophrenia.

It is this second danger that is illustrated in *The Revenger's Tragedy* (ca. 1607), although, unlike other plays that succumb to the danger, here the error lies not in the playwright's mind but in the mind of the revenger-hero, who jests at the dead until he no longer fears Death. But by then, he has gone mad.[14]

The Revenger's Tragedy is unquestionably a play about death. Daniel J. Jacobson has pointed out that the play contains "over eighty-five references to death and dying, and the word *death* itself is the most frequently occurring noun in the play. . . . [E]ven *Hamlet* does not contain as many references to death."[15] Samuel Schoenbaum sees the "essence of *The Revenger's Tragedy*" as "the blending of the motif of lust and the motif of death."[16] And Una

Ellis-Fermor, adapting the imagery of the play to her description of its characters, says:

> [The horror] comes to us . . . from the aroma of evil with which Tourneur by the aid of diction and verbal music surrounds these walking anatomies, these galvanized laboratory subjects, and from the very fact that, being dead, they do so adequately mimic life.[17]

Ellis-Fermor's metaphor of "walking anatomies" is well chosen, and, in fact, as the playwright is to his characters, so Vindice is to the skull of Gloriana, which Marjorie Garber has likened to "a ventriloquist's dummy" in Vindice's hands.[18]

But Vindice is not just a ventriloquist. He is a vaudeville impresario of death. His very opening lines, as he stands with skull in hand watching the procession across stage of the Duke, the Duchess, Spurio, and Lussurioso, are reminiscent of the Mystery *Judgment* plays—the consigning of "types" or "characters" to hell:

> *Vindice:* Duke! royal lecher! Go, gray-hair'd adultery,
> And thou his son, as impious steep'd as he,
> And thou his bastard, true-begot in evil,
> And thou his duchess that will do with devil:
> Four exc'lent characters.
>
> (1.1.1–5)[19]

Vindice will use the imperative mood again and again in staging his productions, assuming in turn the roles of prompting devil, sender of death, tempting Vice, and Dance of Death choreographer; until at last he will look up to Heaven and order his own applause. But in taking up these roles, he will turn all the iconography upside down.

Directly after his apostrophe to the damned souls, Vindice turns his attention to the skull in his hand. His opening address to it is worth quoting at length:

> *Vindice:* Thou sallow picture of my poisoned love,
> My studies' ornament, thou shell of death,
> Once the bright face of my betrothed lady,

When two heaven-pointed diamonds were set
In those unsightly rings—then 'twas a face
So far beyond the artificial shine
Of any woman's bought complexion
That the uprightest man (if such there be,
That sin be seven times a day) broke custom
And made up eight with looking after her.

(1.1.14–25)

The very first line is full of ambiguities. Before the audience discovers that the skull is that of a real "love"—that is, Vindice's lady—"poisoned love" sounds like an abstract phrase, loving that has in some way been thwarted, disappointed, or turned from its ideal purpose. The "sallow picture" then sounds like an emblematic representation: "Thou metaphoric symbol of my disappointed hopes (or warped nature)." Ironically, that is what the skull really is, although Vindice will never realize it; but the third line of his address, meant to clarify and provide exposition, obscures the deeper truth that lies behind the more immediate one.

The ambiguities continue in Vindice's description of the "bright face" with its "heaven-pointed diamonds." In neoplatonic imagery, light is associated not only with beauty but also with virtue and truth—all pointed heavenward to the One. Diamonds are perhaps an unusual jewel to mention in connection with eyes, but even here, the brightness of the many-faceted gem suggests a many-faceted reflection of the One. Unfortunately, the next lines shatter the whole neoplatonic image. Vindice contrasts Gloriana's natural beauty with the "artificial shine" of "bought complexions," a standard poetic figure that leads us to expect an orthodox meditation on the flesh as mask for mortality, as cosmetics are masks for flesh. But instead, Vindice speaks of his lady's beauty only as a temptation to vice. Unlike the neoplatonic ideal, this beauty is not allied to truth; it does not raise men's eyes to Beauty and then to God, but rather pulls the most righteous men down to lust and then to Hell.

In the next passage, even the sacramental kiss of neoplatonism is brought down to the level of dross:

> *Vindice:* O she was able to ha' made a usurer's son
>   Melt all his patrimony in a kiss
>   And what his father fifty yeares told
>   To have consum'd, and yet his suit been cold.
>
> (1.1.26–29)

We have here not only an image of prostitution (and an exorbitantly priced prostitute at that), but an echo of Helen's succubus-kiss in *Doctor Faustus*, further emphasized by the sexual connotations of "melt" and "consum'd."[20] The Gloriana of Vindice's perception, then, emerges as a progressively more corrupt travesty on the ideal love; Vindice's "love" is indeed "poisoned" in more ways than one.

Disgust with the flesh, of course, is standard in the memento mori exercise. But Vindice has transferred his disgust from passive corruption (the decay of the flesh and transience of earthly delights) to active corruption (the turning of the will to sin). As a result, he has lost the traditional sense of contrast between the seemingly beautiful things of the world and the end product of human mortality, from which contrast one concludes that the worldly is insufficient and only the eternal truly beautiful. Instead, he has led the audience to expect an entirely different moral: "The wages of sin is death." It comes as a shock, therefore, to discover in the next passage that Vindice's lady has died because she would *not* sin, because she has rejected the lustful advances of the Duke.

Vindice has inverted all the traditional imagery of love and death, and has drawn all the wrong conclusions from his evidence. He will have everything both ways: Gloriana is both a courtesan and a virgin martyr; her skull is both a murder victim and a murder weapon; for Vindice, these are not contradictions but poetic justice. And in his colloquy to the skull, he continues to miss the point of what he is dealing with. Turning the skull outward, and thereby thrusting death away both literally and metaphorically, he declares his intent to have revenge and falls once more into the imperative mood: "Advance thee, O thou terror to fat folks, / To have their costly three-pil'd flesh worn off / As bare as this" (1.1.45–47). Like Tamburlaine, he will make Death his puppet—but in doing so, he will turn his whole world upside down. Skulls and corpses will become for him the only reality: he will create them in order to mock them. But because he has first made a skull live for him, life and death will become hopelessly confused in his mind.

Vindice is obsessed with the skeletonic symbol that he substitutes for reality, and, as Peter B. Murray notes, by a dramatic sleight of hand the playwright keeps the audience attuned to this obsession even when Vindice is offstage: "Repeated allusions to human brows, faces, and heads keep the image of the skull ever before our minds, as it is constantly before the mind of Vindice."[21] We are therefore prepared to read a third meaning into his words when, in the guise of Piato, he tells Lussorioso that he is a "bone-setter" (1.3.42). His punning explanation, of course, is that he is not a surgeon but "A bawd, my lord. / One that sets bones together" (1.3.43–44); but we know, too, that he is planning to create corpses, and in act 3 we shall discover that he means to play games with the corpses, to "set" them in postures of his own choosing.

It is in the pivotal scene of the play, the killing of the Duke, that we see what this obsession leads to. Vindice, to trap the Duke, has promised him an assignation with a lady, and to keep his promise, he dresses up the skull of Gloriana in a dress and mask. His second address to the skull, then, begins as a pander would speak to a whore:

> *Vindice:* Madame, his grace will not be absent long.—
> Secret? ne'er doubt us, madam. 'Twill be worth
> Three velvet gowns to your ladyship.—Known?
> Few ladies respect that disgrace: a poor thin shell!
>
> (3.5.43–46)

This brief, sarcastic speech is filled with echoes. The "poor thin shell" recalls Vindice's earlier "thou shell of death"; the "Three velvet gowns" is a similar numerically specific offer as the "nine coaches waiting" that he offered to his sister in order to test her virtue (2.1.202); and the very manipulation of the helpless puppet is like the rape of Antonio's wife:

> *Antonio:* Then with a face more impudent than his vizard
> He harried her amidst a throng of panders,
> That live upon damnation of both kinds,
> And fed the ravenous vulture of his lust.
>
> (1.4.41–44)

Vindice, too, wears a "vizard"—the alias of Piato—and has earlier called on "Impudence! / Thou goddess of the palace" for inspiration (1.3.5–14). In effect, he is helping the Duke commit a rape. But what a rape! The skeletonic whore to whom he speaks so insultingly is Gloriana, the woman he once loved. Othello's similar manner of speaking to Desdemona (4.2.24–94) is shocking because deliberate, but since Vindice has focused his attention on the skull rather than on reality, he hardly notices what he is doing, and the audience is liable to overlook it as well.

Vindice's perversity becomes more obvious in his words just prior to his memento mori address proper. Hippolito, echoing Vindice's own praise of Gloriana's beauty, in both Faustian and neoplatonic terms, asks: "Is this the form that, living, shone so bright?" (3.5.66). And Vindice replies:

> *Vindice:* The very same.
> And now methinks I could e'en chide myself
> For doting on her beauty, though her death
> Shall be reveng'd after no common action.
>
> (3.5.67–70)

This is the height of self-deception. Her death, in fact, will not be avenged; it will be made into a piece of mockery—and mockery not only of the Duke but also of his innocent victim. Gloriana, whose virtue and natural beauty were earlier contrasted with the painted complexions of evil women, has been painted in the cosmetics that she once despised, and with poison on her "lips" will be subjected to the embrace of a man whom she died to avoid embracing. But Vindice has almost forgotten Gloriana in his intoxication with skulls; and in this context, his memento mori speech should be all the more chilling, not because it is less orthodox than the first, but because it is more orthodox:

Vindice: Does the silkworm expend her yellow labors
   For thee? for thee does she undo herself?
   Are lordships sold to maintain ladyships
   For the poor benefit of a bewitching minute? . . .
   Does every proud and self-affecting dame
   Camphire her face for this? and grieve her Maker
   In sinful baths of milk, when many an infant starves,
   For her superfluous outside?—all for this? . . .
   Thou may'st lie chaste now! It were fine, methinks,
   To have thee seen at revels, forgetful feasts,
   And unclean brothels. . . .
   Here might a scornful and ambitious woman
   Look through and through herself.—See, ladies, with
      false forms
   Your deceive men, but cannot deceive worms.

                                        (3.5.71–97)

The words of this speech are worthy of Petrus Luccensis or
Hamlet. But the meaning that should animate them is absent.
Hamlet, following the medieval tradition, saw in the dissolution
of the flesh a message that the eternal is all important; that one
must reform oneself and abide the end; that "Heaven will direct
it. . . . Let be." Dekker's Hippolito, in his Renaissance secular-
ism, drew the natural corollary that if there is a corruption, there
must be an ideal state from which it is corrupted; and that since
"good deeds keep men sweet, long above ground," one must work
toward establishing those good deeds, even if only by reforming
others. But Vindice neither absorbs the moral into himself nor
directs it outward to others. Like his real-world counterparts of
the seventeenth century who tried to imitate the Dance of Death
without seeing beyond the skull to the spirit, he has come to view
the human creature simply as part of the food chain: a dish for
worms. But also like those writers, he exempts himself from the
vision; all human endeavor is absurd—except his own. Failing
to see the paradox that he has created, he then condemns himself
in terms of his own meditation: "Now nine years' vengeance crowd
into a minute!" (3.5.121). He has already forgotten his laughter,
barely fifty lines earlier, at mortals who ignore their mortality

in "the poor benefit of a bewitching minute." And, tragically, he no longer cares.

From the moment when Vindice positions the skull to kill (his "poisoned love" now truly bearing poison), his preoccupation with creating more skulls grows to hysterical proportions. He can hardly wait for the caustic poison to eat the flesh off the Duke's skull, and must offer to help it along:

> Vindice: What! Is not thy tongue eaten out yet?
>   Then we'll invent a silence. . . .
>   [To Hippolito:] . . . Now with thy dagger
>   Nail down this tongue. . . .
>   If he but wink, not brooking the foul object,
>   Let our two other hands tear up his lids
>   And make his eyes like comets shine through blood.
>   (3.5.190–99)

Almost, this sounds like an address to a potential skull: "Where is thy cleare shyning eyes? where is thy tongue that so wel could speak?" And pleased with the skull that he is making, Vindice, like God looking upon His created universe, finds it good: "When the bad bleeds, then is the tragedy good" (3.5.200).

The self-appointed revenger has become a self-appointed God—a God of corpses. Whereas in the first part of the play he disguised the living (himself) and tempted them to lust and murder (Castiza, Lussurioso), now his mind turns to disguising the dead (Gloriana, the Duke) and performing all the murders himself. It is as though he must himself respond to the petition in the Book of Common Prayer: "Prevent us in all our doings"; he alone must supervise the revels of the dead.

Now his parodic shows come thick and fast. To Lussurioso, he delivers an emblem straight out of the illustrations in the medieval *Ars moriendi*:

> Vindice: Why, to think how a great rich man lies a-dying, and a
>   poor cobbler tolls the bell for him. How he cannot depart the
>   world and see the great chest stand before him; when he lies
>   speechless, how he will point you readily to all the boxes; and
>   when he is past all memory, as the gossips guess, then thinks

he of forfeitures and obligations; nay, when to all men's hearings he whurls and rottles in the throat, he's busy threat'ning
his poor tenants. (4.2.68–75)

Several medieval traditions are jumbled up in this speech: the
Morality souls dying in avarice, the Mystery devils triumphing
over their prey, and the Death Signs lyrics ("when the throte
roteleth"), with, however, the wrong response of the sinner rather
than the "Miserere" of the penitent. In his own way, Vindice
is giving the warning of the Legend; but again he has perverted
the tradition. He does not want his listener to repent; evil is now
necessary to him as a rationale for creating more corpses.

Unfortunately, Vindice does not notice when the universe
that he is laughing at begins to laugh back; if he hears anything
at all, he assumes that the laughter is *with* him, not *at* him. When
Lussurioso departs, Vindice calls upon the Heaven of his own
making for a sign of vengeance but does not notice that in again
using the word *impudent* he may be giving Heaven an ambiguous
command. Only Hippolito, for a moment, seems to hear an equivocal message in the thunder:

> *Vindice:* O thou almighty patience! 'Tis my wonder
>   That such a fellow, impudent and wicked,
>   Should not be cloven as he stood,
>   Or with a secret wind burst open!
>   Is there no thunder left, or is't kept up
>   In stock for heavier vengeance? [*Thunder.*]
>   There it goes![22]
> *Hippolito:* Brother, we lose ourselves.

(4.2.189–95)

The phrase "we lose ourselves" is itself ambiguous, and in more
ways than Hippolito imagines. To him, it may mean, "we are
straying from the purpose," "we have overestimated our ability,"
or "we are getting hysterical." But to the old audiences of the
Mystery and Morality plays, it would also have meant, "we are
causing our own damnation." And, indeed, even modern criticism
is almost unanimous in sensing that, from this moment, Vindice

has slipped the bonds of all reality and begun to charge headlong to his own destruction.

The final scene of the play is Vindice's final mockery: a parody on the Dance of Death. He and Hippolito will impersonate the masquers at the revels for the new Duke Lussurioso and, entering before them, will kill Lussurioso. The Dance, like so many of Vindice's productions, will have a comic encore. But now fate (or the playwright) is beginning to parody Vindice. Spurio, Ambitioso, and Supervacuo—the masquers to be impersonated—themselves have planned a masque of death for Lussurioso; it is only a question of who gets there first.

Vindice arrives first, of course, and the would-be murderers of the second group fall on each other in suspicion and kill each other. Although the script has run away from Vindice, who had hoped only for the execution of the masquers and an alibi for himself, he has what he wanted: eight corpses at the revels, including four attendant lords. Why, then, having successfully manipulated Death through parody, and thus having emerged safe from death, does he confess to the murder of the Duke and call down death on himself after all?

The most obvious answer is that, like any showman, Vindice requires the applause of an audience. His original response to the thunder indicated such a need—and when the thunder speaks again during his death masque, he delightedly takes another verbal bow:

> Vindice: Mark, thunder!
>   Dost know thy cue, thou big-voic'd crier?
>   Dukes' groans are thunder's watchwords. . . .
>   No power is angry when the lustful die;
>   When thunder claps, heaven likes the tragedy.

> (5.3.42–44; 47–48)

Therefore, when Antonio evinces wonder at the "strangeliest carried" murder of the "old duke" (5.3.90–93), Vindice may be expected to step forward and preen himself again. And so he does:

Vindice: We may be bold to speak it now.
'Twas somewhat witty carried though we say it:
'Twas we two murder'd him.

(5.3.94–96)

It is a rather cavalier confession, and one can hardly blame Antonio for wanting to rid himself of such a casual murderer. But even as he is being led off to be executed, Vindice remains the showman, speaking his curtain line much in the manner of an epilogue to a comedy:

Vindice: We have enough,
I'faith, we're well: our mother turn'd our sister true,
We die after a nest of dukes—adieu.

(5.3.122–24)

And yet, Vindice's showmanship is only part of the reason for his smiling exit. To understand what else has happened to him, let us look at three other characters' variations on the art of dying.

Lussurioso is, of course, the standard Bad Example. We have seen him reject Vindice's blockbook emblem of the dying miser, and before the fatal masque, he denies Death again by encouraging his flattering courtiers to vie with each other in wishing him long life (5.3.30–36; the winner is Third Noble, who hopes that Lussurioso will never die). For both Vindice and the audience, then, Lussurioso has been set up as the classic Herod-figure who must be struck down at the moment of proclaiming his immortality. Vindice knows this, and accordingly strikes him down.

The Duke is another case. When Lussurioso breaks into his room, thinking to find and kill Spurio there, the Duke bargains for his life in words that are patently hypocritical:

Duke: O take me not in sleep!
I have great sins; I must have days,
Nay, months, dear son, with penitential heaves,
To lift 'em out, and not to die unclear.
O, thou wilt kill me both in heaven and here.

(2.3.9–13)

This is the plea of Everyman and Faustus: more time, more time. But Faustus would not repent, no matter how much time he was given, and everyone on- and offstage knows that the Duke will not repent. Vindice in particular knows it, and accordingly strikes the Duke down.

But then there is the odd case of Junior. Condemned to death for the rape of Antonio's wife, he expects to be released by his brothers. But they are tricked into bringing the warrant for his execution,[23] and Junior dies cursing them. His plea is also for more time—but time for curses:

> *First Officer:*   The hour beckons us,
>   The headman waits; lift up your eyes to heaven.
> *Youngest Son:*[24] I thank you, faith; good, pretty-wholesome
>   counsel!
>   I should look up to heaven, as you said,
>   Whilst he behind me cozens me of my head.
>   Ay, that's the trick.
> *Third Officer:*   You delay too long, my lord.
> *Youngest Son:* Stay, good Authority's bastards; since I must
>   Through brothers' perjury die, O let me venom
>   Their souls with curses.
>
>   (3.4.68–76)

This is straightforward impenitence that rejects good counsel at the Summons and mocks Death even at the last moment. The result, however, is unexpected: Junior's amorality leads him not only to a brave death, but to one very like Vindice's in its perverse insistence on his innocence:

> *Youngest Son:* Must I bleed then, without respect of sign?
>   Well—
>   My fault was sweet sport, which the world approves;
>   I die for that which every woman loves.
>
>   (3.4.77–79)

Because of the trickery involved in this death, and Junior's banter at its approach, the impression left is one of almost accidental death, even though, in the strictest sense, Junior's overconfidence has set him up for a fall like Lussurioso's.

But Vindice does not see this last scenario, which plays itself out without his assistance, or the mocking, Vindice-like bow that Junior takes at the end of it. Thus, as far as Vindice can tell, he alone has played the role of Death. He has arranged the bodies, set out the stage, given all the directions, waited for his own cue, and stepped in as Death, to the wild applause of heaven and earth. Like many other actors acclaimed for long-running performances in a single role, Vindice has gradually confused his real identity with his stage identity; to give still another meaning to Hippolito's observation, he has too thoroughly "lost himself" in his role. He does not believe that he can die.

Vindice, then, has overreached himself in staging his Dance of Death—not just the masque but the whole series of comic turns with skulls and corpses. And here I should like to take issue with two important critics who have added much to our understanding of the play, but who, I think, have missed the playwright's culminating irony. Samuel Schoenbaum has compared *The Revenger's Tragedy* to a Dance of Death, but implies that the whole play is a dance staged by the playwright, and Vindice only one of the human dancers: "For in the background of the revels lurks always the leering figure of Death, ever ready to join the dance."[25] To some extent this is true; Vindice certainly does not notice the "leering figure" who waits at his shoulder while he is choreographing his own dance. Again, L. G. Salingar has compared the play to a Morality, in which "The contrast between the skeleton and the specious overlay provided by wealth and sensuality is fundamental."[26] This, too, has some foundation, and I have certainly had enough occasion to note both the playwright's and Vindice's use of medieval tradition. But I should like to suggest that the dance and the morality alike are primarily Vindice's domain, and that the playwright has used Vindice to tell another Pardoner's Tale.

We remember that in Chaucer's tale, the three revelers showed both too much respect and too much disrespect for a personified figure of Death; in seeking to kill the "theef," they forced Death into a finite shape outside themselves and ignored the seeds of death within themselves. Vindice, too, in his obsession with and mockery of dead bodies, fails to see the true death that lies within his corrupt society, exemplified by the playwright in the comedies of errors beyond Vindice's control: Junior's accidental death at the hands of his attempted rescuers, and the melee of sequential killings during the death-masque.[27] Therefore, in arrogating to himself the role of Death (like Chaucer's revelers trying to inflict death on Death), Vindice becomes part of his corrupt society and is subject to the corruption of death. Like the revelers, too, he ignores the supernatural warning—the voice in the thunder—but, with an additional fillip of dramatic irony, he also misses the warning in the skull.

Both *The Revenger's Tragedy* and Rowland's *Terrible Battle*, then, work to the same end, although one makes us shudder and the other makes us laugh.[28] Both reject the literality of skull and skeleton—and *The Revenger's Tragedy*, in addition, rejects the too obsessive rejection. There comes a point in every iconoclastic movement, after all, when the obsession with tearing down idols becomes as superstitious as the idol-worship itself; neither the iconoclast nor the idolator, one might say, can exist without the idol. And yet, it is difficult to depict internal struggle on the stage without recourse to some sort of symbol. How some seventeenth-century dramatists coped with this problem I discuss in my next chapter. Let us now look at others who did not cope very well: those who struggled too hard to abandon the idol and fell into Vindice's traps of beating (as it were) a dead skeleton; and those who, not realizing that the idol had fallen, continued to use a symbol that had become only a bogey—with disastrous results.

Such a result may be seen in a play like Chettle's *The Tragedy of Hoffman* (ca. 1603).[29] Hoffman's father has been killed (whether justly or unjustly is never quite established) by having a "burning crown" set on his head and then his flesh stripped from his bones; Hoffman has been allowed to take the skeleton with him only under a vow not to bury it. As the play opens, we see Hoffman apostrophizing the skeleton, which, with a perverse sort of fidelity to his vow, he has hung from a tree until he can exact vengeance on his dead father's enemies. When he does find one

one of them, he takes pains to use the same methods that killed his father—burning crown, hanging skeleton, and all.

We now have *two* skeletons hanging from the tree, and we may wonder how Hoffman will tell them apart in the future. In the old iconography, nonindividualized skeletons symbolized equality in death. Will Hoffman now either love or hate both dead men equally? Obviously not. Nor can we assume that Chettle is proposing a moral invisible to Hoffman alone, because when the victim's mother, the "virtuous" Martha, discovers her son's skeleton, she reacts just as Hoffman had—leaves it hanging on the tree as a spur to her own revenge. And when Hoffman himself is killed with a burning crown at the end of the play, we may begin to wonder whether we will now see *three* skeletons hanging from the tree. We can barely see the forest for the bones.

But in spite of all the grinning skulls, what is missing from *The Tragedy of Hoffman* is an acknowledgment of mortality. By manipulating the symbols of death, the characters create the illusion that they are in control of death; but in the process, they must also deny their own human response to it. Hence, we see no grief or consolation for grief, no indication that the living or dead are part of the universal human family. The skeletons, symbols that are no longer symbolic, hang from the tree until they are carried off by the stagehands, and the spectators, both on stage and off, go home secure in the thought that such symbols have nothing to do with them.

It is interesting to note that in some later variants, the skull and skeleton almost seem to have nothing to do with their plays. At the wedding that opens Middleton's *The Witch* (1609? 1615?), for example, the Duke toasts the bride and groom in a skull, and then passes the skull around to the rest of the party, excepting only the governor, who has been ill, and the bride "whose health it is"—an unfortunate pun.[30] The women are horrified, the men think the exercise an "ill omen," and everyone except the Duchess refuses to drink, although we discover that the Duchess, of all people, should be the most unwilling:

> Duke: Our duchess, I know, will pledge us, though the cup
> Was once her father's head, which as a trophy,
> We'll keep till death in memory of that conquest.
> He was the greatest foe our steel e'er struck at,
> And he was bravely slain: then took we thee
> Into our bosom's love: thou mad'st the peace
> For all thy country, thou, that beauty did.
>
> (1.1; p. 124)

Such a gruesome bit of quasi cannibalism is hard to understand in the context of the play. The "ill omen" never comes to pass, except for some expected plot complications; no one thinks to moralize on the skull as a "skeleton at the feast"; the Duchess has enough grounds on which to resent her husband without the aid of gratuitous macabre; and, in fact, no one mentions the skull again at all until the last few lines of the play, when the Duke, reconciled to his wife, offers to give her father's remains decent burial. Since everything ends happily, why is the skull introduced in the first place? Middleton seems to have no more idea than the audience does; it is simply a clever and popular piece of scenery.

Middleton, of course, did better than this elsewhere; *The Changeling* and *Women Beware Women* are masterpieces of psychological horror. But that was after he had stopped trying to imitate what had worked for his predecessors, and what could no longer work for him.[31]

Ironically, many scholars credit either Middleton or Tourneur with *The Second Maiden's Tragedy* (ca. 1611), depending on whose hand they have seen in *The Revenger's Tragedy*. And to be sure, the use of a dead lady (in the later play, a corpse rather than a skeleton) to poison a tyrant who has lusted after her might almost be a gloss on the earlier play's implication that overconcern with the relics of the dead is a form of self-deluding idolatry. To a point, in the later play, the device works well.[32]

Govianus's Lady has killed herself rather than accede to the wishes of the Tyrant, and the Tyrant, in grief and frustration, has had her body removed from its tomb, dressed in fine clothing, and brought to his chambers. Here, he subjects it to a grotesque imitation of neoplatonic courtship, bordering on idol-worship:

> [They bring the body in a chair, dressed up in black velvet which sets out the paleness of the hands and face, and a fair chain of pearl 'cross her breast, and the crucifix above it. He stands silent awhile, letting the music play, beckoning the Soldiers that bring her in to make obeisance to her, and he himself makes a low honour to the body and kisses the hand.] (S.D. 5.2.13)

Such a pageant would strike many chords in the Jacobean mind: the Herod and Mariamne story, Tamburlaine's veneration of Zenocrate's body, and, because of the Lady's enthronement and the crucifix that she wears, Catholic veneration of the Blessed Virgin.[33] Significantly, one of the kneeling soldiers, whose words make it clear that he is a Catholic, draws attention to this last implication by his instinctive recoil from it:

> 1 *Soldier:* [Aside] By this hand, mere idolatry. I make curtsy
> To my damnation. I have learned so much,
> Though I could never know the meaning yet
> Of all my Latin prayers, nor ne'er sought for't.
>
> (5.2.20–23)

As the Tyrant and his soldiers kneel, music plays "within" and a chorus intones the traditional *memento mori*:

> Oh, what is beauty that's so much adored?
> A flattering glass that cozens her beholders.
> One night of death makes it look pale and horrid;
> The dainty preserved flesh, how soon it moulders.
> To love it living it bewitcheth many,
> But after life is seldom heard of any.
>
> (5.2.14–19)

Anne Lancashire has suggested that "the song is perhaps sung not at the court and for the Tyrant but outside the action of the play, to the theatre audience, as a moral commentary on the action" (5.2.13.7n.). The moral commentary would indeed have been obvious, particularly since the Lady's true beauty—her soul—

has been "heard of" in act 4, when her ghost appears to Go-vianus. But it is also possible that the Tyrant has ordered the song without realizing what he has ordered. Such an irony would make an even greater moral commentary.

Had the anonymous playwright left his commentary here, the symbol would have worked splendidly. But the temptation to imitate the success of *The Revenger's Tragedy* was apparently too much for him, and so we are treated to another poisonous death-kiss. The Tyrant orders a cosmetician for the Lady's corpse, whose color is rapidly deteriorating, and Govianus enters disguised to do the job. Here again, we have standard themes: the denial of death evinced in a desire to pretend that the dead are still alive, and the use of cosmetics to symbolize the artificial nature of worldly beauty.[34] But Govianus cannot rest with the command of his Lady's ghost, simply to rescue her remains; he poisons the lips of the corpse so that the Tyrant's own wickedness will kill him in the midst of his idolatrous necrophilia. And so it does.

The Lady's ghost returns during the killing to give approval to Govianus's actions (perhaps the playwright's attempt to show that we are not dealing with an evil Vindice here); the courtiers enter, and, rejoicing that the usurping Tyrant is dead, proclaim Govianus as rightful king; and when all is done, the Lady's ghost comes back one last time to make sure that her body will now be suitably interred. The play closes with the only veneration proper to the dead body: a funeral procession to the tomb.

Actually, the final act, for all its macabre, is rather touching, and is easily the most skillful and affecting part of the play; but it just misses being truly great. The playwright, in working out his dramatic irony of the idolator struck down by this own idol, has unfortunately had to use the idol itself as a symbol, and so has diffused his own message. It is all too likely that he has done so for box-office rather than dramatic necessity; significantly, when Govianus formulates his plan, he changes his stated purpose from "rescue" to "revenge." *The Revenger's Tragedy* appears to be heavy on his creator's mind.

The box-office attraction of such a dramatic device cannot be denied; nor, unhappily, can its overuse. By the time Massinger uses it in *The Duke of Milan* (1623), it has degenerated into such a piece of sensationalism that Massinger must wrench his plot and characterization completely out of shape to accommodate it. Toward the end of this play, which is even more obviously modeled on the Herod and Mariamne story than is *The Second Maiden's Tragedy*, Sforza (in utter disjunction with his earlier depiction as a reasonable man and devoted husband) falls prey to jealousy and stabs his wife Marcelia (who, though innocent, encourages his jealousy in a fit of pique contrary to *her* earlier characterization). Overcome with remorse, he refuses to believe that she is dead, forcing the court physicians to play out a charade of nursing her dead body back to health. But this charade cannot go on much longer, as the First Doctor points out: "The body, too, will putrify, and then / We can no longer cover the imposture" (5.2.135–36).[35] Hence they must seek out a way to preserve the body and make it appear alive, at least until they can bring Sforza out of his melancholy.

Enter Francisco, whose character has also changed since the beginning of the play from devoted friend of the Duke to vengeful brother of Eugenia, intent on avenging the Duke's betrayal of her many years before. It was he who first caused Sforza's jealousy and Marcelia's death, and now he has come back in disguise to finish his revenge. Although, as he tells the Doctors, "I am no God, sir, / To give new life to her" (5.2.140–41), he offers to paint the corpse in a way that will simulate life, including a "strange vapor" for her mouth that will give her "a seeming breath" (5.2.142–49). The strange vapor, although the Doctors do not know it, will be poison.

Dismissing the Doctors, Francisco goes to work, his patter an echo of Vindice's, but much more consciously malicious:

Francisco: [Y]our ladyship looks pale
  But I, your Doctor, have a ceruse for you.[36]
  See, my Eugenia, how many faces
  That are ador'd in Court borrow these helps,
  And pass for excellent, when the better part
  Of them are like to this. Your breath smells sour, too,
  But here is that shall take away the scent,

A precious antidote old ladies use
When they would kiss, knowing their gums are rotten.
These hands, too, that disdain'd to take a touch
From any lip whose owner writ not Lord,
Are now but coarsest earth, but I
Am at the charge, my bill not to be paid, too,
To give them seeming beauty. So, 'tis done:
How do you like my workmanship?

(5.2.183–97)

Francisco's satiric disgust with the body, however, is not part of his natural bent. Furthermore, the Duke, whom he will poison, is not really a necrophile but will be tricked into acting like one, thinking that he is embracing a live woman. Nor has the Duke been the kind of tyrannical ruler who deserves to be killed in this gruesome way; he has been acclaimed as just and rational even by his enemies, and his one (admittedly enormous) sin of stabbing Marcelia almost appears to have been introduced into the play to lead to this coffin-trick of Francisco's. In effect, the poisoned corpse is neither a comment on mortality nor poetic justice, but merely a circular argument.

To be sure, poisoned skulls and corpses are not entirely new to the seventeeth-century stage; Kyd had used one in the early *Soliman and Perseda*. But it has progressed from a tactical ploy in a series of murders to an obsession on the part of a murderer and finally to a seeming obsession in the playwright himself. Its culmination may be seen in a particularly revolting variation on the Thyestean feast, the anonymous *The Bloody Banquet* (1639).[37]

In this gruesome tale, the Tyrant has his wife's dead lover quartered—not, as one would suppose, in the normal way with traitors, to display as a warning to the populace, but rather for ease in butchering. Like sides of beef, Tymethes' quarters will hang in the royal larder, and each night the queen will eat a chop or two until the supply is gone:

Tyrant: Lady, you see your cheer, fine flesh, coarse fare.
　　　　Sweet was your lust, what can be bitter there?
　　　　By heaven, no other food thy taste shall have

Till in thy bowels [this] corpse find a grave.

(ll. 1718-21)

It is not even enough for the playwright to describe this horror; he must exhibit it as well:

[Soft music. Enter the Tyrant with the Queen, her hair loose. She makes a curtsey to the table. Sertorio brings in the flesh with a skull all bloody. They all wonder.] (S.D. 1919-22)

Well may they wonder; we may wonder, too. Something more than Senecan horror has occurred here. The whole attention of an age has swung from the moment of death—the separation of soul from body—to the process of causing death and the physical remnant after death. More creative energy (however misplaced) is being spent on the corpse than on the living human creature, until we may suspect the playwright himself of the necrophilia that he describes with such relish.

To some extent, the trend may remind us of the oldest forms of the Legend, in which the corpse beckoned living men to the grave. But in the Legend, the corpse was self-animated; it did not require a human puppeteer to dress it up and shake its limbs at the living. Rather, I think, we are watching one aspect of a growing tendency to deny the moment of death by appropriating Death to one's own uses. In fact, as we shall see, a whole generation of dramatists, in confronting the universal nightmare, took the reins of the nightmare into their own hands and rode it into new territory: a dramatic land of pleasurable dying, gruesome dying, erotic dying, and self-inflicted dying—but very little enlightened dying, and almost no normal death.

XI

A Choice of Deaths

The Last Decades of Renaissance Theater

THE GRADUAL CHANGE in dramatic presentations of death during the seventeenth century is not an easy one to trace. Chronological terms like "Jacobean" and "Caroline" are misleading; styles do not arbitrarily change on a certain date, nor does everyone agree to change. What we think of as the Caroline style, for example, began early in the reign of James I, particularly in the plays of Beaumont and Fletcher; but Webster and even Middleton continued in the old style as late as the 1620s, and consequently fell into disfavor when audiences demanded the revival of Fletcherean rather than Shakespearean drama during the Restoration.[1] And yet, even Webster and Middleton could not easily remain completely in the Marlowe-Shakespeare tradition. Too much had already changed in their own society; and the immediate past, from which all writers draw, was for them no longer the past that had informed the work of their predecessors. In tracing the changes, then, we must deal with the past as well as the present, remembering always that the word *modern* changes its meaning every day, and that yesterday all too rapidly becomes last year.

Henry W. Wells has seen some of this mingling of past and present in the Elizabethans but has curiously overlooked its corollary in what I should like to call, for want of a better term, the New Wave: "While [the Elizabethan theater] combined on an equal footing the medieval and the modern, it remained emancipated and alive. But when Jonson produced a school of realists, when Fletcher succeeded to the laurels of Shakespeare and was followed in turn by Massinger and Shirley, the period of experimentation had passed and that of decadence and imitativeness arrived."[2] The first sentence of this judgment is undoubtedly true. But the second sentence ignores three important points: first, that the New Wave did not seem to its contemporaries "decadent and imitative" but rather so fresh and new that, by the time of the Restoration, Fletcher was considered modern and Shakespeare hopelessly old-fashioned; second, that to "combine . . . the medieval and modern" is in itself a form of imitation; and third, that what the New Wave imitated was neither Shakespeare nor his medieval sources, but rather the immediate heritage that Shakespeare had rejected in his return to the medieval.

In this sense, both *The Duchess of Malfi* and *The Atheist's Tragedy* may be seen as the last steps that a playwright could take in the old style. Both plays demand a background of unified belief, whether Catholic or Protestant; in Webster's play, we must be able to extrapolate from the Duchess's heroics to the "eternal Church" (whatever we think that church may be); and in Tourneur's play, we must see the good and bad characters as Just and Lust, mutually incomprehensible to each other and predestined to reward or punishment. The New Wave, returning with Tourneur to the early Protestant bifurcation of man, could not return with him to the presence of God—and one can only speculate why: lack of belief, uncertainty about doctrine, fear of censure from the Established Church, rebellion against the growing Puritan faction, or simply a feeling, before the increasingly secularized upper-class audience of the private theaters, that to mention God or religion was somehow in bad taste. Whatever the reason, the New Wave split the human creature asunder and then analyzed the parts in terms of this world alone: social rather than divine sanction, and the medical determinism of the humors.

At the same time, as we have seen, death had ceased to be thought of as a threshold, the breathing space between worlds, and now permeated all of life. But although it had come so close, one was no longer permitted to dread it, fear of death being a mark of reprobacy or cowardice. The new Arts of Dying almost uniformly cried "Rejoice!"—run to death, embrace it, long for it as for a bride. And when the New Wave translated this joy to the stage without also translating the reason for the joy, the result was a seeming love of death for its own sake.

Ronald Huebert has attempted to link this almost erotic death-wish to the baroque style in art. For "baroque man," he says, and for Ford's "sweetly suffering heroes and heroines" in particular, "death is the most highly charged emotional experience of all"; and death-longing is merely "an expression of the general baroque bias toward delight in emotion for emotion's sake."[3] This analysis is helpful to a point, and may explain not only the luxuriant deaths of New Wave drama but also the proliferation of bombast in lieu of soliloquy. But we must remember that elaborate rhetoric is not new to the seventeenth-century stage, nor is death the only occasion for emotional outburst. There is as much emotion in Tamburlaine's longing for "the sweet fruition of an earthly crown" as there is in any New Wave heroine's desire for death, and Hamlet can become as overheated about a moral dilemma as the New Wave characters can be about dying. The term "baroque," then, may be a convenient label for the symptoms, but it does not explain the disease.[4]

But is it truly a disease? Or is it, rather, a new cure, a new way to share the nightmare and thus drive it away? Our own view of the New Wave may be colored by our preference for the old style, leading us to see only imitation where novelty exists. Indeed, many of the old symbols appear to continue in the New Wave, particularly the use of the masque as Summons. In Fletcher's *Valentinian* (ca. 1611), Maximus is crowned with a poisoned wreath during a masque; in Massinger's *The Roman Actor* (ca. 1629), the emperor Domitian, having discovered the empress in her attempted seduction of Paris, stages a play in which he kills Paris; in Ford's *'Tis Pity She's a Whore* (ca. 1631), Hippolita plans to kill Soranzo during the course of a masque, although she is foiled by the treachery of Vasques, who hands her the poisoned cup meant for his master; and, again in Ford, Ferentes's

three cast-off mistresses in *Love's Sacrifice* (ca. 1632) take the occasion of a masque to murder him:

> [Enter, in an antic fashion, Ferentes, Roseilli, and Mauruccio at
> several doors. They dance a little. Suddenly to them enter Col-
> ona, Julia, and Morona in odd shapes, and dance. The men gaze
> at them, are at a stand, and are invited by the women to dance.
> They dance together sundry changes. At last they close Ferentes
> in, Mauruccio and Roseilli being shook off, and standing at several
> ends of the stage gazing. The women hold hands and dance about
> Ferentes in diverse complimental offers of courtship. At length they
> suddenly fall upon him and stab him. He falls down, and they
> run out at several doors.][5]

Ford, in fact, for all his late arrival on the dramatic scene,
may be the closest to the old style in his use of the death masque.
Note that the elaborate stage direction given for the masque in
Love's Sacrifice bears an uncanny resemblance to the folk dances
called "dances of death": the self-contained nature of the figure,
limited to the dancers themselves rather than including the
onlookers; the singling out of a "victim," who is surrounded by
the dancers; and the ambiguous alternation of courtship and
mourning. In *The Broken Heart*, too, Ford seems to return to the
medieval Dance, although he inverts the figure so that the victim
at the center of the dance, Calantha, becomes the living receiver
of news about the deaths of others: first her father, then Penthea,
and finally Ithocles. Like Lydgate's Monk, she continues to dance:
"Be chere owtewarde / hard to deuyce" (*Dance of Death*, 391);
but, as she explains later, "Al ben not meri / which that men
seen daunce" (392):

> Calantha: O, my lords,
>   I but deceiv'd your eyes with antic gesture,
>   When one news straight came huddling on another
>   Of death, and death, and death. Still I danc'd forward;
>   But it struck home, and here, and in an instant. . . .
>   These are the silent griefs which cut the heartstrings;
>   Let me die smiling.
>
>   (5.3.67–71; 75–76)[6]

This acknowledgment of grief balances her earlier reaction to the news, a reaction that is orthodox, classical, and admirable, but a bit stark in context, and which in fact hovers on the brink of sounding like Macbeth's despair:

Calantha: Those that are dead
  Are dead; had they not now died, of necessity
  They must have paid the debt they ow'd to nature,
  One time or other.—Use dispatch, my lords;
  We'll suddenly prepare our coronation.

                                                    (5.2.89–93)

Macbeth: She should have died hereafter,
  There would have been a time for such a word.
  Tomorrow, and tomorrow, and tomorrow
  Creeps in this petty pace from day to day
  To the last syllable of recorded time,
  And all our yesterdays have lighted fools
  The way to dusty death.

                                                    (5.5.17–23)

Calantha's repressed grief, her denial that at first refuses catharsis, is not only close to what we admire in the old style, but also one of the most psychologically accurate portraits that Ford has given us. Had he left it there, we might even believe that Calantha could easily die from the combined shock and repression; although we no longer believe in broken hearts, we are familiar, in similar circumstances, with cardiac arrests. But Ford, for all his lingering fondness for the old style,[7] was a man of his time, and Calantha must die, like other New Wave heroines, amid an elaborate scenic production that she has staged for herself. We shall look at some of these productions in a moment.

New Wave playwrights, of course, tinkered as much with the Dance of Death as they did with death's other iconography. Marie Cornelia points out that Shirley's *The Cardinal* deviates from the tradition by having an innocent victim slain by masquers; "it is the wrong perpetrated through the masque," she says, rather than justice (however warped) which is emphasized in the play.[8] Even more important, in some cases the death masque begins to show the defeat rather than the triumph of death, but a defeat by earthly love rather than by Christ. Court masques perhaps emphasized this theme more than did actual plays, but some amateur playwrights, apparently hoping for the favor of the court, embodied the popular masque in their dramas. Henry Glapthorne, for example, in *The Lady Mother* (ca. 1635), uses a death masque to save Lady Marlove and her son from execution for their supposed murder of Thurston. In this masque, Grimes, dressed as Death, invokes Despair and the Furies; but Timothy, as Hymen, chases Death away. They then reveal Thurston, who is alive and married to Clariana, and all ends happily.[9] Although a defeat of Death may seem incompatible with the death-longing then prevalent on the stage, it is significant that the conjunction of love and death remains, and that both are focused on the world of the secular.[10]

To see how subtle the changes in focus can be, we may well compare two sets of star-crossed lovers, early and late. Shakespeare's Romeo, thinking that his Juliet is dead, returns to Verona to die in her tomb. On his arrival, he meets Paris, who has just finished mourning for Juliet in a suitably orthodox manner, one that suggests that Romeo's mourning is as rash as his previous actions and is part of his tragic decline. Paris tries to apprehend Romeo for violating the decree of exile, the two young men fight, Paris is killed, and Romeo drinks poison, first speculating on his other rival, Death:

Romeo: Ah, dear Juliet,
  Why are thou yet so fair? Shall I believe
  That unsubstantial death is amorous,
  And that the lean abhorred monster keeps
  Thee here in dark to be his paramour?

                                        (5.3.101–05)

Note that Death here remains an ugly monster, the perpetrator of a rape—perhaps with overtones of the Persephone legend, with its implied promise of rebirth. And when Romeo dies beside Juliet, he has joined his wife, forestalling not only Paris's but also Death's claims upon her. Death, then, retains its medieval complexity: it is a result of sin, a thing to be feared, but, in the end, a means of justice and reconciliation.

In Ford's *Love's Sacrifice*, however, there is no hint of this complex moral order. Indeed, Bianca and Fernando, the star-crossed lovers, are adulterers in all but consummation of the act. Although Bianca is married to the Duke, Fernando's best friend, she and Fernando have been maintaining a relationship apparently modeled on the fashionable version of "neoplatonism" popularized by Queen Henrietta Maria's court. They exchange vows of love, flirt in public, and, more to the point, swear to die together. When the Duke kills Bianca in a jealous rage exacerbated by her defiant assertion that she loves Fernando, we may therefore expect another Romeo tomb scene, and Ford does not disappoint us. As the repentant Duke approaches Bianca's tomb to mourn for her, up pops Fernando, who has not only brought poison with him but has also dressed for the occasion: "[One goes to open the tomb, out of which ariseth Fernando in his winding-sheet, only his face discovered; as Caraffa is going in, he puts him back.]" (S.D. 5.3.54).

The winding-sheet here is a symbol without a referent, a bit of grue for stage effect, much like the poisoned corpses that we saw earlier. Since Fernando must step out of his burial garment to push the Duke back, and since there is no evidence that nudity was acceptable on the Caroline stage, we must assume that Fernando had wrapped himself up fully clothed—an unorthodox method of laying out a corpse. Either he or Ford has determined to create a pictorial effect for the audience; Romeo's real passion has been translated into an outward show of passion.

It is true that the winding-sheet had become an alternative to the skull as a memento mori by this time; John Donne had ordered his portrait done in a winding-sheet before *Love's Sacrifice* was produced on stage. But neither Fernando nor Bianca seems to be animated by religious impulse; they are merely giving a last gibe at the Duke, the now standard "checkmate" to the tyrant. And Fernando, to complete his pictorial representation, enunciates the progress of his pain as he dies:

Fernando: It works, it works already, bravely, bravely!
Now, now I feel it tear each several joint.
O royal poison, trusty friend, split, split
Both heart and gall asunder, excellent bane!
Roseilli, love my memory.—Well search'd out,
Swift, nimble venom; torture every vein.—
I come, Bianca—cruel torment, feast,
Feast on, do—Duke, farewell. Thus I—hot flames!—
Conclude my love,—and seal it in my bosom!

(5.8.86–94)

This graphic description of the physical pain of dying is one of the curious innovations of the New Wave. It, too, may be associated with the growing masochism of death on the stage, and in Fernando's case may remind us of the mingled anguish and sexuality that runs through the works of such nineteenth-century writers as Flaubert and Swinburne. But Fernando is one of the few "good" characters to die in such vocal pain; normally, it is the bad or expendable figure who entertains us with his or her shrieks of agony. The young Duke in Robert Gomersall's *The Tragedy of Lodovick Sforza* (ca. 1628) spends the better part of the first act screaming on his deathbed.[11] In *'Tis Pity She's a Whore*, the dying Hippolita cries out for eleven lines about the "heat above hell fire / . . . cruel, cruel flames!" that she feels (4.1.90–100), and Bergetto exclaims on the pain in his belly for ten lines (3.7.18–34). In Shirley's *The Maid's Revenge* (ca. 1639), Catalina goes half crazy with pain:

> *Catalina:* Oh, I must walk the dark foggy way that spits fire and brimstone! No physic to restore me? Send for Sharkino [the physician]; a cooler, a cooler; there's a smith's forge in my belly, and the Devil blows the bellows! Snow-water! Berinthia has poisoned me; sink by my own engine; I must hence, hence, farewell! Will you let me die so? Confusion, torment, death, hell! (5.3; pp. 66–67)[12]

And even at the beginning of the New Wave, Fletcher's Aretus, in *Valentinian*, poisons himself before he poisons the Emperor, so that he can let the Emperor know what pains to expect at any given moment. Thus we hear not one but two screams of pain throughout the death scene, in a bizarre sort of echo effect.[13]

If we are tempted to say that the violence of death is as common to the old drama as to the new, we may find it useful to review the manifestations of the violence. We *see* the pain on stage, but we *hear* something different. Humanum Genus and Everyman feel the death signs, but they lament their isolation and spiritual danger more than their pains. Marlowe's Edward II, who undergoes perhaps the most protracted physical torture of any stage figure until the horror films of the twentieth century, is more conscious of mental than of physical torture. Shakespeare's dying characters are more concerned with their states of mind and the workings of their societies than with physical pangs; even Cleopatra, at the beginning of the New Wave, experiences her dying pain as a "lover's pinch" or a lullaby (5.2.298–99; 412–13), and Goneril and Regan, precursors of Shirley's Catalina and Berinthia, confine themselves to understatement before they go offstage to die:

> *Regan:* Sick, oh, sick!
> *Goneril:* [Aside] If not, I'll ne'er trust medicine. . . .
> *Regan:* My sickness grows upon me.
> *Albany:* She is not well. Convey her to my tent.
> (*Lear*, 5.3.95–96; 105–06)

And the grim villains of Webster's plays, so conscious of their vile bodies while they live, think little of them as they die.

Why, then, did the New Wave become so obsessed with physical pain? To speak again of imitation and jaded palates is not entirely fruitful, although we have seen the growth of imitative sensationalism in other shopworn symbols of the day. Again, I think we must look to the source of the imitation: not the medieval or Shakespearean, but the Protestant Morality, in which Moros, Worldly Man, and Lust agonized under God's visitation, to show that the reprobate were more liable to, and less able to cope with, earthly suffering than their elect counterparts. But, again, this explanation does not account for Fernando, the romantic hero who screams as loudly as the wicked, nor can we simply write him off as one of the many anomalies in Ford, who frustratingly refuses to fit into our literary classifications. Before attempting to show how stage agony fits into another New Wave convention, therefore, I should like to indulge in speculation about New Wave society and some of its similarities to our own.

The closing of the theaters in 1642 was not a spur-of-the-moment idea; Puritan leaders had been railing against the immorality of the stage since the 1560s. And if we read the continuing debates between the pro- and anti-theater factions, we may begin to notice how familiar they sound. The prosecution says that seeing immorality onstage will make spectators immoral; the defense replies that, on the contrary, seeing the immoral punished will act as a deterrent to immorality. The prosecution charges that the unreality of the stage warps the spectators' view of reality; the defense counters by pointing to the increasing realism, if not of plot or characterization, then at least of carnage.[14] Thus, the defense can use the prosecution's attack as an excuse for excess, and the more vehement each side becomes, the more delight the opposing side takes in doing what it knows will anger its enemy.

In addition, during this period, the whole composition of the audience began to change.[15] Starting with the leasing of Blackfriars by the King's Men in 1608, serious drama came increasingly to be written for the private theaters and therefore for wealthier audiences; and by the reign of Charles I, all playwrights seem to have written with one eye fixed firmly on the court, where Henrietta Maria not only delighted in seeing plays but even ventured to act in them occasionally, at a time when actresses were unheard of in England. If, as L. G. Salingar claims, the heroes and heroines of New Wave drama "are dwellers in a charmed circle, touchily defensive towards their privileges, but free from any responsiblity outwards,"[16] they are merely a reflection of the "charmed circle" of their audiences, what we may call the Beautiful People of their own day. Such people do not see themselves as "decadent"; rather, they consider themselves the avant-garde, freed from the dull restrictions—legal, moral, and aesthetic—of the boorish masses. It is not that they are trying harder and harder to satisfy increasingly jaded palates; rather (they say), they are more able to "take" reality, to accept with equanimity what would merely inflame the masses. And if the masses fail to be inflamed, the Beautiful People must increase the effort. One must, after all, maintain the image.

And yet, even this societal explanation, so analogous to our own world, does not completely serve. We may begin to see more of the pattern if we examine the New Wave portrayal of soldiering, a glorification of death that paradoxically serves to deny its object. Sanseverin, the Good Soldier of Gomersall's *Tragedy of Sforza*, epitomizes the new feeling about war. Speaking of men who avoid warfare and, by implication, of all civilians, he says:

> *Sanseverin:* And why like these run we an idle race
>   Of threescore years, and then sneak to a death?
>   While soldiers master their mortality
>   And die by men, if that at all they die.
>
> (ll. 593–96)

This is more than Hotspur's exaggerated view of military honor, or Tamburlaine's inflicting of death so that he may avoid it himself. Moreover, Sanseverin is not proven wrong at the end, as Hotspur and Tamburlaine are. Rather, implicit in these lines is a fear of life—the horror of growing old as so dreadful a thought that one must kill and be killed rather than face decay. Sanseverin's last clause, "if that at all they die," would have been a challenge to Death in the old drama; but here the challenge is not answered, and one can only speculate whether or not Gomersall's 1628 audience, like Sanseverin himself, is even more afraid of the ravages of Time than of a violent and sudden death.

Equally significant about the New Wave soldier is that, unlike the patriots and conquerors of earlier times, he is not concerned with fighting for a cause, or for a particular leader, or even for booty. He is fighting for the sake of fighting, for the sake of creating an eternal moment of violent life. He is fighting, although neither he nor his creator seems to realize it, against Death. And, in most cases, he wins.

Caratach, the hero of Fletcher's *Bonduca*, is one of the most elaborately portrayed of these fighting men. A Coriolanus run

amok—and, more important, one approved of by his author—
he has not even Coriolanus's excuse of national pride to spur
him on. He simply loves a battle. Although he is a Briton, he
has little sympathy with his own people and almost seems to prefer
the Romans because they are the better fighters. Indeed, his praise
of them so far exceeds the accepted verbal homage due an enemy
that Bonduca suspects him of treason; but he explains to her,
in what amounts to the only love lyric in the play:

> *Caratach:* I love an enemy: I was born a soldier;
> And he that in the head on's troop defies me,
> Bending my manly body with his sword,
> I make a mistress. Yellow-tressed Hymen
> Ne'er tied a longing virgin with more joy
> Than I am married to that man that wounds me.
>
> (1.1.57–62)

The eroticism of this passage is immediately evident, and it
is the only eroticism sanctioned by the play. The two Roman
soldiers who fall in love are seen as dupes and fools, who ultimately
repent of their folly and return to their proper mistress, war.
Caratach himself is so misogynistic that he cannot abide even
Bonduca, the leader of his own people, and frequently rails at
her for fighting on her own and thereby spoiling his war. But
again, we are not meant to see this perversity as a tragic flaw in
the manner of Coriolanus; it is meant to be honorable and glorious, admired by the gods themselves. During the act 3 sacrifice
scene, for example, Bonduca and her priests are unable to elicit
a response from the gods to their prayers for victory and safety,
but when Caratach addresses the gods in his own way, smoke
immediately rises from the altar:

> *Caratach:* Give us this day good hearts, good enemies,
> Good blows o' both sides, wounds that fear or flight
> Can claim no share in; steel us both with angers,
> And warlike execution fit thy viewing. . . .
> . . . [W]ho does best,

> Reward with honour; who despair makes fly,
> Unarm forever, and brand with infamy.
>
> (3.1.64–67; 71–73)

We may think that any general who prays for a strong enemy and heavy casualties among his own troops should be relieved of command as soon as possible, but within the context of the play, his prayers are seen as admirable. And lest we think that Caratach seeks personal rather than national glory in the battle, we are disabused of this idea in our encounter with Penius, a Roman soldier who temporarily falls prey to martial despair. Sick of the endless trench warfare in Britain, Penius complains that even in victory there is no "fame" to be gleaned from this miserable little war at the ends of the civilized earth, where "one is smother'd with a multitude, / And crowded in amongst a nameless press" (2.1.37–38):

> *Penius:*   Who but fools,
>   That make no difference betwixt certain dying
>   And dying well, would fling their fames and fortunes
>   Into this Britain-gulf, this quicksand-ruin,
>   That sinking, swallows us?
>
> (2.1.46–50)

The art of "dying well" has made a long journey from its original meaning; here, what Penius means is earthly fame.[17] But even fame in this sense, a sense that the sixteenth century would certainly have understood, is no longer sufficient for Fletcher. Penius, after all, represents the bad example; in what amounts to a travesty on the three views of "honor" in *1 Henry IV*, both Bonduca's and Penius's views of war (national and personal glory) are to be seen as the wrong views, offsetting Caratach's which is the right one. And the ultimate irony is that Caratach, the proponent of "dying well" in this newest sense, does not die; like the elect in a Tudor Morality, he comes through the test and is awarded Consolation: an offer to join the Roman army, which he happily accepts. The purpose of the fight does not matter, so long as one can keep fighting. What was a character flaw in Coriolanus is a reward for Caratach.[18]

These professional soldiers appear frequently in New Wave drama: Aecius in *Valentinian*, Sanseverin in Sforza, the soldiers who act as chorus in such Roman tragedies as *Nero*, and so on. We no longer have the glory-seeking armies of Marlowe and his imitators, or the patriotic armies (with their complement of malcontents, philosophers, and ordinary men) of Shakespeare; we have only professional warriors who are proud of their trade and surly when they are idle. Much of this new development may be attributed to the enforced peace during the period; it is easy to be a warhawk during an unpopular peace, particularly since one knows that one will not have to do any of the fighting that one is glorifying. Conversely, since there is no war to observe at first hand, it is difficult to become familiar with actual military behavior or individual reactions to war. One must fantasize instead—or imitate.

But again, topicality is only part of the explanation. Paradoxically, in the very plays where bloody war is glorified we begin to see a rise of pathos, seemingly the direct opposite of the warlike mood intended by the playwright. Increasingly, we are shown protracted and sentimental deathbeds of the helpless; increasingly, New Wave dramatists tell sad stories, not (like Richard II) of the death of kings, but rather of women, children, and mental defectives.[19] In *Bonduca* itself, the mighty Caratach is provided with a young nephew, Hengo, who holds off soldiers with his little sword (much like Coriolanus's son tearing butterflies with his teeth), learns the arts of war, and even absorbs some of his uncle's misogyny. When Hengo dies, taking all of act 5, scene 8 to do it, the scene is so awash with sentimentality that we may imagine ourselves at the bedside of Paul Dombey or Little Nell.

Hengo has been under siege in a cave with Caratach, manfully bearing starvation, but at last he ventures out to find some food and is treacherously slain by a Roman soldier. Earlier, he has catechized his uncle on the meaning of death and has been told that, if we are very good and kind, we will go to the peaceful land of the gods, where we shall meet all our loved ones. (Fletcher does not seem to notice how incongruous this sounds on Caratach's lips.) Now, on his deathbed, Hengo is catechized in turn by Caratach:

> *Caratach:* My dear boy, what shall I lose?
> *Hengo:*   Why, a child,
>   That must have died however: had this scap'd me,
>   Fever or famine; I was born to die, sir.
> *Caratach:* But thus unblown, my boy?
> *Hengo:*   I go the straighter
>   My journey to the gods. So I shall know ye
>   When you come, uncle.
>
>   (5.3.147–53)

And so on for twenty-five more lines. Nor are we meant to see Hengo's acceptance of death as a rebuke to Caratach; it is shortly after this scene that Caratach goes over to the Romans so that he can continue fighting.

Hengo is certainly not the first innocently wise child in drama; there are a host of them in Shakespeare alone: Arthur, Rutland, Macduff's son, and the two princes of *Richard III*. But Hengo is one of the first who longs to die. Here again we can see a departure from the old style, in which even children hung back from Death, resenting his too early arrival, or puzzled at the idea of pain and separation. Children—and other innocents—in New Wave drama become the exemplars of joyful dying, and by looking at another of Fletcher's plays we may begin to see why.

In *Thierry and Theodoret*, Thierry has been told that in order to cure his impotence, he must kill the first woman he sees leaving the temple of Diana. It is all a plot, of course; his impotence has been caused by a drug, and the astrologer, one of the plotters in disguise, has arranged for Ordella, Thierry's bride, to be the first to leave the temple. Ordella, however, is veiled, so that Thierry does not know whom he is addressing. He tells her that she must die for the good of her country, and when she agrees to do so, he tests her virtue by delineating the pangs of annihilation:

> *Thierry:* Suppose it death. . . .
>   and endless parting

With all we can call ours, with all our sweetness,
With youth, strength, pleasure, people, time, nay, reason;
For in the silent grave, no conversation,
No joyful tread of friends, no voice of lovers,
No careful father's counsel, nothing's hard, [heard?]
Nor nothing is, but all oblivion,
Dust, and an endless darkness.

$$(4.1.95-102)$$

Thierry is here proposing the main temptation of the secular:
attachment to worldly goods and companions—attachment even,
in the manner of Everyman's second trial, to the self. Although
it is a test of Ordella's virtue, there is a hint, too, that Thierry
himself wants reassurance: Ordella must contradict him, not only
to assuage his guilt over killing her, but also to comfort him about
his own mortality. In the old style, she might have given this
comfort by speaking of an afterlife or the glory of dying for a cause,
but instead, she speaks in words perilously close to those of
Spenser's Despayre:

Ordella: 'Tis of all sleeps the sweetest,
   Children begin it to us, strong men seek it,
   And kings from height of all their painted glories
   Fall, like spent exhalations, to this center;
   And those are fools that fear it, or imagine
   A few unhandsome pleasures, or life's profits
   Can recompense the place; and mad that stays it
   Till age blow out their lights, or rotten humours
   Bring 'em dispers'd to the earth.

$$(4.1.103-11)$$

"To die, to sleep— / No more." What Hamlet rejected
(3.1.60-61) Ordella accepts. Significantly, she begins by invoking the child, and ends by deploring old age. And if her "Till
age blow out their lights" reminds us of Macbeth's "Out, out,
brief candle," her whole praise of death may remind us of another
of Macbeth's speeches:

Macbeth: Better be with the dead,
   Whom we, to gain our peace, have sent to peace,

> Than on the torture of the mind to lie
> In restless ecstasy. Duncan is in his grave,
> After life's fitful fever he sleeps well.
> Treason has done his worst. Nor steel, nor poison,
> Malice domestic, foreign levy, nothing
> Can touch him further.
>
> (3.3.19–26)

But Macbeth was the voice of evil, and Ordella is the voice of virtue. Nor is she alone. Picinino, the good courtier of *Sforza*, agrees with both Ordella and Macbeth, and, in what amounts to a refutation of Hamlet's most famous soliloquy, comes down firmly on the side of "not to be." During a memento mori exercise, he says of the skull before him:

> Picinino: Then let me think
> What loss I have when I am made like this:
> This fears no French: a piece of ordnance
> Can break but not astonish this; no force
> Can draw a tear, no, not a sigh from hence;
> And can it be a loss to be like this?
> O Death! why art thou fear'd? why do we think
> 'Tis such a horrid terror not to be?
> Why, not to be is not to be a wretch;
> Why, not to be is to be like the heavens,
> Not to be subject to the power of Fate:
> O, there's no happiness but not to be.
>
> (2063–74)

Was New Wave society so irreligious that it saw only Nothing on the other side of the grave? To all appearances, no. Playwrights and playgoers alike continued to attend church regularly, and to buy and read the devotional handbooks that were coming off English presses in ever-increasing numbers. Indeed, one of these handbooks, Henry Montagu's 1631 *Contemplatio Mortis et Immortalitatis*, flatly contradicts Picinino: "To the wicked the best thing of all were not to haue beene. . . . His next best were to liue long. It was ill with him that hee was borne, worse that hee must die: for hee not being sure of a better, would faine bee sure of this. . . . With good men it is otherwise; to them the best thing of life is to haue beene, for this leades the way *ad beatitudinem patriae*, to the fruition of their faith."[20] Religious poetry, too, flowered again in the hands of Donne, Herbert, Vaughan, and Crashaw. And in the later years, when Queen Henrietta Maria arrived from France with her entourage of priests and friars, there seems to have been a religious revival on three fronts: the Puritans, becoming more vocal against not only the episcopal system but also the papistry of the court; the Anglicans, bent on suppressing the Puritans, variously delighted with or suspicious of the new high-church party, and upset by the increased tolerance shown toward papists; and the Roman Catholics themselves, who, counting on the protection of the Court, flocked to the queen's chapel by the thousands to attend Mass openly for the first time in nearly a century.[21] But what is evident even in this apparent intensification of religious fervor is a lack of centrality; that is, belief, however sincere, had become less a matter of internal reality and more a matter of party. We have seen, in the early *Sicke Mannes Salve*, the insecurity that can grow from such doctrinal splintering and its consequent defensiveness. Now, as the splintering increased, so did the insecurity.

In addition, the new "arithmetic" of life—the single reality of the always disappearing moment—can have done little to soothe people's insecurity. It is not, as Philippe Ariès claims, that New Wave society was "less loving of things and people" than were older societies;[22] rather, the love intensified as it was transformed into a desperate clinging to something that was always being snatched away, a sense that the beautiful things themselves were riddled with death. And all the beautiful things that carried the seeds of their own destruction, the most beautiful was self—the self that one must watch disintegrating before one's eyes.

Of all the fears of death, this is perhaps the closest to the fears of our own society; not merely the decay that happens after death, but also the decay that happens before it. We may look at a skeleton as *le mort*, the remnant of someone else who no longer is, and we may even make a joke of it; but we cannot look at it as *la mort*, an impersonal force beckoning to us, because we may take on its form *before* it seizes us. We may revel in stage

violence—the enunciation of pain, the glorification of war—
because it is, as Lupset says, such a violent pain that it is soon
over[23]—and besides, it is the exception, something that will not
happen to us; but we cannot watch someone dying of old age
or plague (in our day, perhaps, heart disease or cancer), because
it is the rule, and *will* happen to us.

Significantly, the Arts of Dying in the seventeenth century
begin administering a caution undreamed of in the old treatises:
not to be afraid of the dead or dying; not to turn from another's
deathbed in aversion, but to approach it in Christian hope and
charity.[24] Such a caution implies almost a fear of contagion—
not of death itself, perhaps, but of predeath disintegration—a fear
of seeing the self grown old and helpless. Obviously, the warning of Elde is unsuitable to such a society in which one covers
one's ears and turns one's face from the elderly. Any warning,
any comfort, must come from the young, who must give an example not only of dying well but also of dying beautifully. We must
be assured that even if we become dead, we will not become ugly.

Furthermore, to increase the distance between Death and
the audience, New Wave playwrights took pains to make the relationship between Death and the dying innocent a highly individualized one. Because death was an escape from a private sorrow,
or an intensely personal encounter between the dying individual
and Death the bridegroom, the audience was removed from the
circle of participants, becoming only spectators of another's sorrow
or joy. The increasingly situational nature of the drama assisted
in this distancing; the more bizarre a situation in which death
occurs, the less likely we are to recognize in it our own death.
Fletcher's plots, based (as Eugene M. Waith has shown) on Senecan *controversiae*, those outlandish moral problems designed more
to show off the skill of an orator than to analyze the normal problems of life,[25] remove even the individualized encounter still further
from the audience; and Ford's psychological anomalies—the incestuous, the obsessed, the humor-driven—almost demand that
the audience reject them as portraits of the self.

Safely cushioned, then, from the dangers of our own decay—
both before and after death—we may weep happily over the
romance of the lovely brides and bridegrooms who go to meet

their betrothed, Death. Indeed, many of the deathbeds are planned with the elaborate care normally given to weddings, and are often conjoined with weddings. During Evadne's preparations for her nuptials in *The Maid's Tragedy*, the jilted Aspatia wanders about in tears, delivering no less than three "when I am dead" speeches: one in the form of a song, one in a general address to the bride and assembled bridesmaids, and once in an encore to Amintor, who has entered too late to hear it the first time. Significantly, both her song and her address to the bridesmaids suggest parallels between the ministrations given to bride and corpse alike:

> *Aspatia*: This is the last time you shall look on me:
> Ladies, farewell. As soon as I am dead,
> Come all and watch one night about my hearse.
> Bring each a mournful story and a tear
> To offer at it when I go to earth;
> With flatt'ring ivy clasp my coffin round;
> Write on my brow my fortune; let my bier
> Be borne by virgins that shall sing by course
> The truth of maids and perjuries of men.
>
> (2.1.99–107)

In Shirley's *The Traitor*, too, a jilted woman interrupts wedding preparations to announce her own forthcoming nuptials. Amidea, whose ex-lover, Pisano, is now leading Oriana to the altar, informs the company that she, too, is about to be wed:

> *Amidea*: To one whom you have all heard talk of.
> Your fathers knew him well. One who will never
> Give cause I should suspect him to forsake me.
> A constant lover, one whose lips, though cold,
> Distill chaste kisses. Though our bridal bed
> Be not adorn'd with roses, 'twill be green.
> We shall have virgin laurel, cypress, yew,
> To make us garlands. Though no pine do burn,
> Our nuptial shall have torches, and our chamber
> Shall be cut out of marble where we'll sleep

> Free from all care forever. Death, my lord,
> I hope shall be my husband.
>
> (4.2.78–90)²⁶

Ironically, Oriana is no happier than Amidea about the marriage; she is in love with Cosmo and faints when he appears on the scene. The ironies increase as Pisano tries to revive her, perhaps unconsciously ringing changes on the old image of death as a divorce from life:

> *Pisano:* Will heaven divorce us ere the priest have made
> Our marriage perfect? We in vain hereafter
> Shall hear him teach that our religion binds
> To have the church's ceremony. She returns.
> *Oriana:* Why were you so unkind to call me from
> A pleasing slumber? Death has a fine dwelling.
>
> (4.2.12–17)

And Penthea, in *The Broken Heart,* prefaces her plea to Calantha, a plea that Calantha accept Ithocles's love, with a fifty-line "legacy" speech (3.5.30–78), in which she announces that she is about to die and bequeaths to Calantha three "jewels": her youth, her fame, and her brother. Surprisingly in this play of the New Wave 1630s, Calantha becomes the commonsense voice of the old style, sympathizing with Penthea's pain but trying to put it into a realistic perspective. We might almost be listening to a conversation between Elinor and Marianne Dashwood in Jane Austen's *Sense and Sensibility* as Calantha gently tries to extricate Penthea from her romantic gloom, even suggesting that if Penthea will "exert herself" (to use Elinor's words), there may be some "remedy" (Calantha's word) for the problem.²⁷ In a startling inversion of the traditional meaning of the term, however—"Is there no remedy?" was once asked of death, not life—Penthea insists, like Shakespeare's Angelo, that there is no door out but death: "That remedy / Must be a winding-sheet, a fold of lead, / And some untrod-on corner in the earth" (3.5.31–33).

Calantha listens patiently, allowing Penthea the catharsis of speech but always keeping such speech in perspective by treating it as a bit of poetry or a theatrical performance:

Calantha: How handsomely thou play'st with harmless sport
Of mere imagination. Speak the last;
I strangely like thy will.

(3.5.66–68)

I do not think that we are meant to see Calantha, here, as an unfeeling woman (although, as in Austen's novel, Penthea may see her so because Calantha will not lend herself completely to unbridled death-longing), or even as a woman as yet untutored in sorrow. Even as Penthea speaks, Calantha is torn between her love for Ithocles and the dynastic necessity of marrying Nearchus, a conflict not unlike Penthea's own. Calantha's father, too, is ailing, and her friends are quite volubly suffering; but Calantha, like Elinor, must maintain her equanimity in order to keep those around her from falling apart.

But "Al ben not meri / which that men seen daunce." There is a hint, even in Calantha's "I strangely like thy will," that she, too, is capable, not only of being crushed by sorrow, but also of giving it vent in words. In her final scene, she is careful (like Elinor—or Hamlet) to explain her self-control and provide for the future well-being of her people; but having exerted herself to the extent necessary, she allows herself to die as theatrically as Penthea. In fulfillment of the oracle's prediction that "The lifeless trunk shall wed the broken heart" (4.1.134), she places her mother's wedding ring on the hand of the dead Ithocles and, kissing him, prepares to die:

Calantha: One kiss on these cold lips, my last—crack, crack!—
Argos now's Sparta's King.—Command the voices
Which wait at th' altar, now to sing the song
I fitted for my end.

(5.3.77–80)

And yet, even in Calantha's apparent submission to New Wave sensibility, she pays homage to old-style sense. Although the first and last sections of her death lyric are allied to Penthea's "Love's martyrs must be ever, ever dying" (4.3.152), the middle section looks beyond the love-death nexus to the whole human condition and echoes the laments of Nashe, Shakespeare, and Spenser:[28]

> Glories, pleasures, pomps, delights, and ease
> Can but please
> Th' outward senses when the mind
> Is not untroubled or by peace refin'd.
> Crowns may flourish and decay,
> Beauties shine but fade away.
> Youth may revel, yet it must
> Lie down in a bed of dust.
> Earthly honors flow and waste;
> Time alone doth change and last.
> Sorrows mingled with contents prepare
> Rest for care;
> Love only reigns in death, though art
> Can find no comfort for a broken heart.

(5.3.81–94)

To the last, Calantha retains the mixed nature of the old Dance of Death, in which the audience is forced to look at itself as well as at the dancers. And it is probably Calantha's blend of Elinor and Marianne—or, we might almost say, of Hamlet and Ophelia—that has earned *The Broken Heart* critical approval through centuries of critical change, being lauded for its realism in ages that rejected romanticism, and for its sentiment in ages that rejected insensibility. It is not merely, as Charles Osborne McDonald has claimed, that "Calantha's actions are certainly meant to set those of all the other characters in a firm moral perspective, to indicate clearly their lesser nobility of action and soul";[29] McDonald, after all, is of the sense party, whereas other critics, of the sensibility party, have taken Penthea as the true heroine and moral exemplar. Rather, Calantha is one of the last of the universal characters of a previous age, an Everywoman of mixed emotions who prevents *The Broken Heart* from slipping over into a drama of types, the deterministic mode of the late Morality in which Just and Lust are immediately recognizable as *them*selves and therefore unrecognizable as *our*selves.

And yet, in spite of Calantha's mixture of old and new, restraint and emotionalism, Ford does place her in the context of his time: the marriage with death that is inextricably linked with earthly marriages. Indeed, it is noteworthy that the death-marriage nexus in these plays is usually presented to the disadvantage of earthly marriage. In all the weddings overshadowed by literal death—the fatal wreath at Maximus's wedding, Aspatia's lament at Evadne's, Amidea's at Oriana's, and so on—there is a core of emotional or spiritual disease. Maximus has murdered his way to the throne and the Empress; the bride Evadne is the king's paramour and forces Amintor to accept an unconsummated marriage bed; Oriana's betrothal is the result of a double betrayal; Thierry is rendered impotent on his wedding day; and Calantha goes to a marriage that has been doomed by a frustrated love before her own.

It is this feeling of doom that pervades both the earthly loves and the death-longings of New Wave drama. In fact, Dorothy Farr has compared *The Broken Heart* to the Oresteian cycles of Greek tragedy, in which all suffer from a crime that has been perpetrated before the play begins.[30] But if we listen to Ithocles's admission of his "crime," the forced marriage of Penthea to Bassanes despite her love for Orgilus, we may hear echoes of something beyond the specific transgression of a cruel brother:

> *Ithocles:* I did the noble Orgilus much injury,
> But griev'd Penthea more. I now repent it;
> Now, uncle, now. This "now" is now too late.
>
> (4.1.8–10)

There is only one place in which repentance is too late: Hell.

Realistically speaking, it is not "too late" for the characters of Ford's play, at least not in the sense that Ithocles and Orgilus mean it. Ithocles has repented, and during the course of the play, he offers to amend his life and make whatever restitution he can to those whom he has injured, a resolution made more striking by the fact that his apology to Penthea takes place on his sickbed, a variation on the old deathbed repentance scene. But in Ford's world, the value of deathbed repentance had long since been rejected; Judgment, in the predestinarian sense, had preceded birth.[31]

Whether Ford himself accepts the idea of fate—either in its classic or its Calvinist form—is a moot point. Giovanni, in *'Tis Pity*, claims that his actions are determined by fate; but Giovanni is an incestuous brother, and both the Friar's exhortations and Annabella's repentance suggest that what Giovanni calls "fate" is only passion controlling will. The lovers in *Love's Sacrifice* speak of their fate; but their downfall is occasioned by well-motivated human machinations. And in *The Broken Heart*, both the oracle's prophecy and Ithocles's "too late" are offset by Tecnicus and Calantha, who speak consistently of free will, control of the passions, repentance, duty, and "remedy." What, then, causes us to accept the determinism of the villains rather than the determination of the heroes? The answer may lie in the very bond that is forged between love and death in New Wave drama—or, rather, the merging of one with the other.

To a certain extent, the attempt to turn the death of beauty *into* beauty is a healthy acceptance of death and (as some have said) the driving force behind art. It is a sign that Good is more powerful than Non-good, because beauty can remake ugliness in its own image, whereas ugliness cannot do the same to beauty. But there comes a point at which acceptance of death, even beautification of death, turns into a rejection of life; as though in purifying contaminated water, we should drink off the poison and pour the water out on the ground. The pivot, as T. S. Eliot pointed out centuries later, is the reason for welcoming death: not for its own sake but for the "right reason."[32] I cannot, therefore, agree with Ronald Huebert, who cites George Herbert's "Death" as another instance of baroque death-longing;[33] the reason for Death's being so "faire and full of grace, / Much in request, much sought for as a good" in this poem is that Death has now become Christ's servant, the porter at the gateway to Heaven. And Herbert's poem concludes, not with an exhortation to run to death, but with an acceptance of whichever pillow God gives: "Downe or dust."[34] This, then, is the precise point of balance, the old refuge between despair and presumption, which

Milton's Michael was to delineate to the fallen Adam: "Nor love thy life, nor hate; but what thou liv'st / Live well, how long or short permit to Heav'n."[35]

But New Wave heroes and heroines seldom permit the choice to Heaven. With the possible exception of Shirley's Sciarrha in *The Traitor*, who is willing to consider an honorable way out of death even after his stoic speech of welcome to martyrdom (4.2.146–59), the new protagonists do not accept death; they long for it, clamor for it, and, if necessary, force others to give it to them. In fact, despite all the sweet melancholy of their "when I am dead" speeches, many of the heroes and heroines are in remarkably good health throughout their plays and must devise elaborate stratagems in order to die. Penthea, it is true, starves herself to death—a relatively simple method of suicide, if, as Huebert suggests, one well calculated to prolong the show of dying and to inflict as much pain as possible on the observers.[36] But Aspatia must dress up as a young man in order to trick Amintor into fighting with her and killing her (*Maid's Tragedy*, 5.3). Philaster, coming upon Arethusa and Bellario in the woods, demands that they kill him, and when they refuse, offers to kill Arethusa, who begs him to do so (*Philaster*, 4.5). When Soranzo discovers Annabella's pregnancy, she goads him into a rage, meanwhile singing, "Che morte più dolce che morire per amore?"— "What death more sweet than to die for love?" (*'Tis Pity*, 4.3; Bianca similarly enrages the Duke in *Love's Sacrifice*). Ordella, reprieved from the death-stroke by Thierry's compassion, is so disappointed that she offers to kill herself (*Thierry and Theodoret*, 4.1). And even the rough soldier Aecius, when Pontius dies rather than carry out the sentence of execution on him, runs about the palace bellowing for death in a manner that is almost comic (*Valentinian*, 4.4).

This lust for death at another's hand easily spills over into the eroticism of lust itself. Both Bellario and Arethusa beg for Philaster's touch, if only the touch of his sword—Bellario, as suits her hopeless love, in the old images of release from a doleful life; and Arethusa, a Philaster's betrothed, in a duet with Philaster that is almost purely sexual:

Bellario: 'Tis less than to be born; a lasting sleep,
A quiet resting from all jealously;
A thing we all pursue; I know, besides,
It is but giving over of a game
That must be lost.

(3.1.254–58)

Arethusa: If my fortune be so good, to let me fall
Upon thy hand, I shall have peace in death.
Yet tell me this, there will be no slanders,
No jealousy in the other world, no ill there?
Philaster: No.
Arethusa: Show me then the way.

(4.5.65–69)

And Aspatia, too, in her "duel" with Amintor, claims that "there
is no place so fit / For me to die as here" (5.3.106–07). Conversely,
Giovanni, by kissing Annabella as he kills her and then tearing
out her heart and ripping up her womb, combines the images
of Death the bridegroom and Death the rapist, bringing to flower
the seeds of death contained in his incestuous love for his sister
and fulfilling the prophecy of the Friar:[37]

Friar: O, Giovanni, hast thou left the schools
Of knowledge to converse with lust and death?
For death waits on thy lust.

(*Tis Pity*, 1.1.57–59)

Sin being made perfect, as Saint Paul or William Perkins might
observe, brings forth death. But in New Wave drama, even virtue made perfect brings it forth; there is a sense that love, like
life, "smelleth with the salt of death."[38] The moment of Judgment
is every moment; it is always "too late"; the nightmare is always
there. The New Wave solution, then, is to turn the unwelcome
guest into a welcome one; to pretend, even, that he has been
invited; but to be sure that the invitation has clearly come (in
the words of the Duchess of Malfi) from the "mad folk" next door.

Epilogue

Some Last Words and a Last Play

IN A BOOK LIKE THIS ONE, it is difficult to draw precise lines of demarcation between periods of thought, or even to make generalizations that are not open to exception and modification. The one generalization that we can make is simply that each age finds its own way of dealing with the universal necessity of death, usually rejecting most of the symbology of its predecessors and using old methods to new ends. To some extent, the process is cyclical: the mixed nature of the soul and the admission of fear are common to the Middle Ages and the Shakespearean period, while the bifurcation of man and the denial of fear (even to the extent of death-longing) recur in the early Tudor and the New Wave periods. To another extent, the process is linear: we begin with a centralized system of belief, progress to a period of religious controversy, finally develop the Anglican settlement of religious compromise, and then split up into religious controversy again— this time in an increasingly pluralistic society; in each case, we must deal with a new system of fears and comforts, and can never completely go back to an older society or to symbols that have lost their original force. If there are any constants in these changing equations, they are the need, first, to take control of the nightmare, to use the very fears against themselves; and second, to absorb the fact of dying into the rationale for living.

To be sure, there are paradoxes and contradictions in every age: dissenting opinions, failures to practice what we preach, and mutually contradictory traditions existing side by side. Even in our own age, as D. J. Enright points out in his introduction to *The Oxford Book of Death*,[1] we seem unable to make up our minds about what we are afraid of or what will comfort us. On one hand, there is a growing fascination with death and dying, beginning with Elisabeth Kübler-Ross's "thanatology" and the hospice movement, and continuing with a spate of articles and books on dying, including *The Hour of Our Death*, *The Oxford Book of Death*, and this book itself. On the other hand, a plethora of health advice articles and appeals for research contributions imply that if we do all the right things, we shall never die.

Shortly after I began the research for this book, a friend, the manager of a cemetery, showed me the new sales-presentation book prepared for his salespeople, and I was amused and delighted to see that the cycle of death literature never stops turning. On one page was an oddly euphemistic memento mori:

We Cannot:
     Predict . . . . *IT*.
     Prevent . . . . *IT*.
     Evade . . . . *IT*.
     Avoid . . . . *IT*.

Or Even:
     Postpone . . . . *IT*.

Therefore—it is better to:
     Prepare . . . . For . . . . *IT*.

Now!   Today!   The RIGHT Way![2]

On the next several pages were descriptions of cemetery plots and mausoleums that should be purchased immediately—or, as the trade jargon says, "pre-need." One wonders what the *Everyman* playwright, Wager, Shakespeare, and Donne would say about this "right way" of preparing for death. But then, buying a cemetery plot may be as valid a preparation for some as sacramental or predestinarian theology, or checkmate to tyrants or emotional death-longing, may be for others. The readiness, as Hamlet would say, is all.

But to bring this study to a close, I should like to present one more play, a play that also uses old methodology to new purposes, and yet contradicts its own age as well as all the others. *The Tragedy of Nero* (ca. 1624), although written in the midst of the New Wave, is a remarkable compendium of ways of dying, both old and new, and combines the mad intensity of *Pride of Life* and the Dances of Death with the unanswered and unanswerable questions of the seventeenth century. Nero himself, a comic grotesque worthy of Webster or Tourneur, may also be considered almost a perverted anti-type of the fourteenth-century King of Life. But although he is the visible villain-hero of the play, Death is the invisible one. At first it may seem that the two are one, that Nero, who issues all the death warrants, is the Summons, portrayed as a monster in the old style. He conducts a Dance of Death in act 3, playing his timbrel over burning Rome while a mother enters with her dead child and a son with his dead father; and as the two victims mourn in alternate strophes, Nero sings and congratulates himself on the symmetry and excellence of his pageant. He orders the execution of all who defy him: conspirators, rivals, and disgruntled audiences at his plays. And when his wife, Poppea, seems to be flirting with a young man, he throws her to the ground and kicks her to death. But in this last act of violence, we begin to see that Nero is at the mercy of the very Death that he imagines himself to represent. He cannot bring the dead back to life again, and is reduced by the death of a loved one (even though he has caused the death himself) to denial, empty raging, and fetishistic destruction:

> *Nero:* Fetch her again; she shall not die.
>   I'll ope the iron gates of hell,
>   And break the imprison'd shadows of the deep,
>   And force from death this far too worthy prey.
>   She is not dead. . . .
>   [To Poppea's body:] [D]o not with wry aspect
>   Look on your Nero, who in blood shall mourn

> Your luckless fate, and many a breathing soul
> Send after you to wait upon their Queen.
> This shall begin, the rest shall follow after
> And fill the streets with outcries and with slaughter.
>
> (4.5.65–69; 84–89)[3]

Finally, it is time for Nero to die. He has been overthrown and sentenced by the Senate to a felon's execution: to be stripped naked and whipped to death. In his hiding place, he agonizes over his fate, first in terms of the pain and ignominy of the sentence—the private aspect of death—and then in terms of the universal Summons, the annihilation of self, the death of all the world:

> *Nero:* Alas, how sharp and terrible is death!
> O, must I die, must now my senses close,
> Forever die, and ne'er return again,
> Nevermore see the sun, nor heaven, nor earth?
> Whither go I? What shall I be anon?
> What horrid journey wanderest thou, my soul,
> Under th' earth, in dark, damp, dusky vaults?
> Or shall I now to nothing be resolv'd?
> My fears become my hopes—O, would I might!
> Methinks I see the boiling Phlegethon. . . .
>
> (5.3.73–82)

Nero's cry of anguish echoes all the cries that we have heard since the earliest Mystery plays. It is the "too late" of the damned souls, the "Whither shall I fly?" of Everyman, the "Is there no remedy?" of Worldly Man, the "Let me breathe awhile" of Faustus, the "Ah, but to die and go we know not where" of Claudio, the journeys into darkness taken by the villains of Webster, Tourneur, and Shirley alike. It is the fear that all will end—followed by the more horrible fear that all will *not* end, that even annihilation is preferable to the "something after death."

Nero is comforted by two Roman citizens who serve as the wise deathbed counselors. Even in the Tudor tradition, where the reprobate rejects such counsel, the counselors themselves must speak with the voice of rectitude; but in *Nero*, this rectitude is the voice of Selimus, scoffing at the punishing gods:

> 1 *Roman:* These are the idle terrors of the night,
>   Which wise men, though they teach, do not believe,
>   To curb our peasures fain, and aid the weak. . . .
> 2 *Roman:* Why should our faults fear punishment from [the gods]?
>   What do the actions of this life concern
>   The other world, with which is no commerce?
>   (5.3.91–93; 99–101)

The important thing to note in this remarkable piece of deathbed comfort is the complete inversion of the Arts of Dying: a sermon against rather than for repentance, the offer of a soulless universe as a universal good—and yet, the Romans' genuine concern for Nero, and Nero's genuine need for such comfort. He is faced with the choice between a quick, honorable death at his own hand and a lingering, ignominious one at the hands of the Senate. He *must* be encouraged to do the better thing; but the better thing, here, is couched in precisely the terms that seventeenth-century audiences would think atheistic.

Nor does the paradox end here. Nero, wanting to believe his comforters but still trembling in terror of death, begs them to help him. If what they say is true, he pleads, will they not accompany him on his journey? "Will you, by dying, teach me to bear death / With courage?" (5.3.111–12). Poor Emperor Everyman. He receives the same reply that his fifteenth-century predecessor did: "No necessity of death / Hangs o'er *our* heads" (5.3.112–13). And the Romans, both true and false friends, leave Nero to make the journey alone, saying, like the old Summons, "there is no remedy." The soldiers approach, and Nero, with a wail of despair, takes—the correct way out of life.

Paradox upon paradox: we, the audience, are forced to choose between two evils as though they were two goods. And even if we accept the counsel of the comforters while rejecting their philosophy, we must still acknowledge that they, like the "wise men" whom they mock, are preaching what they do not believe.

Still, given time, we may untangle the knots of paradox—except that Nero's is not the only paradoxical death in the play.

When the anti-Nero conspiracy is first discovered, Piso, the leader, commits suicide rather than be captured by the Imperial Guard. His rationale is cool and logical, combining the Stoic's free acceptance of death and the leader's sense of cause—and, perhaps, a touch of New Wave reluctance to grow old:

> *Piso:*   O, friends, I would not die
> When I can live no longer. 'Tis my glory
> That free and willing I give up this breath. . . .
> By this you shall my quiet thoughts intend;
> I blame nor earth nor heaven for my end.
>
> (4.2.68–75)

While he speaks, it is easy for us to think of all the heroic deaths in lost causes: the men and women who gave checkmate to the foul tyrant. But when he is dead, his fellow conspirators seem less impressed than we are. They argue—and, we realize with a shock, they are right—that Piso's death leaves them leaderless and scattered, that they are now one fewer against the enemy, and that in fact Piso has taken the easy way out, leaving the rest of them to face the torture chamber alone. What before seemed like strength now seems like weakness, summed up by Lucan's rueful farewell to Piso's body: "O, that this noble courage had been shown / Rather on enemies' breasts than on thy own" (4.2.76–77).

However, if we are now vaguely uneasy about Piso's heroic stoicism, we may yet look forward to the great Seneca's death. We see him among his students, comforting them against his imminent execution, much like any teacher down through the ages who tries to make his students apply their learning to their lives. They cannot be consoled, however; they cannot bear to part with a loved one, or to be left along mindful of their own mortality. Finally, Seneca reminds them of the afterlife, a return of the soul to the Ideal Form, in which are to be found the secrets of the universe. For the scholar, Seneca's may be the best comfort. And yet, we must ask ourselves, why are his students not comforted? Just as the conversion of a skeptic is a dramatic means of convincing a skeptical audience, so the doubts of the convinced must cause us to doubt. And before we have a chance to settle the upheaval in our minds, we are shown still another way of dying: the death of Petronius, the hedonist.

Before Petronius's entrance, his friends Antonius and Enanthe voice great concern over how he will react to his death warrant. He has been so fond of his pleasures, they reason, that for him death will be more horrible than for men less attached to the world. It is easy enough, says Antonius, for "Seneca and such sour fellows" to part with what they never had or wanted in the first place (4.7.7–8), but how will Petronius bear the separation from all that he has held dear? They are astounded, then, when Petronius enters joyfully and tells them that he can hardly wait to die so he can begin to taste the delights of heaven:

> *Petronius:* Death, the grim knave, but leads you to the door,
>   Where, enter'd once, all curious pleasures come
> To meet and welcome you.
>
> (4.7.33–35)

Petronius then goes on to describe these "curious pleasures," envisioning the Elysian fields as a garden of sensual delights. But his friends, who before have feared for him and hoped to comfort him, now perversely try to pick apart the web of comfort that he has spun for himself:

> *Antonius:* What? be not ravish'd with thy fancies, do not
>   Court nothing, nor make love unto our fears.
> *Petronius:* Is't nothing that I say?
> *Antonius:*   But empty words.
>
> (4.7.64–66)

The roles are now completely reversed. In order to face with equanimity the loss of this world, Petronius must convince himself that the next world is better; but in doing so, he must denigrate this world to throw the contrast into sharper relief. Antonius and Enanthe, then, see his paean to death as a betrayal of their epicurean philosophy, and to stave off despair must force Petronius to reject death and return to the praise of life. The irony, of course,

is that Petronius has no choice; he is under sentence of execution and must stave off a different type of despair.

Finally, Petronius invites his friends to go with him to the
happy land that he envisions, slyly intimating that since they live
by the senses only the act of dying will give them tangible proofs
and settle the argument. But Antonius is not persuaded; lapsing
into the hostility common to all such invited companions, he
replies:

> *Antonius:* Nay, I had rather far believe thee here.
>   Others' ambition such discoveries seek;
>   Faith, I am satisfied with the base delights
>   Of common men.
>
> (4.7.71–74)

The two sides of the argument are now committed to an ever-
increasing battle of mutual rejection; and what began for Petronius
as a simple effort to die well has become a need to repudiate life.
He responds to Antonius's defense of living with a warning that
begins like that of the old Legend but ends like the New Wave
fear of decay:

> *Petronius:* Perhaps thou thinkst to live yet twenty years,
>   Which may unlook'd for be cut off, as mine,
>   If not, to endless time compar'd, is nothing;
>   What you endure must ever, endure now;
>   Nor stay not to be last at table set;
>   Each best day our life at first doth go,
>   To them succeeds diseased age and woe.
>
> (4.7.88–94)

Antonius and Enanthe remain unconvinced, however, and hold
firmly to their allegiance to life while Petronius goes off to die
gladly. All the conspirators are now gone, and the only death
remaining is Nero's. Virtually half the play has been given over
to the art of dying, but what is noteworthy about all these deaths
is that none of them can be viewed as completely exemplary or
completely cautionary. Piso, Seneca, and Petronius die bravely
and joyfully; but their followers think them victims of self-
deception. Nero dies correctly; but he has had to become an

atheist to keep from dying fearfully and clumsily. Furthermore, each of the four Morientes has advanced a different view of and rationale for death: Piso, honor and earthly fame; Seneca, the progress into the Ideal Intellect; Petronius, the reward of a sensual paradise; and Nero, total annihilation or eternal pain. They cannot all be right—and they may all be wrong.

One would think that such a mass of paradoxes, such an inconclusive gloss on the ways men die, would make *The Tragedy of Nero* a frightening play, a play that demolishes all the comforts that humankind has ever erected against death. But curiously, it does not. What we see instead is a record of human striving after the eternal, the last great Dance of Death in which any of us may see himself or herself responding to the touch of the skeletonic hand. Like Everyman, Petronius, and Nero, we want company in the Dance, and the skill of the dancers is immaterial as long as they are simply there.

Notes

Chapter One

1. Huizinga, *The Waning of the Middle Ages* (London: Edward Arnold, 1924), 125–26; Kurtz, *The Dance of Death and the Macabre Spirit in European Literature* (New York: Columbia Univ. Press, 1934), 5–6; Spencer, *Death and Elizabethan Tragedy*, chap. 1; Farnham, *The Medieval Heritage of Elizabethan Tragedy* (Berkeley: Univ. of California Press, 1936), chaps. 1–2.
2. *Dombey and Son*, chap. 16.
3. See Philip Aries, *The Hour of Our Death*, trans. Helen Weaver (New York: Knopf, 1981), 112. Louis Edward Jordan III describes some other female Deaths in early iconography but acknowledges that they generally disappear after the fourteenth century; see his Ph.D. dissertation, "The Iconography of Death in Western Medieval Art to 1350," Univ. of Notre Dame, 1980, especially chap. 4 and figs. 66, 67, and 70.
4. In *Select Early English Poems*, ed. Sir Israel Gollancz (London: Oxford Univ. Press, 1930), ll. 165–70. [*farden* = behaved; *leres* = cheeks.]
5. *Prestyle* = readily; *craddantlye* = cowardly.
6. Potter, *The English Morality Play* (London: Routledge & Kegan Paul, 1975), 20.
7. Philippa Tristram, *Figures of Life and Death in Medieval English Literature* (London: Paul Elek, 1976), 163–64. See also Jordan, 99–107.
8. Illustrated in T. S. R. Boase, *Death in the Middle Ages* (London: Thames and Hudson, 1972), 105.

9. John Lydgate, *The Dance of Death*, ed. and intro. Florence Warren (London: EETS, 1931), intro., x.
10. In *Religious Lyrics of the XVth Century*, ed. Carleton Brown (Oxford: Clarendon Press, 1939), 248–49.
11. *Dance of Death*, 11. 665–72. All quotations from Lydgate's *Dance* are taken from the Ellesmere manuscript as given in Warren's edition.
12. *The Four Last Things*, quoted by Warren, xxiv; see also Farnham, 181.
13. Spencer, *Death and Elizabethan Tragedy*, 31.
14. *Dance of Death*, p. 89, l. 320.
15. Lowry Charles Wimberly, *Folklore in the English and Scottish Ballads* (Chicago: Univ. of Chicago Press, 1928), 236.
16. Ariès 114. See also Jordan, figs. 67–70.
17. Ariès 119. See Jordan's chap. 6 and figs. 103, 117–25, although Jordan does not always differentiate among the Summons, the Apocalypse, and the Triumph.
18. We may remember that the Restoration thought Shakespeare a rustic, the nineteenth century thought Donne a barbarian, and even today, some readers persist in calling Chaucer "childlike."
19. *Religious Lyrics of the XVth Century*, 236.
20. *William Dunbar*, "Lament for the Makaris," in *The Poems of William Dunbar*, ed. W. Mackay Mackenzie (London: Faber and Faber, 1932), 20–21 [ll. 9–12, 17–20]. Dunbar lists seventeen types who join this pilgrimage, from the "bab" to the "rhetoris."
21. *The Works of Geoffrey Chaucer*, ed. F. N. Robinson (Boston: Houghton Mifflin, 1957), 152.
22. See Tristram, plates 10 and 19.
23. Unless otherwise noted, the works cited are illustrated in *The World of Dürer: 1475–1528*, ed. Francis Russell (New York: Time, Inc., 1967), on the pages indicated. This plate is on p. 101.
24. Illustrated in Frederick Parkes Weber, *Aspects of Death and Correlated Aspects of Life in Art, Epigram, and Poetry* (1918; rpt. College Park, Md: McGrath, 1971), 70.
25. References are to the Hans Reinhardt edition, *Holbein*, trans. Prudence Montagu-Pollock (London: William Heinemann, 1938), 154–57. The endless popularity of Holbein's *Dance* is attested to by the Dover Press publication of a paperback edition; first published in 1971, the book is still in print as I write, and apparently selling well.
26. See, for example, the portrait of Sir Brian Tuke, illustrated in Weber, 137.
27. Illustrated in Reinhardt, 73; Russell, 154–55.
28. STC 6222. Farnham has an illustration of this broadside facing p. 293, but it is reduced to too small a size to be entirely legible.
29. STC 6223.

30. In *The Complete Works of Samuel Rowlands* (Hunterian Club, 1880; rpt. New York: Johnson Reprint, 1966), vol. 1. Pagination in this edition is not consecutive.

31. STC 6444.

32. STC 5569.

33. "Vppon a deedmans hed, that was sent to hym from an honorable jentyll– woman for a token, deuysed this gostly medytacyon in Englysh, couenable in sentence, comendable, lamentable, lacrymable, profytable for the soule," in *The Poetical Works of John Skelton*, ed. Alexander Dyce (1843; rpt. New York: AMS Press, 1965), 1:18. For a modern-spelling version, see *John Skelton's Complete Poems*, ed. Philip Henderson (London: Dent, 1959), 19.

34. See Spencer, 51–52; Weber, 749–62, illus. 751.

35. Whitney, *A Choice of Emblemes*, ed. Henry Green (New York: Benjamin Blom, 1967), 132.

36. Wither, *A Collection of Emblemes, Ancient and Modern*, ed. and intro. Rosemary Freeman (Columbia: Univ. of South Carolina Press, 1975), intro., vii.

37. "Bethinking hym self of his ende, writeth thus," in *The Paradise of Dainty Devices*, ed. Hyder Edward Rollins (Cambridge: Harvard Univ. Press, 1927), 112.

38. "Thinke to dye," *Paradise*, 52.

39. *The Complete Poetical Works of Spenser*, ed. R. E. Neil Dodge (1908; rpt. Cambridge: The Riverside Press, 1936), III.vi.39–40.

40. William Shakespeare, Sonnet 146, in *The Complete Works*, ed. G. B. Harrison (New York: Harcourt Brace Jovanovich, 1968), 1622.

41. John Donne, Holy Sonnet 6, in *Major Poets of the Earlier Seventeenth Century*, ed. Barbara K. Lewalski and Andrew J. Sabol (New York: Odyssey Press, 1973), 154.

42. George Herbert, "Death," in Lewalski and Sabol, 375–76.

Chapter Two

1. Rosemary Woolf, *The English Religious Lyric in the Middle Ages* (Oxford: Clarendon Press, 1968), 81.

2. Ibid., 82.

3. *The Art of Dying Well: The Development of Ars Moriendi* (New York: Columbia Univ. Press, 1942; rpt. New York: AMS Press, 1966), 4–5.

4. See O'Connor, 18–24; Spencer, 22.

5. STC 789. I have chosen this version because it is the most accessible to the modern scholar, and because a late abridgement usually indicates which part of a book a given society has found most useful or appealing.

6. One may draw a homely analogy here with the pains of childbirth or athletic training. Because such pains have a goal, they are viewed differently—more constructively—than pains associated with disease or accident. In fact, people who have been trained to "cooperate" with goal-oriented pains, to use them as gauges of progress toward the goal, generally report that the gauging process itself distracts the mind to a certain extent from the physical pain.

7. Friends were obviously expected to play a large role during death. In addition to their sections of the Ars moriendi tracts, they were also provided separate manuals to read aloud to the dying, such as the 1498 Doctrynall of Dethe (STC 6932), which is especially directed toward helping Moriens through his bodily pain.

8. STC 6035a.

9. Note that invoking the testimony of the "good pagans" is not new to the sixteenth century; the earliest Artes contain references to them as well. But the reaction against old tradition, coupled with enthusiasm for new learning, does change the emphasis somewhat.

10. John Lydgate, The Assembly of Gods: or, the Accord of Reason and Sensuality in the Fear of Death (London: EETS, 1896), pp. 57–59, ll. 1958–2023.

11. "Lament for the Makaris," Poems, 23.

12. In The Life and Works of Thomas Lupset, ed. John Archer Gee (New Haven: Yale Univ. Press, 1928), 273.

13. STC 1757. O'Connor places the work "before 1560" (Art of Dying Well, 195); Nancy Lee Beaty, "before 1553" (The Craft of Dying: A Study in the Literary Tradition of the Ars Moriendi in England [New Haven: Yale Univ. Press, 1970], p. 108, n. 3).

14. O'Connor points out that "in the 1563 ed. little hands in the margin often emphasize anti-Catholic passages" (Art of Dying Well, p. 195, n. 174).

15. "[T]he heavy-handed, unembellished statement and restatement of doctrinal theses is effective only in so far as the reader is already a committed Christian, emotionally predisposed to respond to dogma itself—and Calvinist dogma at that. However effectively instructed, the unregenerate will remain outside the pale" (Craft of Dying, 146).

16. In Remains of Myles Coverdale, ed. George Pearson, The Parker Society (Cambridge: Cambridge Univ. Press, 1846), 37–132.

17. STC 23474.

18. Eleventh edition, 1619, STC 1603.

19. STC 18024.

20. STC 22949.

21. STC 17294. Versions of the acrostic appear in medieval woodcuts also; the new items are the emblems stressing new life.

22. STC 18073

23. 1632 edition, STC 23365a.

24. "Of Death," in *The Complete Essays of Francis Bacon*, ed. Henry LeRoy Finch (New York: Washington Square Press, 1963), 9.

25. STC 12495.

26. Fifth edition, 1612, STC 12318, p. 660. Overwhelmed by Greenham's eloquence, the reader may not notice how faulty this arithmetic really is. Fourteen from thirty-five yields not sixteen, but twenty-one; furthermore, once we have subtracted thirty-five years for sleep, we must not continue to count fourteen whole years for youth—only seven. But as Greenham points out, none of what we are counting exists anyway, so why make a fuss?

Chapter Three

1. Burgess Meredith et al., Caedmon, TC 1031 (n.d.).

2. See, for example, Richard Axton, *European Drama of the Early Middle Ages* (London: Hutchinson Univ. Library, 1974); Alan Brody, *The English Mummers and Their Plays* (Philadelphia: Univ. of Pennsylvania Press, 1969); J. M. R. Margeson, *The Origins of English Tragedy* (Oxford: Clarendon Press, 1967); William Tydeman, *The Theatre in the Middle Ages* (Cambridge: Cambridge Univ. Press, 1978); and Carolyn L. Wightman, "The Genesis and Function of the English Mystery Plays," *Studies in Medieval Culture* 11 (1977): 133–36.

3. For illustrations of this artistic convention, see especially Boase, *Death in the Middle Ages*, 18–26.

4. *The Chester Mystery Cycle*, ed. R. M. Lumiansky and David Mills (London: EETS, 1974), ll. 89–90, 93–96. All references to the Chester plays will be to this edition.

5. See Caxton, *Arte and Crafte*, esp. A2v–A3v and A4v.

6. *Ludus Coventriae, or the Plaie Called Corpus Christi*, ed. K. S. Block (Oxford: EETS, 1922), ll. 57–58, 68. All references to the N-Town plays will be to this edition. However, for ease of reading, I have made certain emendations in spelling: for the thorn and yok, as usual, I give *th* and *y*, respectively; I have also shortened initial *ff* to *f*, changed initial *h* in third-person plural pronouns to *th*, changed *x* to *sh* as appropriate phonetically, omitted initial *h* in words like "anger," and inserted punctuation where a pause is indicated in mid-line.

7. The nine-line stanza used by the Wakefield Master has many similarities to the "bob and wheel" of the *Gawain* poet, and the use of alliteration and verbal portraiture is often reminiscent of *Piers Plowman*.

8. *The Towneley Plays*, ed. George England and Alfred W. Pollard (1897; rpt. London: EETS, 1952), ll. 550–54, 577–79. All references to the Wakefield plays will be to this edition.

9. See, for example, Bertrand H. Bronson, "*The Book of the Duchess* Re-Opened," *PMLA* 67 (1952): 863–71; Joseph E. Grennen, "Hert-Huntying in the *Book of the Duchess*," *Modern Language Quarterly* 25 (1964): 131–39; P. M. Kean, *Chaucer and the Making of English Poetry*, vol. I: *Love Vision and Debate* (London: Routledge & Kegan Paul, 1972), 59 ff.; James R. Kreuzer, "The Dreamer in the *Book of the Duchess*," *PMLA* 66 (1951): 543–47; John Lawlor, "The Pattern of Consolation in *The Book of the Duchess*," *Speculum* 31 (1956): 626–48; and R. M. Lumiansky, "The Bereaved Narrator in Chaucer's *Book of the Duchess*," *Tulane Studies in English* 9 (1959): 5–17.

10. See, for example, Donald C. Baker, "The Dreamer Again in *The Book of the Duchess*," *PMLA* 70 (1955): 279–82; W. H. French, "The Man in Black's Lyric," *JEGP* 66 (1957): 231–41; Stephen Manning, "The Dreamer Once More," *PMLA* 71 (1956): 540–41; J. Burke Severs, "Chaucer's Self-Portrait in the *Book of the Duchess*," *Philological Quarterly* 43 (1964): 27–39; and James Winny, *Chaucer's Dream-Poems* (New York: Barnes & Noble, 1973), 44–75.

11. The manuscript itself was destroyed in 1922, but fortunately a photograph of it had earlier been included in an 1891 edition of the account rolls onto which a scribe had copied the play.

12. In *Non-Cycle Plays and Fragments*, ed. Norman Davis (London: EETS, 1970), ll. 243–58. All references are to this edition. I have taken some liberties with the spelling, but only where the original would be incomprehensible to the modern reader, as in the inconsistent alternations of *v* and *u*.

13. One of the interesting points about this early play is that the King of Life's folly endangers not only his own soul but his entire kingdom. To be sure, his kingdom may here be understood as the state of being, but the motif of the foolish king will later take on more importance in the secular moralities (e.g., *Magnyfycence*, *Respublica*, and *New Custom*) as well as in the Elizabethan chronical plays and Shakespeare's great histories. The *Pride of Life*, then, may be considered one of the first dramatic attempts to see the human creature as a microcosm of the world, long before the burgeoning of andro-centric imagery in the Tudor age.

14. In *English Morality Plays and Moral Interludes*, ed. Edgar T. Schell and J. D. Shuchter (New York: Holt, 1969), ll. 2785–91. All references are to this edition, although I have retained the original "Humanum Genus" rather than using the translated "Mankind," which may be confused with the name of the hero of *Mankynd*.

15. Death's last colloquial sententia is very like that uttered by the Bishop in *Pride of Life* when he decries the abuses of the day: "Thai farit as ficis in a pol— / The gret eteit the smal" (361–62). The similarity may indicate a connection between the two plays—perhaps in time, perhaps in locality, perhaps in a common source.

Chapter Four

1. "Doctrine and Dramatic Structure in *Everyman*," *Speculum* 32 (1957): 726.
2. *Everyman*: The Way to Life," in *Sudies in Medieval, Renaissance, American Literature* (Fort Worth: Texas Christian Univ. Press, 1971), 53–56.
3. This type of learning process—the formulation of questions—is not only pedagogically but doctrinally sound. In the balance between presumption and despair, we remember, Moriens is cautioned to bear in mind that "none is certayn, yf he be dygne or worthy to haue deserued the loue of god, or the hate of god" (Caxton, *Arte and Crafte*, A4r-v); that is, one must continually reexamine one's conscience and avoid assuming that one is a sharer in God's omniscience.
4. In Schell and Shuchter, ll. 47–51. All references are to this edition. Note, by the way, what has happened to "the big fish eat the small" by this time. The original fresh imagery has faded into what is now obviously a stock phrase.
5. "*Everyman*: A Dramatization of Death," *Quarterly Journal of Speech* 59 (1978): 91.
6. "Doctrine and Structure in *Everyman*," 726.
7. Caxton, *Arte and Crafte*, A4r.
8. "Tetelestai," in *Collected Poems* (New York: Oxford Univ. Press, 1953), 299.
9. *Dance of Death*, 1. 216.

Chapter Five

1. A symbol may be defined as an object or figure that represents something or someone other than itself; an allegory, on the other hand, announces itself *as* itself. Thus, a skeleton that declares, "I hatte Drery Deth" is an allegory, while a skull inscribed "Memento Mori" is more properly termed a symbol. The two may be combined, of course; the Dreary Death may carry an hourglass and dart, or may become a metaphor in absentia, as when we speak of the cold hand of death. For a good treatment of the subject, see Angus Fletcher's *Allegory: The Theory of a Symbolic Mode* (Ithaca, N.Y.: Cornell Univ. Press, 1964).
2. Bernard Spivack, *Shakespeare and the Allegory of Evil* (New York: Columbia Univ. Press, 1958), 67. See also Theodore Spencer, *Death and Elizabethan Tragedy*, especially chapters 3 and 4; and Willard Farnham, *The Medieval Heritage of Elizabethan Tragedy*, 227ff.

3. Among these are Adversity in *Magnificence*, Divine Correction in *The Satire of the Three Estates*, Nemesis in *Respublica*, God's Visitation in *Trial of Treasure*, Correction in *Tide Tarrieth No Man*, Rumor in *Nice Wanton*, God's Judgment in *The Longer Thou Livest*, and Severity in *Like Will to Like*. Oddly enough, there *are* death-figures in some of these plays, but they are not the ones that Houle lists: Confusion in *The Longer Thou Livest*, Time in *Trial of Treasure*, and devil and hangman in *Like Will to Like*. (*The English Morality and Related Drama* [n.p.: Archon Books, 1972], 167–68.)

4. See especially Spivack, *Allegory of Evil*, 207, 243.

5. John Calvin, *Institutes of the Christian Religion*, 2 vols., ed. Ford Lewis Battles (Philadelphia: Westminster Press, 1960), II.v.3.

6. Indeed, in *Tide Tarrieth No Man*, one of the Vices does report the death of another, and then, caught in the paradox between allegory and reality, immediately corrects himself:

> Courage: *Out, alas, these tidings are ill!*
> *My friend Master Greediness hath ended his days!. . .*
> *Why, fool, Greediness will never die*
> *So long as covetous people do live!*
> (In Schell and Shuchter, ll. 1653–54; 1665–66.)

7. One of the best recent discussions of these troublesome times is given by G. R. Elton in *Reform and Reformation: England 1509–1558* (Cambridge: Harvard University. Press, 1977). For the changes in doctrines, see especially pp. 256–60, 274, 287–88, and 366. Elton manages a surprisingly objective account of a time that still—after four hundred and fifty years—calls forth invective and bitter partisanship among otherwise rational scholars.

8. Becon, *Sicke Mannes Salve*. See my chapter 2.

9. "The English Morality Play as a Weapon of Religious Controversy," *Studies in English Literature* 2 (1962): 165. In the reign of Mary, of course, the common enemy became the Reformation.

10. STC 7896.

11. Robert Potter documents the tenuous survival of the fourteenth-century Paternoster Play until it was ignored to death by Archbishop Grindal in 1572; and F. P. Wilson and G. K. Hunter suggest that the N-Town Cycle may have struggled along until 1580. See Potter, *The English Morality Play* (London: Routledge & Kegan Paul, 1975), 23–25; Wilson and Hunter, *The English Drama 1485–1585* (Oxford: Clarendon Press, 1968), 198.

12. Among these plays are *Mankind* (ca. 1485), *Mundus et Infans* (ca. 1510), *Hickscorner* (ca. 1516), *Youth* (ca. 1516), *Lusty Juventus* (ca. 1550), and *Nice Wanton* (ca. 1550). The various Wit and Wisdom (or Wit and Science) plays deal more with secular education than with religious salvation.

13. All references to the two Wager plays are to the Regents Renaissance Drama Series edition, ed. R. Mark Benbow (Lincoln: Univ. of Nebraska Press, 1967).

14. Bernard Spivack, *Allegory of Evil*, 211.

15. I have used the text given in Dodsley's *Old English Plays*, ed. W. Carew Hazlet (1874; rpt. New York: Benjamin Blom, 1964), vol. 3. References in parentheses to "Dodsley" in all cases will include volume and page numbers; no line numbers are given in the text.

16. Perkins, *A Discourse of Conscience* [1596], ed. Thomas F. Merrill (Nieuwkoop: B. De Graaf, 1966), 46.

17. Greenham, *Works*, 106, 232. See also R. T. Kendall, *Calvin and English Calvinism to 1649* (Oxford: Oxford Univ. Press, 1979), 46.

18. The choice of Inclination as the main Vice in *Trial of Treasure* may remind us of the Carthusian's rueful comment, in Lydgate's *Dance of Death*, that despite all preparation each man "Dredeth to dy / by kyndeli mocioun / / After his flessheli / Inclynacioun" (356–57). Throughout *Trial*, Just "bridles" Inclination (with a real bridle), and may therefore be said to achieve, among other things, a loss of the "dred" of Death. Whether or not *Trial*'s playwright had this episode of the *Dance* in mind will, of course, never be known. But the publication of the *Dance* together with the Time-centered *Fall of Princes* in 1554 makes the speculation an interesting one.

19. As early as the reign of Queen Mary, the emblematic figure of Time had begun to infiltrate the stage. In *Respublica*, the Vice Avarice comments sardonically on the impending arrival of Truth by describing Truth's father:

> Avarice: *Old Time's daughter? That shuttle-brained tall long man*
> *That ne'er standeth still but flyeth as fast as he can,*
> *Much like as he swimmed or glided upon ice? . . .*
> *I know him; he carrieth a clock on his head,*
> *A sand glass in his hand, a dial in his forehead. . . .*
> *Old Time the eavesdropper? I know him, pardee!*
> *An ancient turner of houses upside down*
> *And a common consumer of city and town.*
> *Old Time's daughter, quoth he? I shrew his naked heart!*
> *Many of my friends hath he brought to pain and smart.*

(In Schell and Shuchter, 1355–56; 1360–61; 1363–67.) Avarice, as we might expect, pays dearly for his disrespect toward Truth and Time.

20. Calvin, *Institutes*, III.iii.22. This is not to suggest that ignorance was considered an excuse. Ignorance was a sign of reprobacy, too, in that the soul had not been given the grace to know the truth. But seeing truth and denying it was considered even worse.

21. In this context, Ignorance is much like Corceca in Book 1 of *The Faerie Queene:* the "blind devotion" that is actually ignorance of religious truth, and therefore the mother of superstition.

22. Benbow gives the physician the name "Master Flebishiten," a name not included in the original text but one used to the Physician by Covetous. I think Benbow has made an error here. "Flebishiten" is obviously a deliberate malapropism of "Physician," and Covetous, as the Vice, is ridiculing the good Physician by mispronouncing his name. Every time Covetous uses this term, the Physician rebukes him for "jesting." Wager uses the same device in *Longer* to show Moros's folly and incorrigibility.

23. In Schell and Shuchter, ll. 19–30.

24. Spenser was later to use this type of debate with Despair to shattering effect in *The Faerie Queene*. Redcrosse knight is no more match for Despayre's specious reasoning than is Wastefulness; but he, like his predecessor, is saved at the last gasp by an emblem of faith, in his case, Una.

25. See Lily B. Campbell, "Doctor Faustus: A Case of Conscience," *PMLA* 67 (1952): 219–39.

26. In Schell and Shuchter, l. 1997.

27. *Institutes*, III.xx.31. The medieval view had been that even the speaking of the words might open the heart to grace, or at least focus the mind on God. But under the Calvinist system, Philologus cannot benefit from what we may call the medicinally preventive effect of his words.

28. Such withdrawal, while common to minority groups, is itself a result of a double bind: if the ruling society excludes the minority, the only way the minority can assert its existence is to exclude the ruling class in turn, and to insist on its own customs as the mark of excellence.

29. Hamlet insists that Horatio remain alive to tell his story; and even in the early *Appius and Virginia*, the martyred virgin's reward is represented on stage by Reward, Fame, and Memory, who decorate her tomb:

> Reward: *I grant him that the learned pen shall have the aid of me,*
> *To write in learned verse the honour of her name.*
> Fame: *And eke it shall resound by trump of me Dame Fame.*
> *[Here let Memory write on the tomb.]*
> Memory: *I Memory will mind her life: her death shall ever reign*
> *Within the mouth and mind of man, from age to age again.*
> (Dodsley, 4:154)

30. The good are taken away to the Elysian Fields in *The Spanish Tragedy*; the wastrel King Edward II asks God to receive his soul; Richard II bids his soul mount to heaven; Horatio asks "flights of angels" to sing Hamlet to his rest; and so on.

31. *Selimus* (London: Malone Society, 1908), 1829–31.

32. The intervening lines are a long "ubi sunt" litany: "Where's . . . but in my triumph," indicating at least a familiarity with the Triumphs of Death.

33. Wells, *Elizabethan and Jacobean Playwrights* (New York: Columbia Univ. Press, 1939), 15.

34. This folkloric motif has analogues in almost every literature: the mistletoe that kills Baldur; Achilles' heel; and the mustard-seed parable of the Bible. In the fairy tale, the hero (usually a youngest son) discovers that a pin will destroy a magically erected wall that whole armies have been unable to batter down or scale. Interestingly enough, the motif has been used even in modern fairy tales; a magic wall is destroyed by a pin in L. Frank Baum's *The Lost Princess of Oz*.

35. I have used as my text *The Dramatic Works of Thomas Dekker*, 2 vols., ed. Fredson Bowers (Cambridge: Cambridge Univ. Press, 1953), but have modernized spelling and punctuation.

36. Costuming plays an important part in this drama. Virtue and Vice wear allegorical costumes:

> *Enter Vice with gilded face, and horns on her head: her garments long, painted before with silver half-moons, increasing by little and little, till they come to the full; in the midst of them in capital letters this written: CRESCIT EUNDO; her garment painted behind with fools' faces and devils' heads, and underneath it in the middle this written: Ha, ha, he. . . . After her comes Virtue, a cockscomb on her head, all in white before, and this written about the middle: SIBI SAPIT; her attire behind painted with crowns and laurel garlands, stuck full of stars, held out by hands thrust out of bright clouds, and among them this written: DOMINABITUR ASTRIS.*
>
> (S.D. 1.3.1)

Furthermore, the fruits of Vice and Virtue are represented both by literal apples and by more costuming: the apples of Vice produce the stock comic horns on a character's head, and the apples of Virtue remove them.

37. The division of sons into good and bad in this play is not as marked as it would have been in the moralities of the 1560s and 1570s. Even Andelocia has his virtuous moments, and Ampedo some weaknesses. We are probably seeing more folkloric than Calvinistic influence: the older sons who come to nothing and the disregarded younger son who kills the dragon.

38. Slights, " 'Elder in a Deform'd Church': The Function of Marston's Malcontent," *Studies in English Literature* 13 (1973): 360–73; Salomon, "The Theological Basis of Imagery and Structure in *The Malcontent*," *Studies in English Literature* 14 (1974): 271–84.

39. Tom Stoppard notwithstanding, I exclude Rosencrantz and Guildenstern—as well as Polonius—from the list of innocent bystanders. Espionage is a

dangerous business, and death in the performance of these duties may be sad, futile, or even unfair, but it is scarcely accidental.

40. In *Thomas Middleton: Three Plays*, ed. Kenneth Muir (London: Dent, 1975), 5.2.152–53.

41. Conversely, Death may arrive as the *most* likely suspect: the State's mighty messengers, hangman, jailer, and arresting officer.

42. In *Locrine*, the ghost of Albanact strikes food out of Humber's hands to keep him from eating, although death by starvation seems a bit vindictive even for a ghost.

43. *Daemonologie, in the Forme of a Dialogue* (1597), STC 14364, p. 63.

44. (Tudor Facsimile Texts; rpt. New York: AMS Press, 1970), L4v. I have modernized spelling and punctuation.

45. The departure from Calvinist theology is evident even here; Calvin would deny the efficacy of penance.

46. James Boswell, *Life of Johnson*, ed. R. W. Chapman (London: Oxford Univ. Press, 1953), 849.

47. In *The Works of Thomas Nashe*, vol. 3, ed. Ronald B. McKerrow (London: Sidgwick & Jackson, 1910), 246. Note the unusual reference to "good deeds" in the last line, which harks back to the medieval *Everyman*. (I have modernized the spelling and punctuation in *Summer's Last Will and Testament* with regret; the rhymes, especially in the second lyric, are more pleasing to the eye in the original.)

Chapter Six

1. Marlowe, *Tamburlaine the Great*, ed. John D. Jump, Regents Renaissance Drama Series (Lincoln: Univ. of Nebraska Press, 1967), I: 2.7.20. All references to *Tamburlaine* will be to this edition.

2. Marlowe, *Doctor Faustus*, ed. John D. Jump, Revels Plays (London: Methuen, 1962), Prologue, 15:20. I will use this edition throughout my discussion (chapters 6 and 7), because I consider it the best available modern-spelling edition. However, I have worked cautiously with this text, comparing it frequently with Fredson Bowers's old-spelling version in *The Complete Works of Christopher Marlowe*, vol. 2 (Cambridge: Cambridge Univ. Press, 1973), which appears to be textually more thorough and as nearly accurate as any twentieth-century reconstruction of the play can hope to be. As above, I will cite the scene and line numbers in the Revels Edition, followed by a colon and the line numbers in the Bowers edition.

3. The debate has gone on so long and so voluminously that it would be futile to attempt a representative bibliography here. For a sampling of advo-

cates of the "aspiring mind," see Una Ellis-Fermor, *Christopher Marlowe* (London: Methuen, 1927); Paul H. Kocher, *Christopher Marlowe: A Study of His Thought, Learning, and Character* (Chapel Hill: Univ. of North Carolina Press, 1946); Michael Poirier, *Christopher Marlowe* (London: Chatto and Windus, 1951); and Eugene M. Waith, "Tamburlaine, the Herculean Hero," in *Christopher Marlowe's Tamburlaine Part One and Part Two*, ed. Irving Ribner (New York: Odyssey Press, 1974), 237–66. For a sampling of the opposite camp, see Roy W. Battenhouse, *Marlowe's Tamburlaine: A Study in Renaissance Moral Philosophy* (Nashville: Vanderbilt Univ. Press, 1941); Douglas Cole, *Suffering and Evil in the Plays of Christopher Marlowe* (Princeton: Princeton Univ. Press, 1962); Helen L. Gardner, "The Second Part of *Tamburlaine the Great*," *Modern Language Review* 37 (1942): 18–24; Michael Hattaway, "The Theology of Marlowe's *Doctor Faustus*," *Renaissance Drama*, n.s. 3 (1970): 51–78; and Charles G. Masinton, *Christopher Marlowe's Tragic Vision: A Study in Damnation* (Athens: Ohio University Press, 1972). An excellent summary of the conflicting camps can be found in Martha Tuck Rozett's *The Doctrine of Election and the Emergence of Elizabethan Tragedy* (Princeton: Princeton Univ. Press, 1984), especially chapters 5 and 7. Rozett herself points out that deliberate ambiguities are built into *Tambrulaine Part I*; Tamburlaine's world-conquering speeches parody religious treatises on assurance of salvation and so show him as a reprobate, but his conquest of the Turk and his wooing of Zenocrate associate him with the patriotic fervor that surrounded Elizabethan courtier-soldiers.

4. Until act 5, Tamburlaine's "dares" are limited to heroic boasts in the conditional mood:

> *Though Mars himself, the angry god of arms,*
> *And all the earthly potentates conspire*
> *To dispossess me of this diadem,*
> *Yet will I wear it in despite of them.*
>
> (2.2.58–61)

> *Zenocrate, were Egypt Jove's own land,*
> *Yet would I with my sword make Jove to stoop.*
>
> (4.4.71–72)

5. *Selimus*, ll. 1757, 2345, 2539. I have, as always, modernized the spelling for the sake of consistency.

6. Compare the flyting speech that Faulconbridge makes about King John in Shakespeare's play:

> Bastard: *For at hand . . .*
>   *Is warlike John; and in his forehead sits*

> A bare-ribbed Death, whose office is this day
> To feast upon whole thousands of the French.
>
> (King John, 5.2.173–78)

Of course, only a few short scenes later, Death will feast on King John, who will describe himself merely as "a scribbled form, drawn with a pen / Upon a parchment" (5.7.32–33).

7. Bajazeth, Zabina, and Arabia are given "seemly" burials at the end of the play, but almost as an afterthought; Tamburlaine either ignores or boasts over their bodies first and leaves them strewn about the stage until the last five lines of the play.

8. "The Ultimate Source of White, Red, Black and Death?" Notes & Queries; n.s. 5 (April 1958): 146–47. Cutts, it must be noted, is forced by this theory to pass too lightly over the "pale" horse of Death itself.

9. Christopher Marlowe's Tragic Vision, 30.

10. Shakespeare apparently recognized the shock value of a human voice speaking the "too late." Richard II, in the midst of his capricious and suspect banishing of Bolingbroke and Mowbray, says, "After our sentence plaining comes too late" (Richard II, 1.3.175). However, Richard shortly does revise his sentence for Bolingbroke; "Such is the breath of kings" (1.3.215).

11. Dylan Thomas, "Do Not Go Gentle into That Good night," in The Poems of Dylan Thomas, ed. Daniel Jones (New York: New Directions, 1971), 207.

12. The Tragedy of Charles Duke of Byron, 5.4.187–96, in The Plays of George Chapman: The Tragedies, Vol. 1, ed. Thomas Marc Parrott (New York: Russell & Russell, 1961).

13. Waith, "Tamburlaine, the Herculean Hero," passim; Cole, Suffering and Evil, 110–12.

14. See especially Jump, ed., Tamburlaine, intro: xii–xiv.

15. Suffering and Evil, 117.

16. See especially Elijah's daring of Baal in 1 Kings 18 : 17–40.

17. "Tamburlaine, the 'Scourge of God,' " in Ribner, ed., Tamburlaine, 198.

18. Suffering and Evil, 116, n. 53.

19. "Marlowe's Tamburlaine II: A Drama of Death," Modern Language Quarterly 26 (1965): 375–87.

20. Lydgate, Dance of Death, LXXX.

21. See Lupset, Dieyng Well, 279–80: "[A]s Epicure saith, if it be an extreme soore payne, it is shorte. For no vehement peyne can be longe."

22. In The Collected Poems of G. K. Chesterton (London: Cecil Palmer, 1927), 230–31.

Chapter Seven

1. "The Dilettante's Lie in *Doctor Faustus*," *Texas Studies in Literature and Language* 24 (1982): 243–54.
2. See, for example, M. M. Mahood, "Marlowe's Heroes," and Richard Benson Sewall, "Doctor Faustus: The Vision of Tragedy," both in *Doctor Faustus: Text and Major Criticism*, ed. Irving Ribner (New York; Odyssey Press, 1966).
3. "Doctor Faustus and the Ends of Desire," in *Two Renaissance Mythmakers: Christopher Marlowe and Ben Jonson*, ed. Alvin Kernan (Baltimore: Johns Hopkins Univ. Press, 1977), 79.
4. "Marlowe's Faustus: A Reconsideration," in Ribner, ed., *Doctor Faustus*, 92.
5. Rozett suggests that Marlowe's audience was heavily inclined to the Calvinist side of the predestination issue within the Church of England, and so would have seen Faustus's actions as incurably reprobate rather than as a matter of free will (*Doctrine of Election*, 209–46). However, as I show later, the most Calvinist branch of the church would by this time have been avoiding plays, and the official Anglican preaching had already begun to condemn the doctrine on which this view was based.
6. 1592 edition, in Jump, ed., *Doctor Faustus*, app. 2, 137–38.
7. "John Calvin and Doctor Faustus," *Modern Language Review* 68 (1973): 12.
8. "Time and the Timeless in *Everyman* and *Dr. Faustus*," *College English* 22 (1960): 11.
9. "*Doctor Faustus*: A Case of Conscience," 223.
10. *Certaine Sermons or Homilies Appointed to be read in Churches* (1623 ed.), ed. Mary Ellen Rickey and Thomas B. Stroup (Gainesville, Fla.: Scholars' Facsimiles & Reprints, 1968), 2: 264–69.
11. *Treatise on Death*, 101–02.
12. *Practise of Pietie*, 697.
13. Since such a trope makes the audience assume more knowledge than that of the speaker, it is difficult to understand how some critics can continue to urge Faustus's opening soliloquy as a mark of his superior mind. Even the groundlings in the audience know more than Faustus does at this point.
14. It is interesting to note that this passage predicts, too, the eventual Puritan and Cavalier uses of predestination in the mid-seventeenth century: the "strange arithmetick" and the carpe diem philosophy discussed in chapter 2.
15. Quoted by Susan Snyder in "The Left Hand of God: Despair in Medieval and Renaissance Tradition," *Studies in the Renaissance* 12 (1963): 30.
16. Caxton, *Arte and Crafte*, A4v.
17. William Perkins, *A Discourse of Conscience*, 49.
18. STC 6621, 85.
19. Dent, *A Sermon of Repentaunce* [1582], STC 6672, A7r.

20. Perkins, A *Discourse of Conscience*, 63.
21. B-Text, which Bowers gives in prose. The A-Text omits lines 3–4 and gives line 2 as "For he hath given to me all his goods."
22. Notice, too, that Faustus does not leave his goods to a worthy cause, as Epaphroditus does in the *Sicke Mannes Salve*, but bestows them entirely on Wagner, the equally unregenerate Clown.
23. "The Religious Despair of Doctor Faustus," *JEGP* 63 (1964): 634.
24. "Deaths Duell," in *The English Sermon, 1550–1650*, ed. Martin Seymour-Smith (Cheadle, Eng.: Carcanet Press, 1976): 383.
25. The Cardinal, it is interesting to note, has a dying soliloquy similar in many ways to that of Faustus. Mistaking King Henry for the Summons of Death, and with Gloucester's death on his conscience, he cries out:

> *Died he [Gloucester] not in his bed? Where should he die?*
> *Can I make men live whether they will or no?*
> *Oh, torture me no more! I will confess.*
> *Alive again? Then show me where he is.*
> *I'll give a thousand pound to look on him.*
> *He hath no eyes, the dust hath blinded them.*
> *Comb down his hair. Look, look! It stands upright,*
> *Like lime twigs set to catch my winged soul.*

(3.3.9–16)

Compare Faustus's "Couldst thou make men to live eternally / Or being dead raise them to life again" (1.24–25: 52–53); "See, see where Christ's blood streams in the firmament" (xix.146; 1939); and "Look, sirs, comes he not? comes he not?" (xix.29–30: 1826).

Chapter Eight

1. This chapter addresses only the issue of approaches to death, and deals with the other important issues—good governance, justice vs. mercy, etc.— only as they are revealed through the death summons.
2. Cinthio, *Hecatommithi*, 8.5., ed. Geoffrey Bullough, in *Narrative and Dramatic Sources of Shakespeare*, vol. 2 (London: Routledge and Kegan Paul, 1963), 425. All references to Bullough are to this volume; where Bullough gives the old spelling, I have modernized it.
3. The only remnant of the figure is the Duke's "He hath released him, Isabel, from the world. / His head is off, and sent to Angelo" (4.3.114–15). But the Duke offers comfort immediately afterward, and knows, besides, that Claudio is still alive.

4. *De Miseria Condicionis Humane*, ed. Robert E. Lewis (Athens: Georgia Univ. Press, 1978), 1: 19. Translations from this text are mine.

5. *The Mirror of Mans Lyfe*, STC 14093, D3v.

6. *A Dialogue of Dying Wel*, trans. R. Verstepan, STC 19815, A8r–v. Petrus's (or his translator's) reference to the wailing "wretch" may remind the reader of Lupset's coward: "What nowe John? dothe not he seeme vnto you a shamefull cowarde, and a fearfull wretche, a playn kikkes without an harte, that with moche intercession, with many prayers desyrethe a lyttelle delay of death?" (*Dieyng Well*, 281).

7. Compare the final couplet of the 1604 broadside-acrostic, *Map of Mortalitie*: "And feare not death: pale oughlie though he be. / Thou art in thrall, he comes to set thee free." (See chapter 2.)

8. *Revels Plays*, ed. R. W. Van Fossen (London: Methuen, 1961), x.18–20.

9. See especially Arthur H. Scouten, "An Historical Appraoch to *Measure for Measure*," *Philological Quarterly* 54 (1975): 75; and J. W. Lever's introduction to the Arden *Measure for Measure* (London: Methuen, 1965), lxxxvi. I have used the Arden edition for all quotations from the play.

10. Arden *Measure for Measure*, intro., lxxxvii.

11. STC 1403, 186–87; 188–89.

12. *Disce Mori*, 114.

13. *Mirror of Mans Lyfe*, D5r.

14. Whether the Duke knows, at this point, that he will save Claudio's life along with his soul is a fruitless speculation. However, that he does plan to continue his sermon is evident from his parting words: "Dear sir, ere long I'll visit you again" (3.1.46).

15. Hutchins, *David's Sling*, 174.

16. *The Arte or Crafte to Lyue Well or to Deye Well* (Anon., ca. 1506), STC 793, F. lii.

17. See Rosalind Miles, *The Problem of* Measure for Measure (New York: Barnes & Noble, 1976), for an excellent account of the centuries-long argument over Isabella's denunciation of her brother.

18. "*Measure for Measure* and the Protestant Ethic," *Essays in Criticism* 11 (1961): 10–33.

19. Perkins, *Cases of Conscience*, 98.

20. Ibid.

21. Critics who defend Claudio's willingness to lay down Isabella's honor for his life may well take note that even Angelo expects better of him and understands what Claudio's society would demand of him in such a crisis.

22. Gless, *Measure for Measure, the Law, and the Convent* (Princeton: Princeton Univ. Press, 1979), especially chapters 1–3.

23. I do not agree with Lever's substitution of "sisters stood" for "sisterhood" in this line. It seems just as likely that "sisterstood" in F was a typo, since it was corrected to "sisterhood" in F2 and subsequent editions.

24. By caviling upon a few points, I do not mean to undercut the value of Miles's work. Her book is a logical and objective grappling with the problems of the play and its audiences.

25. See, for example, *3 Henry VI*, 2.5; *Richard II*, 3.4; *2 Henry IV*, 2.4; and *Henry V*, 4.1.

26. When I say that the bed-trick "does not work," of course, I do not mean that it does not work for Shakespeare; I mean that it does not work for the Duke. Furthermore, although the new problems posed by its failure provide more rigorous teaching and testing of the characters than the Duke originally planned, we cannot deny that some grave psychic damage is risked along the way. Some modern productions recognize this risk by having Isabella stand stunned and alone at the end of the play instead of going off happily with the Duke. As much as I dislike this sort of tampering with Shakespeare's conventional endings, at least it recognizes that there has been some strain before the happy ending, a strain that cannot suddenly be relieved by the grin and skip that Isabella gives at the end of the recent— otherwise excellent—BBC production.

27. As for Lucio's cry that "Marrying a punk . . . is pressing to death, / Whipping, and hanging" (5.1.520–21), can we really see Lucio choosing death before dishonor? Like the other characters in the play, he has tried to order his own destiny—in this scene, by requesting whipping instead of hanging. After the Duke first offers him both and then remits both, all Lucio can bargain for is a remission of the marriage as well. But he, too, must learn to live with someone else's idea of justice and mercy.

28. Like all proverbs in another language, this is a difficult one to translate accurately. "Meh shtarbt nisht azoi gring; meh lebt un mitchet zich" is, really, a response to both "These troubles will kill me" and "I wish I were dead." The use of the reflexive verb "Mitchen zich" also implies that the troubles or griefs are the function of oneself—not necessarily in the sense of assigning blame, but in the sense that the human condition is inherently a condition of trouble, that we breathe in pain as we breathe in air. But we continue to breathe.

Chapter Nine

1. Don D. Moore's *John Webster and His Critics, 1617–1964* (Baton Rouge: Louisiana State Univ. Press, 1966) gives an excellent account of trends in the controversy up to the mid-1960s. Since then, some of the more interesting works on the play are Peter B. Murray's *A Study of John Webster* (The Hague: Mouton, 1969), which takes a friendly approach to the

Duchess and sees the play almost as a religious allegory; Joyce E. Peterson's *Curs'd Example: "The Duchess of Malfi" and Commonweal Tragedy* (Columbia: Univ. of Missouri Press, 1978), which sees the Duchess as a bad ruler and wicked woman; Nicholas Brooke's *Horrid Laughter in Jacobean Tragedy* (New York: Barnes & Noble, 1979), chap. 4, which places the play in the school of the theater of the absurd; and Jacqueline Pearson's *Tragedy and Tragicomedy in the Plays of John Webster* (New York: Barnes & Noble, 1980) and Lee Bliss's *The World's Perspective: John Webster and the Jacobean Drama* (New Brunswick, N.J.: Rutgers Univ. Press, 1983), both of which view the Duchess's triumph as only partially overcoming her antiheroic world. Don D. Moore has published an expanded summary of pre-twentieth-century Webster criticism in the Critical Heritage Series (London: Routledge & Kegan Paul, 1981).

2. Again, see Moore, *John Webster and His Critics.* Two Jacobean Drama Studies monographs, published within a year of each other, typically take opposing views; Robert Freeman Whitman's *Beyond Melancholy: John Webster and the Tragedy of Darkness* (Salzburg, 1973) sets forth the heavenly moral, while Muriel West's *The Devil and John Webster* (Salzburg, 1974) posits every character as a different variety of devil. Pearson and Brooke see a demonic world out of which the Duchess soars like a (sometimes tattered) angel—a view shared, although in a more seriously religious perspective, by Bettie Anne Doebler in "Continuity in the Art of Dying: *The Duchess of Malfi*," *Comparative Drama* 14 (1980): 203–15. Both Ralph Berry and Richard Hillman describe Webster's world as a "meaningless universe" without a God, while Irving Ribner sees it as a "corrupt, disordered, and chaotic universe" in which the "nobility of the human spirit" nevertheless triumphs. See Berry, *The Art of John Webster* (Oxford: Clarendon Press, 1972), esp. 109, 107; Hillman, "Meaning and Mortality in Some Renaissance Revenge Plays," *Univ. of Toronto Quarterly* 49 (1979): 1–17; and Ribner, *Jacobean Tragedy: The Quest for Moral Order* (London: Methuen, 1962), esp. 109.

3. For the former view, see, in particular, Murray; Robert Ornstein, *The Moral Vision of Jacobean Tragedy* (Madison: Univ. of Wisconsin Press, 1960); and, of course, F. L. Lucas's introduction to his edition of *The Duchess of Malfi* (1927; rpt. London: Chatto & Windus, 1958). Peterson is among the most important of the recent critics to espouse the latter view of the Duchess. See also Clifford Leech, *John Webster* (London: Hogarth Press, 1951).

4. Since Lucas's first proposal of this interpretation of Ferdinand's behavior, no critic has been able to ignore the possibility, even if he or she does not entirely agree with it.

5. Tristram, *Figures of Life and Death*, 156.

6. Chambers, *The Jacobean Shakespeare and "Measure for Measure"* (1937; rpt. Freeport, N.Y.: Books for Libraries, 1970), passim.

7. All references are to the Revels Plays text, ed. John Russell Brown (London: Methuen, 1964), which I consider to be the best available modern-spelling edition. The standard old-spelling edition is still that of Lucas.

8. During the revival of Renaissance drama in New York City in the mid-1960s, I was amused to overhear this reaction among my fellow play-goers at two different performances. Of course, twentieth-century Americans unused to Jacobean conventions may not embody the reactions of blasé Jacobeans, but the point is worth noting.

9. Archer, "The Duchess of Malfi," Nineteenth Century 87 (1920): 126–32. This essay has been anthologized many times and can be found in John Webster: A Critical Anthology, ed. G. K. Hunter and S. K. Hunter (Harmondsworth: Penquin, 1969), 94–98; and in Twentieth Century Interpretations of "The Duchess of Malfi," ed. Norman Rabkin (Englewood Cliffs, N.J.: Prentice-Hall, 1968), 14–20.

10. Regents edition, ed. G. K. Hunter (Lincoln: Univ. of Nebraska Press, 1965).

11. See, for example, Leech, Ornstein, Brown, and Whitman. Brown, in particular, suggests that the Duchess's ghost may even have appeared at line 42, in a sudden "great light" similar to that in The Second Maiden's Tragedy (xxxv). But I think this unlikely. Delio can hear the Echo, and should therefore be able to see it if it is visible. Furthermore, too many of Antonio's other superstitions are called into question during the play to lend credence to this one.

12. Chappell, The Garden of Prudence (1595), STC 4999, B3r.

13. Strode, Anatomie of Mortalitie, 72–73.

14. Southwell, The Fovre Last Things, B4r.

15. See Bliss, 151–58, for a very good analysis of Bosola as a troubled, torn man always hard at work to rationalize his Machiavellian role.

16. See especially Ribner, 113.

17. Doebler, "Continuity in the Art of Dying," 211.

18. Keith Thomas, in his Religion and the Decline of Magic (London: Weidenfeld and Nicolson, 1971), documents the increase of fortune-telling and astrology in sixteenth- and especially seventeenth-century England, as dependence on a central church gave way to pluralism and to the more individualistic and less ritualized denominations of Protestantism. Although clearly favoring the Protestant position, Thomas attributes the growth of predictive superstition primarily to a search for a higher authority than the new churches were willing to claim as churches.

19. In another neat reversal, the horoscope is not only a disordering agent but is patently false. The son for whom is predicted a "short life" and "violent death" (2.3.61–63) survives his whole family and is presented to the audience by Delio at the end of the play as "this young, hopeful gentleman" (5.5.112).

20. One may sometimes be reminded of the Walrus and the Carpenter in
    Through the Looking-Glass:

    > "I weep for you," the Walrus said:
    > "I deeply sympathize,"
    > With sobs and tears he sorted out
    >   Those of the largest size,
    > Holding his pocket-handkerchief
    >   Before his streaming eyes.

    As Tweedledee reminds Alice, even the weeping was a ploy: " 'You see
    he held his hankerchief in front, so that the Carpenter couldn't count how
    many he took' " (Lewis Carroll, *Alice's Adventures in Wonderland* and
    Through the Looking-Glass [New York: Illustrated Editions, n.d.], 165–66).
    Bliss maintains that act 5 of *The Duchess of Malfi* could easily be called
    "Bosola's Revenge" (158).
21. The numerous rhymed *sententiae* in the play are interesting in themselves.
    They are distinctly inferior to the rest of Webster's verse—including the
    other rhymed verse—and often seem to have little to do with the context.
    In view of their uncharacteristically poor craftsmanship, and of the fact
    that so many of them are given to Bosola or other characters of doubtful
    integrity, it is tempting to see them as red herrings drawn across the audi-
    ence's path along with the wax dummies, the coincidences, and the Echo.
22. Regents Renaissance Drama Series edition, ed. N. W. Bawcutt (Lincoln:
    Univ. of Nebraska Press, 1966).
23. See, for example, Leech; Peterson; and James L. Calderwood, "*The Duchess
    of Malfi:* Styles of Ceremony," *Essays in Criticism* 12 (1962): 133–47. Gunnar
    Boklund, too, comes to see the Duchess as a holy martyr during her death
    scene; see The Duchess of Malfi: *Sources, Themes, Characters* (Cambridge:
    Harvard Univ. Press, 1962).
24. Lucas, for example, refers to her as a "Mater Dolorosa" (28), while Murray
    speaks of her in terms of both Job and the Holy Family.
25. Doebler, 208–09.
26. Ornstein, *Moral Vision,* 140.
27. Lupset, *Dieyng Well,* 267.
28. Soldiers in combat often have recourse to the unanswerable question. In
    Vietnam, the standard reply to reprimands was: "So what are you going
    to do to me? Send me to Vietnam?" No matter how many times one heard
    (or said) this, it remained funny. And it could not be answered. The Jews,
    too, have a tradition of answering a question with another question. A
    classic story told about any given persecution, but especially about the
    Holocaust, is this one: The storm troopers are beating up a Jew. When
    they stop to rest, the leader tries to goad the Jew by asking, "Tell me, Jew,
    who caused the war?" The Jew answers promptly, "The Jews and the

pretzel-baker's!" The storm trooper, puzzled, asks, "Why the pretzel-bakers?" And the Jew responds, "Why the Jews?"

29. Lupset, 267.
30. Chesterton, *Ballad of the White Horse*, in *Collected Poems*, 239.
31. Dent, *John Webster's Borrowings* (Berkeley: Univ. of California Press, 1960); see also Brown's note to the passage in the Revels edition, and Muriel West, *The Devil and John Webster*, esp. 206–10.
32. Robert Freeman Whitman identifies Webster's figure with death alone, pointing out that when Bosola enters, directly after these lines, the Cardinal says, "Now! art thou come?" (5.5.7); that is, Bosola is the human representation of the Summons. But Whitman oversimplifies. To explain the "rake," he must make Antonio its human counterpart, since Bosola is carrying the body, and such literalism detracts from the genuinely frightening symbolism that Webster has chosen.
33. Ellis-Fermor, *The Jacobean Drama: An Interpretation* (London: Methuen, 1936), 180.
34. Rabkin, introduction to *Twentieth Century Interpretations*, 5.

Chapter Ten

1. Petrus Luccensis, *Dialogue*, C3v. This is only a small portion of the two-and-a-half-page address to the skull. Although this English translation of the *Dialogue* is dated 1603, the work was originally published in Latin in 1529, and was soon translated into French. I quote it here not only because of its intrinsic verbal charm but also because it is representative of a large class of early sixteenth-century works on the subject.
2. It is possible that Shakespeare had such an image in mind when he had Northumberland say, in a more secular context, "Even through the hollow eyes of death / I spy life peering" (*RII*, 2.2.270–71).
3. I have often wondered whether Shakespeare expected his audience to associate this opening apostrophe with "Alas, poor York," the sarcastic words of Margaret as she tortures the Duke of York in *3 Henry VI* (1.4.84). If so, then the audience would next have expected a parody, and would have been even more unsettled by the quiet pathos of the statement "I knew him, Horatio" that follows.
4. Higgins, "The Influence of Calvinistic Thought in Tourneur's *Atheist's Tragedy*," *Review of English Studies* 19 (1943): 255–62. See also Robert Ornstein, "*The Atheist's Tragedy* and Renaissance Naturalism," *Studies in Philology* 51 (1954): 194–207.
5. I have used the Revels edition, ed. Irving Ribner (London: Methuen, 1964).

6. Theodore Spencer thinks the symbol already obsolete in *The Atheist's Tragedy*, calling the graveyard scene "atmosphere for atmosphere's sake" (*Death and Elizabethan Tragedy*, 188). But if the play is seen in the allegorical terms that I have outlined, the atmosphere serves a definite function.

7. Regents Renaissance Drama Series, ed. M. L. Wine (Lincoln: Univ. of Nebraska Press, 1965).

8. Dekker, *Dramatic Works*, 4 vols., ed. Fredson Bowers (Cambridge: Cambridge Univ. Press, 1953), vol. 1. All references to Dekker's plays are to this edition. I have in all cases modernized spelling and punctuation.

9. *The Plays of Philip Massinger*, ed. William Gifford, rev. Francis Cunningham (London: Chatto & Windus, 1897).

10. Spencer, *Death and Elizabethan Tragedy*, 186.

11. Note, too, how many changes Webster has Bosola ring on this speech in *The Duchess of Malfi*. See my chapter 9, especially Bosola's speeches at 4.2.124–33 and 4.2.186–95.

12. Rowlands, *Works*, vol. 1.

13. Compare Avarice's speech on Time in *Respublica*: "That shuttle-brained tall long man," quoted at length in chapter 5, n. 19. The audience here is expected to realize that Avarice is playing with fire.

14. I have deliberately avoided mentioning the playwright's name in this discussion, for the simple reason that I cannot say with any certainty what it is. The controversy has by now settled down to two names: Tourneur and Middleton. I am inclined to see the hand of Marston at work in some of the physical horrors and the scurrility of Vindice's invective, but there is as much evidence for and against this speculation as there is about any other. Lacking any more definitive evidence than is available at this time, I must echo Lawrence J. Ross and "state with some confidence that [I do] not know who wrote *The Revenger's Tragedy*" (introduction to the play, Regents Renaissance Drama Series [Lincoln: Univ. of Nebraska Press, 1966], xviii). Readers who wish to take up the controversy will find good summaries of the arguments in Ross's introduction, xiv–xix; Peter B. Murray, *A Study of Cyril Tourneur* (Philadelphia: Univ. of Pennsylvania Press, 1964), 144–59; and Samuel Schoenbaum, *Middleton's Tragedies* (New York: Columbia Univ. Press, 1955), 153–82. The battle continues to rage, although scholars are not always averse to changing sides; at the 1980 meeting of the South Central Renaissance Conference (Monroe, La.), Samuel Schoenbaum announced that he now favored Tourneur rather than Middleton as chief candidate for authorship.

15. Jacobson, *The Language of* The Revenger's Tragedy, Jacobean Drama Studies 38 (Salzburg: Univ. of Salzburg, 1974).

16. Schoenbaum, *Middleton's Tragedies*, 16.

17. Ellis-Fermor, *The Jacobean Drama*, 154.

18. Garber, " 'Remember Me': *Memento Mori* Figures in Shakespeare's Plays," *Renaissance Drama*, n.s. 12 (1981): 12.
19. All references are to Ross's Regents Renaissance Drama Series edition.
20. See Eric Partridge, *Shakespeare's Bawdy* (1948; rpt. New York: Dutton, 1960), 105, 153.
21. Murray, *A Study of Cyril Tourneur*, 194–95.
22. Daniel J. Jacobson has suggested that the stage direction, *"Thunder,"* is an erroneous interpolation made by J. Churton Collins in his 1878 edition of the play. According to Jacobson, Vindice's "There it goes!" is simply an ejaculation indicating satisfaction with or delighted anticipation of his own plans. (" 'There It Goes'—or Does It?: Thunder in *The Revenger's Tragedy* and a Catch-Phrase in Shakespeare, Marlowe, and Middleton," *English Language Notes* 13 [1975]: 6–10.) I cannot entirely agree. "There it goes!" without any referent is too much of a disjunction in tone at this point (from indignation to satisfaction); and if we assume a slight pause before the exclamation, to allow for a shift in thought, then Hippolito's protest, obviously directed at Vindice's hysteria, comes too late and is therefore inappropriate. It is apparent that Vindice has heard something in answer to his prayer, and whether Hippolito hears the thunder or not, he certainly sees Vindice hearing something.
23. This scene, with its elaborate play on words meaning either release from prison or release from life, may owe a good deal to the *Measure for Measure* tradition.
24. Ross substitutes *Youngest Son* for *Junior* in his edition "for clarity's sake" (intro., xxxii), and probably for the sake of avoiding modern connotations of diminution and comedy.
25. Schoenbaum, *"The Revenger's Tragedy*: Jacobean Dance of Death," *Modern Language Quarterly* 15 (1954): 206.
26. Salingar, " 'The Revenger's Tragedy' and the Morality Tradition," *Scrutiny* 6 (1938): 404.
27. One of my students has advanced an interesting (but unpublished) theory that one of the ironies surrounding Vindice is that he need not have killed at all; that the rivalries and hostilities among the members of the court would have led them to destroy each other anyway.
28. Nicholas Brooke has suggested that the shudder at Vindice and his society grows out of a "horrid laughter" peculiar to the drama of the Jacobean period. His study of this laughter is a good one, even if it does not take into enough account the horrid laughter present in earlier traditions as well. See Brooke's *Horrid Laughter in Jacobean Tragedy* (New York: Barnes & Noble, 1979), especially chap. 2.
29. Oxford: Malone Society, 1951.

30. Mermaid Series, ed. Havelock Ellis (London: Vizetelly, 1890), l.l; p. 123. A more accurate, if less readable, old-spelling text has been published by the Malone Society (Oxford, 1950).

31. The ineptitude of Middleton's handling of the skull in *The Witch* is one of several reasons for my reluctance to accept him as the author of *The Revenger's Tragedy*. It is hard to imagine anyone doing such a good job with a particular image in 1607 and such a wretched job two to eight years later.

32. I have used the Revels edition, ed. Anne Lancashire (Baltimore: Johns Hopkins Univ. Press, 1978).

33. The Lady's ghost also wears a crucifix, displayed on a white dress rather than a black one. The contrast is interesting: white = correct usage; black = wrong usage. The ghost's crucifix is a sign of her spiritual state rather than an object that she venerates. But the Tyrant's kneeling before a crucifix indicates idolatry.

34. Annette Drew-Bear gives an interesting history of the theme in "Face-Painting in Renaissance Tragedy," *Renaissance Drama*, n.s., 12 (1981): 71–93.

35. In *The Plays and Poems of Philip Massinger*, 5 vols., ed. Philip Edwards and Colin Gibson (Oxford: Clarendon Press, 1976), vol. 1. I have modernized spelling and punctuation.

36. Drew-Bear notes that many cosmetics used by Elizabethan and Jacobean women were corrosives that caused foul breath and shriveled or spotted skin and that sometimes were used at full strength as poisons. She adds, "The increasing use of poisoned cosmetics in Jacobean tragedies also reflects the period's fascination with Italy as the center of both poisoning and cosmetics (the best ceruse came from Italy), as well as actual poisoning attempts like that on Overbury and the bizarre attempts to poison Queen Elizabeth and the Earl of Essex by anointing the pommel of her saddle and the arms of his chair" (89).

37. Oxford: Malone Society, 1961. I have modernized spelling and punctuation.

Chapter Eleven

1. See Emmett L. Avery and Arthur H. Scouten, *The London Stage, 1660–1700* (Carbondale: Southern Illinois Univ. Press, 1968), cxxviii–cxxx.

2. Wells, *Elizabethan and Jacobean Playwrights*, 10.

3. Huebert, *John Ford: Baroque English Dramatist* (Montreal: McGill-Queen's Univ. Press, 1977), 6–7; 48.

4. As with all attempts at labeling, critics other than Huebert have made as good a case for calling this drama "mannerist" as he has made for "baroque."

See especially Cyrus Hoy, "Jacobean Tragedy and the Mannerist Style," *Shakespeare Survey* 26 (1973): 49–67. In a paper delivered before the South Central Renaissance Conference, Paul A. Parrish specifically applied mannerist criticism to *'Tis Pity* (" *'Tis Pity She's a Whore* and the Mannerist Perspective," Monroe, La., 18 April 1980).

5. Ford, *Love's Sacrifice*, ed. Herbert W. Hoskins, Jr. (Washington, D.C.: Univ. Press of America, 1978), S.D. 3.4.18.

6. Ford, *The Broken Heart*, ed. Donald K. Anderson, Jr., Regents Renaissance Drama Series (Lincoln: Univ. of Nebraska Press, 1968).

7. Thomas Marc Parrott and Robert Hamilton Ball point out that Ford was not considered to be among the elite of the New Wave: "There is nothing to show that Ford was either a popular or an influential dramatist. His plays were not welcomed with a chorus of commendatory verses by fellow playwrights, nor were they in sufficient demand to warrant a reprinting." (*A Short View of Elizabethan Drama* [1943; rpt. New York: Scribner, 1958], 251.)

8. Cornelia, *The Function of the Masque in Jacobean Tragedy and Tragicomedy*, Jacobean Drama Studies 77 (Salzburg: Univ. Salzburg, 1978), 70.

9. Glapthorne, *The Lady Mother* (Oxford: Malone Society, 1959), 11. 2476 ff.

10. "Despair," for instance, is in Galpthorne's play more allied with the "straungeness" of the courtly love romance than with the theological despair of the moral allegory.

11. Gomersall, *The Tragedie of Lodovick Sforza* (Louvain: Librairie Universitaire, 1933). I have modernized spelling and punctuation.

12. Shirley, *The Maid's Revenge*, ed. Albert Howard Carter (New York: Garland, 1980). I have modernized spelling and punctuation.

13. Francis Beaumont and John Fletcher, *Valentinian*, 5.1, 5.2, in *Dramatic Works*, 4 vols., ed. Fredson Bowers (Cambridge: Cambridge Univ. Press, 1966). The arithmetic in these two scenes is somewhat amiss. Aretus says that he has taken the poison "two hours before" the Emperor (5.1.4); but when he addresses the Emperor, he tells him, "Thou hast now / A short half hour, no more, and I ten minutes" (5.2.67–68). In actual playing time, the Emperor outlasts Aretus by twenty lines. (Note: All references to the Fletcher canon are to the Bowers edition, but I have modernized the spelling.)

14. One charge against our own early western and crime films was that they made death look too easy: a shot, a puff of dust from the victim's clothing, a spin, and a fall. Where, asked the prosecution, was the pain? How were our children to understand that killing hurts? Were we not promoting a callousness in the audience to the effects of violence? Obediently, film producers began showing those effects: the screams of anguish, the blood and froth of punctured lungs, slow-motion analysis of the progress of bullet or knife—and very shortly, we had a new cause of complaint: too much

violence, too much graphic bloodshed and pain. While the factions continue to argue, audiences continue to ignore them, and the violence remains popular in either form.

15. William A. Armstrong describes the new audiences, and playwrights' attempts to please them, in "The Audience of the Elizabethan Private Theaters," *Review of English Studies*, n.s. 10 (1959): 234–49; reprinted in *The Seventeenth-Century Stage*, ed. Gerald Eades Bentley (Chicago: Chicago Univ. Press, 1968), 215–34. Martin Butler, in *Theatre and Crisis: 1632–1642* (Cambridge: Cambridge Univ. Press, 1984), examines the later theater as an adjunct to the court and a reflection of its politics.

16. Salingar, "The Decline of Tragedy," in *The Age of Shakespeare*, ed. Boris Ford (1955; rpt. Harmondsworth: Penguin, 1975), 430.

17. The scene in which Penius commits suicide in expiation of his martial sin (4.3) is a miniature art of secular dying: a debate over the correct instrument to use. First, Penius says that he will hang himself. Petillius objects, pointing out that hanging is a "dog's death, / An end for slaves" (134–35). Very well, then, says Penius, what about poison? No, replies Petillius, that is "the death of rats, and women, / Lovers, and lazy boys that fear correction" (139–40). They finally agree on the sword.

18. It is tempting to speculate on *Coriolanus* and *Bonduca* as answers to each other. But the dating of the two plays is too uncertain for any valid conclusions; *Coriolanus* has been dated anywhere from 1607 to 1610, and *Bonduca* from 1609 to 1625.

19. When I speak of "mental defectives," I do not refer to lunatics, who were barely considered human at the time, but rather to the minimally retarded, those who, like Bergetto is *'Tis Pity* and the Ward in *Women Beware Women*, seem almost like children themselves.

20. STC 18024, p. 51. Interestingly enough, this passage comes directly after the conventional examination of how "good pagans" managed to live well without benefit of Revelation. The implication is that if even good pagans knew that "to be" was superior, Christians should certainly know better, and if they espouse "not to be," they are not just ignorant but "wicked."

21. See Quentin Bone, *Henrietta Maria: Queen of the Cavaliers* (Urbana: Univ. of Illinois Press, 1972), esp. chaps. 3–4; and J. P. Kenyon, *The Stuarts* (1958; rpt. Fontana: Collins, 1977), 78–79.

22. Ariès, *The Hour of Our Death*, 314–15.

23. Lupset, *Dieyng Well*, 279.

24. See especially Guillemand, *A Combat Betwixt Man and Death*, 27–28.

25. Waith, *The Pattern of Tragicomedy in Beaumont and Fletcher* (New Haven: Yale Univ. Press, 1952), esp. chaps. 3 and 6.

26. Shirley, *The Traitor*, ed. John Stewart Carter (London: Edward Arnold, 1965).

27. I develop this idea further in "Ceremonies of Complement: The Symbolic Marriage in Ford's *The Broken Heart*," *Philological Quarterly* 65 (1986): 23–37.

28. Of the three tetrameter couplets, the first recalls Nashe's "Brightness falls from the air" dirge in *Summer's Last Will and Testament* (283); the second, Shakespeare's "Fear no more the heat o' th' sun" lyric in *Cymbeline* (4.2.258–81); and the third, the Mutabilitie Cantos of Spenser's *Faerie Queene*.

29. McDonald, *The Rhetoric of Tragedy: Form in Stuart Drama* (Amherst: Univ. of Massachusetts Press, 1966), 328.

30. Farr, *John Ford and the Caroline Theatre* (New York: Barnes & Noble, 1979), chap. 5.

31. Even Shirley, whom many scholars have claimed as a convert to Roman Catholicism, and who should therefore be expected to have a more favorable view of repentance (see esp. Stephen J. Radtke, *James Shirley: His Catholic Philosophy of Life* [Washington, D.C.: Catholic Univ. of America, 1962]), does not give repentance good publicity in *The Traitor*. When Amidea wounds herself to forestall the Duke's lustful advances (3.3), the Duke is so amazed at her virtue that he repents and determines to amend his life; but this repentance lasts only until the beginning of the next act, when Lorenzo suggests a new way for him to get at Amidea. Lorenzo himself pretends repentance for his sins, but only to save his own life and have a chance to take Sciarrha's. Even Depazzi renounces his part in the plot only because he is afraid of capture, not because he thinks he is doing anything wrong. And the Duke's dying cry for more time in which to pray is simply the stalling device used by other villains of the time.

32. Eliot, *Murder in the Cathedral*, in *Complete Poems and Plays, 1909–1950* (New York: Harcourt Brace, 1971), 196. Thomas à Beckett, here, has just made the same distinction between martyrdom and suicide that Chesterton makes in *Orthodoxy*: "A martyr is a man who cares so much for something outside him, that he forgets his own personal life. A suicide is a man who cares so little for anything outside him, that he wants to see the end of everything." (*Orthodoxy* [London: Bodley Head, 1908], 117.)

33. Huebert, *John Ford*, 57.

34. Herbert, "Death," in Lewalski and Sabol, 376. A recent article in *Harper's* describes a similar overreaction toward death-longing among the lunatic fringe of the modern hospice movement (Ron Rosenbaum, "Turn on, Tune in, Drop Dead," *Harper's*, July 1982, 32–42). The antihospice bias of Rosenbaum's discussion is evident in his use of terms like "drop-dead chic" and "death 'n' dying" (the latter term implying that the whole subject is mental junk food), and he seems to suggest that if we fight the idea of death hard enough, we will not die; but he does have some valuable points to make about the extremes to which people may go when they fall in love only with the trappings of an idea and lose sight of the context.

35. *Paradise Lost*, 11:553–54, in *Complete Poems and Major Prose*, ed. Merritt Y. Hughes (New York: Odyssey Press, 1957), 445.

36. Huebert, *John Ford*, 66. Penthea has earlier asked her brother to kill her.

37. I cannot agree with critics such as Huebert and Parrish who see the Friar as an overlegalistic inhibitor of Giovanni's natural passion; seventeenth-century audiences did not have our apparent tolerance of incest. Indeed, the whole of Fletcher's *A King and No King* turns on the horrible dilemma of Arbaces's passion for the woman who everyone thinks is his sister, and nowhere is there any hint that the situation is acceptable because love forgives all. Also, among Fletcher's plays, Lelia's wickedness in *The Captain* is seen at its apex when she propositions her father (4.4); and in *Cupid's Revenge*, even the rake Leucippus is horrified when Bacha—once his mistress and now his stepmother—suggests that they resume their old dallying (3.3). In Massinger's *The Bondman*, one of the signs of chaos ensuing from the slaves' revolt is the incestuous flirtation between Corsica and her stepson (2.2). Audiences may have been fascinated by the subject, but they hardly seem to have condoned the act.

38. Guthrum, in Chesterton's *Ballad of the White Horse*, uses this phrase just before he speaks of sending forth death in order to forget death (see my chapter 6): "But every flower, like a flower of the sea, / Smelleth with the salt of death" (*Collected Poems*, 230).

Epilogue

1. (Oxford and New York: Oxford Univ. Press, 1983), xi–xiii.

2. National Association of Cemeteries, 1954.

3. Ed. Elliott M. Hill (New York: Garland, 1979). I have modernized spelling and punctuation. At the risk of sounding like a typical "discoverer" of a neglected play, I should like to suggest that *Nero* has both a balance of paradox and a certain quirkiness that might lend it to profitable revival—if not as a stage performance, since much of the action is static, then at least as a radio play.

Bibliography

Primary Sources

The Arte or Crafte to Lyue Well or to Deye Well. N.p., 1506. STC 793.

Bacon, Francis. *The Complete Essays of Francis Bacon.* Ed. Henry LeRoy Finch. New York: Washington Square Press, 1963.

Barnes, Barnabe. *The Divils Charter.* Tudor Facsimile Texts. 1913. Reprint. New York: AMS Press, 1970.

Bayly, Lewis. *The Practise of Pietie.* 11th ed. London, 1619. STC 1603.

Beaumont, Francis, and John Fletcher. *Dramatic Works.* 4 vols. Ed. Fredson Bowers. Cambridge: Cambridge Univ. Press, 1966.

Becon, Thomas. *The Sycke Mannes Salve.* London, 1561. STC 1757.

Berkeley, Sir William. *The Lost Lady. A Tragycomedy.* London, 1638. STC 1902.

Block, K. S., ed. *Ludus Coventriae, or The Plaie Called Corpus Christi.* 1922. Reprint. London: EETS, 1960.

The Bloodie Banquet, a Tragedie. Oxford: Malone Society, 1961.

Brown, Carleton, ed. *Religious Lyrics of the XVth Century.* Oxford: Clarendon Press, 1939.

Calvin, John. *Institutes of the Christian Religion.* 2 vols. Ed. Ford Lewis Battles. Philadelphia: Westminster Press, 1960.

Campbell, Lily B., ed. *The Mirror for Magistrates.* Cambridge: Cambridge Univ. Press, 1938.

Caxton, William. *The Arte & Crafte to Knowe Well to Dye.* N.p., n.d. [ca. 1490]. STC 789.

Chapman, George. *The Plays of George Chapman: The Tragedies.* 2 vols. Ed. T. M. Parrott. New York: Russell & Russell, 1961.

Chappell, Bartholomew. *The Garden of Prudence*. London, 1595. STC 4999.

Chaucer, Geoffrey. *The Works of Geoffrey Chaucer*. Ed. F. N. Robinson. Boston: Houghton Mifflin, 1957.

Chesterton, G. K. *The Collected Poems of G. K. Chesterton*. London: Cecil Palmer, 1927.

Chettle, Henry. *The Tragedy of Hoffman*. Oxford: Malone Society, 1951.

Child, Francis James, ed. *English and Scottish Ballads*. 4 vols. 1857. Reprint. Boston: Houghton Mifflin, 1885.

Churchyard, Thomas. *A Feast Full of Sad Cheere*. London, 1592. STC 5231.

Colman, Walter. *La Dance Machabre, or Deaths Duell*. London, 1633. STC 5569.

Coverdale, Myles. *Remains of Myles Coverdale*. Ed. George Pearson. The Parker Society. Cambrige: Cambridge Univ. Press, 1846.

Cunliffe, John W., ed. *Early English Classical Tragedies*. Oxford: Clarendon Press, 1912.

[Dance of Death.] "Marke well the effect, purtreyed here in all." N.p., n.d. [ca. 1580]. STC 6223.

The Daunce and Song of Death. N.p., n.d. [1569]. STC 6222.

Davis, Norman, ed. *Non-Cycle Plays and Fragments*. London: Oxford Univ. Press, 1970.

Death and Liffe. In *Select Early English Poems*. Ed. Sir Israel Gollancz. London: Oxford Univ. Press, 1930.

Deaths Daunce. N.p., 1631. STC 6444.

Dekker, Thomas. *Dramatic Works*. 4 vols. Ed. Fredson Bowers. Cambridge: Cambridge Univ. Press, 1953.

Dent, Arthur. *A Sermon of Repentaunce*. London, 1582. STC 6672.

_____. *The Way to Euerlasting Life*. London, 1583. 5th ed. 1624. STC 6621.

The Doctrynall of Dethe. N.p., 1498. STC 6932.

Dunbar, William. *The Poems of William Dunbar*. Ed. W. Mackay Mackenzie. London: Faber and Faber, 1932.

The Dyenge Creature. N.p., 1507. STC 6035a.

Elizabeth I. Proclamation, 16 May 1559. STC 7896.

England, George, and A. W. Pollard, ed. *The Towneley Plays*. 1897. Reprint. London: EETS, 1952.

Enright, D. J. *The Oxford Book of Death*. Oxford and New York: Oxford Univ. Press, 1983.

Erasmus, Desiderius. *Preparation to Deathe*. London, 1538. STC 10505.

Farmer, John S., ed. *Anonymous Plays*. 3rd series. London: EEDS, 1906.

_____, ed. *"Lost" Tudor Plays*. 1907. Reprint. Guildford: Traylen, 1966.

Ford, John. *The Broken Heart*. Ed. Donald K. Anderson, Jr. Regents Renaissance Drama Series. Lincoln: Univ. of Nebraska Press, 1968.

_____. *Love's Sacrifice*. Ed. Herbert W. Hoskins, Jr. Washington, D.C.: University Press of America, 1978.

_____. *'Tis Pity She's A Whore*. Ed. N. W. Bawcutt. Regents Renaissance Drama Series. Lincoln: Univ. of Nebraska Press, 1966.

_____. *The Works of John Ford*. 3 vols. Ed. William Gifford and Alexander Dyce. 1895. Reprint. New York: Russell & Russell, 1965.

Glapthorne, Henry. *The Lady Mother*. Oxford: Malone Society, 1959.

Gomersall, Robert. *The Tragedie of Lodovick Sforza*. Louvaine: Librairie Universitaire, 1933.

Greene, Robert. *The Life and Complete Works in Prose and Verse of Robert Greene*. Ed. A. B. Grosart. New York: Russell & Russell, 1964. Vols. 13–14.

Greenham, Richard. *Works*. 5th ed. London, 1612. STC 12318.

Guillemand, J. *A Combat Betwixt Man and Death*. Trans. Edw. Grimestone. London, 1621. STC 12495.

Gummere, Francis B., ed. *Old English Ballads*. Boston: Ginn & Company, 1894.

Hazlitt, W. Carew, ed. *Dodsley's Select Collection of Old English Plays*. 15 vols. 1874–76. Reprint. New York: Benjamin Blom, 1964.

Heywood, Thomas. *An Apology for Actors* [1612] *With a Refutation of the Apology for Actors by I.G.* [1615]. Ed. Richard H. Perkinson. New York: Scholars' Facsimiles & Reprints, 1941.

_____. *A Woman Killed with Kindness*. Ed. R. W. van Fossen. Revels Plays. London: Methuen, 1961.

Hutchins, E. *David's Sling Against Goliath*. London, 1598. STC 14013.

Innocent III, Pope. *De Miseria Condicionis Humane*. Ed. Robert E. Lewis. Athens: Georgia Univ. Press, 1978.

_____. *The Mirror of Mans Lyfe*. Trans. H. Kirton. London, 1576. STC 14093.

James I. *Daemonologie, In Forme of a Dialogue*. London, 1597. STC 14364.

A Knack to Know a Knave. Tudor Facsimile Texts, 1911. Reprint. New York: AMS Press, 1970.

Kyd, Thomas. *Solimon and Perseda*. Tudor Facsimile Texts, 1912. Reprint. New York: AMS Press, 1970.

_____. *The Works of Thomas Kyd*. Ed. Frederick S. Boas. 1901. Reprint. Oxford: Clarendon Press, 1955.

Lavater, Ludwig. *Of Ghostes and Spirites, Walking by Night. . . .* Trans. R. H. London, 1596. STC 15320.

Legrand, Jacques. *The Book of Good Maners*. N.p., 1494. STC 15395.

Lewalski, Barbara K., and Andrew J. Sabol, eds. *Major Poets of the Earlier Seventeenth Century*. New York: Odyssey Press, 1973.

Locrine. Oxford: Malone Society, 1908.

Lumiansky, R. M., and David Mills, eds. *The Chester Mystery Cycle*. London: EETS, 1974.

Lupset, Thomas. *A Compendious Treatise, Teachyng the Waie of Dyeing Well*. In *The Life and Works of Thomas Lupset*, Edited by John Archer Gee. New Haven: Yale Univ. Press, 1928.

Lydgate, John. *The Assembly of Gods: or, The Accord of Reason and Sensuality in the Fear of Death.* London: EETS, 1896.

————. *The Dance of Death.* Ed. Florence Warren. London: EETS, 1931.

Map of Mortalitie. N.p., 1604. STC 17294.

Marlowe, Christopher. *The Complete Works of Christopher Marlowe.* 2 vols. Ed. Fredson Bowers. Cambridge: Cambridge Univ. Press, 1973.

————. *Doctor Faustus.* Ed. John D. Jump. Revels Plays. London: Methuen, 1962.

————. *Tamburlaine the Great, Parts I and II.* Ed. John D. Jump. Regents Renaissance Drama Series. Lincoln: Univ. of Nebraska Press, 1967.

Marston, John. *Antonio and Mellida.* Ed. G. K. Hunter. Regents Renaissance Drama Series. Lincoln: Univ. of Nebraska Press, 1965.

————. *Antonio's Revenge.* Ed. G. K. Hunter. Regents Renaissance Drama Series. Lincoln: Univ. of Nebraska Press, 1965.

————. *The Malcontent.* Ed. M. L. Wine. Regents Renaissance Drama Series. Lincoln: Univ. of Nebraska Press, 1964.

————. *The Plays of John Marston.* 3 vols. Ed. H. Harvey Wood. Edinburgh: Oliver and Boyd, 1934.

Massinger, Philip. *The Plays and Poems of Philip Massinger.* 5 vols. Ed. Philip Edwards and Colin Gibson. Oxford: Clarendon Press, 1976.

————. *The Plays of Philip Massinger.* Ed. William Gifford. Rev. Francis Cunningham. London: Chatto & Windus, 1897.

Middleton, Thomas. *The Best Plays of Thomas Middleton.* Ed. Havelock Ellis. London: Vizetelly, 1890.

————. *Three Plays.* Ed. Kenneth Muir. London: Dent, 1975.

————. *The Witch.* Oxford: Malone Society, 1950.

Montagu, Henry. *Contemplatio Mortis et Immortalitatis.* London, 1631. STC 18024.

More, John. *A Liuely Anatomie of Death.* London, 1596. STC 18073.

Nashe, Thomas. *Works.* 5 vols. Ed. Ronald B. McKerrow. Rev. F. P. Wilson. Oxford: Basil Blackwell, 1958.

The Paradise of Dainty Devices. Ed. Hyder Edward Rollins. Cambridge: Harvard Univ. Press, 1927.

Perkins, William. *A Discourse of Conscience and the Whole Treatise of Cases of Conscience.* Ed. Thomas F. Merrill. Nieuwkoop: B. De Graf, 1966.

Petrus Luccensis. *A Dialogue of Dying Wel.* Trans. R. Verstegan. London, 1603. STC 19815.

Pikeryng, John. *Horestes.* Oxford: Malone Society, 1962.

Rickey, Mary Ellen, and Thomas B. Stroup, eds. *Certaine Sermons or Homilies Appointed to Be Read in Churches.* 1623 ed. Gainesville, Fla.: Scholars' Facsimiles & Reprints, 1968.

Rowlands, Samuel. *The Complete Works of Samuel Rowlands.* 3 vols. Hunterian Club, 1880. Reprint. New York: Johnson Reprint Corporation, 1966.

Schell, Edgar T., and J. D. Shuchter. *English Morality Plays and Moral Interludes.* New York: Holt, 1969.

The Second Maiden's Tragedy. Ed. Anne Lancashire. Revels Plays. Manchester: Manchester Univ. Press, 1978.

Selimus. [Robert Greene?] Oxford: Malone Society, 1908.

Seymour-Smith, Martin, ed. *The English Sermon, 1550–1650.* Cheadle, Eng.: Carcanet Press, 1976.

Shakespeare, William. *The Complete Works.* Ed. G. B. Harrison. New York: Harcourt Brace Jovanovich, 1968.

––––––. *Measure for Measure.* Ed. J. W. Lever. The Arden Shakespeare. London: Methuen, 1965.

Shirley, James. *The Cardinal.* Ed. Charles R. Forker. Bloomington: Indiana Univ. Press, 1964.

––––––. *Love's Cruelty.* Ed. John Frederick Nims. New York: Garland, 1980.

––––––. *The Maid's Revenge.* Ed. Albert Howard Carter. New York: Garland, 1980.

––––––. *The Politician.* Ed. Robert J. Fehrenbach. New York: Garland, 1980.

––––––. *The Traitor.* Ed. John Stewart Carter. London: Edward Arnold, 1965.

Skelton, John. *The Complete Poems of John Skelton, Laureate.* Ed. Philip Henderson. London: Dent, 1959.

––––––. *The Poetical Works of John Skelton.* 2 vols. Ed. Alexander Dyce. 1843. Reprint. New York: AMS Press, 1965.

Smith, Lucy Toulmin, ed. *York Plays.* Oxford: Clarendon Press, 1885.

Southwell, Robert. *A Fovre-Fold Meditation of the Fovre Last Thinges.* London, 1606. STC 22949.

Spenser, Edmund. *The Complete Poetical Works of Spenser.* Ed. R. E. Neil Dodge. 1908. Reprint. Cambridge: Riverside, 1936.

Strode, George. *The Anatomie of Mortalitie.* 1618. Reprint. London, 1632. STC 23365a.

Sutton, Christopher. *Disce Mori. Learne to Die.* London, 1600. STC 23474.

Thomas, R. George, ed. *Ten Miracle Plays.* Evanston: Northwestern Univ. Press, 1966.

Tourneur, Cyril. *The Atheist's Tragedy.* Ed. Irving Ribner. Cambridge: Harvard Univ. Press, 1964.

––––––. *The Revenger's Tragedy.* Ed. R. A. Foakes. Revels Plays. London: Methuen, 1966.

The Tragedy of Nero. Ed. Elliott M. Hill. New York: Garland, 1979.

The Tragedy of Tiberius. Oxford: Malone Society, 1914.

The Trial of Treasure. London: Tudor Facsimile Texts, 1908.

Wager, W. *The Longer Thou Livest* and *Enough Is as Good as a Feast.* Ed. R. Mark Benbow. Regents Renaissance Drama Series. Lincoln: Univ. of Nebraska Press, 1967.

A Warning for Fair Women. Tudor Facsimile Texts, 1912. Reprint. New York: AMS Press, 1970.

Webster, John. *The Duchess of Malfi.* Ed. John Russell Brown. Revels Plays. London: Methuen, 1964.

———. *The Duchess of Malfi.* Ed. F. L. Lucas. 1927. Reprint. London: Chatto & Windus, 1958.

———. *The White Devil.* Ed. F. L. Lucas. 1927. Reprint. London: Chatto & Windus, 1958.

Whitney, Geoffrey. *A Choice of Emblemes.* Ed. Henry Green. New York: Benjamin Blom, 1967.

Wither, George. *A Collection of Emblemes, Ancient and Moderne.* Ed. Rosemary Freeman. Columbia: Univ. of South Carolina Press, 1975.

Woodes, Nathaniel. *The Conflict of Conscience.* Tudor Facsimile Texts, 1911. Reprint. New York: AMS Press, 1970.

Yarrington, Robert. *Two Lamentable Tragedies.* Tudor Facsimile Texts, 1913. Reprint. New York: AMS Press, 1970.

Secondary Sources

Aries, Philippe. *The Hour of Our Death.* Trans. Helen Weaver. New York: Knopf, 1981.

Avery, Emmett L., and Arthur H. Scouten. *The London Stage, 1660–1700.* Carbondale: Southern Illinois Univ. Press, 1968.

Beaty, Nancy Lee. *The Craft of Dying: A Study in the Literary Tradition of the Ars Moriendi in England.* New Haven: Yale Univ. Press, 1970.

Bentley, Gerald Eades, ed. *The Seventeenth-Century Stage.* Chicago: Univ. of Chicago Press, 1968.

Bergeron, David M. "The Wax Figures in *The Duchess of Malfi.*" *Studies in English Literature* 18 (1978): 331–39.

Berry, Ralph. *The Art of John Webster.* Oxford: Clarendon Press, 1972.

Bevington, David M. *From "Mankind" to Marlowe.* Cambridge: Harvard Univ. Press, 1962.

———. *Tudor Drama and Politics.* Cambridge: Harvard Univ. Press, 1968.

Bliss, Lee. *The World's Perspective: John Webster and the Jacobean Drama.* Brighton, Eng.: Harvester Press, 1983.

Bluestone, Max, and Norman Rabkin, eds. *Shakespeare's Contemporaries.* Englewood Cliffs, N.J.: Prentice-Hall, 1970.

Boase, T. S. R. *Death in the Middle Ages.* London: Thames and Hudson, 1972.

Boklund, Gunnar. *"The Duchess of Malfi": Sources, Themes, Characters.* Cambridge: Harvard Univ. Press, 1962.

Bone, Quentin. *Henrietta Maria: Queen of the Cavaliers.* Urbana: Univ. of Illinois Press, 1972.

Bowers, Fredson. *Elizabethan Revenge Tragedy, 1587–1642.* Princeton, N.J.: Princeton Univ. Press, 1940.

Bradbrook, M. C. "Fate and Chance in *The Duchess of Malfi.*" *Modern Language Review* 42 (1947): 281–91.

_____. *Themes and Conventions of Elizabethan Tragedy.* 1935. Reprint. Cambridge: Cambridge Univ. Press, 1969.

Bronson, Bertrand H. *Rasselas, Poems, and Selected Prose.* New York: Holt, 1971.

Brooke, Nicholas. *Horrid Laughter in Jacobean Tragedy.* New York: Barnes & Noble, 1979.

Brown University, Department of Art. *Europe in Torment: 1450–1550.* Providence: Brown Univ., 1974.

Bryant, James C. *Tudor Drama and Religious Controversy.* N.p.: Mercer Univ. Press, 1984.

Bullough, Geoffrey, ed. *Narrative and Dramatic Sources of Shakespeare.* London: Routledge and Kegan Paul, 1963. Vol 2.

Butler, Martin. *Theatre and Crisis: 1632–42.* Cambridge: Cambridge Univ. Press, 1984.

Calderwood, James L. "*The Duchess of Malfi*: Styles of Ceremony." *Essays in Criticism* 12 (1962): 133–47.

Camoin, François André. *The Revenge Convention in Tourneur, Webster, and Middleton.* Jacobean Drama Studies 20. Salzburg: Univ. of Salzburg, 1972.

Campbell, Lily B. "*Doctor Faustus*: A Case of Conscience." *PMLA* 67 (1952): 218–89.

Chambers, Raymond W. *The Jacobean Shakespeare and* Measure for Measure. 1937. Reprint. Freeport, N.Y.: Books for Libraries Press, 1970.

Cole, Douglas. *Suffering and Evil in the Plays of Christopher Marlowe.* Princeton, N.J.: Princeton Univ. Press, 1962.

Corder, Jim. "*Everyman*: The Way to Life." In *Studies in Medieval, Renaissance American Literature.* Fort Worth: Texas Christian Univ. Press, 1971: 53–56.

Cornelia, Marie. *The Function of the Masque in Jacobean Tragedy and Tragicomedy.* Jacobean Drama Studies 77. Salzburg: Univ. of Salzburg, 1978.

Craik, T. W. *The Tudor Interlude: Stage, Costume, and Acting.* London: Leicester Univ. Press, 1958.

Cutts, John P. *The Left Hand of God: A Critical Interpretation of the Plays of Christopher Marlowe.* Haddonfield, N.J.: Haddonfield House, 1973.

_____. "The Ultimate Source of Tamburlaine's White, Red, Black and Death?" *Notes and Queries,* n.s. 5 (1958): 146–47.

Diehl, Huston. "The Iconography of Violence in English Renaissance Tragedy." *Renaissance Drama,* n.s. 11 (1980): 27–44.

Doebler, Bettie Anne. "Continuity in the Art of Dying: *The Duchess of Malfi.*" *Comparative Drama* 14 (1980): 203–15.

Doran, Madeleine. *Endeavors of Art: A Study of Form in Elizabethan Drama.* Madison: Univ. of Wisconsin Press, 1954.

Drew-Bear, Annette. "Face-Painting in Renaissance Tragedy." *Renaissance Drama,* n.s. 12 (1981): 71–93.

Ellis-Fermor, Una. *The Jacobean Drama: An Interpretation.* London: Methuen, 1936.

Elton, G. R. *Reform and Reformation: England 1509–1558.* Cambridge: Harvard Univ. Press, 1977.

Farnham, Willard. *The Medieval Heritage of Elizabethan Tragedy.* Berkeley: Univ. of California Press, 1936.

Farr, Dorothy M. *John Ford and the Caroline Theatre.* New York: Barnes & Noble, 1979.

Fletcher, Angus. *Allegory: The Theory of a Symbolic Mode.* Ithaca, N.Y.: Cornell Univ. Press, 1964.

Garber, Marjorie. " 'Remember Me': *Memento Mori* Figures in Shakespeare's Plays." *Renaissance Drama,* n.s. 12 (1981): 3–25.

Gardner, Helen. "The Second Part of *Tamburlaine the Great." Modern Language Review* 37 (1942): 18–24.

Gless, Darryl F. *"Measure for Measure,"* the Law, and the Convent. Princeton, N.J.: Princeton Univ. Press, 1979.

Godshalk, W. L. *The Marlovian World Picture.* The Hague: Mouton, 1974.

Goldhammer, Allen D. "*Everyman:* A Dramatization of Death." *Quarterly Journal of Speech* 59 (1973): 87–98.

Grierson, Sir Herbert. *Cross-Currents in Seventeenth Century English Literature.* New York: Harper, 1958.

Haller, William. *The Rise of Puritanism.* 1938. Reprint. Philadelphia: Univ. of Pennsylvania Press, 1972.

Harris, William O. *Skelton's Magnyfycence and the Cardinal Virtue Tradition.* Chapel Hill: Univ. of North Carolina Press, 1965.

Hattaway, Michael. "The Theology of Marlowe's *Doctor Faustus." Renaissance Drama,* n.s. 3 (1970): 51–78.

Higgins, Michael H. "The Influence of Calvinistic Thought in Tourneur's *Atheist's Tragedy." Review of English Studies* 19 (1943): 225–62.

Hillman, Richard W. "Meaning and Mortality in Some Renaissance Revenge Plays." *University of Toronto Quarterly* 49 (1979): 1–17.

Holmes, David M. *The Art of Thomas Middleton.* Oxford: Clarendon Press, 1970.

Holmes, Elizabeth. *Aspects of Elizabethan Imagery.* Oxford: Basil Blackwell, 1929.

Honderich, Pauline. "John Calvin and Doctor Faustus." *Modern Language Review* 68 (1973): 1–13.

Houle, Peter J. *The English Morality and Related Drama: A Bibliographical Study.* Hamden, Conn.: Archon Books, 1972.

Hoy, Cyrus. "Jacobean Tragedy and the Mannerist Style." *Shakespeare Survey* 26 (1973): 49–67.

Huebert, Ronald. *John Ford: Baroque English Dramatist.* Montreal: McGill-Queen's Univ. Press, 1977.

Huizinga, J. *The Waning of the Middle Ages.* London: Edward Arnold, 1924.

Hunter, G. K. *Dramatic Identities and Cultural Tradition: Studies in Shakespeare and His Contemporaries.* New York: Barnes & Noble, 1978.

———, and S. K. Hunter, eds. *John Webster: A Critical Anthology.* Harmondsworth: Penguin, 1969.

Jacobson, Daniel Jonathan. *The Language of* The Revenger's Tragedy. Jacobean Studies 38. Salzburg: Univ. of Salzburg, 1974.

———. " 'There It Goes'—or Does It?: Thunder in *The Revenger's Tragedy* and a Catch-Phrase in Shakespeare, Marlowe, and Middleton." *English Language Notes* 13 (1975): 6–10.

Jones, Robert. *Engagement with Knavery: Point of View in* Richard III, The Jew of Malta, Volpone, *and* The Revenger's Tragedy. Durham, N.C.: Duke Univ. Press, 1986.

Jordan, Louis Edward. "The Iconography of Death in Western Medieval Art to 1350." Ph.D. diss., Univ. of Notre Dame, 1980.

Kaufmann, R. J. "Ford's 'Waste Land': *The Broken Heart.*" *Renaissance Drama,* n.s. 3 (1970): 167–87.

Kaula, David. "Time and the Timeless in *Everyman* and *Dr. Faustus.*" *College English* 22 (1960): 9–14.

Kendall, R. T. *Calvin and English Calvinism to 1649.* Oxford: Oxford Univ. Press, 1979.

Kenyon, J. P. *The Stuarts.* 1958. Reprint. Fontana: Collins, 1977.

Kinghorn, A. M. *Medieval Drama.* London: Evans Brothers, 1968.

Kistner, Arthur L., and M. K. Kistner. "Morality and Inevitability in *The Revenger's Tragedy.*" *Journal of English and Germanic Philology* 71 (1972): 36–46.

Knights, L. C. *Drama and Society in the Age of Jonson.* New York: George W. Stewart, 1937.

Kurtz, Leonard P. *The Dance of Death and the Macabre Spirit in European Literature.* New York: Columbia Univ. Press, 1934.

Layman, B. J. "Tourneur's Artificial Noon: The Design of *The Revenger's Tragedy.*" *Modern Language Quarterly* 34 (1973): 20–35.

Leech, Clifford. *The John Fletcher Plays.* Cambridge: Harvard Univ. Press, 1962.

———. *John Ford and the Drama of His Time.* London: Chatto & Windus, 1957.

———. *John Webster.* London: Hogarth Press, 1951.

Levin, Harry. *The Overreacher: A Study of Christopher Marlowe.* Boston: Beacon Press, 1952.

McDonald, Charles Osborne. *The Rhetoric of Tragedy: Form in Stuart Drama.* Amherst: Univ. of Massachusetts Press, 1966.

Mackenzie, W. Roy. *The English Moralities from the Point of View of Allegory.* 1914. Reprint. New York: Gordian Press, 1966.

Margeson, J. M. R. *The Origins of English Tragedy*. Oxford: Clarendon Press, 1967.

Masinton, Charles G. *Christopher Marlowe's Tragic Vision: A Study in Damnation*. Athens: Ohio Univ. Press, 1972.

Miles, Rosalind. *The Problem of "Measure for Measure": A Historical Investigation*. New York: Barnes & Noble, 1976.

Moore, Don D. *John Webster and His Critics, 1617–1964*. Baton Rouge: Louisiana State Univ. Press, 1966.

———, ed. *Webster: The Critical Heritage*. London: Routledge & Kegan Paul, 1981.

Morris, Brian, ed. *John Webster*. Mermaid Critical Commentaries. London: Ernest Benn, 1970.

Morris, Harry. *Last Things in Shakespeare*. Tallahassee: Florida State Univ. Press, 1985.

Murray, Peter B. *A Study of Cyril Tourneur*. Philadelphia: Univ. of Pennsylvania Press, 1964.

———. *A Study of John Webster*. The Hague: Mouton, 1969.

Murrin, Michael. *The Veil of Allegory*. Chicago: Univ. of Chicago Press, 1969.

Neil, Michael. " 'The Simetry, Which Gives a Poem Grace': Masque, Imagery, and the Fancy of *The Maid's Tragedy*." *Renaissance Drama*, n.s. 3 (1970): 111–35.

O'Connor, Sister Mary Catherine. *The Art of Dying Well: The Development of the Ars Moriendi*. New York: Columbia Univ. Press, 1942. Reprint. New York: AMS Press, 1966.

Oliver, H. J. *The Problem of John Ford*. Melbourne: Melbourne Univ. Press, 1955.

Ornstein, Robert. "*The Atheist's Tragedy* and Renaissance Naturalism." *Studies in Philology* 51 (1954): 194–207.

———. *The Moral Vision of Jacobean Tragedy*. Madison: Univ. of Wisconsin Press, 1960.

Parrish, Paul A. " '*Tis Pity She's a Whore* and the Mannerist Perspective." South Central Renaissance Conference, Monroe, La. 18 April 1980.

Parrott, Thomas Marc, and Robert Hamilton Ball. *A Short View of Elizabethan Drama*. 1943. Reprint. New York: Scribner, 1958.

Peterson, Joyce E. *Curs'd Example: the Duchess of Malfi and Commonweal Tragedy*. Columbia: Univ. of Missouri Press, 1978.

Piehler, Paul. *The Visionary Landscape: A Study in Medieval Allegory*. London: Edward Arnold, 1971.

Pineas, Rainer. "The English Morality Play as a Weapon of Religious Controversy." *Studies in English Literature* 2 (1962): 157–80.

Potter, Robert. *The English Morality Play*. London: Routledge & Kegan Paul, 1975.

Prosser, Eleanor. *Drama and Religion in the English Mystery Plays: A Re-Evaluation*. Stanford, Calif.; Stanford Univ. Press, 1961.

Rabkin, Norman, ed. *Twentieth Century Interpretations of "The Duchess of Malfi."* Englewood Cliffs, N.J.: Prntice-Hall, 1968.

Radtke, Stephen J. *James Shirley: His Catholic Philosophy of Life.* Washington, D.C.: Catholic Univ. of America Press, 1962.

Reed, Robert Rentoul, Jr. *The Occult on the Tudor and Stuart Stage.* Boston: Christopher, 1965.

Reinhardt, Hans. *Holbein.* Trans. Prudence Montagu-Pollock. London: William Heinemann, 1938.

Ribner, Irving, ed. *Christopher Marlowe's Doctor Faustus: Text and Major Criticism.* New York: Odyssey Press, 1966.

———, ed. *Christopher Marlowe's Tamburlaine Part One and Part Two.* New York: Odyssey Press, 1974.

———. *Jacobean Tragedy: The Quest for Moral Order.* London: Methuen, 1962.

Richards, Susan. "Marlowe's *Tamburlaine II*: A Drama of Death." *Modern Language Quarterly* 26 (1965): 375–87.

Rosenbaum, Ron. "Turn On, Tune In, Drop Dead." *Harper's*, Aug. 1982, 32–42.

Rossiter, A. P. *English Drama from Early Times to the Elizabethans.* 1950. Reprint. New York: Barnes & Noble, 1967.

Rozett, Martha Tuck. *The Doctrine of Election and the Emergence of Elizabethan Tragedy.* Princeton, N.J.: Princeton Univ. Press, 1984.

Russell, Francis. *The World of Dürer: 1471–1528.* New York: Time, Inc., 1967.

Ryan, Lawrence V. "Doctrine and Dramatic Structure in *Everyman*." *Speculum* 32 (1957): 722–45.

Sachs, Arieh. "The Religious Despair of Doctor Faustus." *Journal of English and Germanic Philology* 63 (1964): 625–47.

Salingar, L. G. "The Decline of Tragedy." In *The Age of Shakespeare*, edited by Boris Ford. 1955. Reprint. Harmondsworth: Penguin, 1975.

———. " 'The Revenger's Tragedy' and the Morality Tradition." *Scrutiny* 6 (1938): 402–24.

Salomon, Brownell. "The Theological Basis of Imagery and Structure in *The Malcontent*." *Studies in English Literature* 14 (1974): 271–84.

Sanders, Wilbur. *The Dramatist and the Received Idea.* Cambridge: Cambridge Univ. Press, 1968.

Sargeaunt, M. Joan. *John Ford.* New York: Russell & Russell, 1966.

Schoenbaum, S. *Middleton's Tragedies.* New York: Columbia Univ. Press, 1955.

———. "*The Revenger's Tragedy*: Jacobean Dance of Death." *Modern Language Quarterly* 15 (1954): 201–07.

Scouten, Arthur H. "An Historical Approach to *Measure for Measure*." *Philological Quarterly* 54 (1975): 68–84.

Sensabaugh, G. F. *The Tragic Muse of John Ford.* Stanford, Calif.: Stanford Univ. Press, 1944.

Slights, William W. E. " 'Elder in a Deform'd Church': The Function of Marston's Malcontent." *Studies in English Literature* 13 (1973): 360–75.

Snyder, Susan. "The Left Hand of God: Despair in Medieval and Renaissance Tradition." *Studies in the Renaissance* 12 (1965): 18–59.

Southall, Raymond. "*Measure for Measure* and the Protestant Ethic." *Essays in Criticism* 11 (1961): 10–33.

Spencer, Theodore. *Death and Elizabethan Tragedy*. 1936. Reprint. Pageant Books, 1960.

Spinrad, Phoebe S. "The Dilettante's Lie in *Doctor Faustus*." *Texas Studies in Literature and Language* 24 (1982): 243–54.

Spivack, Bernard. *Shakespeare and the Allegory of Evil*. New York: Columbia Univ. Press, 1958.

Spivack, Charlotte. *The Comedy of Evil on Shakespeare's Stage*. Rutherford, N.J.: Fairleigh Dickinson Univ. Press, 1978.

Stagg, L. C. *The Figurative Language of the Tragedies of Shakespeare's Chief 17th Century Contemporaries: An Index*. 3d ed. New York: Garland, 1982.

———. *The Figurative Language of the Tragedies of Shakespeare's Chief 16th Century Contemporaries: An Index*. New York: Garland, 1984.

Stavig, Mark. *John Ford and the Traditional Moral Order*. Madison: Univ. of Wisconsin Press, 1968.

Stevenson, David Lloyd. *The Achievement of Shakespeare's "Measure for Measure."* Ithaca, N.Y.: Cornell Univ. Press, 1966.

Stilling, Roger. *Love and Death in Renaissance Tragedy*. Baton Rouge: Louisiana State Univ. Press, 1976.

Symonds, John Addington. *Shakespeare's Predecessors in the English Drama*. 1924. Reprint. New York: Greenwood Press, 1969.

Thomas, Keith. *Religion and the Decline of Magic: Studies in Popular Beliefs in Sixteenth and Seventeenth Century England*. London: Weidenfield and Nicolson, 1971.

Tillyard, E. M. W. *Shakespeare's Problem Plays*. 1950. Reprint. Toronto: Univ. of Toronto Press, 1971.

Tomlinson, T. B. *A Study of Elizabethan and Jacobean Tragedy*. Cambridge: Cambridge Univ. Press, 1964.

Toole, William B. *Shakespeare's Problem Plays: Studies in Form and Meaning*. The Hague: Mouton, 1966.

Tristram, Philippa. *Figures of Life and Death in Medieval English Literature*. London: Paul Elek, 1976.

Trombetta, James. "Versions of Dying in *Measure for Measure*." *English Literary Renaissance* 6 (1976): 60–76.

Waith, Eugene M. *The Pattern of Tragicomedy in Beaumont and Fletcher*. New Haven: Yale Univ. Press, 1952.

Walker, D. P. *The Decline of Hell: Seventeenth-Century Discussions of Eternal Torment*. Chicago: Univ. of Chicago Press, 1964.

Wallis, Lawrence B. *Fletcher, Beaumont & Company: Entertainers to the Jacobean Gentry*. New York: King's Crown Press, 1947.

Weber, Frederick Parkes. *Aspects of Death and Correlated Aspects of Life in Art, Epigram and Poetry*. 1918. Reprint. College Park, Md.: McGrath, 1971.

Wells, Henry W. *Elizabethan and Jacobean Playwrights*. New York: Columbia Univ. Press, 1939.

West, Muriel. *The Devil and John Webster*. Jacobean Drama Studies 11. Salzburg: Univ. of Salzburg, 1974.

West, Robert Hunter. *The Invisible World: A Study of Pneumatology in Elizabethan Drama*. Athens: Univ. of Georgia Press, 1939.

Whitman, Robert Freeman. *Beyond Melancholy: John Webster and the Tragedy of Darkness*. Jacobean Drama Studies 4. Salzburg: Univ. of Salzburg, 1973.

Williams, Arnold. *The Drama of Medieval England*. N.p.: Michigan State Univ. Press, 1961.

Wilson, F. P., and G. K. Hunter. *The English Drama, 1485–1585*. Oxford: Clarendon Press, 1968.

Wimberly, Lowry Charles. *Folklore in the English and Scottish Ballads*. Chicago: Univ. of Chicago Press, 1928.

Woolf, Rosemary. *The English Mystery Plays*. Berkeley: Univ. of California Press, 1972.

———. *The English Religious Lyric in the Middle Ages*. Oxford: Clarendon Press, 1968.

Index

Appius and Virginia, 108, 295n.29

Ars moriendi. See Art of Dying

Art of Dying: Christian humanist, 37–39, 252; corruptions of, 252, 262, 268, 281; medieval, 27–36; Protestant, 39–49, 252; In plays: *Bonduca*, 262; *Everyman*, 82–85; *Measure for Measure*, 165–71, 182; Mystery plays, 54; *The Revenger's Tragedy*, 236–37

Austen, Jane: *Sense and Sensibility*, 270–71

Bacon, Sir Francis, 46

Barnes, Barnabe: *The Devil's Charter*, 118–20

Bayly, Lewis: *Practise of Piety*, 43

Beaumont and Fletcher. See Fletcher, John

Becon, Thomas: *Sicke Mannes Salve*, 39–42, 93

Bloody Banquet, The, 248–49

Calvin, John. See Calvinism

Calvinism: and despair, 105; and doubt, 138, 154; and perseverance in grace, 88–89, 98–99, 105, 174; and predestination and bifurcation of Morality hero, 88–102,

218–21, 251, 258; and presumption, 156; repentance and conversion, 88, 104; and temptation, 161

Cannibalism, 244, 248–49

Carpe diem, 103

Castle of Perseverance, 64–67, 76, 85, 87, 116, 258

Chapman, George: *Bussy D'Ambois*, 117; *The Tragedy of Byron*, 121, 133–34

Chappell, Bartholomew: *The Garden of Prudence*, 190

Chaucer, Geoffrey: *Book of the Duchess*, 57; *The Pardoner's Tale*, 15-17, 61, 91, 116, 148, 241–42

Chesterton, G. K.: *The Ballad of the White Horse*, 141–42; *Orthodoxy*, 313n.32

Chettle, Henry: *The Tragedy of Hoffman*, 242–43

Cinthio, Giraldi, 163

Colman, Walter: *La Dance Machabre*, 21

Coverdale, Myles: *Treatise on Death*, 42–43, 149–50

Dance of Death: as drama, 7, 110, 120, 272, 285; as folk dance,

6–7, 253; as masque in secular plays, 114–16; origins and development of, 4–11, 13, 69, 96, 214. In plays: *The Duchess of Malfi*, 192–93; John Ford, 11, 253, 272; *The Revenger's Tragedy*, 230, 238, 241; *Tamburlaine*, 136; *The Tragedy of Nero*, 279, 285. *See also* Holbein, Hans; Lydgate, John

"*The Daunce and Song of Death*," 18

De contemptu mundi, 2, 4, 46, 103, 164–68, 190–93. *See also* Innocent III, Pope

Death and Liffe, 2–3, 59

Death of Herod (N-Town), 51, 59–61, 85, 116

Death-longing. *See* Dying, eroticism in; Suicide

Death-signs lyric, 28–29, 81, 84, 237

Deathbed: attendants, 33–34, 42, 55–58, 101, 131–33, 139, 194, 280–85; temptations, 31–49, 82. *See also* Repentance, deathbed

"Deaths Daunce," 20

Debate of Body and Soul, 34, 64

Dekker, Thomas: *The Honest Whore*, 223–26 235; *Northward Ho*, 223; *Old Fortunatus*, 112–14

Dent, Arthur, on repentance, 152–53

Despair: as allegory, 103–04, 194, 202, 265; as temptation, 31, 103–06, 117–18, 155–58, 177, 194. *See also* Suicide

Doctrynall of Death, 95, 289n.7

Donne, John, 25, 159

Dreary Death, 13, 18, 58, 60, 126, 189–90

Dürer, Albrecht, 17, 96, 130, 210

Dunbar, William: "Lament for the Makaris," 15, 36

The Dyenge Creature, 34–35

Dying: eroticism in, 261, 268–70, 275–76; stages of, 73–75, 83–84, 96, 144

Elde, warning of, 16, 113, 148, 268

Eliot, T. S.: *Murder in the Cathedral*, 313n.32

Elizabeth I, Queen: proclamation against religious and political plays, 90

Everyman, 50, 68–85, 87, 95, 168, 258

Fame, as immortality, 108, 132–33

Fletcher, John: *Bonduca*, 260–64; and *controversiae*, 268; *The Maid's Tragedy*, 269, 275; *Philaster*, 275–76; *Thierry and Theodoret*, 264–66, 275; *Valentinian*, 252, 257–58, 275

Ford, John: *The Broken Heart*, 114, 253–54, 270–75; and fate, 274; *Love's Sacrifice*, 252–53, 256–57; *'Tis Pity She's a Whore*, 199, 252, 257, 275

Gerson, Jean, *De arte moriendi*, 29–30

Ghosts, 3–4, 11, 117–18, 188, 246

Glapthorne, Henry: *The Lady Mother*, 255

Gomersall, Robert: *The Tragedy of Lodovick Sforza*, 257, 260, 266

Greene, Robert: *Selimus*, 86, 108–09, 125–26

Greenham, Richard: on time and death, 48–49, 267; on tribulation, 94

Guillemand, J.: *A Combat Betwixt Man and Death*, 46–47

Henrietta Maria, Queen: and neoplatonism, 256, 259; and resurgence of Catholicism, 267

Herbert, George: "Death," 26, 274
Heywood, Thomas: A Woman Killed
    with Kindness, 165
Hidden Death, 17–19, 202
Holbein, Hans, 17–18
Homilies, Book of, Anglican, 149–51
Horestes, 108
Horsemen of the Apocalypse, 12,
    17, 129–30, 210. See also Dürer,
    Albrecht
Hutchins, E.: David's Sling Against
    Goliath, 166, 171

Iconography, 1–26, 214–49. See also
    Dance of Death; Dreary Death;
    Horsemen of the Apocalypse;
    Legend of Three Living and
    Three Dead; Memento Mori;
    Skeletons; Triumph of Death
Innocent III, Pope: De Miseria Con-
    dicionis Humane, 164, 167

James I: Daemonologie, 117–18
Johnson, Samuel: Idler, no. 103, x;
    Life, 120

Kyd, Thomas: Soliman and Perseda,
    86, 108–09, 112; The Spanish
    Tragedy, 112, 114

Langland, John: Piers Plowman, 16,
    53
Last Judgment, 2, 126, 129, 210
Last Judgment plays, 51–54, 69, 230,
    237
Lazarus plays, 51, 54–59, 85
Legend of Three Living and Three
    Dead, 4–5, 13, 17, 58, 60, 91,
    249, 284
Locrine, 117
Lupset, Thomas: The Waie of Dieyng
    Well, 37–39, 128, 169–70,
    206–07
Luther, Martin: on conversion, 104;

on despair, 151
Lydgate, John: Assembly of Gods, 36;
    Dance of Death, 8–11, 36, 47,
    77, 84, 139, 253, 271; Fall of
    Princes, 8

The Map of Mortalitie, 44–45
"Marke Well the Effect," 19
Marlowe, Christopher: Doctor
    Faustus, 123, 143–62; Edward II,
    62, 121, 258; Tamburlaine, 121,
    123–43, 260
Marston, John: Antonio's Revenge,
    117, 188, The Dutch Courtesan,
    223; The Malcontent, 114–15
Massinger, Philip: The Duke of
    Milan, 246–48; The Old Law,
    223; The Roman Actor, 252
Memento mori, 22–23, 133, 201–02,
    214–49, 256, 278–79
Middleton, Thomas: The Witch,
    243–44; Women Beware Women,
    115
Military, glorification of, 260–64
Milton, John: Paradise Lost, 275
Montagu, Henry: Contemplatio Mor-
    tis, 43, 266–67
Moral interludes. See Morality plays
Morality plays, 50, 61–106, 229,
    237, 258
More, John: A Liuely Anatomie of
    Death, 45
Mystery plays, 50–61; as background
    for Moralities, 102–03; disap-
    pearance of, 89–90

Nashe, Thomas: Summer's Last Will
    and Testament, 121–22
Necrophilia, 246–48
Nice Wanton, 89

Perkins, William: on doubt, 154; on
    frivolity, 94, 158; on hope, 152;
    on presumption, 153; on

progression of sin, 175-76
Petrus Luccensis, Dialogue of Dying Well, 164-65, 214-15, 222
The Pride of Life, 50, 61-64, 85, 116, 291n.13
Puritanism, 107, 175, 259

Repentance: as act of will, 147; Anglican, 80, 103, 148-61, 204-05; Catholic, 78-79; deathbed, 27-49, 64-67, 101-02, 108, 119, 148, 273-74; general, 118-20, 167, 313n.31. See also Calvinism
Respublica, 294n.19, 309n.13
The Revenger's Tragedy, See Tourneur, Cyril
Rowlands, Samuel: Looke to It, 20; A Terrible Battel Betweene Time and Death, 20, 226-29

The Second Maiden's Tragedy, 244-46
Shakespeare, William: Antony and Cleopatra, 258; Coriolanus, 260-62; Hamlet, 80, 85, 115, 118, 121, 171, 188, 215-18, 235, 265; 1 Henry IV, 260; 2 Henry IV, 222-23; 2 Henry VI, 159-60; 3 Henry VI, 115, 121; Julius Caesar, 117; King John, 298n.6; King Lear, 62, 85, 116-18, 121, 258; Macbeth, 116, 188, 254, 265-66; Measure for Measure, 162-86, 213; Othello, 62, 120-21; Richard II, 110-11, 121, 298n.10; Richard III, 117, 121; Romeo and Juliet, 255-56; Sonnet 146, 25
Shirley, James: The Cardinal, 254; The Maid's Revenge, 257; The Traitor, 269-70, 275
Skeletons, 2-26, 71, 110-11, 140, 210, 214-49
Skelton, John: "On a Deedmans Hed," 22
Skulls. See Skeletons

Southwell, Robert: Foure Last Things, 43-44, 190
Spenser, Edmund: The Faerie Queene, 24-25, 194, 265
Strode, George: Anatomie of Mortalitie, 45-46, 190
Suicide: and death-longing, 275-76; despairing, 103-04, 194; honorable, 127-28, 134-36
Sutton, Christopher: Disce Mori, 43, 167

The Tide Tarrieth No Man, 102-04
Time the Destroyer, 24, 26, 48, 97-98, 141, 226-29, 260, 267-68, 294n.19
Timor mortis lyric, 14, 36
Tomb inscriptions, 3
Tourneur, Cyril: The Atheist's Tragedy, 117, 218-21, 251; The Revenger's Tragedy, 115, 229-42
The Tragedy of Nero, 279-85
Treasonable Utterances Act, 90
Trial of Treasure, 89, 93-98, 220-21
Triumph of Death, 12-13, 17, 96, 115-16, 126
Two Lamentable Tragedies, 112

Ubi sunt, 2, 54

Vado mori lyric, 6, 14

Wager, W.: Enough Is as Good as a Feast, 87, 98-102, 157, 172; The Longer Thou Livest, the More Fool Thou Art, 91-93, 219-20
A Warning for Fair Women, 112
Webster, John: The Duchess of Malfi, 115, 117, 184-213, 251
Whetstone, George: Promos and Cassandra, 163-64
Whitney, Geffrey: A Choice of Emblems, 23
Wither, George: A Collection of Emblemes, 23-24
Woods, Nathaniel: Conflict of Conscience, 104-06